CHRONICLE OF THE POPES

P. G. MAXWELL-STUART

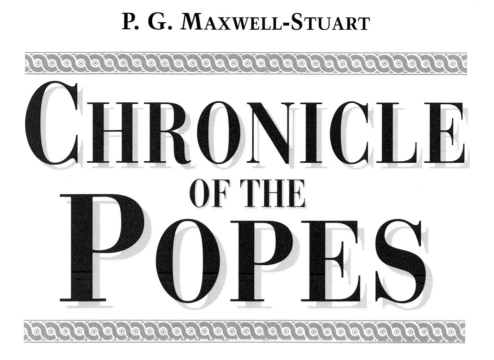

CHRONICLE
OF THE
POPES

THE REIGN-BY-REIGN RECORD OF THE PAPACY FROM ST. PETER TO THE PRESENT

WITH **308** ILLUSTRATIONS
105 IN COLOR

THAMES AND HUDSON

Author's Note
I should like to thank all those who
have assisted in the preparation and
realization of this book

(*Half-title*) The keys of St Peter; mould
for impressing bricks used to wall up the
Holy Door in St Peter's Basilica in 1750.

(*Frontispiece*) Christ handing the keys
to St Peter. This is the earliest extant
picture by Perugino and was painted in
c. 1482. It is the fifth fresco on the north
wall of the Sistine Chapel, and is one of
the few pieces remaining from the
original decoration, much having been
destroyed to make way for
Michelangelo's *Last Judgment*.

First published in the United States of
America in hardcover in 1997 by
Thames and Hudson Inc., 500 Fifth
Avenue, New York, New York 10110

Library of Congress Catalog Card
Number 97-60230

ISBN 0-500-01798-0

Printed and bound in Slovenia by
Mladinska Knjiga

CONTENTS

St Peter

Innocent III

Clement IX

Pius VII

Avignon; the scandals of having several popes at once; recovery and active promotion of papal authority

Special Features

pages 154–207

FROM GLORY TO INFIRMITY
AD 1492–1769

The popes of the Renaissance: patrons, builders, warriors; how the papacy met the challenge of the Protestant reformers; the Counter Reformation; increasing political weakness in a turbulent Europe

Special Features

pages 208–232

TRYING TO COME FULL CIRCLE
AD 1769–1997

How the popes managed to survive Napoleon, two world wars, and Communism; John XXIII and Vatican II; the Polish papacy

Special Feature

97597

PREFACE:
THE MANY
FACES OF THE PAPACY

It is an observable fact that almost any great institution imprints itself on the popular imagination by means of scandal. Nearly everyone has at least heard of the notorious female 'Pope' Joan, even though she never existed. Mention Avignon and one tends to remind people of the time when the Church had several popes at once, each claiming to be genuine. Say 'Borgia', and inevitably the word 'poison' leaps to everyone's lips. There are, alas, many such associations. Formosus (891–896) is considered to be a pattern of vanity for calling himself 'Handsome' (*formosus*) when he became pope: but who recalls that he was a highly intelligent man and a remarkable preacher of the Gospel? Leo X (1513–1521) is credited with saying, upon his election, 'God has given Us the Papacy. Now let Us enjoy it': and yet his election was enormously popular because of his liberality and personal kindness. What is more, he was one of the greatest patrons of the Renaissance. Urban VIII (1623–1644) conducted a full-scale magical ritual in the Lateran Palace with the assistance of one of the most famous magicians of the day – there is no lack of material for those who enjoy mere titillation. But scandal, of course, does not define an institution.

The papacy came to be defined by its history. When the Western Roman empire collapsed in the 5th century, Christian Rome remained a focal point for Christian Europe and its bishop, the pope, its central figure. Successive popes exercised increasing secular as well as spiritual power. In Italy they had lands over which they ruled as Italian princes, continuing to do so until the mid-19th century. They preached crusades and thereby opened increasing communication, partly hostile, partly cultural, between Christian West and Muslim Middle East, largely to the benefit of the former. They encouraged learning and persecuted radical deviation from official teaching. They were great builders and over the centuries encouraged artists of all kinds to expend their skills on the Church. Mention almost any one of the foremost painters, sculptors and architects of the Renaissance, for example, and it is likely he was employed or animated at some time in his career by one of the popes.

Women, too, have played a part in the papal story, albeit their roles have been somewhat various. There is the ever-notorious 'Pope' Joan and the mystery of why a respectable monk should have taken the trouble to invent her; St Catherine of Siena, adviser of and influence upon both Gregory XI and Urban VI; and Giulia Farnese, famous for her luminous beauty, one of Alexander VI's mistresses. In modern times we have Mother Pasqualina, one of the nuns of the household of Pius XII, who was perceived as enjoying increasing significance as his pontificate progressed; and John Paul II made clear at the very

'Pope' Joan gives birth to a child, and thereby reveals her previously hidden identity as a woman; a 15th-century manuscript illustration (Bibliothèque de l'Arsenal, Paris). The story of this mythical popess first emerged in the *Universal Chronicle of Metz* (*c.* 1240–50), and went through numerous versions before its exposure in the 17th century as a fabrication.

Raphael painted Leo X in 1518 (Uffizi Gallery, Florence). It is perhaps typical that Leo, who so shamelessly advanced his relatives, should here be seen flanked by two of his cousins, Giulio de' Medici (on the left) who later became Pope Clement VII, and Cardinal Luigi de' Rossi (on the right). Raphael also seems to offer other, more subtle criticisms – the expanse of fur-lined damask and lace, the head slightly too large for the body, the flabby cheeks and the double chin. It is a picture of a worldly prince rather than that of a devout churchman, and thus succinctly sums up his patron.

start of his reign his devotion to the Virgin Mary by incorporating her initial into the papal coat-of-arms.

Just as interesting and diverse are papal statistics. There have been 266 popes and 39 antipopes (that is, rival popes elected at the same time as another but whose candidature is considered for various reasons to be invalid). Seventy-eight have been declared saints as well as, oddly enough, 2 antipopes; 8 have been pronounced 'Blessed'. There have been 77 Roman popes, 100 Italian, 14 French, 11 Greek, 6 German, 6 Syrian, 3 Sicilian, 2 Sardinian, 2 Spanish, 2 African, 1 English, 1 Dutch, 1 Portuguese, and 1 Polish. Fifteen have been monks, 4 friars, 2 laymen, and 1 a hermit. Four have abdicated, 5 have been imprisoned, 4 murdered, 1 openly assassinated, 1 deposed, and 1 subjected to a public flogging. One died of wounds he received in the midst of battle, and another after a ceiling collapsed and fell on him. The sheer variety of the ways they began and ended is riveting in itself.

The popes, then, are a major part of the fabric of history. During the last 2,000 years there can be scarcely a place on earth which has not, at some time, felt their touch or found itself changed for better or worse, for a short time or permanently, by their pronouncements, decrees and sometimes personal presence. They claim extraordinary titles – 'supreme pontiff', 'vicar of Christ', 'servant of the servants of God' – and during their long existence some have laid stress upon one and some on another. But when all is said and done, viewed from the end of the second millennium the papacy seems to have travelled a circular route. It began as a spiritual office, grew by degrees and sometimes by design into a major secular power, and reached the extremes of worldly learning and corruption. Then slowly it began to contract its political role, shed its materialistic pretensions, and return to an affirmation of its spiritual leadership.

According to a 16th-century forgery, 'The Prophecy of St Malachy', there would be 110 popes after Celestine II. That means there is one left to follow John Paul II. The papacy, however, has survived many a storm and scandal and can take such insubstantial chicanery in its stride. No doubt when the third millennium dawns there will still be an occupant of Peter's throne. No other institution on earth can boast such a history. Therefore, approve or disapprove of them as we may, the popes have a unique claim to merit our close attention.

The Meaning of 'Pope'

The word 'pope' means 'father'. In ancient Greek it was a child's term of affection but was borrowed by later Latin as an honorific. Both Greek-speaking Eastern and Latin-speaking Western Christians then applied it to priests and bishops and patriarchs ('head of the family'); and still today priests of the Orthodox Churches of Greece, Russia and Serbia call their parish priests 'pope'. Gradually, however, Latin started to restrict its usage. At the beginning of the 3rd century, *papa* was a term of respect for churchmen in high positions; by the 5th century, it was applied particularly to the bishop of Rome; and after the 8th, as far as the West was concerned, the title was exclusively his. With the Reformation that exclusivity became a sore point and Protestants tended to object to its usage, preferring to refer to the pontiff by his older (and still relevant) title, 'bishop of Rome'. Often the word 'pope' was sufficient to ignite in them a blaze of indignation. An English dictionary published in 1589, for example, gives the following definition of the term: 'Pope, head bishop of the church malignant, Satan's chief vicar on earth'.

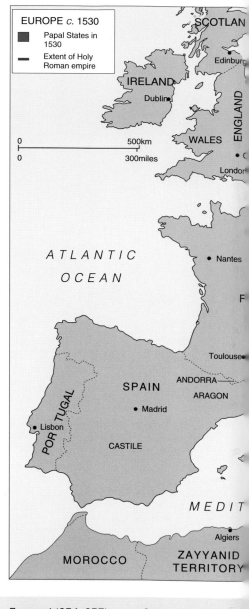

EUROPE *c.* 1530 — Papal States in 1530; Extent of Holy Roman empire

Canonized Popes

Name	Feast Day
Peter (died *c.* 64/68)	29 Jun
Linus (*c.* 66–*c.* 78)	23 Sept
Anacletus (*c.* 79–*c.* 91)	26 Apr/ 13 Jul
Clement I (*c.* 91–*c.* 101)	23 Nov
Evaristus (*c.* 100–*c.* 109)	26 Oct
Alexander I (*c.* 109–*c.* 116)	3 May
Sixtus I (*c.* 116–*c.* 125)	3 Apr
Telesphorus (*c.* 125–*c.* 136)	5 Jan
Hyginus (*c.* 138–*c.* 142)	11 Jan
Pius I (*c.* 142–*c.* 155)	11 Jul
Anicetus (*c.* 155–*c.* 166)	17 Apr
Soter (*c.* 166–*c.* 174)	22 Apr
Eleutherius (*c.* 174–189)	26 Mar
Victor I (189–198)	28 Jul
Zephyrinus (198/9–217)	26 Aug
Callistus I (217–222)	14 Oct
Urban I (222–230)	25 May
Pontian (230–235)	13 Aug
Anterus (235–236)	3 Jan
Fabian (236–250)	20 Jan
Cornelius (251–253)	16 Sept
Lucius I (253–254)	4 Mar
Stephen I (254–257)	2 Aug
Sixtus II (257–258)	7 Aug
Dionysius (260–268)	26 Dec
Felix I (269–274)	30 May
Eutychian (275–283)	7 Dec
Gaius (283–296)	22 Apr
Marcellinus (296–304)	2 Jun
Marcellus I (306–308)	16 Jan
Eusebius (310)	17 Aug
Miltiades (311–314)	10 Dec
Silvester I (314–335)	31 Dec
Mark (336)	7 Oct
Julius I (337–352)	12 Apr
Damasus I (366–384)	11 Dec
Siricius (384–399)	26 Nov
Anastasius I (399–401)	19 Dec
Innocent I (401–417)	28 July
Zosimus (417–418)	26 Dec
Boniface I (418–422)	4 Sept
Celestine I (422–432)	6 Apr
Sixtus III (432–440)	28 Mar
Leo I (440–461)	10 Nov
Hilarus (461–468)	28 Feb
Simplicius (468–483)	10 Mar
Felix III/II (483–492)	1 Mar
Gelasius I (492–496)	21 Nov
Symmachus (498–514)	19 Jul
Hormisdas (514–523)	6 Aug
John I (523–526)	18 May
Felix IV/III (526–530)	22 Sept
Agapitus I (535–536)	22 Apr
Silverius (536–537)	20 Jun
Gregory I (590–604)	3 Sept
Boniface IV (608–615)	25 May
Adeodatus I (615–618)	8 Nov
Martin I (649–653)	13 Apr
Eugene I (654–657)	2 Jun
Vitalian (657–672)	27 Jan
Agatho (678–681)	10 Jan
Leo II (682–683)	3 Jul
Benedict II (684–685)	7 May
Sergius I (687–701)	8 Sept
Gregory II (715–731)	11 Feb
Gregory III (731–741)	28 Nov
Zacharias (741–752)	15 Mar
Paul I (757–767)	28 Jun
Leo III (795–816)	12 Jun
Paschal I (817–824)	now dropped

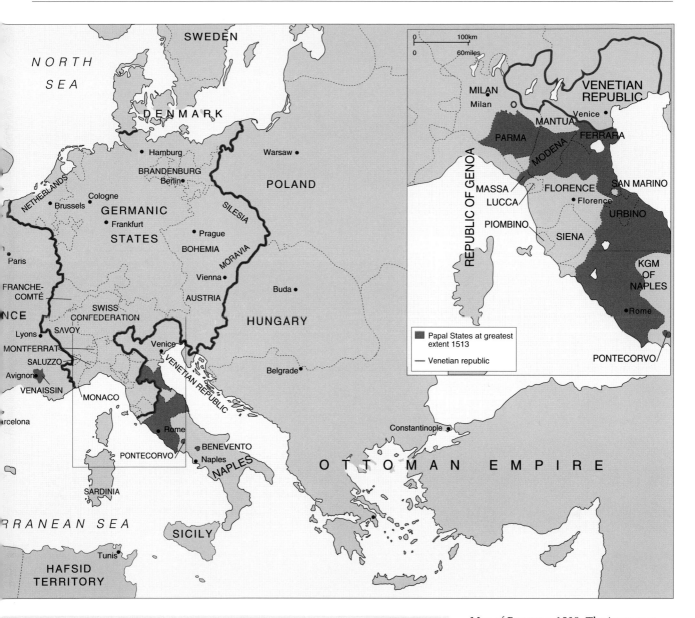

Map of Europe *c.* 1530. The inset map shows Italy *c.* 1513 when the Papal States reached their greatest extent under Pope Julius II.

Leo IV (847–855)	17 Jul
Nicholas I (858–867)	13 Nov
Hadrian III (884–885)	8 Jul
Leo IX (1049–1054)	19 Apr
Gregory VII (1073–1085)	25 May
Celestine V (1294)	19 May
Pius V (1566–1572)	30 Apr
Pius X (1903–1914)	21 Aug

ANTIPOPES

| Hippolytus (217–235) | 13 Aug |
| Felix II (355–365) | 29 Jul |

BEATIFIED POPES

Name	Feast Day
Victor III (1086–1087)	16 Sept
Urban II (1088–1099)	29 Jul
Eugene III (1145–1153)	8 Jul
Gregory X (1271–1276)	9 Jan
Innocent V (1276)	22 Jun
Benedict XI (1303–1304)	7 Jul
Urban V (1362–1370)	19 Dec
Innocent XI (1676–1689)	12 Aug

St Peter
died between late 64
and mid-68

Linus
c. 66–*c.* 78
Anacletus
c. 79–*c.* 91
Clement I
c. 91–*c.* 101
Evaristus
c. 100–*c.* 109
Alexander I
c. 109–*c.* 116
Sixtus I
c. 116–*c.* 125
Telesphorus
c. 125–*c.* 136
Hyginus
c. 138–*c.* 142
Pius I
c. 142–*c.* 155
Anicetus
c. 155–*c.* 166
Soter
c. 166–*c.* 174
Eleutherius
c. 174–189

Victor I
c. 189–*c.* 198
Zephyrinus
c. 198/9–217
Callistus I
217–222
Urban I
222–230

Pontian
230–235
Anterus
235–236
Fabian
236–250
Cornelius
251–253
Lucius I
253–254
Stephen I
254–257
Sixtus II
257–258
Dionysius
260–268
Felix I
269–274
Eutychian
275–283
Gaius
283–296
Marcellinus
296–304
Marcellus I
c. 306–*c.* 308/9
Eusebius
c. 310
Miltiades
311–314
Silvester I
314–335
Mark
336
Julius I
337–352
Liberius
352–366

Damasus I
366–384

Siricius
384–399
Anastasius I
399–401
Innocent I
401–417
Zosimus
417–418
Boniface I
418–422
Celestine I
422–432
Sixtus III
432–440

Leo I
440–461

Hilarus
461–468
Simplicius
468–483
Felix III (II)
483–492
Gelasius I
492–496
Anastasius II
496–498
Symmachus
498–514
Hormisdas
514–523

John I
523–526
Felix IV (III)
526–530
Boniface II
530–532
John II
533–535
Agapitus I
535–536
Silverius
536–537

Vigilius
537–555

Pelagius I
556–561
John III
561–574
Benedict I
575–579
Pelagius II
579–590

Gregory I
590–604

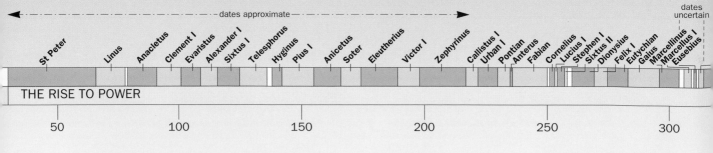

dates approximate

dates
uncertain

St Peter · Linus · Anacletus · Clement I · Evaristus · Alexander I · Sixtus I · Telesphorus · Hyginus · Pius I · Anicetus · Soter · Eleutherius · Victor I · Zephyrinus · Callistus I · Urban I · Pontian · Anterus · Fabian · Cornelius · Lucius I · Stephen I · Sixtus II · Dionysius · Felix I · Eutychian · Gaius · Marcellinus · Marcellus I · Eusebius

THE RISE TO POWER

50   100   150   200   250   300

St Peter

Sixtus I

Damasus I

Gregory I

THE RISE TO POWER
AD 64/68–604

The papacy began with a personal conversation between Jesus and Peter. Peter figured prominently during Jesus's ministry and after Jesus was crucified, Peter's role of leader became ever more clearly acknowledged so that those who succeeded him consistently tried to identify themselves with him and the position he had held in the infant Church. The new Church's initial concern was to survive, and to cope with both the indifference and hostility of the Roman State. Each successor of Peter – or 'bishop of Rome' – was forced to seek some kind of accommodation with the secular power while maintaining his claim to supremacy over all other figures in the growing Church. The Church tried to centralize itself in Rome, the seat of secular power and the place where St Peter had died, and in doing so inevitably made the bishop of Rome, or 'pope' as he was becoming known, a political figure and, to some extent, a secular ruler in his own right.

When the Roman empire split into a Western half and an Eastern half with Christianity the State religion of both, it was the pope alone, with his claims to supremacy over the whole Church, who might provide a unifying force in a disintegrating and changeable world. Under Pope Leo I (440–461), the Western emperor recognized that the pope enjoyed primacy over all bishops of the empire. But Leo's successors had to fight to maintain this pre-eminent position until the accession of one of the greatest of the early popes, Gregory I (590–604), ensured that the papacy once again revived its flagging spirits and prestige.

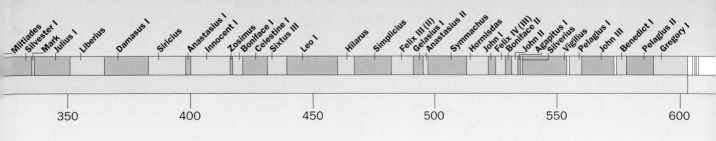

Miltiades Silvester I Mark Julius I Liberius Damasus I Siricius Anastasius I Innocent I Zosimus Boniface I Celestine I Sixtus III Leo I Hilarus Simplicius Felix III (II) Gelasius I Anastasius II Symmachus Hormisdas John I Felix IV (III) Boniface II John II Agapitus I Silverius Vigilius Pelagius I John III Benedict I Pelagius II Gregory I

350   400   450   500   550   600

St Peter
died between late 64 and mid-68

A 12th-century stone sculpture of St Peter holding his emblem – the keys to the kingdom of heaven – from the abbey of Cluny. Keys have always been significant symbols of spiritual or supernatural power, and designate the holder as a warder of life after death. Before Jesus died he appointed Peter leader of the Apostles, asking him to carry on the work that he had started as this passage from John's gospel shows: 'When they had dined, Jesus saith to Simon Peter, son of Jonas, lovest thou me more than these? He saith unto him, Yea, Lord; thou knowest that I love thee. He saith unto him, Feed my lambs.'

ST PETER

Born
c. 4 BC in Bethsaida, by the Sea of Galilee

Work
A fisherman, with his brother Andrew and the sons of Zebedee, John and James. All four became followers of Jesus

Status
Married; legend implausibly credits Peter with a daughter, Petronilla

Education
Little or none. The *Acts of the Apostles* (4.13) describes Peter as 'unlearned and ignorant', although this may be derived from a hostile source

Died
Martyred, possibly in 64 after the Christians were blamed for the Great Fire of Rome, or in the chaos following Nero's suicide in 68; traditionally crucified upside down as an act of humility

As [Peter] went out of the gate he saw the Lord entering Rome; and when he saw him, he said, Lord, where are you going? And the Lord said to him, I am coming to Rome to be crucified. And Peter said to him, Lord, are you being crucified again? He said to him, Yes, Peter, I am being crucified again. And Peter regained his senses; and he saw the Lord ascending into Heaven. Then he returned to Rome rejoicing and giving praise to the Lord, because he said, I am being crucified [since] this was to happen to Peter.

Acts of Peter 35

St Peter is an important figure in the history of the Christian Church. While Jesus was alive, Peter was prominent among the rest of the disciples, often singled out by Jesus for special attention. He seems to have been a head-strong, emotional man, but one of deep faith and fearlessness once Jesus had finally departed. During the early years of the Church he took the lead in preaching and spreading the Christian message both in and beyond the Levant. He successfully defended himself and others when they were arrested and brought before the religious authorities of the day; and so potent was his reputation as a healer that people carried their sick to him on stretchers and laid them

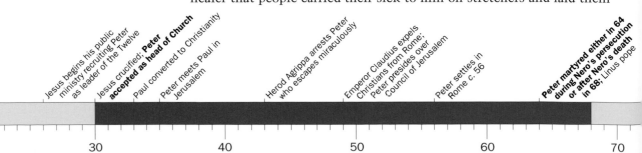

Jesus begins his public ministry recruiting Peter as leader of the Twelve

Jesus crucified; **Peter accepted as head of Church**

Paul converted to Christianity

Peter meets Paul in Jerusalem

Herod Agrippa arrests Peter who escapes miraculously

Emperor Claudius expels Christians from Rome; Peter presides over Council of Jerusalem

Peter settles in Rome c. 56

Peter martyred either in 64 during Nero's persecution or after Nero's death in 68; Linus pope

20   30   40   50   60   70

Then took they [Jesus] and led him, and brought him into the high priest's house. And Peter followed afar off.... A certain maid beheld him as he sat by the fire ... and said, This man was also with him. And he denied him, saying, Woman, I know him not.... And immediately, while he yet spake, the cock crew. And the Lord turned and looked upon Peter.... And Peter went out, and wept bitterly.

Luke 22.54–62

When Peter was leaving Rome during Nero's persecution, we are told, he met Christ on the Via Appia, going in the opposite direction. 'Where are you going, Lord?' he asked. 'To Rome, to be crucified again', was the reply. Whereupon Peter turned back and suffered his own death on the cross. The Church of San Sebastiano near the place of the encounter still displays the marks of Christ's feet, imprinted on a stone. Painting (*above*) by Caracci – *Domine, quo vadis?* (National Gallery, London).

on the ground, hoping that his shadow might fall on them, and thus cure them, as he passed.

The bones found in the grave beneath St Peter's Basilica (see p. 16) are those of someone in his late 60s. If they do belong to Peter, it suggests that he and Jesus were about the same age, although if theories about Christ's being born in 7 or 5 BC are correct, Peter may have been somewhat younger. He came from Bethsaida, a town on the northern shore of the Sea of Galilee, not far from the River Jordan. Its name means 'the house of fishing' or 'the house of the fisherman'. His father's name was Jonas and he himself was called Symeon or Simon until Jesus changed his name to 'Peter'. With his brother Andrew, and in partnership with James and John, sons of Zebedee, he earned his living as a fisherman.

By the time Jesus began his ministry, however, Peter had married and moved to Capernaum to live with his mother-in-law. After being called to discipleship he travelled with Jesus, gradually acquiring the foremost place among the Twelve Apostles, a place which seems to have been rendered unassailable when, according to *Matthew* (16.13–20), Jesus asked his disciples who they thought he was and Simon answered, 'Thou art the Christ, the Son of the living God'. Jesus's reply to that has echoed down the ages and his words have formed the basis of all subsequent papal claims to supremacy: 'Thou art Peter [Greek for 'rock'], and upon this rock I will build my church; and the gates of hell shall not prevail against it. And I will give unto thee the keys of the kingdom of heaven: and whatsoever thou shalt bind on earth shall be bound in heaven: and whatsoever thou shalt loose on earth shall be loosed in heaven.'

Henceforth Peter, despite his impulsive nature, clearly plays the leading role among the growing band of the disciples. Three times Jesus committed them to his care. Peter was the first to enter the empty tomb, the first of the Apostles to whom the resurrected Jesus showed himself, the first to perform a miracle of healing. It was Peter who explained the meaning of Pentecost to the crowd; who took the lead in electing Matthias to fill the place of Judas; who sat in judgment upon Ananias and Sapphira who had tried to cheat the Church. Warm-hearted, prickly, impulsive, but profoundly faithful, he possessed a leader's charisma. As the early Church struggled to find its feet, Peter travelled widely, preaching, converting, curing the sick, raising the dead and ministering to fledgling Christian communities throughout the northern Levant. Specific details of his movements, however, become increasingly sketchy. In 43, he was arrested by King Herod Agrippa I but released from prison by miraculous means. In 49, he presided over a Church council in Jerusalem where he decided that Gentiles should be admitted to full membership of the Church without needing to submit themselves first to the full rigour of the Jewish ritual law. Thereafter he seems to have gone to Antioch which, according to tradition, claimed him as its first bishop.

Finally, he went to Rome. In spite of the silence of the New

Testament on this point, early Church writers are in agreement that he worked and died there; and according to the historian Eusebius (*c.* 260–*c.* 340) he was executed during the reign of Nero (54–68). This probably indicates that he died during the persecution of 64, following the immense fire which destroyed three of the capital's 14 districts and damaged seven more, and for which, rightly or wrongly, the Christians were blamed. Jesus had prophesied long before that Peter would be crucified (*John* 21.18). The tradition that he asked to be crucified upside down (presumably to avoid invidious comparison with the crucifixion of Jesus), goes back to the Alexandrian theologian Origen (*c.* 184–*c.* 253). It could be true. But the legend, recorded by the apocryphal 2nd-century *Acts of Peter*, that he was executed because he induced the concubines of the city prefect Agrippa to leave him and henceforth remain chaste, need not be taken seriously.

The *Acts* go on to say that when Peter died, an important Roman convert, Marcellus, took down his body from the cross, washed him in milk and wine, and buried him in a marble coffin full of mastic (a type of

Masaccio's *Martyrdom of St Peter* (1426), a painted panel illustrating the legend that Peter was crucified upside down. The other half of the panel shows the beheading of St John the Baptist (Staatliche Museum, Berlin). Crucifixion was a mode of execution common in the ancient world. A person hanging on a cross was not expected to die at once. Jewish law, for example, assumed that a crucified man had sufficient time to be redeemed by a rich matron, or to divorce his wife. Nails taken from crosses were believed to have therapeutic powers.

A 12th-century Catalan panel painting which depicts St Peter wearing a mitre. The mitre as a symbol of episcopal dignity was first officially granted to Christian bishops by Emperor Constantine I (the Great). The three fingers raised in blessing are representative of the Holy Trinity.

resin), myrrh, aloes and Attic honey. Within 20 years, we are told, Pope Anacletus, third in the pontifical succession, had raised a memorial shrine over the grave: and thus the scene was set for a long and tangled archaeological history which was to lead to Pope Paul VI's announcement and the reburial of a man's skeleton beneath St Peter's Basilica (see p. 16).

THE EXCAVATION OF
ST PETER'S TOMB

On 22 August 1949 the *New York Times* carried the announcement that the bones of St Peter had been found under the altar of his basilica, and were being guarded by Pope Pius XII. Nineteen years later on 26 June 1968 Pope Paul VI let it be known that the skeletal remains of Peter had been satisfactorily identified, and the following day officiated at their replacement in their ancient resting place. These two sets of bones were not, however, one and the same. The first was a mixture of farm animals and three humans, two men and a woman. The second set, found in a different spot but still within the ground now widely

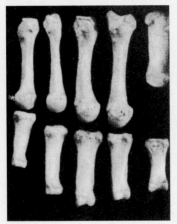

agreed to be Peter's grave, were those of a man dating to the 1st century AD.

It was the burial of Pope Pius XI in 1939 which started the archaeological investigation of the area beneath the basilica's high altar.

Bones from the left hand of the skeleton reservedly identified as that of St Peter. About half the skeleton remains.

During alterations to the burial crypt called the 'Sacred Grottoes' an extraordinary series of ancient tombs was uncovered, revealing a cemetery which had been in use since very early times, and a red wall complex, which turned out to be part of the edifice containing St Peter's tomb. A canopy-like structure – the *Tropaion* (*right*) – had been built into the wall *c.* AD 150, marking the place wherein it was believed Peter was buried. Beside this complex the archaeologists discovered a wall covered in graffiti. Many of these refer to Peter, and it is clear that early pilgrims had scratched prayers and religious symbols as near the sacred spot as possible.

The most exciting find came from a niche within the red wall – the bones of a 1st-century AD man in his late to mid-60s, of powerful build, originally wrapped in cloth of imperial purple and embroidered with gold thread. The Vatican has been cautious, but there is a very good chance that these are indeed the remains of the leading Apostle.

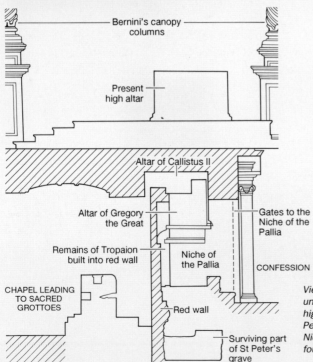

View of the levels directly underneath the present high altar of the basilica. St Peter's grave is below the Niche of the Pallia, in the foundations of the red wall.

Bernini's canopy columns

Present high altar

Altar of Callistus II

Altar of Gregory the Great

Gates to the Niche of the Pallia

Remains of Tropaion built into red wall

Niche of the Pallia

CONFESSION

CHAPEL LEADING TO SACRED GROTTOES

Red wall

Surviving part of St Peter's grave

Archaeologists have uncovered an ancient burial-ground underneath the present basilica. Originally many of the tombs stood beside a road running across the valley and parts of this 'street' still exist below St Peter's floor as shown above.

Linus
c. 66–c. 78

Anacletus
c. 79–c. 91

Clement I
c. 91–c. 101

Evaristus
c. 100–c. 109

Alexander I
c. 109–c. 116

Sixtus I
c. 116–c. 125

Telesphorus
c. 125–c. 136

Hyginus
c. 138–c. 142

Pius I
c. 142–c. 155

Anicetus
c. 155–c. 166

Soter
c. 166–c. 174

Eleutherius
c. 174–189

PAPAL NAMES	
LINUS	**EVARISTUS**
Nationality	*Nationality*
Italian?	Greek?
Elected pope	*Elected pope*
c. 66	c. 101
Died	*Died*
c. 78 in Rome	c. 109
Length of pontificate	*Length of pontificate*
c. 11 years	c. 8 years
ANACLETUS	**ALEXANDER I**
Nationality	*Nationality*
Greek?	Italian, from Rome?
Elected pope	*Elected pope*
c. 79	c. 109
Died	*Died*
c. 91 in Rome	c. 116
Length of pontificate	*Length of pontificate*
c. 12 years	c. 7 years
CLEMENT I	**SIXTUS I**
Nationality	*Nationality*
Italian, from Rome?	Italian, from Rome?
Elected pope	*Elected pope*
c. 91	c. 116
Died	*Died*
c. 101	c. 125
Length of pontificate	*Length of pontificate*
c. 10 years	c. 9 years

In accordance with the injunction of the Apostle [Paul], he [Pope Anicetus] forbade the clergy to grow their hair long.

Liber Pontificalis

There follows a sequence of more or less shadowy popes, all based in Rome, about some of whom not a great deal is known beyond pious legend. All have been canonized.

Linus (*c.* 66–*c.* 78) is supposed to have been appointed pope by Peter and Paul acting in concert, and if these dates are anywhere near correct, he will have been pontiff when Jerusalem was destroyed by Titus in August 70, and may have seen the hordes of prisoners in Rome, labouring on the massive new Flavian amphitheatre (the Colosseum). He was succeeded by **Anacletus** (*c.* 79–*c.* 91), to judge by his name a Greek and perhaps originally a slave. Dubious tradition says that he, like Linus, was martyred for his faith. Next in the line of succession is **Clement I** (*c.* 91–*c.* 101). There is a tradition that he was ordained by St Peter and acted as a kind of auxiliary bishop to Linus and Anacletus. But suggestions that he was a cousin of Emperor Domitian, martyred for his adherence to Christianity, must be counted simply as legend. Excavations in Rome, however, raise the possibility that the Church of San Clemente may

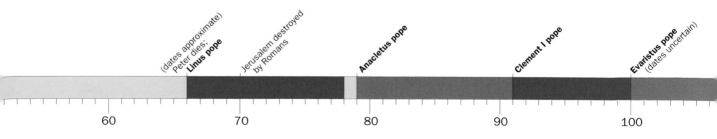

PAPAL NAMES

TELESPHORUS
Nationality
  Greek?
Elected pope
  c. 125
Died
  c. 136, martyred
Length of pontificate
  c. 11 years

HYGINUS
Nationality
  Greek?
Early career
  Philosopher
Elected pope
  c. 138
Died
  c. 142
Length of pontificate
  c. 4 years

PIUS I
Nationality
  Italian, from
  Aquileia?
Elected pope
  c. 142
Died
  c. 155
Length of pontificate
  c. 13 years

ANICETUS
Nationality
  Syrian, from
  Emesa?
Elected pope
  c. 155
Died
  c. 166
Length of pontificate
  c. 11 years

SOTER
Nationality
  Italian, from
  Campania?
Elected pope
  c. 166
Died
  c. 174
Length of pontificate
  c. 8 years

ELEUTHERIUS
Nationality
  Greek, from Epirus?
Early career
  Deacon
Elected pope
  c. 174
Died
  189
Length of pontificate
  c. 15 years

11th-century fresco from the Church of San Clemente in Rome. It has been suggested that the Church of San Clemente was actually built over the site of Pope Clement I's house in Rome.

actually have been built on the site of his house. Of the various writings attributed to him, only one seems to be authentic, the *Epistle to the Corinthians*, written because there had been some kind of a revolution among the Christian community at Corinth; and we may perhaps conjecture that it was Clement's personal prestige in the early Church which caused later historians to attribute other works to him. Accounts of his martyrdom are equally late and equally legendary.

Then come **Evaristus** (*c.* 100–*c.* 109), whose Greek name means 'pleasing' or 'acceptable'; the completely obscure **Alexander I** (*c.* 109–*c.* 116); and **Sixtus I** (*c.* 116–*c.* 125), who may have got the name 'Sixth' because he was counted as being the sixth in line after St Peter. With Peter as the first pope, however, his name does not quite fit. Nor does it go with what seems to have been a trend at this time for Greek names among the popes. The alternative for 'Sixtus', however, is 'Xystus', a Greek word meaning 'shaved', and perhaps the epithet indicates a personal peculiarity. For Sixtus lived during the reign of Emperor Hadrian who, after a long time during which shaven cheeks had been the norm, had brought back into fashion the full beard. **Telesphorus** (*c.* 125–*c.* 136) is another Greek name meaning 'bringing fruit to perfection' or 'accomplishing one's purpose'. There appears to be a gap of two years between his reign and that of **Hyginus** (*c.* 138–*c.* 142), but all dates of this period are highly conjectural. Hyginus means 'wholesome, sound, healthy'. Irenaeus, the Catholic theologian, tells us that during his reign the heretic Valentinus came to Rome. Valentinus was the most prominent

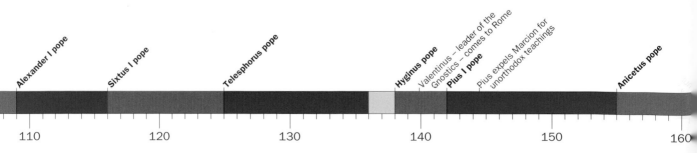

PAPAL NAMES

Why did so many early popes have Greek names? It is most unlikely that they were all Greek and indeed the *Liber Pontificalis* – a collection of papal biographies compiled to enhance papal prestige, the earliest dating to the 6th century – says that seven of them were Roman or Italian, and one was Syrian. It is possible they changed their real names for Greek epithets in memory of St Peter who had had his name changed to Greek by Jesus. The custom, if that is what it was, did not cease with Eleutherius, and one can find 'Greek' names well into the Middle Ages. The further one recedes from Peter, however, the less likely it is that the choice of Greek was significant.

List of popes from the Liber Pontificalis written at St Amand, c. 800 (University Library, Leiden).

6th-century mosaic from Sant' Apollinare Nuovo in Ravenna showing Pope Sixtus I carrying the wreath of martyrdom. According to the *Liber Pontificalis*, Sixtus decreed that no one except the clergy should touch any of the sacred vessels used during the mass.

leader of a group of Gnostics – people who claimed superior knowledge of things spiritual – who counted themselves as members of the Church but worshipped a Mother Goddess and acknowledged a complex hierarchy of heavens and angelic powers. Christ, in this system of belief, was a redeemer but not one recognizable by orthodox Christian theology. Valentinus himself was keen to remain within the Church, but it is scarcely surprising that circumstances eventually compelled him to leave it. He stayed, however, in Rome, a potential thorn in the flesh not only for Hyginus but for the next two popes as well.

There followed **Pius I** (*c.* 142–*c.* 155), whose Latin name means 'dutiful' and is unusual in that it is only the second Latin name or title in the list of the first 12 popes. Could he have chosen it because he was elected pontiff during the reign of Emperor Antoninus (138–161) who acquired the sobriquet 'Pius' as a title of respect? Pope Pius, however, unlike the emperor who had a remarkably peaceful reign, had a great deal to contend with during his pontificate. Not only was Valentinus still active in Rome; so also were other highly unorthodox teachers such as Cerdo, a Syrian, who taught that there were two equal gods, one good, the other evil, and that Jesus was the son of the former: and Marcion who said that the Church was wrong to pay any attention to the Old Testament (or, indeed, to most of the New), and that Jesus was not the Messiah foretold by the Jewish prophets. **Anicetus** (*c.* 155–*c.* 166) – the Greek name means 'unconquered' – was followed by **Soter** (*c.* 166–*c.* 174), whose Greek name means 'deliverer' or 'preserver', and we have a letter which records

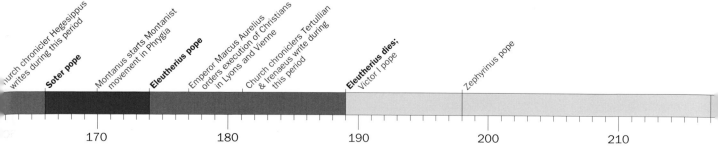

A CARING PONTIFF

The following is a letter to the Roman community from Dionysius, bishop of Corinth:

From the start, this has been your custom: to do good in all kinds of different ways to all the brethren, and to send contributions to the many churches in every city, in some places relieving the poverty of those in need and giving extra help to the brethren in the mines.... Your blessed Bishop Soter has not only maintained this custom, but has even added to it.

Eusebius *History of the Church*
4.23.10

the pastoral care given by Rome, and by Soter in particular, to poor and unfortunate Christians wherever they were in the empire. After him came **Eleutherius** (*c.* 174–189). The Greek means 'free-spirited, frank'. Hegesippus, the 2nd-century historian, tells us he had been deacon to Anicetus. During Soter's pontificate the heretic Montanus had made an appearance in Phrygia. He and his followers were notable for their religious raptures during which they spoke in strange tongues and uttered prophecies. Convulsions and mass hysteria seem to have been hallmarks of Montanist meetings, and the notion that these enthusiasts were under the direct guidance of the Holy Spirit and constituted an élite whose task was to restore the primitive simplicity of the Church proved immensely popular in both eastern and western parts of the empire. Eleutherius, according to Tertullian – an important Church writer and a convert to Montanism – was at first favourably inclined to the sect but later rejected it. In doing so, he made a significant choice. Henceforth it would be seen that spiritual governance was to be done by a hierarchical institution rather than by the dictates of individual feeling, however charismatic.

PROSPECTS

When these popes looked out on Rome, what did they see? Peace abroad and heresy at home might be the general impression. The emperor, upon whose indifference the pope's own safety and that of his flock largely depended, was frequently absent from the capital for long periods. Antoninus Pius, it is true, did not stray far from it during the 23 years of his reign; but Trajan (98–117) and Hadrian (117–138) spent much time at war, and Antoninus's successor, Marcus Aurelius (161–180), was also absent for years. What is more, Marcus was not well-disposed towards Christians. 'Miracle-mongers, magicians, and exorcisers' (*Meditations* 1.6) was one of his opinions, a view possibly based on the Christians' constantly boasting of their power to cast out demons. In 177, when brutal persecution broke out at Lyons and Vienne in the Rhône Valley, the emperor supposedly instructed that the Christians there be tortured to death. Even if this story is not true, we know he did not approve of the histrionic way many Christians embraced martyrdom. 'They kill us,

11th-century ivory triptych of the 40 martyrs of Sebaste, put to death in 320 during the reign of Emperor Licinius (Staatliche Museum, Berlin).

they cut us limb from limb, they hunt us with curses!' he records them as crying (*Meditations* 8.51), to which he replies: 'How does that prevent your mind from continuing to be pure, sane, sober, and just?'

But people in general, too, could turn hostile. 'If the Tiber rises too high', wrote Tertullian, full of sarcasm, 'or the Nile too low, the cry is, "The Christians to the lion!" All of them to a single lion?' Anything less than imperial indifference, then, could make things difficult.

There was, however, an additional danger. Heresy in various forms not only existed: it flourished. Christianity remained a capital offence, and if the authorities were to be persuaded to tolerate it, they must not be given cause to show their contempt. Some kind of centralized control over the Church, therefore, was becoming increasingly desirable.

The persecution of Christians during the reign of Marcus Aurelius (above) is recorded by several Christian apologists.

Victor I
c. 189–c. 198

Zephyrinus
c. 198/9–217

Callistus I
217–222

Urban I
222–230

Pontian
230–235

Anterus
235–236

Fabian
236–250

Cornelius
251–253

Lucius I
253–254

Stephen I
254–257

Sixtus II
257–258

Dionysius
260–268

Felix I
269–274

Eutychian
275–283

Gaius
283–296

Marcellinus
296–304

Marcellus I
c. 306–c. 308/9

Eusebius
c. 310

Miltiades
311–314

Silvester I
314–335

Mark
336

Julius I
337–352

Liberius
352–366

They say that Fabian ... because of the most extraordinary workings of divine and heavenly grace ... inherited the [papal] office. For the brethren had all assembled for the purpose of appointing someone to succeed to the episcopate, and many people were thinking of a number of distinguished men.... Fabian was present, but no one was thinking of him. Suddenly, they say, a dove flew down and settled on his head, just as the Holy Spirit had descended upon the head of the Saviour in the form of a dove. At this, everyone, as if moved by a single divine inspiration, eagerly and whole heartedly called out that Fabian was worthy and immediately took him and placed him on the episcopal throne.

Eusebius *History of the Church* 6.29.3–4

Victor I (*c.* 189–*c.* 198) was an African by birth and a great upholder of

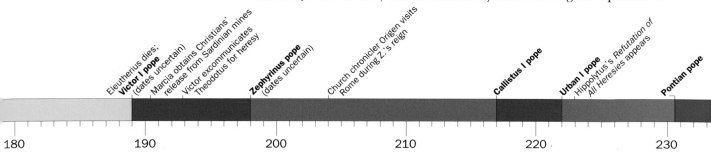

Mosaic of St Victor in the golden sky, in the eponymous chapel of the basilica of Sant' Ambrosio, Milan. Pope Victor excommunicated, among others, Theodotus the cobbler, who denied the Godhead in Jesus and said that Christ was simply a man.

PAPAL NAMES

VICTOR I	URBAN I
Nationality	*Nationality*
African	Italian, from
Elected pope	Rome
c. 189	*Elected pope*
Died	222
c. 198	*Died*
Length of pontificate	230
9 years	*Length of pontificate*
	8 years
ZEPHYRINUS	*Antipope*
Nationality	St Hippolytus
Italian, from	(217–235)
Rome?	
Elected pope	PONTIAN
c. 198/9	*Nationality*
Died	Italian, from
217	Rome
Length of pontificate	*Elected pope*
18/19 years	21 July 230
	Abdicated
CALLISTUS I	28 September
Nationality	235
Italian?	*Died*
Early career	While in prison
Slave; deacon	on Sardinia
Elected pope	*Length of pontificate*
217	5 years,
Died	2 months,
222	9 days
Length of pontificate	*Antipope*
5 years	St Hippolytus
Antipope	(217–235)
St Hippolytus	
(217–235)	

the Western, as opposed to the Eastern, ecclesiastical tradition. This can be seen from his decision that Easter should be observed on a set Sunday each year in accordance with Roman practice. Hitherto, it could be commemorated weekly or be celebrated on a particular date, regardless of the day of the week on which that fell. Victor, however, did not seek to impose his will without consultation. Synods were held in all the chief Christian centres, East and West. The West agreed: the East, on the whole, did not. This refusal by the churches of Asia Minor angered the pope and he excommunicated them. It was a remarkable display of vigour and authority and shows how much the papacy was growing in self-confidence.

Zephyrinus (*c.* 198/9–217) was a complete contrast. With him we return to a tradition of Greek papal names and in him the vigorous exercise of authority which characterized Victor seems to have been lacking entirely. Heresies arose and Zephyrinus wrung his hands. A work attributed to Hippolytus the Martyr (*The Refutation of All Heresies*), indeed, goes so far as to call Zephyrinus 'ignorant and greedy', 'a receiver of

M. Thrax deports Pontian
Anterus pope
Fabian pope
Fabian brings Pontian's body back for burial in Rome
Fabian dies during Emperor Decius's persecution
Cornelius pope
Lucius I pope
Stephen I pope
S. quarrels with Cyprian over rebaptism of ex-heretics
Sixtus II pope
Sixtus II beheaded
Dionysius pope
Felix I pope
Eutychian pope
Gaius pope

240   250   260   270   280

4th-century gilded glass disk showing the head of Pope Callistus I (Cabinet des Médailles, Paris). Pope Callistus was the first pope, except for St Peter, to be commemorated as a martyr in the earliest Church martyrology, the *Depositio Martyrum* (c. 354).

ANTIPOPES

An antipope is someone who claims or exercises the office of pope without any valid authority to do so. Some antipopes were deliberately elected by factions of cardinals; others because of genuine confusion during a period in which the rules for election were fluid or not well understood, or when the legitimate pontiff had been deposed or sent into exile. One antipope, however, Constantine (767), actually seized the position by force. The first appearance of the term seems to occur in c. 1192.

bribes and a lover of money', a man easily led by his *éminence grise*, the archdeacon, Callistus, 'unlearned and unskilled in the Church's rules'. It is a damning catalogue but, in fairness to the pope, one must recognize here the authentic note of prejudice. Tradition has assigned to his reign one of the earliest references to the graves of Peter and Paul. A Church historian called Gaius wrote to a leader of the Montanist heresy, 'I can point out the trophies [i.e. "monuments"] of the Apostles, for if you will go to the Vatican or to the Ostian Way, you will find the trophies of those who founded this Church'. It is possible that Origen, one of the greatest of the early Church Fathers, who came to Rome at this time, will have seen these tombs for himself.

With **Callistus I** (217–222) – sometimes 'Calixtus' – we return to a pope with a stronger character. The name is Greek and means 'very handsome'. The *Refutation of All Heresies* tells us the following story about Callistus's early life. He was the house-slave of a Christian called Carpophorus who was attached to the imperial household. The two men entered a business arrangement whereby Carpophorus entrusted his slave with quite a large sum of money in return for Callistus's promise that he would make his master a profit from what we would call banking. Several Christians made deposits but Callistus embezzled the cash, and when Carpophorus asked to see the accounts, he tried to escape abroad. He was waiting on a cargo-ship when he was captured and handed over to Carpophorus. Back in Rome, he was sentenced to death, but members of the Christian community pleaded with Carpophorus and eventually won their case. Callistus was released, although kept under strict watch. He found this intolerable and determined he would seek death as a way of escape. So one Sabbath, he rushed into a synagogue and began to abuse the congregation. Naturally, a fight broke out and Callistus was arrested, and after being hauled before the city prefect, he was condemned to the mines in Sardinia. Released by the kind actions of Marcia, Emperor Commodus's mistress, he was sent to live in Antium by Pope Victor who paid him a monthly allowance. After Victor's death, Callistus ingratiated himself with Pope Zephyrinus and thus set himself on the road to power and influence in the Church.

Urban I (222–230) also escaped imperial persecution. Much of the supposed information about him is fantasy, including that of his martyrdom. His election was contested and a formidable scholar, *Hippolytus*, set himself up as an alternative bishop of Rome (antipope). Urban's successor, **Pontian** (230–235), however, fell foul of Maximinus Thrax who became emperor in 235, and who deliberately set about attacking the

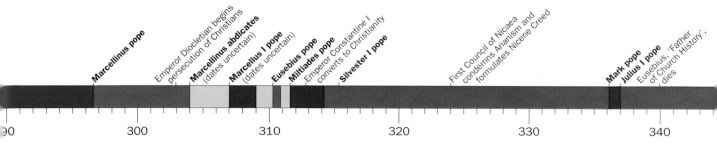

Marcellinus pope

Emperor Diocletian begins persecution of Christians

Marcellinus abdicates (dates uncertain)

Marcellus I pope (dates uncertain)

Eusebius pope

Miltiades pope

Emperor Constantine I converts to Christianity

Silvester I pope

First Council of Nicaea condemns Arianism and formulates Nicene Creed

Mark pope

Julius I pope

Eusebius, 'Father of Church History', dies

90   300   310   320   330   340

(*Above*) Epitaph of Pope Pontian in the catacombs of St Callistus, Rome. It reads: 'Pontianus Bi[shop] M[arty]r'.

(Above right) Epitaph of Pope Fabian in the catacombs of St Callistus, Rome. It reads: 'Phabianos Bi[shop] M[arty]r'.

(*Above*) Pope Fabian was martyred under Emperor Decius (249–251). (National Gallery, London.)

leaders of the Christian community in Rome. Pontian and Hippolytus were arrested and sent to Sardinia. Since he never expected to be released, Pontian resigned the papacy – he is the first pope to have done so – and later died as a result of the appalling conditions he endured during imprisonment. Pontian was succeeded by **Anterus** (235–236). His name is interesting. It is Greek, referring to the son of Venus and Mars (or a kind of amethyst), and is thus clearly unlike the Greek epithets we have noticed in earlier popes. The likelihood is, therefore, that Anterus was actually a Greek. It is virtually the only thing that can be said about him with any degree of confidence.

During the pontificate of **Fabian** (236–250), with a change of emperor, persecution ceased for a time and Fabian was able to turn his attention to diocesan affairs in Rome. He tightened administration, organized building-works in the cemeteries, and arranged (probably through friendly contacts at the imperial court) for the return of Pope Pontian's body from Sardinia. With another change of emperor, however, persecution sprang up again and Fabian was arrested. His grave-slab, discovered in 1854, has the abbreviation for 'martyr' engraved upon it.

So violent was the persecution initiated by Emperor Decius (249–251) that Fabian's successor, **Cornelius** (251–253), was not elected for a full 14 months. During the interval the Church was governed by a committee, and was troubled by the claims of an antipope, *Novatian*, like Hippolytus, an excellent scholar. **Lucius I** (253–254) was caught by Emperor Trebonianus Gallus's persecution, but managed to return safely to Rome when Emperor Valerian (253–260) relaxed official hostility towards Christians. As far as we can tell, he continued Cornelius's general policies. More important is the next pope, **Stephen I** (254–257), who overtly made attempts to assert the primacy of Rome. One of his opponents, Firmilian, bishop of Caesaerea, tells us that Stephen used to boast

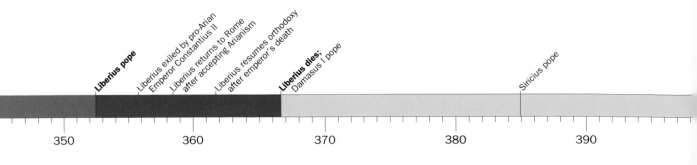

Liberius pope
Liberius exiled by pro-Arian Emperor Constantius II
Liberius returns to Rome after accepting Arianism
Liberius resumes orthodoxy after emperor's death
Liberius dies; Damasus I pope
Siricius pope

350   360   370   380   390

PAPAL NAMES	

ANTERUS
 Nationality
  Greek
 Elected pope
  21 November 235
 Died
  3 January 236
 Length of pontificate
  1 month, 12 days
 	
 FABIAN
 Nationality
  Italian, from Rome
 Elected pope
  10 January 236
 Died
  20 January 250, in
  prison in Rome
 Length of pontificate
  14 years
 	
 CORNELIUS
 Nationality
  Italian, from Rome
 Elected pope
  March 251
 Died
  June 253
 Length of pontificate
  c. 2 years, 3 months
 Antipope
  Novatian (251–258)
 	
 LUCIUS I
 Nationality
  Italian, from Rome
 Elected pope
  25 June 253
 Died
  5 March 254
 Length of pontificate
  8 months, 10 days
 Antipope
  Novatian (251–258)
 	
 STEPHEN I
 Nationality
  Italian, from Rome
 Elected pope
  12 May 254
 Died
  2 August 257
 Length of pontificate
  3 years, 2 months,
  21 days
 Antipope
  Novatian (251–258)
 	
 SIXTUS II
 Nationality
  Greek
 Elected pope
  August 257
 Died
  6 August 258,
  beheaded
	Length of pontificate
	  c. 1 year
	 Antipope
	  Novatian
	  (251–258)
	
	 DIONYSIUS
	 Nationality
	  Greek?
	 Elected pope
	  22 July 260
	 Died
	  26 December 268
	 Length of pontificate
	  8 years, 5 months,
	  5 days
	
	 FELIX I
	 Nationality
	  Italian, from Rome
	 Elected pope
	  3 January 269
	 Died
	  30 December 274
	 Length of pontificate
	  6 years
	
	 EUTYCHIAN
	 Nationality
	  Italian, from
	  Tuscany
	 Elected pope
	  4 January 275
	 Died
	  7 December 283
	 Length of pontificate
	  8 years, 11
	  months, 4 days
	
	 GAIUS
	 Nationality
	  Uncertain
	 Elected pope
	  17 December
	  283
	 Died
	  22 April 296
	 Length of pontificate
	  12 years, 4
	  months, 6 days
	
	 MARCELLINUS
	 Nationality
	  Uncertain
	 Elected pope
	  30 June 296
	 Deposed/abdicated
	  Date unknown;
	  Marcellinus was
	  an apostate and
	  almost certainly
	  forced from office
	 Died
	  25 October 304
	 Length of pontificate
	  Uncertain

about the place of his bishopric and the claim that he held his succession from Peter 'on whom the foundations of the Church were laid'. The phrase *cathedra Petri* ('the chair of Peter'), although coined by someone else, was seized on by Stephen to symbolize the primatial rights and authority of Rome. In consequence, it is not surprising that he made enemies of rival bishops. Nevertheless, slowly and gradually the claims he was advancing were taking on a reality which Christian communities were being forced to confront and either reject or acknowledge.

Sixtus II (257–258) seems to have been less of an unbending character than Stephen, for he succeeded in repairing relations between the papacy and Cyprian, bishop of Carthage in Africa (249–258), who had quarrelled with Pope Stephen over whether supporters of Novatian who had seen the error of their ways should be rebaptized or not. Sixtus also seems to have made a start on patching up the breach between Rome and some of the other churches, which Stephen's quarrels with Cyprian had opened. Unfortunately, however, he became pope just when Emperor Valerian was turning persecutor. Christian bishops, priests and deacons were, by imperial order, to be executed, and on 6 August 258 Pope Sixtus was killed while he was in the middle of preaching a sermon in the cemetery of Praetextatus in Rome. An epitaph by one of his successors, Damasus I, describes how he was beheaded along with four of his deacons.

Sixtus was succeeded by several popes whose pontificates we need summarize only briefly. **Dionysius** (260–268) could not be elected, because of the severity of the imperial persecution, until news of Valerian's death abroad had reached Rome. As pope, he managed to take advantage of the reversal of hostility to Christians by Emperor Gallienus (260–268) to reorganize the Church and maintain Rome's traditional support of Christians in distress throughout the empire. **Felix I** (269–274) is quite obscure and the pontificate of **Eutychian** (275–283) is equally lost in shadows. One may observe, however, that he was fortunate in enjoying a pontificate entirely free from persecution by the State. **Gaius** (283–296), too, seems to have had a peaceful pontificate, but virtually all other information about him turns out, on closer examination, to be suspect. **Marcellinus** (296–304), on the other hand, appears to have fallen victim to the first wave of Emperor Diocletian's extended persecution. The emperor's hand was heavy. He ordered that churches be destroyed, sacred books be delivered to the secular authorities, and that sacrifice be offered to pagan gods by anyone attending a law-court. Marcellinus, for reasons unknown, bowed to the imperial command early in 303. He handed over the Scriptures and is said to have offered incense to the gods. It was apostasy on the grandest possible scale and as such must have been galling to any Christian who acknowledged Rome's peculiar ecclesiastical authority. Marcellinus died in 304. It is unlikely he died as pope. Abdication or deposition must surely have followed his surrender to the State. What is clear, however, is that the Church was without its Roman primate for over three years, as the next pope was not elected until c. 306. Under the circumstances, one must

4th-century gold glass disk showing Pope Marcellinus (Vatican Museums). After his death, Donatist heretics spread the story that he had repented his apostasy and sought martyrdom by way of expiation.

PAPAL NAMES

MARCELLUS I	*Elected pope*
Nationality	31 January 314
Italian, from Rome?	*Died*
Elected pope	31 December 335
November/	*Length of pontificate*
December 306 (or	21 years, 11
May/June 308)	months
Died	
16 January 308 (or	**MARK**
16 January 309)	*Nationality*
Length of pontificate	Uncertain
Uncertain	*Elected pope*
	18 January 336
EUSEBIUS	*Died*
Nationality	7 October 336
Greek?	*Length of pontificate*
Early career	8 months, 20 days
Physician	
Elected pope	**JULIUS I**
18 April 310	*Nationality*
Died	Italian, from Rome
21 October 310,	*Elected pope*
while a deportee in	6 February 337
Sicily	*Died*
Length of pontificate	12 April 352
6 months, 3 days	*Length of pontificate*
	15 years, 2
MILTIADES	months, 2 days
Nationality	
Italian, from Rome?	**LIBERIUS**
Elected pope	*Nationality*
2 July 311	Italian, from Rome
Died	*Elected pope*
10 January 314	17 May 352
Length of pontificate	*Died*
2 years, 6 months,	24 September 366
8 days	*Length of pontificate*
	14 years, 4
SILVESTER I	months, 6 days
Nationality	*Antipope*
Uncertain	Felix II (355–365)

14th-century mosaic from Santa Maria Maggiore, Rome, showing Pope Liberius blessing John the Patrician. Liberius gave his name to one of the earliest versions of the *Liber Pontificalis*. It is known as the 'Liberian Catalogue' and attributes a reign of 25 years to St Peter.

regard Marcellinus's later canonization as something of a miracle.

Marcellus I (*c.* 306–*c.* 308/9) started to reorganize and regroup the Church under the tolerant rule of Emperor Maxentius (306–312), but his attempts ended in disorder and bloodshed and he was driven from Rome. **Eusebius** (*c.* 310) fared no better and he, too, was exiled by Maxentius. **Miltiades** (311–314), however, enjoyed what was to be a protracted period of imperial favour, and it was during his reign that Emperor Constantine (306–337), just before engaging in the Battle of the Milvian Bridge, had the vision of a cross of light in the sky with the words 'Conquer by means of this', which led to his apparent conversion to Christianity. Constantine also made the ancient city of Byzantium the official seat of secular power – renaming it Constantinople – a move which would have long-lasting repercussions and which marked a decline in the political importance of Rome and the western provinces of the empire as a whole. **Silvester I** (314–335), despite his long reign, is oddly obscure. Indeed, he is most notable for his absences. He did not attend the Church council at Arles, nor the First Council of Nicaea (324–325) which promulgated the Nicene Creed and condemned the heretic Arius; and even the famous *Donation of Constantine*, a document purporting to give Silvester and his successors primacy over all other patriarchs and temporal command over the empire of the West, was a late fabrication. **Mark** (336), too, is obscure. His reign must have been overshadowed by the internal rows arising from Nicaea.

Julius I (337–352), on the other hand, set about imposing order again and reinforcing the claims of Rome to primacy over the bishoprics of the East. **Liberius** (352–366), the first pope not to be canonized – almost certainly because he was considered to have compromised himself with heresy – at first manifested that stubbornness which often accompanies weakness of character. But then, bullied by Emperor Constantius II (337–361) and sent into exile, he finally gave way to Eastern demands and entered into communion with the heretic Arians. He was allowed to

CONSTANTINE AND THE BATTLE OF THE MILVIAN BRIDGE

He said that at midday, when the sun was sloping towards the west, he saw in the sky before his very eyes the triumphal sign of a cross made of light. It was placed above the sun and had the following written upon it: 'Conquer by means of this'. At this sight both he and all the soldiers who were accompanying him on this march and who had also been witnesses of the miracle were astonished.

Eusebius *Life of Constantine* I.27–28

The significance of Constantine's conversion to Christianity is three-fold. First, he extended toleration to the Christians. This had been done by earlier emperors, but the fact that his mother (St Helena) was an open and devout Christian strengthened the likelihood that imperial favour would last. Secondly, he granted privileges to Christian communities. This gave them increased influence in the machinery of the State. Thirdly, with the agreement of Silvester I, he summoned the First Council of Nicaea which condemned the Arian heresy and formulated orthodox teaching in the Creed which was named after it. Thus Christianity was incorporated into the structure of the imperial State and the fabric of imperial thinking.

(Left) Head of Emperor Constantine, found in the Basilica Nova, Rome.

(Above) Legend said that Silvester I baptized Constantine in the baths of the Lateran Palace and, at the same time, cured him of leprosy.

(Below) The Donation of Constantine was a document taken to be a grant from the emperor to the pope of imperial power, the Lateran Palace, and rule over Rome, Italy and the Western world. Constantine supposedly made the gift in gratitude for his baptism and his miraculous cure. The donation was not proved a forgery until the 15th century.

FIRST COUNCIL OF NICAEA (324–325)

Emperor Constantine was much disturbed by the teachings of a priest from Alexandria in Egypt, a man called Arius who said that God the Father had existed before the Son and therefore the Son must be lesser than the Father: that he was, in fact, a creation of the Father. The bishops of Egypt and Libya were outraged by this notion and summoned Arius to a synod in *c.* 320 at which he proved stubborn and was therefore excommunicated. Arius then went to Syria where he was received amicably by several important ecclesiastical figures and thus his influence grew and controversy with it.

Since Constantine was eager to extend imperial protection to Christianity, he perceived it as his duty to settle the Arian question and when his preliminary attempts failed to bring about a solution, he summoned a general council of the most important bishops in the world. They met in Nicaea (modern Iznik in northwest Turkey). Arius's teachings were not the only matters on their agenda. Defining the articles of the faith was the council's principal concern, and out of its

The heretic Arius prostrates himself in front of the emperor and a number of bishops during the Council of Nicaea. While Arianism had virtually disappeared in the Roman empire by the 4th century, pockets of Arians survived among Germanic peoples, and via them Arianism was able to enter the West once more in force.

deliberations issued the formulae now known as the Nicene Creed – the first official definition of faith promulgated by the Christian Church. The date of Easter, hitherto celebrated on different days and including Jewish observances, was to be fixed: all Christians must celebrate it on the same day and without Jewish customs. A variety of other details, largely concerned with the status of the clergy and matters of baptism, also received consideration.

As for Arius, he was condemned as a heretic and while Constantine lived, the controversy Arius had stirred was more or less silenced. It flared up again, however, during the 5th century before being finally wiped out in the 6th.

The Arian heresy gained ascendancy under certain of Constantine's successors, and while it enjoyed imperial favour, its orthodox opponents were forced to flee (above). By 381, however, Arianism had disappeared from much of the Roman empire.

return to Rome where the antipope *Felix II* had been elected in his stead, but, despite a late volte-face to orthodoxy, he died with his reputation in tatters.

One particularly significant point emerges from this long list of popes. Waves of State persecution taught Christian communities, especially those in Rome itself, that the favour of the State was unreliable. Therefore a firm grip was needed from some other authority: and who better than the pope? The more authoritative the papacy was seen to be, the more (after local resistance) it was accepted as such, until finally even the State acknowledged, to some extent, the nascent papal claims.

Damasus I
366–384

Late 11th-/early 12th-century manuscript showing Pope Damasus (Bibliothèque Nationale, Paris). Damasus is addressing St Jerome who stands to the left (unseen). Damasus built several churches, restored the catacombs and encouraged the cult of the martyrs. He was also interested in literature and composed several poems in honour of past popes and the martyrs of the Church.

DAMASUS I	
Nationality	*Age at election*
Italian, from Rome	c. 61
Date of birth	*Died*
c. 305	11 December 384
Family background	*Length of pontificate*
Son of a priest	18 years, 2
Early career	months, 11 days
Deacon	*Antipope*
Elected pope	Ursinus (366–367)
1 October 366	

Damasus and Ursinus, burning with a desire more than human to seize the office of bishop, were arguing very bitterly because of their conflicting points of view, and the supporters of each party, in their disagreements, went to the point of inflicting fatal wounds [on each other] ... Damasus was victorious in the dispute through the efforts of the party which favoured him; and it is well known that in the basilica of Sicininus, where the assembly of the Christian sect is held, there were found in a single day 137 corpses of those who had been killed.

Ammianus Marcellinus *History* 27.3.12–13

He was spitefully accused of adultery, and a synod was held at which he was cleared by 44 bishops who also condemned his accusers, the deacons Concordius and Callistus, and expelled them from the Church.

Liber Pontificalis

Damasus I (366–384) restarts the list of saints. Riots broke out in Rome when Liberius died and Damasus hired thugs to massacre the supporters of his rival, the antipope *Ursinus*. The violence continued after Damasus's consecration until finally the new pope was firmly in control. He then entered upon a pontificate during which, supported by the imperial court, he vigorously advanced the claims of the Roman primate, referring often to Rome as 'the Apostolic See'. 'The East may have sent the Apostles', he said in verses engraved on a tablet which he set over the very spot where Peter and Paul lay buried, 'but because of the merit of their martyrdom Rome has acquired a superior right to claim

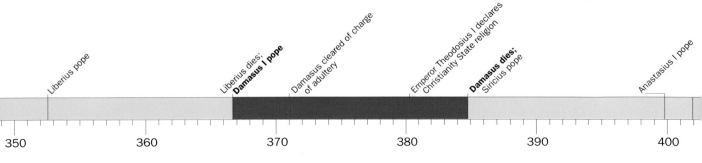

Liberius pope

Liberius dies; **Damasus I pope**

Damasus cleared of charge of adultery

Emperor Theodosius I declares Christianity State religion

Damasus dies; Siricius pope

Anastasius I pope

350   360   370   380   390   400

them as citizens.'

But Damasus also had charm which he exercised upon upper-class women in particular – a tactic which may have lent superficial weight to a charge of adultery he once had to face. His line of reasoning was obvious. Convert the ladies and their men-folk will follow. It was a policy which met with some degree of success. Christianity became, if not exactly fashionable, at least acceptable in aristocratic circles. This, in turn, could not but reinforce the growing prestige and power of the pope, which the regality of Damasus's personal life and the richness of his churches 'gleaming with gold' and 'ornamented with precious marbles' both displayed and emphasized.

Struggle with heresy and schism, however, was not a thing of the past. Throughout his pontificate Damasus continued to combat those who took a deviant line or refused to acknowledge the See of Peter as preeminent, and on 28 February 380 he received a qualified reward for his efforts. For on that day Emperor Theodosius I (379–395) ordered 'all the inhabitants of the empire' to follow 'the form of religion handed down by the Apostle Peter to the Romans, and now followed by Bishop Damasus and Peter of Alexandria'.

His charm and forcefulness, perhaps his two most dominant traits, can be seen from the reactions to him. St Jerome wrote to him in 376, 'Though your eminence alarms me, your kindness draws me to you', and in the following year agreed to become his secretary. It was by Damasus's orders that Jerome corrected and translated into Latin both the Septuagint – a Greek version of the Old Testament – and the New Testament and thus provided the Western Church with its authoritative edition of the Scriptures, the Vulgate – an important centralizing measure, as it happened, and one which helped to enshrine Latin as the principal liturgical language at Rome, and Rome as the focus of biblical

The Crypt of the Popes in the catacombs of St Callistus. Pope Damasus composed an epitaph for Sixtus II whose name 'Xysti Pon' (Pope Sixtus) can be seen here. One version of Sixtus's death says he was run through with a sword. The 4th-century poet Prudentius mistakenly thought he was crucified.

Episodes from the Life of St Jerome, the First Bible of Charles the Bald, 9th century. The bottom picture shows Jerome distributing copies of his Latin version of the Bible, the Vulgate.

scholarship. St Basil, on the other hand, found Damasus irritating and impossible to deal with. He was reminded, he wrote in a letter to a friend, of what Diomedes said about Achilles: 'You ought not to entreat him because, they say, the man is arrogant.'

Siricius
384–399

Anastasius I
399–401

Innocent I
401–417

Zosimus
417–418

Boniface I
418–422

Celestine I
422–432

Sixtus III
432–440

PAPAL NAMES	
SIRICIUS	Family
Nationality	Son = Innocent I,
Italian, from	the next pope
Rome	*Died*
Early career	19 December 401
Deacon	*Length of pontificate*
Elected pope	2 years, 9 months,
December 384	23 days
Died	
26 November 399	INNOCENT I
Length of pontificate	*Nationality*
14 years, *c.* 10	Italian, from Rome
months, 26 days	*Elected pope*
	21 December 401
ANASTASIUS I	*Died*
Nationality	12 March 417
Italian, from Rome	*Length of pontificate*
Elected pope	15 years, 2
27 November 399	months, 22 days

This inscription from the top of a pillar in St Paul's Basilica reads: 'Siricius, the bishop, completely devoted to Christ'. Siricius restored the great basilica of St Paul on the Ostian Way, beginning in 386.

We carry the burdens of all those who are heavily laden. For undoubt-edly the blessed Apostle Peter carries these things in us and, we are sure, protects us in all things to do with his government, and watches over his heirs.

Siricius *Letters* 1.13

When Damasus died, the former antipope Ursinus once again stood for election, and even St Jerome entertained hope of succeeding his erst-while patron. But neither realized his ambition. **Siricius** (384–399) was preferred and throughout his pontificate continued the emphasis of his predecessor upon Roman supremacy. His answers to queries by other bishops on a variety of matters were peremptory and authoritative, and his attitude to heresy was uncompromising. He was also the first Roman bishop to use the title 'pope' in its modern sense, and it may well be that such an overt exercise of primacy contributed to the hostile opinion of Paulinus of Nola that Siricius was both haughty and reserved.

SIRICIVSEPISCOPVS☩TOTAMENTEDEVOTVS

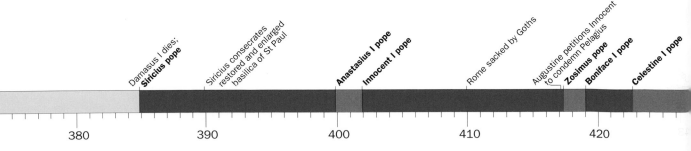

THE EMPIRE DIVIDED

Not long after Constantine became sole emperor in 324, he removed the imperial capital from Rome to a refounded Byzantium, now to be called 'Constantinople'. Constantine did this partly as a result of his conversion to Christianity, which suggested the desirability of a new Christian capital free from pagan associations, but mainly because the nature of the sprawling Roman empire required a centre of civil and military administration further east. The effect was gradually to split the empire, with separate administrations and eventually emperors, and separate religious traditions. From about the 6th century, the five major Christian bishoprics – Rome, Constantinople, Alexandria, Antioch and Jerusalem – were supreme over all others, and their incumbents were known as 'patriarchs', although the title was not used in Rome; here the bishop was the pope. Since Constantinople was an imperial capital, its patriarch regarded himself equal in status to the pope. Because papal claims to supremacy could not accommodate themselves to this point of view, the holders of the two offices were inevitably hostile to each other, a hostility which ended in a breach between the Western and Eastern Churches in 1054, which has continued, with minor attempts to heal the rift, until modern times.

In 410, Rome was sacked by a Visigothic army. St Jerome wrote: 'The city which had captured the whole world was captured itself. Indeed, it perished by famine before it perished by the sword, and very few were found to be taken captive.' *Letter* 127.

Anastasius I (399–401) is particularly notable for his involvement in a bitter controversy over the translation of certain writings by the 3rd-century Alexandrian theologian Origen. One can see factions at work here, because both Jerome and Theophilus, the patriarch of Alexandria, were ruthless in bringing pressure to bear on the pope to anathematize Origen's works as erroneous and dangerous; and because Anastasius was under the eye of Jerome's friends and supporters in Rome, he eventually acquiesced in the condemnation, even though he himself had not read a word of the works he was condemning. Jerome was duly grateful and after Anastasius's death consecrated his memory as a saintly and blessed bishop 'of very rich poverty and Apostolic solicitude' who had successfully governed the Roman Church during a time of tempestuous Eastern heresy.

With **Innocent I** (401–417), reputedly the son of the previous pope, came an immense disaster which challenged the pope's character and abilities to the full. In 410, Rome was sacked. The instrument was Alaric I, king of the Visigoths; the cause was the empire's debility at this

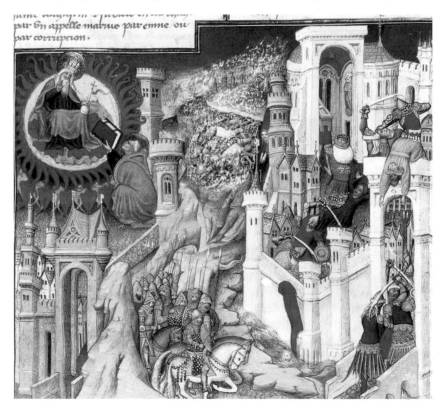

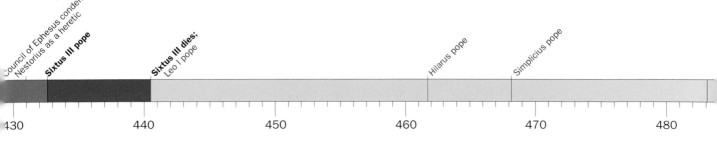

Council of Ephesus condemns Nestorius as a heretic

Sixtus III pope

Sixtus III dies; Leo I pope

Hilarus pope

Simplicius pope

430   440   450   460   470   480

PAPAL NAMES

ZOSIMUS
Nationality
  Greek
Family background
  Perhaps Jewish
Elected pope
  18 March 417
Died
  26 December 418
Length of pontificate
  1 year, 9 months,
  8 days

BONIFACE I
Nationality
  Italian, from Rome
Family background
  Son of a priest
Elected pope
  28 December 418
Died
  4 September 422
Length of pontificate
  3 years, 8 months,
  7 days
Antipope
  Eulalius (418–419)

CELESTINE I
Nationality
  Italian, from
  Campagna
Early career
  Archdeacon of
  Rome
Elected pope
  10 September
  422
Died
  27 July 432
Length of pontificate
  9 years,
  10 months, 10
  days

SIXTUS III
Nationality
  Italian, from
  Rome
Elected pope
  31 July 432
Died
  19 August 440
Length of pontificate
  8 years, 19 days

juncture. The empire had been divided into two, with Honorius, the Western emperor, resident in Ravenna from 404, and the Eastern emperor resident in Constantinople. The talented Western general Stilicho kept the Visigoths in check, but his murder and Honorius's weakness gave Alaric a chance to attack, and in 408 Rome found itself under siege. Alaric reduced the city to the extremities of famine before accepting the offer of a prodigious ransom. Pope Innocent went to Ravenna to persuade Honorius that this ransom would have to be paid if Rome were to survive.

Honorius, however, temporized, and in 409 Alaric again advanced on Rome, seizing the port of Ostia where corn was stored to feed the capital. A second siege began. In August 410 the gates were opened by traitors and Alaric entered the city. For three days it was pillaged. Alaric, a Christian, spared Christian buildings but destroyed those belonging to the pagan population. Innocent, who had been in Ravenna throughout this catastrophe, returned when the Visigoths had left and set about works of public charity.

During his final years a British heresy, Pelagianism, disturbed the Church in Africa and hundreds of letters were sent to the pope from St

ST AUGUSTINE

St Augustine (354–430) was born in north Africa. After a dissolute youth, he became fascinated by Manichaeism – the notion that the world is engaged in a battle between good and evil and that each person must choose to fight for one or the other. Disappointment soon set in, however, and Augustine moved to Milan where he met its bishop Ambrose who converted him to Christianity. He eventually became the bishop of the African city of Hippo (*right*). During his life he wrote voluminously, his most famous works being *Confessions* (397–401), which gave an account of his spiritual restlessness and subsequent conversion, and *The City of God* (413–427), a complex examination of the battle between the love of self and the love of God. He himself had to fight against many heresies – Manichaeism, Donatism, Pelagianism and Arianism – and in the process was obliged to develop new theories on theological questions and formulate their implications. These theories were to attract later theologians, such as Martin Luther.

HERESIES

The word heresy comes from the Greek *hairesis* which has two different meanings: 1) capturing or acquisition, and 2) a system of philosophy or religious sect, and can be neutral or pejorative according to use. Heresy quickly came to be associated with pride and wilfulness, an arrogant opposition to the true, orthodox teaching of the Church. Thus heresy was both immoral and reprehensible since it stemmed from personal stubbornness, and threatened the integrity of the Church and of the faithful.

The heresies listed below are just a few of those which plagued the early Church:

Donatism: A 4th-century heresy which believed that a priest without the true grace of God could not administer valid sacraments.

Pelagianism: A 5th-century heresy which believed that the human will was completely free and equally ready to do good or evil.

Nestorianism: A 5th-century heresy which thought of Christ as two entities, one divine, the other human. It spoke of Mary, not as 'Mother of God', but as mother of the human Christ only.

Monophysitism: This heresy stated that Christ had only one nature (divine) rather than two (divine and human). This theory started more or less in the 5th century, and was one of several attempts to come to terms with the notion of two disparate natures simultaneously and wholly present in the same person.

Monothelitism: This began in the 7th century as part of an attempt to bring Monophysites back into the orthodox fold. It said that Christ had a single will, despite his two natures, and tended to exalt his divine nature at the expense of the human.

Augustine and other African bishops, asking him to repudiate Pelagius's teachings. Innocent's claims that all important religious questions must be referred to him as pope were, it seems, beginning to take effect.

Zosimus (417–418), too, was drawn into the Pelagian controversy but handled it tactlessly and managed to quarrel with the African bishops. **Boniface I** (418–422) had to contend with an antipope, *Eulalius,* and for a while had to leave Rome in the face of powerful political hostility. But he, too, had friends at court and once he managed to reassert his authority, he grappled with the mess left behind by Zosimus. Like his predecessors, Boniface promoted the claims of the papacy and handed to his successor, **Celestine I** (422–432), a Church in somewhat better frame of mind to receive a pope's directives. Celestine's major challenge was yet another heresy – Nestorianism. Nestorius was patriarch of Constantinople (428–451) – an office which was recognized in 381 as being second only to the papacy in deciding Christian matters – and initiated a far-ranging quarrel about whether the Virgin Mary could be called *Theotokos* ('Mother of God') or not. He wrote to Celestine himself and others sent the pope copies of his sermons; but eventually he was condemned as a heretic by the Council of Ephesus in 431, even though Celestine had originally given his approval to Nestorius's appointment as patriarch. Celestine was equally unfortunate in his dealings with the Church in Africa, which continued to assert its freedom of action. **Sixtus III** (432–440) continued Celestine's policies and left a permanent memorial of his reign in Rome by building the church of Santa Maria Maggiore, whose mosaics begin to show the growing influence of the Virgin in Catholic devotion.

A portion of a mosaic of Sixtus III in Santa Maria Maggiore. The church was commissioned by Sixtus. The mosaic illustrates the way in which the Church increasingly appropriated imperial symbols. The arch over the high altar is strongly reminiscent of the Roman triumphal arch.

Leo I
440–461

Detail of a 13th-century manuscript called *The Saxon World Chronicle* showing Pope Leo I greeting Attila the Hun (to the left, out of view). Leo was the first pope to be buried in St Peter's, and his body has been moved four times to different parts of the basilica. On the third removal in 1607, the body was found in almost perfect condition.

LEO I	
Nationality	absence in Gaul
Italian, from Rome	while on a
Early career	diplomatic mission
Deacon	*Died*
Elected pope	10 November 461
August/September	*Length of pontificate*
440. He was	21 years, 2 or 3
elected during his	months, 10 days

No one, dearly beloved, may flatter himself on having any merits of a good life if he is without the works of charity; nor may he rest secure in the purity of his body if he does not cleanse it by the purification of alms-giving. Alms-giving expunges sin, destroys death, and quenches the punishment of eternal fire.

Leo I *Sermon 10*

Rome was left undefended and Gaiseric got hold of it. The holy bishop Leo went forth to meet him outside the gates and his prayers, by God's help, so softened him that though all was in his power, as the city had been handed over to him, he refrained from fire and slaughter and punishment.

Prosper of Aquitaine *Chronicles to the Year 445*

After Pope Sixtus III came the first of only two popes to be known as 'the Great'. **Leo I** (440–461) had worked for both Celestine I and Sixtus III and gained useful experience in dealing with heresies whether they were continuing problems from those earlier reigns, revivals from the previous century, or Christological controversies in the present. Indeed, when it came to the latter especially, he brooked no nonsense. One can see this in his dealings with an heretical Eastern monk, Eutyches, who had been teaching a form of Monophysite heresy – the belief that Christ had had only one nature, the human having been absorbed by the divine. The patriarch of Constantinople, Flavian, condemned this and immediately Eutyches stirred up trouble and appealed to Rome. A council was summoned to Ephesus in 449 to deal with this problem.

Leo did not condescend to come himself to the council but sent dele-

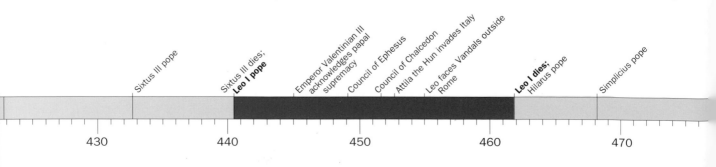

Sixtus III pope
Sixtus III dies; **Leo I pope**
Emperor Valentinian III acknowledges papal supremacy
Council of Ephesus
Council of Chalcedon
Attila the Hun invades Italy
Leo faces Vandals outside Rome
Leo I dies; Hilarus pope
Simplicius pope

430   440   450   460   470

PAPAL SUPREMACY

It is certain that the only defence for us and our empire is the favour of the God of heaven; and to deserve it our first care is to support the Christian faith and its venerable religion. So, because the pre-eminence of the Apostolic See is assured by the merit of the prince of bishops St Peter, by the leading position of the city of Rome, and also by the authority of a sacred synod, let none presume to attempt anything contrary to the authority of that see. For then at last the peace of the churches will be preserved everywhere if the whole body recognizes its ruler.

Leo *Letters* 11 (quoting the Order of Valentinian III)

Pope Leo's views on the papacy are important. He was a man grounded in Roman law and sought to clarify the notion of papal succession in terms of the existing Roman law of inheritance. Each pope, in law, succeeded St Peter, not the immediately preceding pope, and thus inherited St Peter's powers. This view had the effect of separating the papal office from the person holding it, so that the prestige and the authority of the papacy would remain untouched (at least legally) by the individual failings or virtues of any particular pope. Hence the pope became executor of the office and his personality was of no account in the execution of papal powers inherited directly from Peter.

gates armed with a doctrinal statement (*Tome*) asserting the orthodox teaching that the incarnate Christ's two natures were separate. At the same time Leo sent instructions that he did not expect his *Tome* to be subjected to any inquiry or discussion. 'Rome has spoken; the subject is closed' is not one of his sayings, but there is little doubt he would have applauded its sentiment. He had imperial support. Emperor Valentinian III acknowledged the claim to papal supremacy in an edict (445) which enabled Leo to confine to his diocese a troublesome Gallic bishop, Hilary of Arles.

But Leo does not appear to have become arrogant. He took his pastoral duties seriously and was a busy preacher, his 96 extant sermons revealing his eagerness to promote charitable giving to the poor, fasting and avoidance of sun-worship on the steps of St Peter's. He was also personally courageous. In 452, for example, when northern Italy was under attack by Attila the Hun, Leo faced him near Mantua and persuaded him to withdraw his army. Again, in 455 he confronted Gaiseric the Vandal outside the walls of Rome and, by his intervention, mitigated somewhat the sack of the city which followed.

The impression carried away by anyone who reads an account of his pontificate is that of a man who had no doubts that he was exercising the full authority of St Peter as transmitted to the bishops of Rome, and that this authority overrode that of all other patriarchs and bishops. When he died he was buried within the porch of St Peter's, but in 668 his tomb was removed and a monument erected inside the basilica itself – a great honour, and Leo was the first pontiff to whom it was accorded.

17th-century sculpture of Pope Leo I facing Attila the Hun, by Alessandro Algardi, St Peter's Basilica, Rome. Attila had a wry sense of humour. Bishop Lupus and Pope Leo I were the two people who had been most persuasive in getting the king to spare the cities of Troyes and Rome. 'I can conquer men', said Attila, 'but not the Lion (*Leo*) and the wolf (*Lupus*)'.

Hilarus
461–468

Simplicius
468–483

Felix III (II)
483–492

Gelasius I
492–496

Anastasius II
496–498

Symmachus
498–514

Hormisdas
514–523

John I
523–526

Felix IV (III)
526–530

Boniface II
530–532

John II
533–535

Agapitus I
535–536

Silverius
536–537

He [Pope Gelasius I] gave himself up to no vain, idling, and wasteful banquets which bring maladies of soul and body. This pastor was an imitator of the great Good Shepherd, an outstanding bishop of the Apostolic See, who lived the divine precepts and taught them.

Dionysius Exiguus *Decretals of the Roman Pontiffs*

PAPAL NAMES

HILARUS
Nationality
  Sardinian
Early career
  Archdeacon
Elected pope
  19 November 461
Died
  29 February 468
Length of pontificate
  6 years, 3 months, 12 days

SIMPLICIUS
Nationality
  Italian, from Tivoli
Elected pope
  3 March 468
Died
  10 March 483
Length of pontificate
  15 years, 7 days

FELIX III (II)
Nationality
  Italian, from Rome
Family background
  Aristocratic; son of a priest
Elected pope
  13 March 483
Marital status
  Widower
Offspring
  At least two children – ancestors of Agapitus I and Gregory I
Died
  1 March 492
Length of pontificate
  8 years, 11 months, 18 days

Succeeding a great pope cannot have been easy, but **Hilarus** (461–468) had worked closely with Leo and modelled himself upon him, not hesitating, for example, to confront the Western emperor Anthemius (467–472) when he seemed to be on the point of favouring heretics in the heart of Rome itself. Hilarus also consolidated Rome's authority over the churches in Gaul and Spain, emphasized Roman supremacy in his letters to the bishops of the East, and fought against heresies abroad as well as at home. **Simplicius** (468–483) saw the last Roman emperor of the West, Romulus Augustulus, deposed in favour of a German general, Odoacer, a heretic, and the disintegration of the Western empire into separate romanized but non-Roman principalities. This was a significant moment, for it left the Church as the most likely heir to Roman imperial authority and prestige. In the East, however, Monophysite teaching, so firmly opposed by Leo I, was in the ascendant and Simplicius became

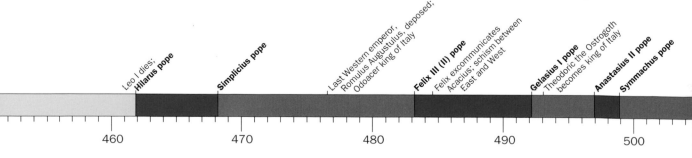

Leo I dies; **Hilarus pope**

Simplicius pope

Last Western emperor, Romulus Augustulus, deposed; Odoacer king of Italy

Felix III (II) pope
Felix excommunicates Acacius; schism between East and West

Gelasius I pope
Theodoric the Ostrogoth becomes king of Italy

Anastasius II pope

Symmachus pope

460   470   480   490   500

PAPAL NAMES

GELASIUS I
Nationality
  African, born in
  Rome
Early career
  Archdeacon
Elected pope
  1 March 492
Died
  21 November 496
Length of pontificate
  4 years, 8 months,
  21 days

ANASTASIUS II
Nationality
  Italian, from Rome
Family background
  Son of a priest
Early career
  Deacon
Elected pope
  24 November 496
Died
  19 November 498
Length of pontificate
  1 year, 11 months,
  26 days

SYMMACHUS
Nationality
  Sardinian
Religious status
  Convert from

paganism
Early career
  Deacon
Elected pope
  22 November 498
Died
  19 July 514
Length of pontificate
  15 years,
  7 months, 28 days
Antipope
  Lawrence
  (498–499;
  501–506)

HORMISDAS
Nationality
  Italian, from
  Frosinone
Family background
  Aristocratic;
  wealthy
Elected pope
  20 July 514
Marital status
  Married before his
  ordination
Family
  Son=later became
  Pope Silverius
Died
  6 August 523
Length of pontificate
  9 years, 17 days

Pope Gelasius I, from the frontispiece of a hymnal illuminated at Fulda, *c*. 975 (Göttingen University Library). Gelasius was a prolific writer of letters as well as theological treatises. He developed a theory that there were two powers in the world, one episcopal and one royal. The latter was held in particular by the emperor, the former, superior to it, by the pope.

Theodoric, king of the Ostrogoths and viceroy of Italy for the Eastern emperor Zeno I (474–491), overthrew Odoacer in 493 to become king of Italy. The inscription reads: 'King Theodoric, the pious ruler'. Theodoric was actually an Arian heretic, but protected Catholics against the Eastern emperor's desire to promote Monophysitism.

increasingly helpless to do anything about it. The Eastern emperor simply ceased to consult or inform him.

Felix III (483–492) – or II if one discounts the earlier antipope of the same name – quickly found that Constantinople had little respect for either him or his office, and reacted angrily by excommunicating the patriarch Acacius for appointing a Monophysite to the see of Antioch to replace its orthodox bishop. Acacius ignored the sentence and thus began a split between East and West which lasted for 35 years. Felix, however, maintained a resolute antagonism to Monophysite influence, even in the face of a new emperor's attempts at *rapprochement*. His resistance is notable. It marks how far the papacy had come from the days when it either had to lie low or win a lofty accommodation from the imperial secular power.

During the pontificate of **Gelasius I** (492–496), the second pope of African descent, the schism between East and West continued and deepened. While Odoacer the German was replaced by Theodoric the Ostrogoth, thus distancing the remnants of the Western empire even further from the East, Gelasius stubbornly refused to compromise with Constantinople, warning his legate there about the sly tricks and obstinate heresy of the 'Greeks'. Fortunately, perhaps, Gelasius managed to form an excellent relationship with Theodoric who, in spite of being (or maybe because he was) a heretic, allowed Gelasius a free hand in regulating the Church. But even in Rome not everyone agreed with the pope's unbending stance, and his successor, **Anastasius II** (496–498), initiated a conciliatory approach to the Eastern emperor. 'We do not want the disagreement among the churches to continue any longer', he wrote and

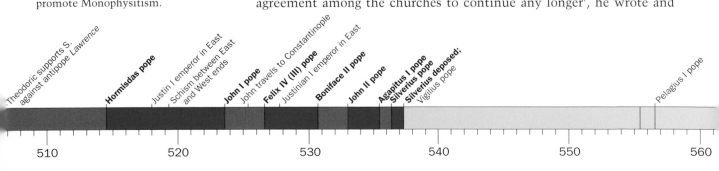

(*Right*) Mosaic in the Church of Sant' Apollinare Nuovo in Ravenna, showing Theodoric's palace at Ravenna. Theodoric and his courtiers have been obliterated. This took place after the conquest of Ravenna by the Eastern emperor's military commander, Belisarius, in 540.

(*Below*) A brick from the Church of San Martino ai Monti, inscribed with Theodoric's stamp. It was made during Theodoric's restoration of Rome. It reads: 'During the reign of our lord Theodoric, for the good of Rome.'

And there, because of the dreadful and outrageous stench which the deep abyss threw up, we drew together behind a lid covering a great tomb, on which I saw writing which said, 'I hold Pope Anastasius'.

Dante *Inferno* Canto 11

PAPAL NAMES

JOHN I
Nationality
  Tuscan
Early career
  Deacon
Elected pope
  13 August 523
Age at election
  Elderly
Died
  18 May 526 in Ravenna
Length of pontificate
  2 years, 9 months, 4 days

FELIX IV (III)
Nationality
  Italian Samnite
Early career
  Deacon
Elected pope
  12 July 526
Died
  22 September 530

Length of pontificate
  4 years, 2 months, 10 days

BONIFACE II
Nationality
  German, born in Rome
Family background
  Wealthy
Early career
  Archdeacon
Elected pope
  22 September 530
Died
  17 October 532
Length of pontificate
  2 years, 25 days
Antipope
  Dioscorus (September 530–October 530)

---

followed his letter with an embassy. At the same time, Theodoric suggested to the emperor that he recognize his (Theodoric's) claim to the kingship of Italy. A quid pro quo was offered; the emperor would recognize Theodoric on the understanding that the pope would adopt a softer line on Monophysitism: one notes the assumption that Anastasius would fall into line. But almost at once Anastasius was in trouble. Rome had split into hard-liners and compromisers, and the pope's somewhat inept forays into diplomacy produced internal schism. It is not, therefore, surprising that when the pope suddenly died at the height of the crisis, his enemies attributed his death to the wrath of God.

The schism meant a divided election. **Symmachus** (498–514) was opposed by the antipope *Lawrence* amid violent scenes which brought Theodoric into the process. He declared for Symmachus who was then accused by Lawrence's supporters of celebrating Easter on the wrong day, being unchaste and misusing Church property. Summoned by Theodoric to explain himself, Symmachus foolishly fled to Rome and locked himself in St Peter's. Needless to say, this caused another split among the clergy and it was not until 502 that Symmachus was vindicated. But Theodoric was displeased by this verdict and for a while Lawrence and Symmachus coexisted in Rome, ruling by virtue of the violence of their respective adherents. Then in 506 Theodoric changed his mind and transferred his support wholly to Symmachus. Lawrence fled to a farm owned by his principal patron, and not long after died. The bitterness of these early years soured the rest of Symmachus's pontificate. **Hormisdas** (514–523), however, was able to act as a peacemaker not only between the factions in Rome but also between Rome and Constantinople. In his reign the long quarrel started under Felix III was brought to an end, helped by the accession of a new Eastern emperor, Justin I (518–527), who was no supporter of Monophysitism.

However, **John I** (523–526), a former admirer of the antipope Lawrence, was immediately faced by a major political challenge.

PAPAL NAMES

JOHN II
Nationality
  Uncertain
Original name
  Mercurius
Elected pope
  2 January 533
Age at election
  Elderly
Died
  8 May 535
Length of pontificate
  2 years, 4 months,
  6 days
Notable feature
  John may have
  been the first pope
  since St Peter to
  have a change of
  name, unless the
  Greek names of
  some of the earliest
  popes indicate a
  similar tradition of
  name-changing

AGAPITUS I
Nationality
  Italian, from Rome
Family background
  Aristocratic; son of
  a priest
Elected pope
  13 May 535

Early career
  Archdeacon
Died
  22 April 536, in
  Constantinople
Length of pontificate
  11 months, 10 days

SILVERIUS
Nationality
  Italian, from
  Frosinone
Family background
  Son of Pope
  Hormisdas
Early career
  Subdeacon
Elected pope
  8 June 536
Deposed
  11 March 537;
  exiled to Patara, a
  seaport in
  southwest Anatolia
Abdicated
  11 November 537
  on Palmaria, an
  island in the Gulf of
  Gaeta
Died
  2 December 537
Length of pontificate
  1 year, 5 months,
  2 days

A 14th-century fresco in the Church of Santa Maria in Porto Fuori, Ravenna, depicting John I being judged by King Theodoric. A companion fresco shows the pope in prison. The pictures record a dubious tradition that Theodoric had John arrested and put to death. A miniature of the 15th century shows the pope being executed.

Justin I had begun to persecute Arians, followers of the 4th-century heretic Arius who denied that Jesus was consubstantial with God (i.e. had the same essence or substance as the Father), which would mean, of course, that Jesus was inferior to God. This teaching had proved popular in certain quarters and had spread. King Theodoric himself was an Arian and resented Justin's attempts to suppress his beliefs. So he ordered the pope to go to Constantinople and negotiate a settlement with the Eastern emperor. John was the first pope to go to the East and was accorded a brilliant welcome. Nevertheless, his mission ended in failure and, on his return to Italy, he had to face Theodoric's anger. Mercifully for him, perhaps, he died before the king could decide what to do with him.

A member of John's delegation to Constantinople became the next

Pope Felix IV. Detail from a heavily restored 6th-century mosaic in the Church of SS. Cosma and Damiano, Rome. Felix was the first pope to adapt pagan buildings in the Roman Forum to Christian worship. The Temple of the Sacred City and its adjoining Shrine of Romulus, for example, were turned into a church dedicated to the martyrs Cosma and Damiano. This portrait in the apse of that church is the earliest surviving papal likeness. Unfortunately, however, it has been much altered by later hands.

pope. **Felix IV** or III (526–530) seems to have been Theodoric's preferred choice and continued to enjoy favour at the Gothic court. But the next pontificate began badly. **Boniface II** (530–532), the first pope of German descent, had been unconstitutionally nominated by Felix as his successor and was opposed by an antipope *Dioscorus* who received the votes of a worryingly large number of clergy. He died, however, after 22 days and Boniface made those who had voted for him sign a letter, confessing their mistake. Thereafter, the pope set about reconciliation but almost threw it away by trying to nominate his successor. Faced with potential revolt, he retreated and thus saved himself from Gothic disfavour.

For two months and 15 days after Boniface's death, the most scandalous election campaign yet waged for the papal office saw intrigue, chicanery and corruption busying themselves about Rome. Large-scale bribing of royal officials and influential senators reached such a pitch that Theodoric's successor, King Athalaric, passed a law to prevent its reoccurrence. Out of this mess came **John II** (533–535), a man on good terms with both Athalaric and the new Eastern emperor, Justinian I (527–565). The latter published a decree favourable in its tone to the Monophysites, and John, in spite of an appeal from monks in Constantinople, ratified the document in clear contradiction of the line taken earlier on the subject by Pope Hormisdas. **Agapitus I** (535–536), a cultured aristocrat, was not so accommodating and turned his face against Justinian's declared intention of invading Italy and incorporating it once more into the empire. He went to Constantinople to see if the emperor might be persuaded to drop his plan but because the Church's wealth had been squandered during the election battles in 532, he was obliged to pawn sacred vessels to pay for his deputation. This was, as it turned out, a failure. Certainly he managed to convince Justinian that the patriarch of Constantinople, Anthimus, was a heretic, and have him deposed; but the key-point of his mission was refused. Italy, said Justinian, would still be invaded.

Agapitus died in Constantinople and Empress Theodora, a Monophysite who had favoured the deposed patriarch, offered a Roman deacon, Vigilius, the papal throne if he agreed to reinstate her favourite. Rome, however, had meanwhile elected **Silverius** (536–537) pope. This contretemps proved short-lived, as did the pope. Justinian's military commander, Belisarius, now in Rome, tried to persuade Silverius to resign quietly and when the pope refused, deposed him by force and sent him into exile. An appeal, however, was lodged with Justinian. The emperor ordered that Silverius be returned to Rome and stand trial for allegedly plotting with the Goths against him. Vigilius, now pope, took immediate steps to have him officially abdicate and Silverius, exiled a second time, soon after died from starvation.

Vigilius
537–555

Boniface II named Vigilius (*right*) – then a deacon – as his successor, but it was decided that the papacy could not be treated by its incumbent as though it were a piece of personal property, and the nomination was cancelled.

VIGILIUS	
Nationality Italian *Family background* Aristocratic; a consular family *Early career* Deacon *Elected pope* 29 March 537	*Died* 7 June 555 at Syracuse in Sicily, from gallstones *Length of pontificate* 18 years, 2 months, 10 days

A gold medallion of Emperor Justinian as conqueror (British Museum).

Theodora summoned Vigilius and secretly urged him to promise that if he became pope, he would dismiss the Council [of Chalcedon, held in 451], write to Theodosius, Anthimus and Severus [leading Monophysites] and pledge his loyalty to them in his letter. She promised to give him an order for Belisarius to have him ordained pope and present him with 700 gold pieces. Vigilius, therefore, willingly made his promise, for love of the papal office and of gold; and when he had given his word, he set out for Rome where he found that Silverius had already been ordained pope.

Liberatus of Carthage *Breviarium* 22

With Vigilius there is no disguising the fact that we reach a low point in papal history. True, our sources are largely hostile to him, but even after one discounts the bias, there is still much to be hostile about. Three things are clear: Vigilius was a creature of Justinian and Theodora; the basic motivation of his career was his desire to become pope and he was complicit to some degree in the downfall of Silverius. Nevertheless, a measure of sympathy may be appropriate. With the military aggrandizement of the imperial court in Constantinople, the determined resistance to it of the Gothic court in Italy, and the battle between pro-Gothic and

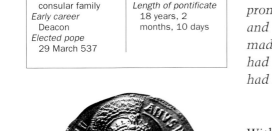

John I pope
Felix IV (III) pope
Boniface II pope
John II pope
Agapitus I pope
Silverius pope
Silverius deposed; **Vigilius pope**
Justinian issues decree against 'Three Chapters'
Church council at Constantinople
Vigilius dies
Pelagius I pope
John III pope

520   530   540   550   560   570

EMPRESS THEODORA

Theodora resolutely fixed her mind without cease upon cruelty. She was never persuaded by anyone, nor forced, to do anything but carried out her own wishes herself by the full force of her own will. No one dared intercede for any person who had displeased her. Neither passage of time, nor surfeit of punishment, nor any art of supplication, nor threat of death … would persuade her to lay aside any part of her rage. In short, no one ever knew Theodora ever to reconcile herself with anyone who had given her offence, even after he had left the land of the living. The child of the dead man inherited the empress's hatred, just as he inherited anything else belonging to his father, and bequeathed it to the third generation.

Procopius *Secret History* 15

Detail from a 6th-century mosaic in the Church of San Vitale, Ravenna, showing Empress Theodora.

pro-imperial factions in Rome itself, not to mention the wider struggle of orthodox teaching and Monophysite heresy to capture hearts and minds, the papacy must have feared being reduced to the status of a meaty bone torn by two quarrelling dogs.

Vigilius had first made the acquaintance of Theodora – who had begun life as an actress and a prostitute, catching Justinian's eye while he was still heir to the throne and marrying him shortly after he became emperor – when he was sent as a papal representative to Constantinople by Boniface II. During the intrigues which followed the death of Agapitus I, Vigilius eventually emerged as pope on the spears of Belisarius's army and thus owed much to imperial favour. Unfortunately for him, emperor and empress were on opposite sides of the doctrinal controversy, and while Vigilius wrote to Justinian that he supported wholeheartedly the emperor's theological stance, privately, through the offices of the former patriarch of Constantinople, he assured Theodora of his goodwill towards and approval of the Monophysite position. It was not a balancing-act he could maintain forever.

In 543, Justinian issued an official repudiation of the writings of three individuals, all of whom supported the orthodox line on the two-fold nature of Christ. This initiated what is known as the 'Three Chapters' controversy and proved fatal to Vigilius's ability to survive without further dishonour. Justinian may have been hoping that his anti-orthodox decree would please (and thus pacify) the large number of Monophysites in the empire, but what it actually did was to deepen further the already profound division between East and West. Vigilius, to do him justice, did try at first to resist the emperor's demand that he ratify this decree. But Justinian was in no mood for recalcitrance, and had the pope arrested and eventually brought to Constantinople. It took a long time to wear down his resistance, but at length he gave in – although even then he temporized. He would condemn the Three Chapters, he said, but maintain the orthodox position.

The West saw this as a betrayal and such was the furore aroused that Justinian agreed that a Church council should be summoned to resolve it. During the long delay which ensued Justinian impatiently reissued his condemnation of the Three Chapters, only to be met by Vigilius's outright refusal to support him. This was the beginning of Vigilius's end. Attacked by soldiers, he fled into exile, and when the council was finally called in Constantinople in 553, he thought it best not to attend in person. The council, in Justinian's pocket, decreed as the emperor wished. As for the pope, he was brought back to house arrest in the Eastern capital and eventually forced to comply with Justinian's demands.

He remained in exile for about seven years until, broken and ill, he was told he might return to Rome. He died before he reached it. We are told that he died in Syracuse of an attack of gallstones. The exact date of his death is unknown. It happened either late in 554 or early in 555. His body was taken on to Rome and buried in the Church of San Marcello on the Via Salaria.

Pelagius I
556–561

John III
561–574

Benedict I
575–579

Pelagius II
579–590

Pelagius II restored the Basilica of San Lorenzo fuori le Mura, Rome, and is here shown in one of the church's 6th-century mosaics with a model of the restored building.

PAPAL NAMES

PELAGIUS I
Nationality
  Italian, from Rome
Family background
  Aristocratic; wealthy
Elected pope
  16 April 556
Age at election
  Elderly
Died
  3 March 561
Length of pontificate
  4 years, 10
  months, 17 days

JOHN III
Nationality
  Italian, from Rome
Family background
  Senatorial family;
  son of a provincial
  governor
Original name
  Catelinus
Elected pope
  17 July 561
Died
  13 July 574

Length of pontificate
  12 years, 11
  months, 27 days

BENEDICT I
Nationality
  Italian, from
  Rome
Elected pope
  2 June 575
Died
  30 July 579
Length of pontificate
  4 years, 1 month

PELAGIUS II
Nationality
  Goth, born in
  Rome
Elected pope
  26 November 579
Died
  7 February 590 in
  Rome, of the
  plague
Length of pontificate
  10 years, 2
  months, 12 days

So great are the calamities and tribulations we suffer from the treachery of the Lombards in spite of their solemn promises, that no one could adequately describe them.... The empire is in so critical a state that unless God prevails on the heart of our most pious prince to show to his servants the pity he feels and to grant us a commander or general, then we are lost. For the territory around Rome is completely undefended and the exarch writes that he can do nothing for us, since he himself is unable to defend the region round Ravenna. May God bid the emperor to come to our aid as quickly as possible before the army of that impious nation, the Lombards, seize the lands which still form part of the empire.

A letter from Pelagius II to his representative in Liguria

Vigilius was not the only one to suffer imperial displeasure. His deacon, Pelagius, had been thrown into gaol by Justinian to help undermine Vigilius's obstinacy, and when Vigilius died, Pelagius was sent to Rome as the emperor's candidate for the papacy. No one there greeted him with delight. He was never elected to the papal throne, and was consecrated only after two bishops had been hustled into performing the ceremony. **Pelagius I** (556–561), therefore, had an inauspicious start, but he

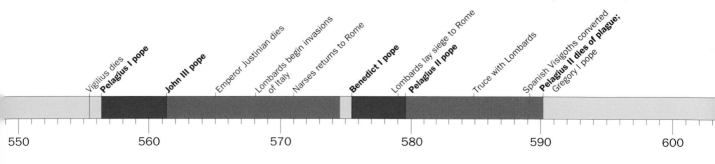

Vigilius dies **Pelagius I pope** | **John III pope** | Emperor Justinian dies | Lombards begin invasions of Italy | Narses returns to Rome | **Benedict I pope** | Lombards lay siege to Rome | **Pelagius II pope** | Truce with Lombards | Spanish Visigoths converted **Pelagius II dies of plague; Gregory I pope**

550   560   570   580   590   600

PLAGUE IN LIGURIA

There began to appear in people's groins and in other somewhat tender places, a swelling of the glands, which looked like a nut or a date. Soon there followed a fever so hot and unbearable that upon the third day the person died. But if anyone got through the third day, he had a hope of living. Everywhere there was grief; everywhere there were tears. For as common report had it, people fled to avoid the plague; houses were left deserted by their inhabitants, and only young dogs looked after them. The flocks remained alone in the pastures with no shepherd at hand.... Sons fled, leaving the dead bodies of their parents unburied; parents, forgetful of their duty, abandoned their children in burning fever. If by chance a long-standing sense of duty did penetrate anyone's feelings deeply enough to persuade him to bury his relative, he himself remained unburied, and while he was performing the funeral rites, he perished.... The crops survived the time of the harvest and waited, untouched, for the reaper. The vineyard remained undisturbed, its leaves fallen, its grapes glistening, while winter came on.... Pastoral places had been turned into a burial ground, and human habitations had become places of refuge for wild beasts.

Paul the Deacon *History of the Lombards* 2.4

Detail of a 10th-century Spanish manuscript showing a Visigothic king. The Visigoths originally came from Sweden, but by the 2nd century AD they had moved into southern Russia. Constantine I made them allies of the empire, but by the beginning of the 5th century they were strong enough to invade Italy and sack Rome in 410. The Visigoths were Arian heretics, and their kingdom in Spain was a stronghold of Arianism from the middle of the century until 711 when it was conquered by the Arabs.

worked immensely hard to rescue Rome and Italy from the ravages of their recent wars, reorganize the papal finances, and reform monastic and clerical behaviour, both of which were much in need of it. Great harm had been done to papal authority by Vigilius's temporizing and so Pelagius's achievements, although not spectacular, must under the circumstances be regarded as considerable. **John III** (561–574), his successor, saw Italy invaded again. This time it was the Lombards who were on the move. They ravaged a territory already turned into a graveyard by plague, which had visited the area three years before. At their approach, John fled south to Naples and there persuaded the former Byzantine governor of Italy, Narses, to venture out of an enforced retirement and come back to Rome to organize a defence. Narses, however, had originally been dismissed from his post because he was unpopular and this return caused fresh disturbances during which the pope, fearful of becoming embroiled in the violence, retired from Rome and conducted the rest of his pontificate from a church 2 miles away.

Relations between Rome and Constantinople, meanwhile, improved a little. Nevertheless, the upheavals in Italy meant that **Benedict I** (575–579) had to wait for 11 months before imperial approval of his consecration as pope. Throughout his reign, the Lombards were thrusting south and in 579 they were able to lay siege to Rome. An army sent by the Eastern emperor proved ineffectual, and grain from Egypt relieved the situation only briefly. Famine invested Rome and Pope Benedict died in the midst of its afflictions. His successor, the Gothic pope, **Pelagius II** (579–590), thus inherited a desperate crisis. His appeals to Constantinople were fruitless as the emperor had problems of his own in fending off Persian attacks, and it was not until 585 that Constantinople reached an accommodative truce with the Lombard leaders. One papal success – the conversion of the Visigoths in Spain – was accompanied by the start of yet another controversy. This involved a title, 'Ecumenical Patriarch', adopted in 588 in accordance with custom by the patriarch of Constantinople, but which Pelagius viewed as a subtle derogation of papal supremacy. He objected but did not have long to pursue the question. In the autumn of 589, records the *Liber Pontificalis*, 'there were such heavy rains that everyone said the waters of the flood had overflowed; and such fearful carnage that no one remembered that its like had ever been seen in the world'. There followed plague which carried off the pope, and the Church was left for nearly a year without a sovereign pontiff.

The votive crown of Recceswinth, the Visigothic king of Spain, 653–672 (Archaeological Museum, Madrid). During the reign of Pelagius II the Visigoths of Spain were successfully converted to Christianity. Note the cross hanging from the crown.

Map showing the territories of the Lombards in Italy between the 6th and 8th centuries AD. The Lombards came originally from the shores of the Baltic, moving south to settle in what was to become the Avar empire. Forced to leave this region because of Avar expansion, the Lombards began encroaching on Italian territories – an invasion which would have significant consequences for the popes, although the Lombards never managed to conquer Rome.

Early kingdom of the Lombards; area evacuated in 568, due to Avar expansion, leading to Lombard invasions of Italy

Lombard conquests of Byzantine territory *c.* 590

Lombard conquests of Byzantine territory *c.* 730

Byzantine empire *c.* 730

Gregory I
590–604

Detail of an 11th-century manuscript showing Gregory the Great. Gregory was the first pontiff to employ the phrase, 'speaking *ex cathedra*', meaning, with the full weight and authority of the papal office. A *cathedra* was originally a high-backed chair, and then came to refer to a bishop's throne.

GREGORY I	
Nationality	*Length of pontificate*
Italian, from Rome	13 years,
Family background	6 months,
Aristocratic; wealthy	8 days
Early career	*Notable feature*
Prefect of Rome	Gregory was
c. 572–574; after	the first monk
father's death, he	to become a
became a monk;	pope, and is one
deacon	of only two popes
Elected pope	(the other being
3 September 590	Leo I), to be called
Died	'the Great'
12 March 604	

He [Gregory] was of ordinary height and well proportioned.... He was rather bald, so that in the middle of his forehead he had two small neat curls, twisted towards the right.... His cheeks were well shaped, and his chin protruded in a comely fashion from the limit of his jaws. His colour was swarthy and full of vital force, not pale and sickly, as it afterwards became.

John the Deacon *Vita Sancti Gregorii Magni*, 4.84

Under the pretence of being made a bishop, I have been brought back into the world, and I devote myself to the interests of secular things to a much greater extent than I recall even having done when I was a layman. I have lost the deep joy of my peace and quiet, and while I seem outwardly to have risen, inwardly I am in a state of collapse.... Behold my most serene lord the emperor has ordered a monkey to become a lion. But while a lion it may be called at his command, a lion it cannot become. Therefore he must assign the blame of all my faults and negligences, not to me, but to his kindly feeling which led him to commit the exercise of power to a fragile man.

Gregory *Registrum Epistularum* 1.5

After his initial reluctance at being elected pope, **Gregory I** (590–604) set about his duties with vigour. First he had to deal with the current starvation in Rome, and in the course of providing relief he also reorganized the management of the large, widely scattered papal estates so that money would be reliably available to the Holy See to help to feed people in any time of crisis. In the absence of sufficient imperial forces to protect Rome against incursions from the north, Gregory saw to its defences, paid for troops and, in 591 and 593, even bribed the Lombards

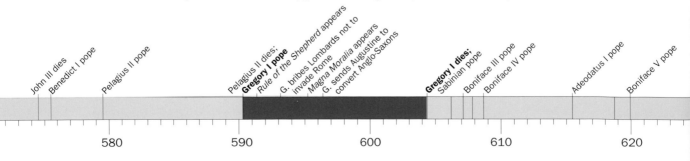

John III dies
Benedict I pope
Pelagius II pope
Pelagius II dies; **Gregory I pope**
Rule of the Shepherd appears
G. bribes Lombards not to invade Rome
Magna Moralia appears
G. sends Augustine to convert Anglo-Saxons
Gregory I dies; Sabinian pope
Boniface III pope
Boniface IV pope
Adeodatus I pope
Boniface V pope

580   590   600   610   620

'SERVANT OF THE SERVANTS OF GOD'

The only pope, apart from Leo I, to be called 'the Great', came from a wealthy, aristocratic Roman family. We know little about his early years, but he was well-educated and his writings reveal a keen interest in natural science, and a knowledge of history, Classical literature and music. His Latin was fluent, but in spite of his spending several years in Constantinople, he never learned Greek, which shows how far apart the West and East were drifting; and indeed the popes' lack of Greek – for Gregory was not the only one at this period without it – was beginning to place them at a disadvantage in their dealings with Eastern theologians.

After a secular career in urban administration, Gregory became a monk (c. 574) and turned his family home into a monastery. There he entered upon a rigorous regime of prayer and fasting which he would continue all his life, and which would play a part in undermining his constitution. In about 579 he was sent to Constantinople by Pelagius II as a papal representative and there got to know the principal power-brokers of the Eastern empire. In c. 585 he was recalled to Rome to act as an advisor to Pope Pelagius, especially in a delicate matter involving the schism of certain Italian bishops who had been disgusted by Pope Vigilius's handling of the 'Three Chapters' affair.

A 10th-century German ivory panel showing Gregory at work. Perched on his shoulder and whispering in his ear is the Holy Spirit in the form of a dove (Kunsthistorisches Museum, Vienna).

When Pelagius died the papal electors unanimously cast their votes in Gregory's favour. He was horrified and wrote to Emperor Maurice (582–602) asking him to withhold his consent. Imperial confirmation of his election arrived, however, and Gregory was duly consecrated pontiff on 3 September 590 – the first monk to occupy the papal throne.

Detail of the Lombard king Agilulf's helmet (Bargello, Florence).

to call a halt to their depredations. But Emperor Maurice, who should have been grateful for these efforts, merely grumbled about what he saw as interference and received a well-deserved papal rebuke in return for his captiousness. Outside Italy, too, there was much to claim the pope's attention. Africa, for example, was seeing a resurgence of the 4th-century Donatist heresy which maintained that its clerics alone could validly confer the sacraments, and the pope sought to contain this rise and turn the heretic

Coin portrait of Emperor Maurice (British Museum). Maurice was born in Cappadocia, although a legend makes him an Armenian. A decentralizer, in contrast to Justinian I, he successfully defended the empire against Persia, but was unable to resist the Lombard encroachment in northern Italy. He was executed by his successor, Phocas.

It is now a long time since I have had the strength to rise from my bed. For at one time the pain of gout tortures me, and at another a fire (of what kind I do not know), spreads itself with pain through my whole body. Usually at one and the same time a painful, burning heat afflicts me, and both body and mind fail me. I am unable to count how many other great distresses of illness are visited upon me in addition to those I have mentioned. In a few words, however, I can say that the infection of a poisonous humour drinks me up to such an extent that it is a punishment for me to live, and I look longingly for death which I believe is the only thing which can provide a cure for my groans.

Gregory *Registrum Epistularum* 11.20 (letter to Marianus, bishop of Arabia, February 601)

tide. With Spain and Gaul, however, he was able to establish amicable relations, and to England he sent the prior of his Roman monastery, Augustine, in 596, to convert the Anglo-Saxons to Christianity there; while with Constantinople he kept up the lengthy disagreement over the title 'Ecumenical Patriarch', which had exercised his predecessor, Pelagius II.

Such domestic and foreign problems, however, were not the pope's only concerns. Gregory also had to deal with discipline within the Church, and, spurred by a conviction that the world would soon come to an end, he set about preparing souls for the Second Coming. Thus, in a book which was to prove lastingly influential, *The Rule of the Shepherd* (c. 591), he laid down rules for the election and proper conduct of bishops, and degraded, without hesitation, clerics who failed to maintain the high moral standards he expected. In particular, he enforced clerical celibacy which had been obligatory for bishops, priests and deacons since the reign of Siricius, and for subdeacons since that of Leo I.

Further writings poured from his pen. Various *Homilies* provided comment both on the Gospels and on selected books of the Old Testament; his *Dialogues*, which relate the lives and miracles of some of the saints, were produced in c. 593; and *Magna Moralia* (An Extensive Consideration of Moral Questions), an exposition of the Book of Job in 35 volumes, and perhaps his best-known work, appeared in 595. It was much admired but considered far too long, even then, and was excerpted almost at once for greater accessibility. Finally, we have 854 of his *Letters* gathered into 14 books, which provide invaluable insights into Gregory's character, his reaction to the chequered events of his reign and the increasingly complex and varied range of papal responsibilities.

All this took its toll and by 604 Gregory was worn out. Once again the Lombards were preparing to strike and, as it had been in 590 when he ascended the papal throne, Rome was in the grip of a dreadful famine. The people, panic-stricken, turned against him for want of someone else to blame. When he died in March 604, this alienation showed. The East revered him as a saint, Spain as a great writer, England as its true apostle. Only Rome more or less ignored him, an injustice which would not be rectified until the 9th century. There is, however, a story, related first by John of Salisbury, that Gregory was fiercely hostile to astrologers and not only had them banished from the papal court, but also burned the contents of the Palatine Library, which had been one of the glories of pagan Rome. Such vandalism seems unlikely, although it is true that Gregory set little store by literature for its own sake, and repudiated the Latin classics because they were heathen writings. But his legacy was rich and could not be passed over: the transmission of a venerable tradition of exegetical literature; the development of popular homiletic preaching; the promotion of monasticism in the West; a more effective papal administration; and the conservation of a particularly Roman view of what constitutes order under law. No wonder, then, his epitaph called him 'God's consul'. Gregory, however, adopted a less exalted title. 'Servant of the servants of God' was his self-description.

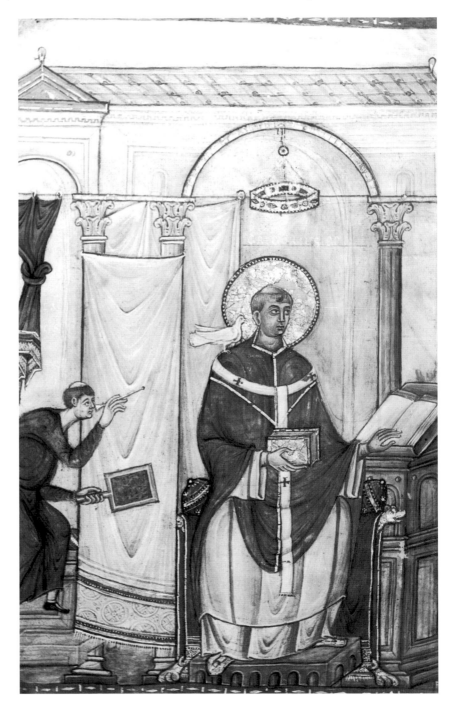

A 10th-century manuscript, the *Registrum Gregorii*, showing Pope Gregory, dictating to the deacon Peter (Stadtbibliothek, Trier). The customary Holy Spirit in form of a dove can be seen on his right shoulder. Peter is famous as a prolific forger. Many works attributed to earlier authorities in fact came from his pen. His handwriting is known, which makes detection of his forgeries somewhat easier.

Sabinian
604–606
Boniface III
607
Boniface IV
608–615
Adeodatus I
615–618
Boniface V
619–625
Honorius I
625–638

Severinus
640
John IV
640–642
Theodore I
642–649
Martin I
649–653
Eugene I
654–657
Vitalian
657–672
Adeodatus II
672–676
Donus
676–678
Agatho
678–681
Leo II
682–683
Benedict II
684–685
John V
685–686
Conon
686–687
Sergius I
687–701
John VI
701–705
John VII
705–707

Sisinnius
708
Constantine
708–715
Gregory II
715–731
Gregory III
731–741
Zacharias
741–752
Stephen (II)
752
Stephen III (II)
752–757
Paul I
757–767
Stephen IV (III)
768–772

Hadrian I
772–795
Leo III
795–816

Stephen V (IV)
816–817
Paschal I
817–824
Eugene II
824–827
Valentine
827
Gregory IV
827–844
Sergius II
844–847
Leo IV
847–855
Benedict III
855–858
Nicholas I
558–867
Hadrian II
867–872
John VIII

872–882
Marinus I
882–884
Hadrian III
884–885
Stephen VI (V)
885–891
Formosus
891–896
Boniface VI
896
Stephen VII (VI)
896–897
Romanus
897
Theodore II
897
John IX
898–900
Benedict IV
900–903
Leo V
903
Sergius III
904–911
Anastasius III
911–913
Lando
913–914
John X
914–928
Leo VI
928
Stephen VIII (VII)
928–931
John XI
931–935/6
Leo VII
936–939
Stephen IX (VIII)
939–942
Marinus II
942–946
Agapitus II
946–955

John XII
955–964
Leo VIII
963–965
Benedict V
964
John XIII
965–972
Benedict VI
973–974
Benedict VII
974–983
John XIV
983–984
John XV
985–996
Gregory V
996–999
Silvester II
999–1003

John XVII
1003
John XVIII
1003–1009
Sergius IV
1009–1012
Benedict VIII
1012–1024
John XIX
1024–1032
Benedict IX
1032–1044; 1045;
1047–1048
Silvester III
1045
Gregory VI
1045–1046
Clement II
1046–1047
Damasus II
1048
Leo IX
1049–1054

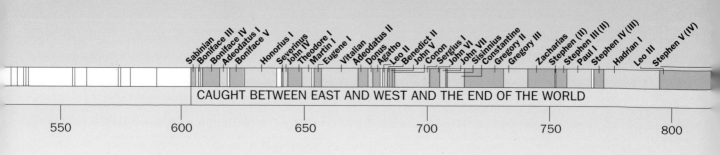

CAUGHT BETWEEN EAST AND WEST AND THE END OF THE WORLD

Honorius I

Paschal I

Leo IV

Silvester II

CAUGHT BETWEEN EAST AND WEST AND THE END OF THE WORLD
AD 604–1054

At the beginning of the 7th century the papacy had achieved a position of remarkable prestige. It was still living in the shadow of Constantinople and the complexion of the papacy for much of the 8th century reflected an Eastern leaning. Nevertheless, the popes had a constant notion of the primacy of the Holy See and were seeking to edge away from Eastern imperial control. Perpetual invasions from the north by Lombard kings encouraged the popes to look West for help, and after the creation of a Latin empire by Charlemagne – which counter-balanced the Eastern empire centred upon Constantinople – each pope found himself faced by the need to maintain a delicate equilibrium between East and West. Gradually the papacy acquired the status of secular as well as spiritual ruler. But with temporal responsibilities came political problems. The papacy was sucked into the violent inter-familial struggles of the Roman aristocracy, and in its efforts to extricate itself from their control fell under the hand of the Western emperors. The millennium thus saw the pontiff as sometimes little better than a Roman or imperial puppet, although the primacy of his spiritual office had long been agreed. In 1054, however, disaster struck Christendom as the Western and Eastern Churches excommunicated one another.

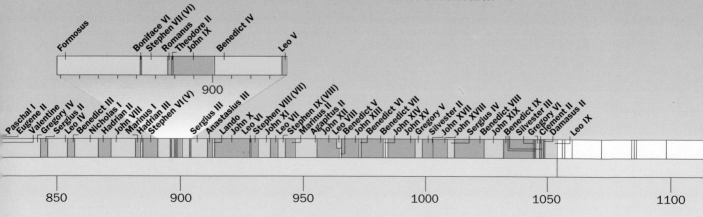

Sabinian
604–606

Boniface III
607

Boniface IV
608–615

Adeodatus I
615–618

Boniface V
619–625

Honorius I
625–638

A 7th-century mosaic showing Honorius I holding a model of the Church of Sant' Agnese fuori le Mura in Rome, which he had built. Honorius beautified several other churches in Rome, and founded the monastery of St Andrew and St Bartholomew.

PAPAL NAMES

SABINIAN
Nationality
Italian, from Volterra, Tuscany
Elected pope
13 September 604
Died
22 February 606
Length of pontificate
1 year, 5 months, 8 days

BONIFACE III
Nationality
Greek, born in Rome
Elected pope
19 February 607
Died
12 November 607
Length of pontificate
8 months, 22 days

BONIFACE IV
Nationality
Italian, from

L'Aquila
Family background
Son of a physician
Elected pope
15 September 608
Died
8 May 615
Length of pontificate
6 years, 7 months, 24 days

ADEODATUS I
Nationality
Italian, from Rome
Family background
Son of a subdeacon
Elected pope
19 October 615
Age at election
Elderly
Died
8 November 618
Length of pontificate
3 years, 21 days

The popes who followed Gregory the Great swung between imitation of his example and deliberate contrast with it. Some favoured monasticism, for example, while others did not. All managed to establish good relations with Constantinople, although the Eastern emperors were often distracted by war and did not always respond quickly to changes of pope in Rome.

Little is known for certain about **Sabinian** (604–606). He was elected amid the emotional turbulence of a Rome which was under threat of invasion and gripped by famine, and we are told that instead of imitating Gregory's open-handed charity and distributing grain free of charge from the papal granaries, he sold it at high prices. All this, however, may be invention by Gregory's biographers who wanted to enhance Gregory's posthumous reputation even more. **Boniface III** (607) waited nearly a year for imperial confirmation of his election, but had the satisfaction of an official declaration by Emperor Phocas (602–610) that Rome was the head of all the Churches. **Boniface IV** (608–615) also had to wait for imperial approval. Like Gregory I, he favoured monasticism and lived the life of a monk even after his election. It was during his reign that the

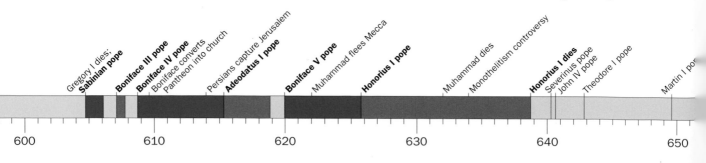

Gregory I dies;
Sabinian pope
Boniface III pope
Boniface IV pope
Boniface converts Pantheon into church
Persians capture Jerusalem
Adeodatus I pope
Boniface V pope
Muhammad flees Mecca
Honorius I pope
Muhammad dies
Monothelitism controversy
Honorius I dies
Severinus pope
John IV pope
Theodore I pope
Martin I po[pe]

600   610   620   630   640   650

Emperor Phocas (602–610) made the declaration that Rome was the head of all the Churches during the reign of Pope Boniface III. Contemporary Byzantine historians, however, described him as no better than a bloody tyrant.

Interior of the Pantheon. Originally a pagan temple, the first Pantheon in Rome was built in 27 BC. After it was damaged by fire, the present building was created by Emperor Hadrian. It was given to Pope Boniface IV in 609 and consecrated to the Virgin Mary and all the martyrs, under the name Santa Maria Rotunda or Santa Maria Ad Martyres.

Pantheon was converted into a church and dedicated to the Virgin and all the martyrs. **Adeodatus I** (615–618) – the name means 'given by God' – is obscure and throughout his pontificate, as throughout the three before him, Italy continued to be plagued by natural disasters and military reverses. **Boniface V** (619–625), who took a particular interest in the English Church, waited for over a year for imperial confirmation of his election, while the Eastern emperor waged war with the Persians. **Honorius I** (625–638), by contrast, was consecrated almost at once. Like Gregory, he employed monks rather than secular clergy to assist him and, like Boniface IV, turned his home into a monastery. He is best known, unfortunately, for his embroilment in a theological controversy. He believed that Christ did not possess simultaneously a divine will and a human will, but only one which he exercised through both his divine and human natures. The view he formulated and published is known as Monothelitism, which was later condemned as heretical by the Third Council of Constantinople (680–681), an embarrassment for subsequent pontiffs and councils of the Church.

ISLAM

It was during the reign of Honorius I that Muhammad died in Medina (632). During his lifetime he had carried his message to the furthest corners of the Arabian peninsula, and by 750 Islam had spread westwards as far as France and eastwards as far as modern Pakistan (see map). The next 21 popes would see the spectacle of a new religion seeming to sweep all before it, and whole areas such as north Africa, Syria and Spain were lost to Rome for a considerable time. Some, indeed, never returned.

It is noticeable that during the first century of Islamic expansion in particular, Rome and Constantinople drew closer together. In the hundred years before 650, for example, most of the popes had been Roman or Italian in origin. During the hundred years after, most of them came from the East. Moreover, the disappearance of ancient rivals for prestige – the bishops of Antioch, Jerusalem and Alexandria, all washed away by the Islamic tide – left Rome and Constantinople without peers in the Christian world.

Nevertheless, disunity bubbled under the surface. The very fact that so many late 7th- and early 8th-century popes were non-Roman, non-Italian, was not pleasing to the West. Differences in doctrinal teaching and religious practice between West and East would not be tolerated indefinitely by either side. Nor would the secular overlordship of the Eastern emperor remain for ever unchallenged. With Constantinople increasingly obliged to look to her defences in the East, Rome would be left to make her own accommodation with the rising powers of Europe. Essentially, therefore, the advent of the Islamic empire drove Christian East and Christian West apart, and after a time this division could no longer be concealed.

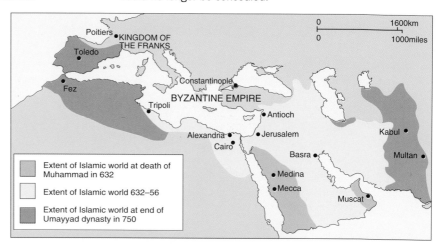

Extent of Islamic world at death of Muhammad in 632

Extent of Islamic world 632–56

Extent of Islamic world at end of Umayyad dynasty in 750

(Right) We are told that Muhammad, accompanied by the angel Gabriel, made the journey from the mosque at Mecca to Jerusalem and then back again in a single night. 16th-century manuscript showing the ascension of Muhammad (British Library).

(Below) A Turkish tile depicting the Ka'ba in the centre of the Great Mosque in Mecca. Originally a pagan temple, the Ka'ba was cleansed by Muhammad.

10th-century pen drawing of an Arab horseman (National Library, Vienna).

Severinus
640

John IV
640–642

Theodore I
642–649

Martin I
649–653

Eugene I
654–657

Vitalian
657–672

Adeodatus II
672–676

Donus
676–678

Agatho
678–681

Leo II
682–683

Benedict II
684–685

John V
685–686

Conon
686–687

Sergius I
687–701

John VI
701–705

John VII
705–707

Sisinnius
708

Constantine
708–715

Gregory II
715–731

Gregory III
731–741

Zacharias
741–752

Stephen (II)
752

Stephen III (II)
752–757

Paul I
757–767

Stephen IV (III)
768–772

PAPAL NAMES	

SEVERINUS
Nationality
  Italian, from Rome
Family background
  Aristocratic
Elected pope
  28 May 640
Age at election
  Elderly
Died
  2 August 640
Length of pontificate
  2 months, 6 days
	JOHN IV
	Nationality
	  Dalmatian
	Early career
	  Archdeacon of
	  Rome
	Elected pope
	  24 December 640
	Died
	  12 October 642
	Length of pontificate
	  1 year, 9 months,
	  20 days

He [Theodore I] was a lover of the poor, generous, the kindliest of men, and very compassionate.

Liber Pontificalis

We begin with heresy. **Severinus** (640) endured the usual wait for imperial approval. Pressed by Constantinople to accept Monothelitism – the dispute over which had done so much damage to Honorius I – and besieged at home by angry soldiers demanding that their arrears of pay be disbursed from the papal treasury, he survived his consecration by just over two months, leaving **John IV** (640–642) to pick up the pieces. He vigorously condemned Monothelitism and wrote to the Eastern emperor, making an ingenious but unconvincing attempt to defend Pope

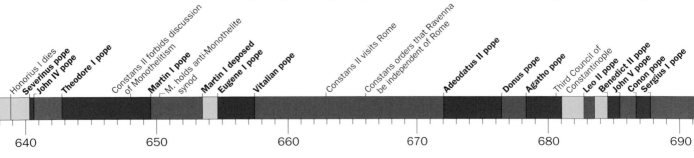

PAPAL NAMES

THEODORE I
Nationality
Greek, born in Jerusalem
Family background
Son of a bishop
Elected pope
24 November 642
Died
14 May 649
Length of pontificate
6 years, 5 months, 21 days

MARTIN I
Nationality
Italian, from Todi
Early career
Deacon
Elected pope
5 July 649
Deposed
17 June 653; tried in Constantinople, condemned to death, flogged and then deported
Died
16 September 655, in the Crimea
Length of pontificate
3 years, 11 months, 13 days

EUGENE I
Nationality
Italian, from Rome
Elected pope
10 August 654
Age at election
Elderly
Died
2 June 657
Length of pontificate
2 years, 9 months, 23 days

VITALIAN
Nationality
Italian, from Segni
Elected pope
30 July 657
Died
27 January 672
Length of pontificate
14 years, 5 months, 28 days

ADEODATUS II
Nationality
Italian, from Rome
Early career

Monk
Elected pope
11 April 672
Age at election
Elderly
Died
17 June 676
Length of pontificate
4 years, 2 months, 6 days

DONUS
Nationality
Italian, from Rome
Elected pope
2 November 676
Age at election
Elderly
Died
11 April 678
Length of pontificate
1 year, 5 months, 8 days

AGATHO
Nationality
Sicilian
Early career
Monk
Elected pope
27 June 678
Died
10 January 681
Length of pontificate
2 years, 6 months, 14 days

LEO II
Nationality
Sicilian
Elected pope
17 August 682
Died
3 July 683
Length of pontificate
10 months, 18 days
Notable feature
Leo took a special interest in Church music

BENEDICT II
Nationality
Italian, from Rome
Early career
Priest
Elected pope
26 June 684
Died
8 May 685
Length of pontificate
10 months, 13 days

Honorius's reputation. Even before he was consecrated he had taken a firm line on theological divagations, adding his signature to a letter to the Irish Church, warning it to beware of Pelagianism, a British heresy on the nature of human will which left God as a mere spectator of human affairs.

Theodore I (642–649), a Greek from Jerusalem, then reinforced John's condemnation of Monothelitism and quarrelled with the patriarch of Constantinople to such effect that Emperor Constans II (641–668) forbade all further discussion of the subject. **Martin I** (649–653), however, continued papal opposition and so annoyed Constans that he refused to recognize Martin as pope. Martin then held a synod which condemned the heresy and wrote to Constans, asking him to repudiate it. Constans replied by ordering his arrest and so Martin, bedridden through illness, was seized and carted to Constantinople where he was tried for treason, found guilty, flogged, and sent into exile.

Eugene I (654–657) sought a compromise. Constantinople was inclined to accept, but when the details came back to Rome, the assembled clergy and people rejected them and forced Eugene to reject them too. Constans, his hands filled for the moment with the business of war, threatened the pope with arrest and deportation. Death, however, intervened and it was left to **Vitalian** (657–672) to endeavour to effect a reconciliation. He was successful to the extent that Constans actually visited Rome for 12 days in 663 – the last Eastern emperor to do so for 700 years – and was received with every mark of respect and amicability. Nevertheless, he ordered that Ravenna, the seat of imperial government in Italy, be henceforth independent of Roman control – a warning, perhaps, to Vitalian and those who would come after him. **Adeodatus II** (672–676), however, continued the line of papal resistance to the heresy promoted by Constantinople, while **Donus** (676–678), whose reign is otherwise obscure, managed to persuade Ravenna at least to contemplate surrender of its new independence from Rome.

It was high time for this episode to end. Under **Agatho** (678–681), Emperor Constantine IV (668–685) had come to the conclusion that imperial support for Monothelitism no longer served any useful purpose and in consequence he invited the pope to send representatives to Constantinople to settle the matter once and for all. Agatho readily agreed, having first held a Western synod to make sure everyone there was united on the subject, and at the Third Council of Constantinople (680–681) the Monothelite heresy was finally declared anathema. There was also an unexpected bonus in that Ravenna agreed to return to

Eastern Church council
Justinian II forced into exile
John VI pope
Lombards invade Campania
John VII pope
Justinian II restored
Sisinnius pope
Constantine pope
C. and Justinian meet in Nicomedia
Gregory II pope
Leo III becomes Eastern emperor
G. commissions restoration of abbey of Monte Cassino
Leo supports iconoclasm
Lombards threaten Rome
Gregory III pope
G. condemns iconoclasm
Ravenna falls to Lombards
Lombards threaten Rome
Zacharias pope

700   710   720   730   740

PAPAL NAMES

JOHN V
Nationality
Syrian, from Antioch
Early career
Archdeacon
Elected pope
23 July 685
Died
2 August 686
Length of pontificate
1 year, 10 days

CONON
Nationality
Sicilian
Early career
Priest
Elected pope
21 October 686
Age at election
Elderly
Died
21 September 687
Length of pontificate
11 months
Antipopes
Theodore (687),
Paschal (687)

SERGIUS I
Nationality
Syrian, born in
Palermo in Sicily
Early career
Priest

Elected pope
15 December 687
Died
9 September 701
Length of pontificate
13 years, 8
months, 25 days
Antipope
Paschal (687)

JOHN VI
Nationality
Greek
Elected pope
30 October 701
Died
11 January 705
Length of pontificate
3 years, 2 months,
12 days

JOHN VII
Nationality
Greek
Family background
Son of official in
imperial palace
Elected pope
1 March 705
Died
18 October 707
Length of pontificate
2 years, 7 months,
18 days

An 8th-century mosaic of John VII from the Vatican Grottoes.

Roman control. The renewed harmony between Rome and Constantinople may be reflected in the origins of the next 16 popes. Only four popes between 682 and 772 would come from Rome. The rest would be mainly Syrian, Sicilian or Greek.

Since Agatho died while the council was still in progress, his successor, **Leo II** (682–683) had to wait until it was over for imperial ratification of his election. Part of the delay was caused by Constantinople's insistence on condemning Honorius I's opinions, and only when Rome gave way on this point did the emperor grant his consent to Leo's elevation. **Benedict II** (684–685), too, had a long wait but he secured for the Holy See an important concession. Imperial approval of the election of a new pope would come hereafter from the emperor's representative in Ravenna rather than from Constantinople itself. **John V** (685–686), who had been one of Agatho's delegates at the general council, was ill for much of his pontificate, as was **Conon** (686–687) who also had to face an antipope, *Theodore*. The turmoil caused by this and by the pope's mishandling of a clerical appointment meant that **Sergius I** (687–701) had an unhappy start to his reign. He, too, faced Theodore, as well as another antipope, *Paschal*, and it was only after scenes of violence and acts of bribery that the opposition retired and Sergius was confirmed in his office. Moreover, tensions between Rome and Constantinople were about to grow again as Emperor Justinian II (685–695) tried to assert his control over the universal Church. Sergius refused to endorse the acts of another, essentially Eastern, Church council (692) and Justinian sent a military commander with orders to extract the pope's compliance by force if necessary. Imperial troops in Italy, however, rallied to the pope and not long after Justinian himself was driven into exile (695).

John VI (701–705), a Greek, profited from the emperor's fall from power but was careful not to alienate Constantinople: a wise decision, as Justinian was restored in 705. Some Italian troops mutinied against imperial rule and John found himself trying to pacify them and the imperial commander, Theophylact – who had come to exact punishment – and dealing with yet another Lombard invasion close to Rome. **John VII** (705–707), also Greek, had no trouble from the Lombards but met an imperious demand from Emperor Justinian II (705–711), in power for a second time, to approve what Sergius I had refused to sanction. The pope temporized by returning the documents to Constantinople without comment or signature, and for this was accused of cowardice and complaisance. His successor, **Sisinnius** (708), a Syrian, was old when elected and crippled with gout, and his death was sudden. **Constantine**

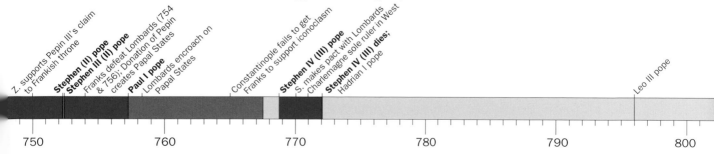

Z. supports Pepin III's claim to Frankish throne

Stephen (II) pope
Stephen III (II) pope
Franks defeat Lombards (754 & 756); Donation of Pepin creates Papal States

Paul I pope
Lombards encroach on Papal States

Constantinople fails to get Franks to support iconoclasm

Stephen IV (III) pope
S. makes pact with Lombards
Charlemagne sole ruler in West
Stephen IV (III) dies;
Hadrian I pope

Leo III pope

750 760 770 780 790 800

(708–715), a Syrian too, thus inherited the problem of whether or not to agree to Justinian's demand that Rome endorse the decisions of the council of 692. In the event, negotiation proved successful. Constantine and Justinian met at Nicomedia (711) where the emperor kissed the pope's foot, and the pope administered communion to the emperor.

The peace, however, was soon shattered, for in 711 Justinian was murdered and the new emperor was an adherent of the Monothelite heresy. Violence flared in Rome and the pope had to act as a pacifier. Fortunately this emperor did not last and was replaced by one who was eager to proclaim his orthodoxy; and so the crisis passed.

Gregory II (715–731), a Roman, had been one of Pope Constantine's principal negotiators with Justinian, but when Emperor Leo III (717–741) tried to impose enormous taxes on Italy, Gregory was in the vanguard of opposition. He also had to resist further encroachments by the Lombards and was successful in persuading their king to abandon his siege of Rome. Leo, however, was an iconoclast, a 'breaker of images'. He disapproved of the use of statues and pictures in worship, and ordered the pope to agree officially. Gregory said no, and northern Italy rose in his defence. **Gregory III** (731–741) was made pope by acclamation and was the last pope to ask for Eastern imperial approval. War attended his refusal to support iconoclasm, and when the Lombards attacked once more, Gregory appealed to the Franks for assistance. They, however, unwilling to help since the Lombards had aided them against Muslim invasions of Provence, politely refused and Rome was left dangerously open to depredation.

Zacharias (741–752), however, was able to retrieve the situation. He made peace with the Lombards and also with Constantinople, in spite of

ICONOCLASM

Iconoclasm, literally 'breaking images', objected to any representation of humans by statues, picture, engraving or embroidery, and to the veneration of such images. The movement, arising from the belief that veneration of images might easily turn into worship and hence pagan idolatry, exercised its strongest influence during the 8th century, and was especially associated with the Eastern empire. The emperors Leo III and Constantine V were particularly fervent iconoclasts, and an Eastern Church council in 754 denounced all images as idols. The movement lost support, however, when the Second Council of Nicaea in 787 declared the legitimacy of cult images of the saints.

Iconoclasts painting out an image. The inscription reads: 'those who wage war on images'.

After his predecessor and brother, King Ratchis, retired to a monastery in 749, the Lombard king Aistulf had plans to conquer the whole of Italy. In 754, however, the Frankish king, Pepin III, overcame him in battle, and when Aistulf threatened Rome again in 756, he was once more defeated. Here he capitulates to Pope Stephen III (II) in a 12th-century manuscript illumination (Vatican Library).

PAPAL NAMES

ZACHARIAS
Nationality
  Greek, born in
  Calabria
Early career
  Deacon
Elected pope
  3 December 741
Died
  15 March 752
Length of pontificate
  10 years, 3
  months, 12 days
Notable feature
  The last Greek pope

STEPHEN (II)
Nationality
  Uncertain
Elected pope
  22/23 March 752
Age at election
  Elderly
Died
  25/26 March 752,
  from a stroke
Length of pontificate
  2 or 3 days
Comment
  Since Stephen died
  before he could be
  consecrated, there
  is disagreement
  over whether he
  should be included
  in the list of popes

STEPHEN III (II)
Nationality
  Italian, from Rome
Family background
  Aristocratic; wealthy
Early career
  Deacon

Elected pope
  26 March 752
Died
  26 April 757
Length of pontificate
  5 years, 1 month

PAUL I
Nationality
  Italian, from
  Rome
Family background
  Aristocratic;
  wealthy; Paul was
  the younger brother
  of the previous
  pope
Early career
  Deacon
Elected pope
  29 May 757
Died
  28 June 767
Length of pontificate
  10 years, 1
  month

STEPHEN IV (III)
Nationality
  Sicilian
Early career
  Priest
Elected pope
  7 August 768
Died
  24 January
  772
Length of pontificate
  3 years, 5 months,
  17 days
Antipopes
  Constantine
  (767–768),
  Philip (768)

the fact that Emperor Leo's successor was also an iconoclast. Moreover, he strengthened relations between himself and the Franks, and supported the claim of Pepin III to the Frankish throne – a decision replete with moment for the future, since relations between the new dynasty and the Holy See were thus warmed by royal indebtedness. **Stephen (II)** (752) lasted for just over three days after his election, and as a stroke took him off before he could be consecrated, it is a moot point whether he should be counted as pope or not. **Stephen III** (752–757) – or II according to the official lists – drew further away from Constantinople and closer to the Franks. This served him well, for when Rome was menaced by the Lombards in 753, he was able to visit the Frankish king in person and beg for his protection against the invaders. The king agreed and in two campaigns (754 and 756) defeated the Lombards and restored to the papacy lands which they had taken from it.

Paul I (757–767), Pope Stephen's younger brother, was faced not only by similar struggles against Lombard encroachment, but also by Constantinople's continuing support of iconoclasm and her ominous attempt to court both Franks and Lombards. This attempt, as it happened, proved unsuccessful, but faction flourished and Paul's death was attended by a contest for the papal throne. Two antipopes, *Constantine* and *Philip*, made a brief appearance before the legitimate **Stephen IV** – or III – (768–772) emerged victorious. He, like his immediate predecessors, found himself battling constantly against Lombard intrigues until, perhaps worn down and exhausted by them, he eventually cast aside his Frankish friends and threw in his lot with the Lombards. It was a grave mistake: for the principal Frank he had chosen to desert was Charlemagne, the greatest of all the early Medieval rulers in Europe.

Hadrian I
772–795

Leo III
795–816

When Hadrian I died, Charlemagne was overcome by grief and sent to Rome a marble monument engraved with memorial verses. It can be seen in the portico of St Peter's Basilica.

HADRIAN I	
Nationality	*Died*
Italian, from Rome	25 December
Family background	795
Aristocratic	*Length of pontificate*
Early career	23 years,
Deacon	10 months,
Elected pope	26 days
1 February 772	

He [Charlemagne] honoured more than any of the other holy and venerable places the church of St Peter in Rome. He piled up in its treasury a large sum of money, in gold as well as in silver, not to mention precious stones. He sent innumerable gifts to the popes, and throughout the whole of his reign nothing was more important to him than that the city of Rome, by her own efforts, should exert her former authority, and that the church of St Peter should not only be safe under his protection, but that by his wealth she should be adorned and endowed more than any other church.

Einhard *Vita Karoli Magni*, 27

HADRIAN I

In that same winter died the supreme Roman pontiff Hadrian, of holy memory, and when [Charlemagne] had ceased weeping for him, he asked that prayers be said by every Christian throughout his empire. Charlemagne also sent many charitable offerings for him, and in France ordered that his name be engraved on marble in golden letters, so that he might send it to adorn Pope Hadrian's tomb in Rome.

Annales Lauseshamenses for the year 795

Since Pope Stephen IV (III) had made an unfortunate error in deciding to trust the Lombard rather than the Frankish king, **Hadrian I** (772–795) found himself in an extremely awkward position. He began the process of extrication by getting rid of the Lombard king's agent in Rome and then demanding that the king fulfil his promise to Pope Stephen to restore certain lands to the Holy See. King Desiderius, however, refused and moved against Rome itself, desisting only when the pope threatened to excommunicate him. Then Charlemagne, moved by appeals from Hadrian, descended on Pavia, the Lombard capital, besieged it (773–774), captured it, and destroyed the Lombard kingdom. This done,

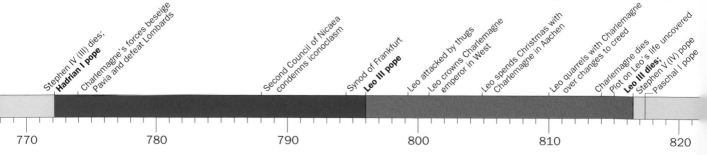

Stephen IV (III) dies; **Hadrian I pope**

Charlemagne's forces beseige Pavia and defeat Lombards

Second Council of Nicaea condemns iconoclasm

Synod of Frankfurt **Leo III pope**

Leo attacked by thugs

Leo crowns Charlemagne emperor in West

Leo spends Christmas with Charlemagne in Aachen

Leo quarrels with Charlemagne over changes to creed

Charlemagne dies

Plot on Leo's life uncovered **Leo III dies;**

Stephen V (IV) pope

Paschal I pope

770　　　　780　　　　790　　　　800　　　　810　　　　820

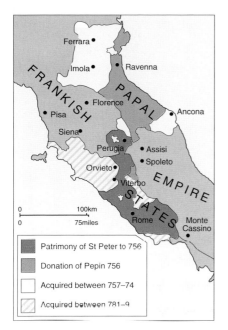

Map showing the creation and expansion of the Papal States to the end of the reign of Charlemagne.

Charlemagne paid a visit to Rome and handed to the pope a document which, in effect, promised to make over to the papacy a very large portion of the Italian peninsula. Nevertheless, Charlemagne did not relinquish control over his donation and insisted that Hadrian give up certain other areas such as Tuscany and Spoleto.

Encouraged by this Frankish alliance, the pope felt able to propose, at the Second Council of Nicaea (787), that iconoclasm – for so long favoured by Constantinople – be condemned and that a proper veneration of images be restored to worship and usage. Ironically this nearly

Hadrian I greeting Charlemagne during his visit to Rome in 774 after the defeat of the Lombards. Between them, Hadrian and Charlemagne embodied the notion of a new empire looking back to Rome but wholly Christian – a Holy Roman empire. Hadrian sent the emperor documents which formed the basis of ecclesiastical law, and Charlemagne promulgated this code throughout his domains.

LEO III	

Nationality
  Italian, from Rome
Early career
  Cardinal priest. The
  meaning of
  'cardinal' varies
  somewhat at
  different times in
  the early Church. At
  this time in Rome it
  seems to have
  designated bishops
	of certain sees,
	who had extra
	responsibilities
	attached to the
	Lateran Church
	Elected pope
	  26 December 795
	Died
	  12 June 816
	Length of pontificate
	  20 years, 5
	  months, 17 days

caused a skirmish with Charlemagne who was not over-pleased at the prospect of a reconciliation between pope and Eastern emperor; but when the subject was raised at Charlemagne's Synod of Frankfurt (794), iconoclasm was declared anathema and all parties, except the Easterners, were satisfied.

LEO III

When the birthday of Our Lord Jesus Christ arrived, they all assembled again in the church of St Peter the Apostle; and on this occasion the venerable and gentle pontiff [Leo III] crowned him with his own hands

St Peter with Pope Leo III and Charlemagne, illustrating the division of spiritual and temporal power. A copy by Grimaldi of a lost 9th-century mosaic in the Lateran (Vatican Library).

with a most precious crown. Then all the loyal Romans, seeing that great love and care which he showed for the holy Church of Rome and for its vicar, inspired by God and by St Peter ... cried out aloud with one voice, 'To Charles, most pious Augustus crowned by God, mighty and peaceable emperor, long life and victory!'.

Liber Pontificalis

Leo III (795–816), however, did not enjoy such a happy pontificate. It began well, but then Leo alienated the Roman aristocracy, and under the aegis of Paschalis, a nephew of Pope Hadrian and one of the principal officers in the papal administration, a gang of bravos attacked Leo as he went to say mass in St Peter's in April 799. It was a very violent assault. The hired thugs tried, amid much else, to gouge out his eyes and cut away his tongue. He was left for dead in the street, but later dragged into the Church of San Silvestro where he was assaulted again and then locked up in the adjoining monastery. The conspirators, however, fearful that he would be discovered, transferred him to another monastery whence he escaped at night.

It seemed prudent to seek Charlemagne's protection, and Leo set out for Germany. Both he and representatives of the rebels found Charlemagne at Paderborn. There Leo heard his enemies charge him with perjury and adultery, accusations which Charlemagne dismissed for the present but arranged to have investigated when Leo was safely back in Rome. In December 800 a solemn convention was held in St Peter's at which Leo swore an oath to his innocence. Two days later, during the mass of Christmas Day, the pope crowned Charlemagne emperor in the West, after which he did homage to the monarch.

Thereafter, Leo's pontificate was more peaceable, although Charlemagne exercised his imperial authority to direct such ecclesiastical and papal affairs as he saw fit, and Leo, to judge by the way he dated the papal coinage by Charlemagne's regnal years, was unable to forget that technically he was Charlemagne's subject. A final conspiracy to murder the pope was uncovered in 815. By this time Charlemagne was dead and Leo tried the conspirators himself, condemning many of them to death.

A denier coin of Pope Leo III minted at Rome after Charlemagne's coronation in 800. It has 'CARLUS' on one side set around a monogram standing for 'imperator', and 'PETRUS SCS' (sanctus) on the other encircling Leo's monogram, an interesting reference to the perceived partnership between empire and papacy.

It had been an interesting pontificate. The question was now, had Rome, in withdrawing from Constantinople and allying herself with Aachen, really managed to create a new, independent, pivotal role between East and West; or had she merely exchanged one master for another?

CHARLEMAGNE AND THE CAROLINGIAN EMPIRE

For almost a century, the popes had been pursuing (perhaps not always consistently or consciously), three interrelated policies: to ease the Church from Eastern imperial control; to free themselves from constant Lombard incursions; and to forge an alliance with secular powers in the West. Gradual success in all three endeavours proved, however, to be a mixed blessing.

Charlemagne (Charles the Great) was king of the Franks from 768 to 814. From 800 he was emperor in the West. His father was King Pepin III who died in 768 leaving his sons Charles (Charlemagne) and Carloman as joint rulers. When Carloman died in 771, Charles was left sole ruler and immediately embarked on a career of military expansion. He was principally a soldier, but also laboured to create and maintain order and good governance in the Church as well as in his growing empire. But he began to make claims over the Church, which were as complete as any which had been made by an Eastern Roman emperor, and Pope Leo III actually paid homage to him – although it is also true that the same Leo crowned Charlemagne emperor on Christmas Day 800. Clearly Charlemagne saw himself as both protector and reformer of Christendom, and in pursuit of these roles did not hesitate to appoint bishops and abbots in France, summon Church councils, and regularly issue

instructions to clergy on their behaviour, duties, finances and even beliefs. In exchanging Constantinople for Aachen, therefore, the popes had, in a manner of speaking, stepped from the frying pan into the fire. Still, on balance, the papacy benefited from the change, if only because Charlemagne was very pious and acknowledged without question the primacy of Rome.

Frankish empire 768

Conquests of Charlemagne 768–814

Dependencies of the Frankish empire 768–814

Byzantine empire 814

(Above) The Carolingian empire to the end of Charlemagne's reign.

(Left) Reliquary bust of Charlemagne c. 1350 (Domschatz, Aachen). The contemporary chronicler Einhard, described him as tall but well proportioned, with a round skull, a big nose, large lively eyes, and a pot belly. Until his final years, he enjoyed good health, but then he became subject to fevers and at the end he dragged one foot.

(Above) Charlemagne's stone throne in the tribune at Aachen once contained relics.

(Right and bottom) Charlemagne's palace chapel at Aachen, an octagonal building reminiscent of San Vitale in Ravenna, stood opposite the rest of the palace buildings at one end of a courtyard large enough to hold 7,000 people.

(Left) Gilt cover of the 12th-century Golden Book of Prüm *(Stadtsbibliothek, Trier). Jesus sits enthroned in the centre, with Pepin III (Charlemagne's father) to his right and Charlemagne to his left. Charlemagne's descendants – Louis the Pious, Lothair I, Louis II (the German) and Charles the Bald – stand below (from left to right). The abbey of Prüm was one of the most important of the Carolingian political and intellectual centres. Charlemagne imprisoned his son Pepin there, and the* Annales Prumienses *provide a very good historical account of the 10th century. The abbey's cloister school was particularly famous.*

Stephen V (IV)
816–817

Paschal I
817–824

Eugene II
824–827

Valentine
827

Gregory IV
827–844

Sergius II
844–847

Leo IV
847–855

Benedict III
855–858

Nicholas I
858–867

Hadrian II
867–872

John VIII
872–882

Marinus I
882–884

Hadrian III
884–885

Stephen VI (V)
885–891

Formosus
891–896

Boniface VI
896

Stephen VII (VI)
896–897

Romanus
897

Theodore II
897

John IX
898–900

Benedict IV
900–903

Leo V
903

Detail of a mosaic of Paschal I, who had the apses of the Church of Santa Prassede in Rome decorated with mosaics.

Paschal [I] ... sent [the emperor] a letter in which he averred that he had not only been unwilling to have the dignity of the papacy as it were thrust upon him, but that he had also struggled very hard against it.

Einhard *Annales Fuldenses*, year 817

Stephen V or **IV** (816–817) crowned and anointed Charlemagne's successor, Louis the Pious. **Paschal I** (817–824) was hastily consecrated in order to circumvent possible interference by Louis, but the two seem to have struck up a friendship and harmony reigned, save for a touch of abrasion between the pope and Louis's son, Lothair (who thought the pope too independent), and the absolute hatred of the Roman populace which rioted when Paschal died. Lengthy disturbances and intrigues after Paschal's death eventually produced an acceptable candidate, **Eugene II** (824–827), whose reign saw the acme of Frankish control of the papacy. He agreed, for example, that henceforth the pope-elect should take an

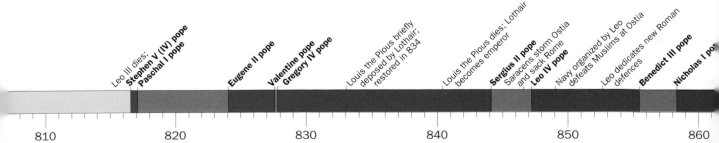

Leo III dies; **Stephen V (IV) pope**; **Paschal I pope**

Eugene II pope

Valentine pope; **Gregory IV pope**

Louis the Pious briefly deposed by Lothair; restored in 834

Louis the Pious dies; Lothair becomes emperor

Sergius II pope; Saracens storm Ostia and sack Rome; **Leo IV pope**

Navy organized by Leo defeats Muslims at Ostia

Leo dedicates new Roman defences

Benedict III pope

Nicholas I pope

810   820   830   840   850   860

Sergius III 904–911	**Leo VII** 936–939	**John XIII** 965–972
Anastasius III 911–913	**Stephen IX (VIII)** 939–942	**Benedict VI** 973–974
Lando 913–914	**Marinus II** 942–946	**Benedict VII** 974–983
John X 914–928	**Agapitus II** 946–955	**John XIV** 983–984
Leo VI 928	**John XII** 955–964	**John XV** 985–996
Stephen VIII (VII) 928–931	**Leo VIII** 963–965	**Gregory V** 996–999
John XI 931–935/6	**Benedict V** 964	**Silvester II** 999–1003

A 9th-century illuminated manuscript showing the abbot of Fulda presenting his book to Pope Gregory IV. From a miniature painting on vellum preserved in the monastery of Fulda.

oath of loyalty to the Western emperor, although one must add that Eugene remained immovable in the face of Louis's request that he defer to the iconoclasm which was once more making itself felt in the Eastern empire and had gained some support in the West. **Valentine** (827) appears to have reigned for less than a month. **Gregory IV** (827–844) was equally dependent on the Western emperor, later known as 'the Holy Roman emperor', even though the imperial family was riven by dynastic struggles during his pontificate. Gregory supported Lothair, the eldest son of Louis the Pious and hence the natural heir, in preference to Lothair's brothers, Pepin and Louis the German. But most of the Frankish bishops pointed out that Gregory had taken an oath of loyalty to Emperor Louis and therefore had no business to be supporting a son who (along with his brothers) was in revolt against him. Duplicity, however, ruled the field and in 833 Gregory discovered that his attempts to negotiate a peace between father and sons had been circumvented by Lothair's treachery. Emperor Louis was briefly deposed, and even after

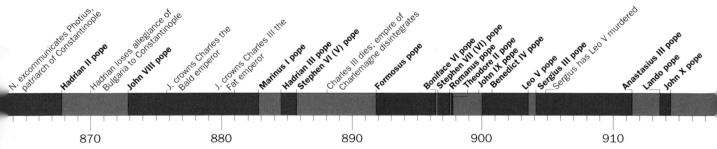

N. excommunicates Photius, patriarch of Constantinople

Hadrian II pope

Hadrian loses allegiance of Bulgaria to Constantinople

John VIII pope

J. crowns Charles the Bald emperor

J. crowns Charles III the Fat emperor

Marinus I pope

Hadrian III pope

Stephen VI (V) pope

Charles III dies; empire of Charlemagne disintegrates

Formosus pope

Boniface VI pope

Stephen VII (VI) pope

Romanus pope

Theodore II pope

John IX pope

Benedict IV pope

Leo V pope

Sergius III pope

Sergius has Leo V murdered

Anastasius III pope

Lando pope

John X pope

870   880   890   900   910

Raphael's *Fire in the Borgo*. In the 9th century fire threatened to engulf the Vatican, but Leo IV (who can be seen in the background), gave a gesture of benediction which quenched the blaze.

PAPAL NAMES	

STEPHEN V (IV)
Nationality
  Italian, from Rome
Family background
  Aristocratic
Early career
  Deacon
Elected pope
  22 June 816
Died
  24 January 817
Length of pontificate
  7 months, 2 days
 	
PASCHAL I
Nationality
  Italian, from Rome
Early career
  Priest, abbot
	Elected pope
	  24 January 817
	Died
	  11 February 824
	Length of pontificate
	  7 years, 19 days
	
	EUGENE II
	Nationality
	  Uncertain
	Early career
	  Archpriest
	Elected pope
	  June 824
	Died
	  August 827
	Length of pontificate
	  3 years, c. 2
	  months

his restoration conflict with Lothair continued in spite of the pope's attempts to intervene.

At Gregory's death, an antipope, *John*, was acclaimed pope by the Roman populace, but the aristocracy elected **Sergius II** (844–847) and crushed all opposition; then the first stirrings of papal independence appeared. Lothair, now emperor, was angry when Sergius was consecrated without his consent and threatened to invade Rome with an army. But Sergius managed to smooth things over and to crown Lothair without swearing fealty to him – a notable achievement. This pontificate was marred, however, by rampant simony and when Saracen Muslims were able to storm and pillage Ostia, everyone took it as a sign of God's displeasure. **Leo IV** (847–855) did not wait for Lothair's approval either – largely because he was busy fortifying Rome against possible Saracen attack – and, in spite of an outward deference to the emperor, managed to assert himself to greater effect than his immediate predecessors, executing imperial representatives who were guilty of murder, restoring Church discipline and transforming Rome itself by his building works.

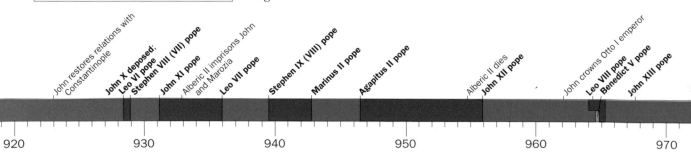

John restores relations with Constantinople

John X deposed; Leo VI pope

Stephen VIII (VII) pope

John XI pope

Alberic II imprisons John and Marozia

Leo VII pope

Stephen IX (VIII) pope

Marinus II pope

Agapitus II pope

Alberic II dies

John XII pope

John crowns Otto I emperor

Leo VIII pope

Benedict V pope

John XIII pope

920   930   940   950   960   970

PAPAL NAMES

VALENTINE
Nationality
  Italian, from Rome
Family background
  Aristocratic
Early career
  Archdeacon
Elected pope
  August 827
Died
  September 827
Length of pontificate
  c. 1 month

GREGORY IV
Nationality
  Italian, from Rome
Family background
  Aristocratic
Early career
  Cardinal priest
Elected pope
  Late 827
Died
  25 January 844
Length of pontificate
  16 years, c. 25 days

SERGIUS II
Nationality
  Italian, from Rome
Family background
  Aristocratic
Early career
  Archpriest
Elected pope
  January 844
Age at election
  Elderly
Died
  27 January 847
Length of pontificate
  3 years, c. 27 days
Antipope
  John (844)

LEO IV
Nationality
  Italian, from Rome
Early career
  Benedictine monk,
  cardinal priest
Elected pope
  10 April 847
Died
  17 July 855
Length of pontificate
  8 years, 3 months,
  6 days

BENEDICT III
Nationality
  Italian, from Rome
Early career
  Cardinal priest
Elected pope
  29 September 855
Died
  17 April 858
Length of pontificate
  2 years, 6 months,
  20 days
Antipope
  Anastasius
  Bibliothecarius
  (855)

NICHOLAS I
Nationality
  Italian, from Rome
Date of birth
  c. 820
Family background
  Son of a leading
  city official
Elected pope
  24 April 858
Age at election
  c. 38
Died
  13 November 867
Length of pontificate
  9 years, 6 months,
  19 days

HADRIAN II
Nationality
  Italian, from Rome
Date of birth
  792
Family background
  Aristocratic
Status
  Married before
  ordination
Early career
  Cardinal priest
Elected pope
  14 December 867
Age at election
  75
Died
  November/
  December 872
Length of pontificate
  4 years, c. 11
  months, c. 17
  days

(*Left*) 15th-century Flemish manuscript showing Saracens attacking Rome. The worst ever sack of Rome took place during the reign of Sergius II. Saracens entered the city and despoiled the shrine of St Peter. In the Middle Ages, 'Saracen' was a term for anyone, regardless of race, who was a Muslim. The original Greek usage referred to an Arab tribe of the Sinai Peninsula.

Benedict III (855–858) was elected after a previous choice had refused the papal office. An antipope, *Anastasius Bibliothecarius*, briefly enjoyed imperial support amid the customary violence and mayhem. But popular feeling ran with Benedict who was eventually consecrated. His reign, though short, still demonstrated than even an infirm papacy could act with firmness towards imperial pretensions, and with the advent of **Nicholas I** (858–867) this firmness brooked no opposition. Nicholas clashed with the archbishops of Ravenna and Rheims, deposed two others in a dispute over a royal divorce, and defied the Western emperor who supported the royal side. He also refused to accept the appointment of Photius as patriarch of Constantinople, and left the Eastern emperor in no doubt about his opinion.

The line of popes since Hadrian I had been Roman by birth and was to continue thus almost uninterrupted until the millennium. It is a mark, perhaps, of the papacy's retreating into its heartland, the better to avoid control by outside powers.

Nevertheless, there were some very difficult moments and these tended to multiply. **Hadrian II** (867–872) was weak and vacillating, and hence the psychological gains made by Nicholas I were thrown away. He leaned heavily on, of all people, the antipope Anastasius, whose imperious lack of tact sowed discord between the pope and the imperial family which was rent, at the time, by one of its periodic internal feuds; while in the East, Hadrian lost control of Bulgaria which henceforth owed allegiance to Constantinople. **John VIII** (872–882) appeared to halt the sudden decline, defending Italy against further Saracen raids, and crowning

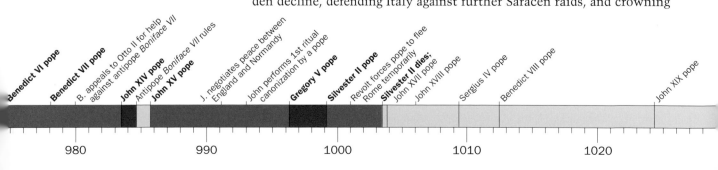

Benedict VI pope

Benedict VII pope

B. appeals to Otto II for help against antipope Boniface VII

John XIV pope

Antipope Boniface VII rules

John XV pope

J. negotiates peace between England and Normandy

John performs 1st ritual canonization by a pope

Gregory V pope

Silvester II pope

Revolt forces pope to flee Rome temporarily

Silvester II dies;

John XVII pope

John XVIII pope

Sergius IV pope

Benedict VIII pope

John XIX pope

980   990   1000   1010   1020

Charles the Bald emperor in 875 in the hope that he would return the favour by securing the papacy against intrigue and violence. But Charles died in 877 and his former rival for the imperial crown occupied Rome and imprisoned the pope. John escaped and turned to Constantinople for help, for which he was made to pay a high price – recognition of Photius as patriarch being included. His pontificate ended in catastrophe. John was the first pope to be assassinated, poison and clubbing, we are told, being the methods employed. **Marinus I** (882–884) was an experienced diplomatist before he became pope and thus seems to have avoided making a delicate situation worse. **Hadrian III** (884–885) is obscure. Violence characterized his pontificate, a sign of the times.

Stephen VI or V (885–891) was nearly deposed by Emperor Charles the Fat, but the empire founded by Charlemagne was disintegrating and after Charles died Stephen was obliged to rely on unreliable Western princes and Constantinople to keep the papacy safe. His successor, **Formosus** (891–896) – his name means 'good-looking' – was a pope of exceptional qualities, maintaining and promoting amicable relations with Constantinople, Paris and the new Western emperor, although he soon had to appeal to Arnulf, king of the eastern Franks, for help against the third of these. Arnulf, however, had some kind of stroke and was left paralyzed, so the alliance fell to ashes. Moreover, Formosus collected enemies who hated him virulently. This did not appear during the brief reign of **Boniface VI** (896), an unsavoury character, who died 15 days after his election; but **Stephen VII** or **VI** (896–897) proceeded to exhume Formosus's corpse, have it dressed in pontifical vestments, propped up on a throne, and stand trial for supposed offences committed during Formosus's reign. Obsessed by hatred of Formosus, Stephen was deposed during a popular uprising, thrown into prison and strangled.

Of **Romanus** (897) we know little for certain. The same can be said of **Theodore II** (897) whose reign was even shorter. **John IX** (898–900) was elected amid controversy with the aid of Lambert, king of Italy, and set about rehabilitating Formosus's reputation and revalidating his acts. A synod was held at Ravenna to confirm these proceedings to which Lambert was favourable. All was thrown into doubt, however, by the sudden death of the king, and the accession of **Benedict IV** (900–903) was thus attended by strife and bitterness, as pro- and anti-Formosus factions fought each other. Benedict belonged to the former and battled manfully not only with ecclesiastical problems in Italy, but also with the dynastic turmoil consequent upon Lambert's death. But he chose to crown the wrong candidate, thus passing on to **Leo V** (903) a muddle of turbulence, and it is perhaps a mark of the confusion in Rome that the electors chose for pope a simple parish priest instead of the usual Roman aristocrat. He faced an antipope, *Christopher*, who threw him into gaol and 'reigned' until January 904 when he was replaced by **Sergius III** (904–911). Sergius had actually been elected pope in December 897, but had had to give way to John IX who enjoyed imperial support. A hater of Formosus, Sergius regarded all popes from John IX onwards as interlopers, and set about

PAPAL NAMES

BENEDICT IV
Nationality
  Italian, from Rome
Family background
  Aristocratic
Elected pope
  May/June 900
Died
  August 903
Length of pontificate
  3 years,
  c. 2 months

LEO V
Nationality
  Uncertain
Early career
  Parish priest
Elected pope
  August/September
  903
Died
  Early 904,
  murdered in
  prison
Length of pontificate
  c. 6 months?
Antipope
  Christopher
  (September
  903–January 904)

SERGIUS III
Nationality
  Italian, from Rome
Family background
  Aristocratic
Early career
  Bishop of Caere
Elected pope
  29 January 904
Died
  14 April 911
Length of pontificate
  7 years, 2 months,
  17 days

ANASTASIUS III
Nationality
  Italian, from Rome
Elected pope
  c. June 911
Died
  c. August 913
Length of pontificate
  2 years,
  c. 2 months

LANDO
Nationality
  Italian, from Sabine
  territory
Family background
  Aristocratic;
  wealthy; Lombard
Elected pope
  c. August 913
Died
  c. March 914
Length of pontificate
  c. 6 or 7 months

JOHN X
Nationality
  Italian, from
  Tossignano
Early career
  Archbishop of
  Ravenna
Elected pope
  March/April 914
Deposed
  May 928;
  imprisoned in
  Castel Sant'
  Angelo
Died
  929; probably
  suffocated
Length of pontificate
  14 years, c. 1
  month?

LEO VI
Nationality
  Italian, from Rome
Family background
  Aristocratic; son of
  a lawyer
Early career
  Cardinal priest
Elected pope
  May 928
Age at election
  Elderly
Died
  December 928
Length of pontificate
  5 or 6 months

STEPHEN VIII (VII)
Nationality
  Italian, from Rome
Early career
  Priest
Elected pope
  December 928
Died
  February 931
Length of pontificate
  2 years, c. 2 months

JOHN XI
Nationality
  Italian, from Rome
Family background
  John was possibly
  the illegitimate son
  of Pope Sergius III
  and Marozia
Early career
  Cardinal priest
Elected pope
  February/March
  931
Age at election
  Early 20s
Died
  December 935/
  January 936
Length of pontificate
  4 years, c. 9 or 10
  months

overturning their actions. Violence accompanied his decrees, but he seemed to be immune from prosecution because of his servile adherence to the Roman aristocracy, and in particular to a high-ranking woman named Marozia, by whom (so scandal averred) he had a son.

Anastasius III (911–913) made little impact on the times and his successor, **Lando** (913–914), a Lombard, was equally transient. **John X** (914–928), on the other hand, seems to have been somewhat more vigorous. Secure in his friendship with Berengar I, king of Italy, he set about uniting the Roman aristocracy against the continual Saracen invasions which were ruining central Italy. In 915, his efforts were successful and the Saracens were defeated. With Berengar crowned as the Western emperor, John managed to re-establish papal discipline in parts of the West which were slipping out of control; and in 923 he even restored amity with Constantinople which had once again quarrelled with Rome a decade before. But his relations with the Roman aristocracy deteriorated and in 928 John was deposed and probably murdered. **Leo VI** (928), too, was murdered, and **Stephen VIII** or VII (928–931) was under the thumb of Marozia, the supposed mistress of Sergius III. **John XI** (931–935/6) was Marozia's son and was elected pope through her influence. Whether he was also Sergius's son is open to question. He is notable for his support of the Cluniac order, a body of reforming monks founded in 909 and dedicated to halting a decline in monastic discipline. His patroness, however, overstepped the mark with her second marriage to the new king of Italy, for this incited the Roman mob to riot and in the aftermath both king and pope were imprisoned.

The key note of these last 19 reigns had been violence, whether arising from internal feuding among members of the Western imperial family, or from the factionalism of the Roman aristocracy whose fissiparousness produced new popes in the twitch of an eye. The papal successors of the next 50 years were, alas, to enjoy no greater harmony, an impotence which can be illustrated by the next four popes, all of whom were in thrall to a powerful Roman nobleman, Alberic II, a son of Marozia by her first husband.

Leo VII (936–939) owed his office to Alberic who was particularly interested in reviving Italian monasticism. To this end, the great abbot of Cluny was invited to Rome where he seized the opportunity to institute a reform of the monasteries. **Stephen IX** or VIII (939–942) was also appointed by Alberic, and continued to support the Cluniac abbot's reform of monasteries both in Rome and in central Italy. He came, however, to an unpleasant end – in the ominous words of Martin of Oppau, 'mutilated by certain Romans' – almost certainly the result of a falling-out with Alberic. **Marinus II** (942–946) suffered the same complete lack of influence as his predecessors, as did **Agapitus II** (946–955), nominated, like the others, by Alberic. During his pontificate, monastic reform continued apace, and when Otto I of Germany swept into Italy to assume

PAPAL NAMES

LEO VII
Nationality
  Italian, from Rome
Early career
  Cardinal priest,
  Benedictine monk?
Elected pope
  3 January 936
Died
  13 July 939
Length of pontificate
  3 years, 6 months,
  10 days

STEPHEN IX (VIII)
Nationality
  Italian, from Rome
Family background
  Perhaps the half-
  brother of Pope
  John XI
Early career
  Cardinal priest
Elected pope
  14 July 939
Died
  Late October 942;
  he was imprisoned
  and mutilated and
  probably died of his
  injuries
Length of pontificate
  3 years, *c.* 3
  months

MARINUS II
Nationality
  Italian, from Rome
Early career
  Cardinal priest
Elected pope
  30 October 942
Died
  Early May 946
Length of pontificate
  3 years, *c.* 6
  months

AGAPITUS II
Nationality
  Italian, from Rome
Elected pope
  10 May 946
Died
  December 955
Length of pontificate
  9 years, *c.* 4 or 5
  months

JOHN XII
Nationality
  German
Date of birth
  c. 937
Original name
  Octavian
Family background
  Illegitimate son of
  Alberic II, prince of
  Rome

Elected pope
  16 December 955
Age at election
  c. 18
Deposed
  4 December 963
Died
  14 May 964, from a
  stroke
Length of pontificate
  7 years, 11
  months, 20 days

LEO VIII
Nationality
  Uncertain
Early career
  Lawyer
Status
  Layman
Elected pope
  4 December 963
Deposed
  26 February 964
Died
  1 March 965
Length of pontificate
  Either 2 months, 22
  days or 1 year, 2
  months, 28 days,
  according to the
  validity of his
  deposition
Notable features
  Because he was a
  layman when he
  was elected, Leo
  had to be rushed
  through holy orders
  in a single day

BENEDICT V
Nationality
  Italian, from Rome
Early career
  Deacon
Elected pope
  22 May 964
Deposed
  23 June 964, and
  exiled to Hamburg.
Died
  4 July 966, in
  Hamburg
Length of pontificate
  1 month, 2 days

JOHN XIII
Nationality
  Italian, from Rome
Early career
  Librarian, bishop of
  Narnia
Elected pope
  1 October 965
Died
  6 September 972
Length of pontificate
  6 years, 11
  months, 5 days

Otto I the Great, chosen as German king in 936, was waited on by four dukes at his coronation banquet. One of his principal aims was to make himself supreme in Germany. Another was to subordinate the papacy to the empire. Here he is shown offering a model of Magdeburg Cathedral to Christ. 10th-century ivory plaque (Metropolitan Museum of Art).

the royal title there, Agapitus, in what was perhaps a feeble bid for some measure of independence, willingly and actively sought to confer upon him the imperial crown of the West. Alberic, however, succeeded in delaying Otto's accession to this honour, although he could not prevent Agapitus from granting the German ruler a remarkable jurisdiction over both monastic and episcopal affairs. Still, Alberic had the last word. When he knew he was on his deathbed, he brought together the pope and representatives of both clergy and nobility, and made them swear they would elect his bastard son, Octavian, as pope after Agapitus died. Supinely they all agreed and in 955 Octavian ascended the papal throne and took the name 'John'.

John XII (955–964) was a scandal, both in his election and in his private life; even after his elevation to the papacy, John continued to give himself to lechery, so much so that the Lateran was openly described as a brothel. This, surprisingly, did not seem to affect his standing outside Italy. At home, however, the political situation was highly unstable and he was obliged to seek Otto's assistance, promising him in return the imperial crown. Otto agreed to help and quickly restored order to the volatile north, receiving his reward on 2 February 962 when John crowned him emperor in the West. The emperor was pleased to confirm a large proportion of Italy as a separate papal state. Otto then left Rome to attack Berengar, king of Italy, and in his absence John started colluding with Berengar's son – presumably as a gesture of independence. Otto returned, furious, and engineered John's deposition, consecrating **Leo VIII** (963–965) in his place. A revolt by Rome in John's favour briefly restored him, but not for long. A stroke carried him off, and it says much for his reputation that his death, occurring in the midst of an act of adultery, was attributed to a blow on the head delivered by Satan. He was only 27.

It is a moot point whether Leo or his successor, **Benedict V** (964), should be considered an antipope. Was John's deposition valid? If not, then Leo's election was illegitimate. But when John died, the Romans

PAPAL NAMES

BENEDICT VI
Nationality
  Italian, from Rome
Family background
  Son of a man who
  later became a
  monk
Early career
  Cardinal priest
Elected pope
  19 January 973
Died
  July 974; Benedict
  was arrested and
  imprisoned in June
  974 in Castel Sant'
  Angelo, and
  strangled
Length of pontificate
  1 year, *c.* 5 or 6
  months
Antipope
  Boniface VII
  (June–July 974;
  August 984–July
  985)

BENEDICT VII
Nationality
  Italian, from Rome
Family background
  Aristocratic
Early career
  Bishop of Sutri
Elected pope
  October 974
Died
  10 July 983
Length of pontificate
  8 years, *c.* 9
  months

JOHN XIV
Nationality
  Italian, from Pavia
Original name
  Peter Canepanova
Early career
  Bishop of Pavia
Elected pope
  December 983
Deposed
  April 984;
  assaulted and then
  imprisoned in
  Castel Sant' Angelo
Died
  20 August 984;
  starved or poisoned
Length of pontificate
  c. 4 or 5 months

JOHN XV
Nationality
  Italian, from Rome
Family background
  Son of a priest
Early career
  Cardinal priest
Elected pope
  Mid-August 985
Died
  March 996, of fever
Length of pontificate
  10 years, *c.* 6 or 7
  months

GREGORY V
Nationality
  German
Date of birth
  972
Original name
  Bruno
Family background
  Cousin to Emperor
  Otto III
Early career
  Priest
Elected pope
  3 May 996
Age at election
  24
Died
  18 February 999, of
  malaria?
Length of pontificate
  2 years, 9 months,
  15 days
Antipope
  John XVI (February
  997–May 998)

SILVESTER II
Nationality
  French, from
  Auvergne
Date of birth
  c. 945
Original name
  Gerbert
Family background
  Humble
Early career
  Archbishop of
  Ravenna
Elected pope
  2 April 999
Died
  12 May 1003
Length of pontificate
  4 years, 1 month,
  10 days

Otto II, son of Otto the Great, giving the bishop's staff to Adalbert, detail from a 12th-century bronze door in Gnesen Cathedral. Otto was crowned king of Germany at the age of six in 961, and in 967 joint-emperor with his father during a ceremony at which Pope John XIII officiated.

ignored Leo as Otto's puppet and elected Benedict instead, and he in turn was deposed by an outraged Otto. Not until **John XIII** (965–972), then, can we be comfortable with the validity of the papal succession. This pope, however, seen as another imperial tool, quickly became hateful to the Romans who drove him into exile. Restored with Otto's assistance, John remained more or less in the emperor's pocket but managed to direct ecclesiastical affairs without further rebellion from Rome. **Benedict VI** (973–974) also relied on Otto, but when the emperor died in May 973 Rome immediately stirred against him. The new emperor, Otto II, was too preoccupied with difficulties in Germany to help, and so nothing prevented Benedict from being arrested, imprisoned and then strangled by order of his 'successor', the antipope *Boniface VII*.

Benedict VII (974–983) succeeded amid scenes of chaos, a not unusual circumstance during this period. The antipope Boniface was active and dangerous throughout his pontificate, and in 980 so threatened the pope's safety that Benedict was forced to appeal to Otto for assistance. But during the intervals of what passed for calm, Benedict managed to carry out such ecclesiastical duties as conformed to the emperor's pleasure. Upheaval, however, was never far away and when Benedict died, the customary turbulence surfaced. Otto offered the papal throne to the abbot of Cluny who refused it, and then to one of his former ministers who became **John XIV** (983–984). Unfortunately, Otto died almost at once and John, without friends or allies, proved an easy victim for Boniface who rushed to Rome, arrested the pope, deposed him, threw him in prison and allowed him to starve to death. Boniface then ruled until July 985 when, to the relief of many, he died. His body was flayed, pierced with lances, dragged naked through the streets and finally dumped in front of the Lateran.

John XV (985–996) was the nominee of certain powerful Roman families. Hobbled by such ties at home, John made more of a mark abroad. In

Otto III receiving the obeisance of the realms. Miniature from the Gospels of Otto III, 997–1000 (Bayerische Staatsbibliothek, Munich). Otto III is enthroned between two priests and two soldiers. The picture neatly symbolizes the influence of the Church, especially through Abbot Heribert of Brogne who was his chancellor and principal adviser, and the army, on which he relied for his multiple campaigns.

991, he negotiated a peace between Normandy and England; in 992, he accepted Poland as a gift from its ruler to St Peter; in 993, he canonized a German saint in the first recorded ritual of such an event; and in 993/4, he successfully resisted the first stirrings of Gallicanism, the attempt by the Church in France to act independently of papal authority. After 991, however, his position in Rome was becoming difficult. His friends were dying and those who came after held him in no respect. His successor, **Gregory V** (996–999), was the second German pope, a young relative of Otto III, the new Western emperor. But, having managed to alienate Otto and having failed to make friends in Rome, Gregory soon found himself obliged to leave the city and reside in Lombardy, which gave his enemies a chance to elect an antipope, *John XVI*, in his place. Gregory was restored only with the help of imperial arms, and during the rest of his short reign he cooperated (though uneasily) with imperial policies.

On Gregory's death, Otto chose the first Frenchman to become pope, **Silvester II** (999–1003). He was a dazzling and versatile scholar, and, although a Gallican prior to his election, Silvester quickly transformed into a champion of papal prerogatives and worked hard with Otto to reform abuses in the Church. But in 1001 a revolt in Rome forced both pope and emperor to leave the city; Rome came under the control of John II Crescentius. Otto died of malaria not quite one year later, and Silvester was permitted to return only under close supervision.

A PAPAL PACT WITH THE DEVIL?

Curious legends gathered about Silvester II after his death. According to one of them, he studied astrology and various other mathematical subjects among the Saracens, and he was particularly eager to lay his hands on one particular book:

He begged and pleaded [with the owner] by God and by friendship. He offered much: he promised more. When this had scarcely any effect, he tried trickery at night. Having carefully prepared the way by cultivating a close friendship with the owner's daughter (who then turned a blind eye), he made him drunk, seized the book which the man had put under his pillow, and fled. But the owner shook off sleep and, by using his expert knowledge of the stars, set off in pursuit of the fugitive. [Silvester] looked back, used astrology and recognized his danger, and hid

himself under a wooden bridge which was close by, wrapping his arms round it and hanging down so that he touched neither the water nor the land. Thus his pursuer's ardour was frustrated and the man went home. Then [Silvester] quickened his journey and came to the sea. There he summoned the Devil by means of incantations, and agreed to offer him perpetual homage if he would transport him across the sea, away from the man who was starting to pursue him once again: and it was done.

William of Malmesbury *Gesta Regum Anglorum*, 2.167

11th-century ivory situla belonging to Otto III in the cathedral at Aachen. Pope Silvester II is the upper central enthroned figure.

THE MILLENNIUM

Silvester's pontificate saw the close of the first 1,000 years of Christian history. According to a Frankish monk, Adso, when the Apocalypse approached, a Frankish king would unite the Roman empire, become the greatest of all rulers, and reign in peace until the arrival of the Antichrist heralded the Last Days and Final Judgment. People looked for signs of the four horsemen of the Apocalypse – War, Famine, Disease and Death – and found it easy to see them.

What, then, was the condition of the papacy at this juncture? At various times in the past, the popes had been given (or had claimed to have been given) imperial or princely powers. The spurious *Donation of Constantine* (8th century) had made Silvester I a kind of emperor of the West, while the genuine *Donation of Pepin* (754) and of *Otto* (962) created a fiefdom in Italy which was later to be known as 'the Papal States'.

The pope, therefore, was a secular Italian ruler as well as being the Vicar of Christ. His secular authority and dignity, however, were severely curtailed by the factiousness of the Roman aristocracy and by his consequent reliance upon Western imperial power to uphold his person and office. As a religious authority, too, the pope found himself held in check by a multiplicity of worldly powers, but in particular by the emperor in the West. Constantinople, dominant during the early centuries, had drifted into the background. It could still be a potent force in papal politics, but it was from the West that the popes received directives and read their fates.

The battle for prestige, however, had been long conceded. Rome was recognized far and wide as the head of the Church, in practice if not altogether in theory, and as a figure of religious dignity the pope had no equal anywhere in the Christian world.

Behold a white horse: and he that sat on him went forth to conquer. There went out another horse that was red: and power was given to him that sat thereon to take peace from the earth. Lo, a black horse: and he that sat on him had a pair of balances in his hand. Behold, a pale horse: and his name that sat on him was Death.

Apocalypse *6.2–8*

A 12th-century Spanish manuscript illumination of the Four Horsemen of the Apocalypse (British Library).

John XVII
1003

John XVIII
1003–1009

Sergius IV
1009–1012

Benedict VIII
1012–1024

John XIX
1024–1032

Benedict IX
1032–1044; 1045; 1047–1048

Silvester III
1045

Gregory VI
1045–1046

Clement II
1046–1047

Damasus II
1048

Leo IX
1049–1054

Henry II was the last of the Saxon emperors. Pope Benedict VIII crowned him emperor in February 1014.

[The bishop of Caprea] saw the late Pope Benedict [VIII] seated upon a black horse, as if he were still in the flesh. When he realized that his journey had been interrupted, the bishop said, 'Good gracious! Aren't you the Pope Benedict we thought was drowned?'
'I am indeed,' he replied, 'and I am an unhappy man.'
'In what way, Father?'
'I am visited by grave torments,' he said, 'but I have a hope of deliverance if help is forthcoming. Go, I beg, to my brother John who now occupies the Apostolic seat and tell him to distribute amongst the poor, for my salvation, the sum of money which is hidden in a certain chest … because what he has already given the needy on my behalf has not benefited me at all, since it was acquired by acts of plunder and injustice.'

St Peter Damian *De abdicatione episcopatus,* 3

John XVI is missing. He was an antipope, but somehow acquired a number, like Boniface VII. **John XVII** (1003) is quite obscure and **John XVIII** (1003–1009), like his predecessor, was beholden to the Crescentii clan in

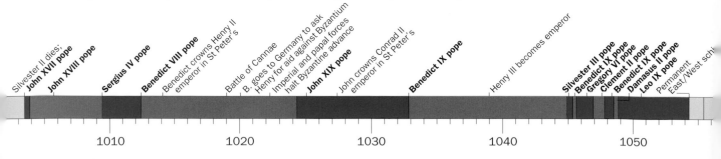

Silvester II dies; **John XVII pope**
John XVIII pope
Sergius IV pope
Benedict VIII pope
Benedict crowns Henry II emperor in St Peter's
Battle of Cannae
B. goes to Germany to ask Henry for aid against Byzantium
Imperial and papal forces halt Byzantine advance
John XIX pope
John crowns Conrad II emperor in St Peter's
Benedict IX pope
Henry III becomes emperor
Silvester III pope
Benedict IX pope
Gregory VI pope
Clement II pope
Benedict IX pope
Damasus II pope
Leo IX pope
Permanent East/West schism

1010   1020   1030   1040   1050

PAPAL NAMES

JOHN XVII
Nationality
  Italian, from Rome
Original name
  John Sicco
Elected pope
  16 May 1003
Died
  6 November 1003
Length of pontificate
  5 months, 22 days

JOHN XVIII
Nationality
  Italian, from Rome
Original name
  John Fasanus
Early career
  Cardinal priest
Elected pope
  25 December 1003
Died
  June/July 1009
Length of pontificate
  5 years, 6 or 7
  months, 7 days
Notable feature
  It is recorded that
  John retired or
  abdicated and
  ended his days as a
  monk

SERGIUS IV
Nationality
  Italian, from Rome
Original name
  Peter
Family background
  Son of a shoemaker
Early career
  Bishop of Albano
Elected pope
  31 July 1009
Died
  12 May 1012, by
  violence?
Length of pontificate
  2 years, 9 months

13 days

BENEDICT VIII
Nationality
  Italian
Date of birth
  c. 980
Original name
  Theophylact
Family background
  Aristocratic
Religious status
  Layman
Elected pope
  17 May 1012
Age at election
  c. 32
Died
  9 April 1024
Length of pontificate
  12 years, 10
  months, 24 days
Antipope
  Gregory 'VI'
  (May–December
  1012)

JOHN XIX
Nationality
  Italian
Original name
  Romanus
Family background
  John was the
  younger brother
  of Pope Benedict
  VIII
Religious status
  Layman
Early career
  Senator, consul
Elected pope
  19 April 1024
Age at election
  Younger than 32
Died
  20 October 1032
Length of pontificate
  8 years, 6 months

John XIX (*above*) was widely condemned for his greed, especially in demanding money for ecclesiastical posts.

Rome for his elevation to the papacy. The Crescentii family had come to prominence at a synod held in 963, convened by Emperor Otto I to depose Pope John XII. They were to play a crucial part in Roman politics for the next few decades. The details of Pope John XVIII's life are somewhat cloudy, but he is said to have ended his days in retirement as a monk, which presumably means he abdicated first. **Sergius IV** (1009–1012) was yet another client of the Crescentii, but by the time **Benedict VIII** (1012–1024) became pope, a revolution in Rome had swept the Crescentii away and raised up the family 'Tusculani' in their place. The Tusculani were generally supporters of the Western emperor, and their nominal founder, Gregory de Tusculana, was the father of the new pope Benedict. Needless to say, this situation produced an antipope, *Gregory 'VI'*; but Benedict and his faction were firmly in control and when the German king, Henry II, recognized him as pope, Gregory disappeared. Benedict then invited Henry to Rome and crowned him emperor in February 1014. The two men then went to Ravenna whence a synod, clearly acting under their instructions, issued decrees relating to clerical discipline. It is perhaps a mark of the dual nature of the papacy at this period that Benedict spent much of his time in armour or on horseback, operating as a soldier in quest of secular territories. He also took part in a sea battle against Saracen marauders (1016), but when, in 1019, Constantinople won a land battle at Cannae in southern Italy, he was obliged to go to Germany in person and ask for Henry's help against further Byzantine incursions in Italy. Together, in 1022, pope and emperor halted the Byzantine advance, and thus ended the pontificate on a note of something like triumph.

Benedict's brother then bribed his way to the papal throne. As he was a layman, his startling assumption of the highest sacerdotal office gave cause for alarm and resentment. Nor did his pontificate, in spite of its outward show of confidence, give cause for satisfaction. **John XIX** (1024–1032), therefore, must be regarded with reserve. We are told, perhaps dubiously, that he actually wavered a little in the face of a delegation from the Byzantine emperor requesting papal recognition of Constantinople's primacy in the East. True, he refused; but it is clear that the Western emperor, Conrad II, regarded him with scant respect and on more than one occasion compelled the pope to cancel his own decisions and fall in with imperial wishes on the subject.

After his death, the papacy stayed in the family, for his nephew now became pope as **Benedict IX** (1032–1044; 1045; 1047–1048). Another layman: another scandal. Nevertheless, he was less obliging to Conrad than his uncle had been, and when Conrad was succeeded by Henry III, the new emperor found him just as prickly. But Benedict's private life eventually caused a riot and in January 1045 he was replaced by **Silvester III**. To exchange a Tusculan candidate for a Crescentian, however, proved no solution and by March Benedict was back in power. But his grip was weak and in May he abdicated in favour of his godfather who became **Gregory VI** (1045–1046). A huge sum of money passed between them.

PAPAL NAMES

BENEDICT IX
Nationality
Italian
Original name
Theophylact
Family background
Nephew of Popes
John XIX and
Benedict VIII
Status
Layman
Elected pope
21 October 1032
Age at election
20s?
Expelled
September 1044
Resumed office
10 March 1045
Abdicated
1 May 1045
Deposed
24 December 1046
Resumed office
8 November 1047
Ejected
16 July 1048
Died
Late 1055/early
1056
Length of pontificate
Impossible to gauge

SILVESTER III
Nationality
Italian?
Original name
John
Early career
Bishop of Sabina
Elected pope
20 January 1045
Expelled
10 March 1045
Died
1063
Length of pontificate
c. 1 month, 27 days

GREGORY VI
Nationality
Italian
Original name
John Gratian
Family background
Wealthy bankers
Early career
Archpriest
Elected pope
1 May 1045
Age at election
Elderly
Deposed
20 December 1046

Died
Late 1047
Length of pontificate
1 year, 7 months,
20 days

CLEMENT II
Nationality
German
Original name
Suidger
Early career
Bishop of Bamberg
Elected pope
24 December 1046
Died
9 October 1047 of
lead poisoning
Length of pontificate
9 months, 17 days

DAMASUS II
Nationality
German, from
Bavaria
Original name
Poppo
Early career
Bishop of Brixen
Elected pope
17 July 1048
Died
9 August 1048, at
Palestrina, possibly
of malaria
Length of pontificate
24 days

LEO IX
Nationality
German, from
Alsace
Date of birth
21 June 1002
Original name
Bruno
Family background
Aristocratic; related
to the imperial
family
Early career
Bishop of Toul
Elected pope
12 February 1049.
Leo was still in his
diocese at the
time
Age at election
46
Died
19 April 1054
Length of pontificate
5 years, 2 months,
5 days

Did Gregory buy the office? The matter is open to question, although a synod presided over by the Western emperor pronounced him guilty and therefore deposed him. The emperor then appointed **Clement II** (1046–1047), a fellow German. Henry's aim was clearly to rescue the papacy from the factious Roman nobility, and indeed Clement began a rigorous programme of reform with particular emphasis on simony. But progress was slow, and on Clement's death a mixture of emotionalism

Pope Leo IX blessing a monastic foundation offered by Warinus, abbot of St Arnulf, Metz. German miniature, second half of 11th century (Burgerbibliothek, Bern).

and bribery in Rome brought Benedict back for a third time. Henry was furious and had him removed by force, nominating another German as pope in his place. **Damasus II** (1048) had a remarkably short reign of 23 days, so **Leo IX** (1049–1054), a German candidate once again, succeeded as the emperor's nominee.

Leo was a great reformer. To further his aims he made use of like-minded clerics to help him in Rome, called several synods at important ecclesiastical centres, and took the unusual step of travelling himself through Europe to promote his message; clerical celibacy, simony and papal supremacy being the three points he addressed with especial vigour. At first all went well, but in 1053 he made the mistake of leading a poor and inadequate army against Normans who were ravaging southern Italy. His army was defeated. He himself was captured on 18 June 1053 and imprisoned, he then had to watch while the patriarch of Constantinople – Michael Cerularius, a rabid anti-westerner – closed Latin churches in Constantinople and fulminated against Latin liturgical practices. The quarrel, ostensibly over such details as the use of unleavened bread in the mass, but exacerbated by Leo's attempt to free southern Italy – an area claimed by Byzantium – was actually about the right of Rome to claim primacy over all other sees, and Michael's personal resolve never to play second fiddle to anyone. 'I will not serve', was his motto. Reconciliation was attempted but failed completely. The main players were too entrenched, too intransigent. Then, on 16 July 1054, Rome excommunicated the patriarch and his party, and was in its turn declared anathema. The die was cast: the breach was to be permanent.

It was a disaster the pope himself fortunately did not live to see. He died on 19 April 1054, only a month after being brought back to Rome from captivity in the south. He was canonized not long after, the first papal saint since Hadrian III nearly 170 years before.

11th-century chessman in the shape of a Norman knight, from southern Italy (Cabinet des Médailles, Paris). The Norman achievements were spectacular. Originally Vikings, the Normans established themselves in Normandy in 911 and in 1130 created the Kingdom of the Two Sicilies under Roger II – a creation which lasted until the mid-19th century. They thus developed a distinctive culture in Europe, and via the first crusade, in which their contribution played a decisive role, in the Holy Land as well. When Pope Leo IX attempted to oust them from the south of Italy in 1053 he was taken prisoner and humiliated.

Victor II
1055–1057
Stephen X (IX)
1057–1058
Nicholas II
1058–1061
Alexander II
1061–1073
Gregory VII
1073–1085

Victor III
1086–1087
Urban II
1088–1099

Paschal II
1099–1118
Gelasius II
1118–1119
Callistus II
1119–1124
Honorius II
1124–1130
Innocent II
1130–1143
Celestine II
1143–1144
Lucius II
1144–1145

Eugene III
1145–1153

Anastasius IV
1153–1154
Hadrian IV
1154–1159
Alexander III
1159–1181
Lucius III
1181–1185
Urban III
1185–1187
Gregory VIII
1187
Clement III
1187–1191

Celestine III
1191–1198
Innocent III
1198–1216

Honorius III
1216–1227
Gregory IX
1227–1241
Celestine IV
1241
Innocent IV
1243–1254
Alexander IV
1254–1261

Urban IV
1261–1264
Clement IV
1265–1268
Gregory X
1271–1276

Innocent V
1276
Hadrian V
1276
John XXI
1276–1277
Nicholas III
1277–1280
Martin IV
1281–1285
Honorius IV
1285–1287
Nicholas IV
1288–1292
Celestine V
1294
Boniface VIII
1294–1303
Benedict XI
1303–1304
Clement V
1305–1314

John XXII
1316–1334

Benedict XII
1334–1342
Clement VI
1342–1352
Innocent VI
1352–1362
Urban V
1362–1370
Gregory XI
1370–1378

Urban VI
1378–1389
Boniface IX
1389–1404
Innocent VII
1404–1406
Gregory XII
1406–1415
Martin V
1417–1431
Eugene IV
1431–1447
Nicholas V
1447–1455
Callistus III
1455–1458
Pius II
1458–1464
Paul II
1464–1471
Sixtus IV
1471–1484
Innocent VIII
1484–1492

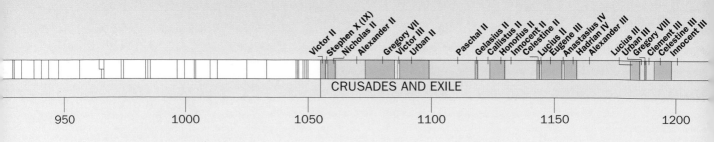

CRUSADES AND EXILE

950   1000   1050   1100   1150   1200

Victor III

Innocent III

John XXII

Clement VI

CRUSADES AND EXILE

Low Point and Recovery AD 1055–1492

The long 400 years which separated the schism of East and West from the blossoming of the Renaissance saw the papacy become more deeply involved in worldly affairs. Its independence was threatened from various quarters: the Holy Roman emperor, the Normans in Sicily and southern Italy, the kings of France and the turbulent noble families of the Italian city-states and of Rome itself. Several popes gave way under the conflicting pressures and became creatures of one or other of these competing interests, the most notorious example being the exile to Avignon between 1309 and 1377 when political conditions were such that the popes either willingly or perforce abandoned Rome and made their residence in the south of France. This was also the period of the scandal of rival popes – at one point, three reigned simultaneously. During this time simony, nepotism and the scandalous sale of indulgences besmirched the reputation of the papacy.

The period was not one of complete disreputable gloom, however. Many popes were saintly, many were learned. They founded universities, developed canon law, were patrons of the arts and promoted attempts to liberate the Holy Land from the rule of the ungodly. Nor did they all succumb willingly to political influences, but made some serious attempts to prevent the papacy from falling into the hands of those who would abuse it for their own ends. Thus, during the Avignon exile it seemed that the institution was at its nadir, but by 1492 there were signs that recovery, both spiritual and secular, might be on the way.

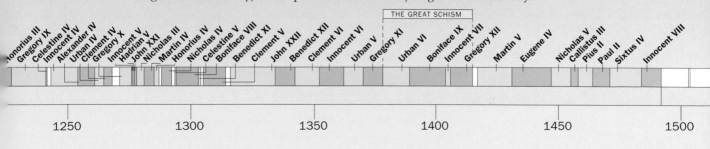

Victor II
1055–1057

Stephen X (IX)
1057–1058

Nicholas II
1058–1061

Alexander II
1061–1073

Gregory VII
1073–1085

Gregory VII (*above*) was one of the great rejuvenators of the Church. He was canonized in 1606 by Pope Paul V. 11th-century manuscript (University Library, Leipzig).

VICTOR II	

Nationality
  German, from
  Swabia
	Elected pope
	  13 April 1055

Date of birth
  c. 1018
	Age at election
	  c. 37

Original name
  Gebhard of
  Dollnstein-
  Hirschberg
	Died
	  28 July 1057,
	  in Arezzo of
	  fever

Family background
  Aristocratic
	Length of pontificate
	  2 years, 3 months,
	  15 days

Early career Bishop of Eichstätt	

VICTOR II

The subdeacon dropped poison meant for the pope [Victor II] into the chalice. After the consecration, when Victor wanted to raise the chalice he could not do so, and in order to ask God what was the reason for this, he and the people prostrated themselves in prayer. At once his poisoner was seized by an evil spirit and the reason was thus made plain.

Bernold of St Blaise *Chronicon*

The disaster of the break with Constantinople did not make itself felt immediately. Why should it? There had been breaches between East and West before: this, presumably, would simply be another. So the line of German popes and imperial nominees continued with **Victor II** (1055–1057), nobly born and a distant relative of the Western emperor, Henry III, although he himself did not make much of the connection. He became bishop of Eichstätt in Bavaria when he was about 24 and at once displayed remarkable administrative gifts which made him one of the principal voices in imperial councils. But then Pope Leo IX died and the Romans sent delegates to Henry III, asking him to name Bishop Gebhard of Eichstätt as pope. It was a request which gave pause to both nomina-

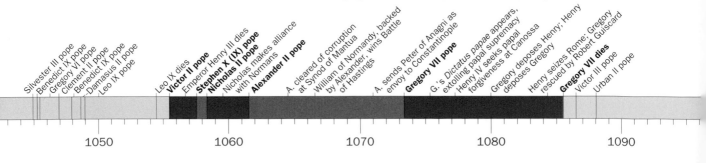

Silvester III pope
Benedict IX pope
Gregory VI pope
Clement II pope
Benedict IX pope
Damasus II pope
Leo IX pope
Leo IX dies
Victor II pope
Emperor Henry III dies
Stephen X (IX) pope
Nicholas II pope
Nicholas makes alliance with Normans
Alexander II pope
A. cleared of corruption at Synod of Mantua
William of Normandy, backed by Alexander, wins Battle of Hastings
A. sends Peter of Anagni as envoy to Constantinople
Gregory VII pope
G.'s *Dictatus papae* appears, extolling papal supremacy
Henry IV seeks papal forgiveness at Canossa
Gregory deposes Henry; Henry deposes Gregory
Henry seizes Rome; Gregory rescued by Robert Guiscard
Gregory VII dies
Victor III pope
Urban II pope

1050 1060 1070 1080 1090

After Pope Victor II died at Arezzo in July 1057, some of his entourage wanted to take his body back to Eichstätt in Germany, where he had earlier been bishop, to bury it in the cathedral there. The citizens of Ravenna, however, would not allow this and seizing the body they interred it in the Church of Santa Maria Rotunda (*above*). Originally this building was the mausoleum of King Theodoric who had died in 526.

tor and nominee. The former did not want to lose a trusted minister: the latter was awed by the burden of the papacy; for nearly five months procrastination ruled. At last, however, Gebhard gave way to become Victor II. Henry III could see the advantage of having his man in the Lateran.

There were two situations which needed to be addressed. One was Church discipline; the second was Norman expansion. In the 11th century, 'Italy' was a geographical expression rather than a territorial entity. First Lombard, then Frankish invasions had drawn the north and centre into the whirlpool of Western politics, while the south still looked to Constantinople as its fount of authority, and Sicily had become a province of the Fatimid caliphate. Normans had started to make their presence felt in southern Italy in 1016, and thereafter their expansion was rapid. Indeed, by 1073 the south was a Norman kingdom.

Leo IX's defeat by the Normans in 1053 had left both Victor and Henry with this problem and when Henry had to return to Germany in November 1055 to deal with opposition to his authority, it was not long before Victor followed, in need of assistance against the Norman threat. Other events, however, overtook them. In October 1056, while the pope was still in Germany, the emperor died, leaving his five-year-old son to Victor's care: and it says much for Victor's diplomatic skill that he not only managed to have the child crowned at Aachen, but also reconciled to the empire two of its most persistently restless vassals, Godfrey of Lorraine and Baldwin of Flanders. On Henry's death, Godfrey's became the most significant voice in Italy and so it was perhaps a stroke of luck that the important post of abbot of Monte Cassino became vacant and so cleared the way for the pope to consecrate Frederick of Lorraine – Godfrey's brother and a monk of the abbey – and make him a cardinal, too. Lorraine was thus bound to the pope by gratitude.

STEPHEN X (IX)	
Nationality German, from Lorraine	librarian of the Church, abbot of Monte Cassino
Original name Frederick of Lorraine	*Elected pope* 2 August 1057
Family background Aristocratic	*Died* 29 March 1058, in Florence
Early career Chancellor and	*Length of pontificate* 7 months, 26 days

STEPHEN X (IX)

As chance would have it, six weeks after Frederick's promotion the pope died and Frederick found himself elected pope as **Stephen X** or IX (1057–1058). His reign was short and while he was pope he did not cease to be abbot of Monte Cassino. But this does not indicate an unseemly hunger for power. Like Victor, he was solidly on the side of reforming abuse in the Church, and seems to have expected fierce opposition: he wrote in one of his letters, 'We await the brute savagery of evil-doers who at this time meet no resistance in their hostility towards the pastors of the Lord's sheep.' He was assisted in his reforming ventures by Peter Damian (later canonized). Damian was a man of formidable intelligence, an ardent communicator, and a keen reformer strongly in favour of ascetic monasticism. Another adviser was Humbert of Silva Candida, the man who had excommunicated the patriarch of Constantinople, Michael Cerularius, and thus (perhaps unwittingly) precipitated the schism between East and West. A third was Hildebrand, later to be pope himself, a Cluniac monk advanced in papal circles by Leo IX. In the summer of 1057, Stephen sent him on a complex diplomatic journey. He was to do two things: (i) investigate a reforming movement in Milan, the so-called Patarines ('rag-bags'), who were much needed but perhaps too impetuous to be altogether welcome; and (ii) announce Stephen's election to the imperial court in Germany. This was slightly delicate, as it had taken place without reference to the emperor and, as we have seen, the Western throne had become accustomed to indicating its wishes regarding who was elected pope.

Even more delicate, however, were the pope's future intentions to expel the Normans from southern Italy, using the treasures of Monte Cassino to finance the venture, and to win the support of his brother Godfrey of Lorraine by crowning him Western emperor in place of the luckless child, Henry IV, then wearing the crown. Such, at any rate, was current belief. But Stephen's health was failing and in March 1058 he died in Florence, having first made the Romans promise not to elect a successor until Hildebrand had returned from Germany.

NICHOLAS II

NICHOLAS II	
Nationality	*Age at election*
German, from	c. 48
Lorraine	*Died*
Date of birth	19/26 July 1061,
c. 1010	in Florence
Original name	*Length of pontificate*
Gerard	2 years, 7 months,
Early career	13 or 20 days
Bishop of Florence	*Antipope*
Elected pope	Benedict X
6 December 1058	(1058–1059)

He [Nicholas II] went to Rome where in the second Lateran Council he procur'd a Law to be enacted, very wholesom for the Church of Rome, which is to be seen among the Decrees, to this purpose, 'That if any one either by Simony, or by the favour of any powerful Man, or by any tumult either of the People or Soldiery shall be placed in S. Peter's Chair, he shall be reputed not Apostolical, but an Apostate, one that transgresses the rules even of common Reason; and that it shall be lawful for the Cardinals, Clergy, and devout Laity, with Weapons both spiritual and material, by Anathema's and by any humane aid him to drive out and depose; and that Catholicks may assemble for this end in any place whatsoever, if they cannot do it in the City.'

Bartolomeo Platina *Lives of the Popes*

An antipope, *Benedict X*, took advantage of the vacuum caused by Hildebrand's absence and the Romans' promise to wait for his return, and seized power for just over nine months. In December 1058, however, **Nicholas II** (1058–1061) was canonically elected and Benedict fled, later to suffer public trial and degradation at the request of Hildebrand. Nicholas, a reformer like his predecessors, presumably with the intention of lessening the opportunities for simony in future papal elections, promulgated a decree on 13 April 1059, which said that henceforth the pope would be chosen by the cardinal bishops, with the remaining clergy and the people assenting to their decision. Interestingly enough, imperial confirmation does not seem to have been envisaged as an essential concomitant of the procedure.

So far, Nicholas was pursuing Stephen's general trend, aided by the same trio of strong characters who had advised and helped Pope Stephen.

11th-century fresco from the Church of San Clemente showing Nicholas II. Nicholas, we are told, washed the feet of 12 poor men every day of his pontificate, and if he had no time to do this during the day, he did it at night.

The abbey of Monte Cassino, cradle of the Benedictine Order, was founded by St Benedict in *c.* 529. It was destroyed by the Lombards in *c.* 581 and restored in *c.* 717. Saracens destroyed the abbey in 883 and it was rebuilt yet again under Abbot Alignerus (947–986). Under Desiderius (later Pope Victor III), the abbey reached the height of its splendour and intellectual eminence (*above*).

But with regard to the Normans, Nicholas performed something of an about-turn. For on the advice of Desiderius, the new abbot of Monte Cassino, and Hildebrand, he made an alliance with Robert Guiscard, the Normans' principal leader, and thus secured peace. Alas, all could not remain well. The Western imperial court and the German bishops were embittered by the terms of the oath sworn by Robert to the pope, wherein he recognized the supreme authority of the papacy over his Italian territories and possessions. This the Germans saw as an encroachment on their presumed political rights over those self-same territories, and in the summer of 1060 a synod of German bishops declared the pope's decrees null and void and even went so far as to suggest that he be deposed. The pope pressed ahead regardless. In July 1061, however, Nicholas was taken ill and died. The conditions were right for the appearance of an antipope and sure enough, *Honorius II*, a German nominee of Empress Agnes, emerged in Basel. Meanwhile, an Italian, Anselm of Lucca, strongly supported by Hildebrand – who was irritated by the sight of a Roman delegation sneaking off to Germany to ask the youthful emperor to make a choice for them – was elected, consecrated and enthroned with the help of Norman troops.

ALEXANDER II	
Nationality	*Died*
Italian, from Baggio	21 April 1073
Original name	*Length of pontificate*
Anselm	11 years, 6
Early career	months, 22 days
Bishop of Lucca	*Antipope*
Elected pope	Honorius II
30 September	(1061–1064)
1061	

PAPAL BULLS

The Latin word *bulla* refers to a seal attached to an official document, stamped with a device which is meant to guarantee the document's authenticity. Early papal bulls were made of lead and carried the papal signature on one side and his motto or picture on the other. After the 13th century, the name extended itself to the document as a whole. Since 1878 the leaden bull has been largely replaced by a red ink stamp. Bulls are written in Latin, the official language of the Church, and are referred to by their opening Latin words.

Detail of a papal bull of Alexander II. The pope's name appears in the circle below those of St Peter and St Paul.

GREGORY VII	
Nationality	*Elected pope*
Italian, from	22 April 1073
Tuscany	*Age at election*
Date of birth	*c.* 53
c. 1020	*Died*
Original name	25 May 1085
Hildebrand	*Length of pontificate*
Family background	12 years, 1 month,
Humble	3 days
Status	*Antipope*
Monk	Clement III (1080;
Early career	1084–1100)
Archdeacon	

ALEXANDER II

The new pope, **Alexander II** (1061–1073), thus faced a serious rift in the Church: imperial court against Roman cardinalate, self-interest against reform. Nor was the rift easily mended. Honorius set himself to buy support in Italy and was largely successful, so much so that two 'papal' armies (for Alexander had not been slow to muster aid) came to blows in Rome and left the city divided. The impasse was ended by Godfrey of Lorraine who sent the two men away to await an imperial decision on their claims. Two years passed before Alexander managed to clear himself of charges of corruption in obtaining the papacy; but relations with the imperial court continued to be strained and Alexander made tentative approaches to Constantinople, although nothing came of them.

GREGORY VII

At length, with no display of enmity or of recklessness [King Henry] came with a few attendants to the town of Canossa in which I was staying, and there he remained for three days in front of the gate, a pitiable figure who had laid aside all kingly attire and, as is natural for a penitent, was without shoes and clad in woollen garments.

Gregory *Letters* 4.12 (year 1077)

(*Right*) From top to bottom: Henry IV and Guibertus of Ravenna, later elected antipope Clement III, with a German soldier expelling Gregory VII, 'while the king is in a rage'. Gregory VII in exile surrounded by faithful bishops. Gregory VII on his death-bed. Miniature from the *Weltchronik* by Otto of Friesling, 1170 (University Library, Jena).

(*Opposite bottom*) Henry IV petitioning Matilda of Tuscany at Canossa to intercede on his behalf with Pope Gregory. 12th-century manuscript (Vatican Library).

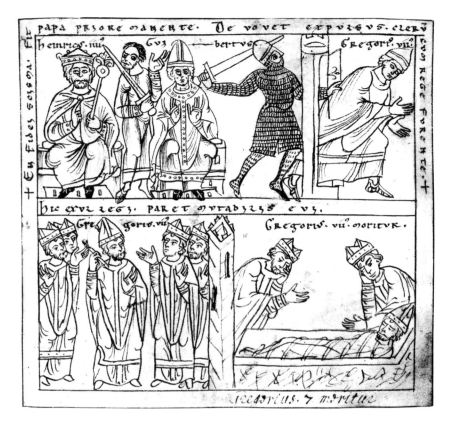

THE INVESTITURE DISPUTE

A hostile view of the quarrel between Gregory and Emperor Henry:

The pope of Rome, whose office is an honourable one and who is guarded by a large number of armies, quarrelled with Henry, the king of Germany.... The reasons for this disagreement between the king and the pope were as follows: the pope accused King Henry of not granting church preferments free of charge but of selling them for money, and of conferring episcopal office from time to time on unworthy individuals. The king of Germany, for his part, accused the pope of being an usurper, on the grounds that he had taken possession of the Apostolic throne without imperial consent. Moreover, the king added insults to this injury and said that if Gregory did not give up the papacy of his own free will, he would be expelled ignominiously from it. When these remarks were reported to the pope, he immediately exposed the royal envoys to his fury. He started by maltreating them savagely, then cut their hair with scissors and their beards with a razor, and finally crowned his conduct with a dreadful outrage, well beyond the bounds of civilized behaviour, and sent them away. I would give details of this outrage, but the modesty which belongs to a woman and to a woman of the imperial house, prevents me from doing so.

Anna Comnena *Alexiad* 1.13

Alexander's death brought Hildebrand at last to the papal throne as **Gregory VII** (1073–1085).

His career had been distinguished and he was to prove an exceptional pontiff. Like his predecessors, he was a reformer and had an exalted opinion of the papacy. Both characteristics were to bring him into conflict with entrenched interests in both Church and State. This can best be illustrated by the 'Investiture Dispute'. Who was to have the right to nominate bishops: emperor or pope? Henry IV pursued his own perceived privilege; Gregory rebuked him. Henry summoned a synod of German bishops who obediently deposed the pope. Gregory countered this move by excommunicating Henry in 1076. Henry bought forgiveness, however, by humbling himself in January 1077 at the castle of Canossa in northern Italy, where he petitioned Matilda, countess of Tuscany – Canossa being her hereditary fief – to intercede with Pope Gregory on his behalf. Matilda was married to Godfrey of Lorraine, the brother of the earlier pope, Stephen X, and hence maintained the position of the pope against the emperor during the dispute. Henry's humility, however, was feigned and three years later Gregory not only excommunicated Henry again, but also deposed him. German bishops retaliated by deposing Gregory and electing an antipope, *Clement III*, in his place. Henry marched on Rome and took it; Gregory was rescued by the Norman Robert Guiscard whose troops so antagonized the people that the pope was obliged to flee. He died in Salerno.

Victor III
1086–1087

Urban II
1088–1099

Late 12th-century French manuscript showing Pope Urban II dedicating the third abbey church of Cluny (Bibliothèque Nationale, Paris). The Benedictine abbey of Cluny, situated in the Rhône Valley, became a major centre of Church reform during the Middle Ages, blending pastoral concern with an ascetic otherworldliness. By the 12th century it had more than 400 monks.

VICTOR III	
Nationality Italian	*Consecrated pope* 9 May 1087
Date of birth c. 1027	*Died* 16 September 1087, in Monte Cassino
Original name Daufer	
Early career Abbot of Monte Cassino, cardinal priest	*Length of pontificate* 1 year, 3 months, 24 days
Elected pope 24 May 1086	*Antipope* Clement III (1080; 1084–1100)
Age at election c. 59	

URBAN II	
Nationality French, from Châtillon-sur-Marne	*Elected pope* 12 March 1088
Date of birth c. 1035	*Age at election* c. 53
Original name Odo	*Died* 29 July 1099
Family background Aristocratic	*Length of pontificate* 11 years, 4 months, 17 days
Early career Prior of Cluny, cardinal bishop	*Antipope* Clement III (1080; 1084–1100)

VICTOR III

Gregory's death was followed by 12 months of shambles until Desiderius became pope as **Victor III** (1086–1087). Even this decision, however, proved abortive since Rome was in such chaos that Victor decided to abandon the papacy and return to Monte Cassino as its abbot. It took until spring 1087 to persuade him to renew himself as pontiff, and it was not until May that he received his consecration in St Peter's, the antipope Clement III having first been ousted by Norman troops. Yet still Clement's influence flourished, along with rumours that Henry IV was coming to Italy: and so Victor trudged back and forth between Rome and Monte Cassino and his health declined. That he managed to govern the Church at all in these conditions is a tribute to his courage.

URBAN II

The cardinal-bishops of Porto, Tusculum and Albano, who were the directors of this conclave, rose to their feet and climbed up into the pulpit. When silence had fallen, all three together proclaimed that it was their wish Otto, bishop of Ostia, be elected Roman pontiff. When they

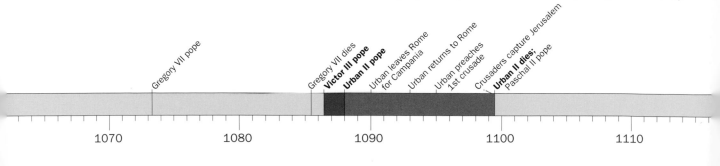

Gregory VII pope

Gregory VII dies
Victor III pope
Urban II pope
Urban leaves Rome for Campania
Urban returns to Rome
Urban preaches 1st crusade
Crusaders capture Jerusalem
Urban II dies; Paschal II pope

1070   1080   1090   1100   1110

'POPE JOAN'

This is probably as good a time as any to deal with the mythical pontiffess who, according to one version of the tale, supposedly succeeded Victor III, although the following narrative places her after Leo IV.

John the Englishman ... reigned for two years, seven months, and four days.... This man, it is claimed, was a woman and when she was a girl had been taken to Athens by one of her lovers who had dressed her in men's clothing. In this fashion she made progress in various branches of knowledge, to the extent that her equal could not be found ... and because there was in Rome a high opinion of her life and erudition, she was elected pope with general approbation. But during her papacy she was made pregnant by her companion, and because she did not know exactly when the birth would take place, she produced in a narrow lane between the Colosseum and San Clemente while she was making her way from St Peter's to the Lateran. It is said that when she died, she was buried at that same spot.... She is not included in the list of holy pontiffs as much for the disgrace as for the fact that she was a woman.

Martin von Troppau *Chronicle of the Popes and Emperors*

Delicious material for polemic, it is nevertheless nothing more than myth, although it was not exposed as such until as late as the 17th century.

The 'Popess' tarot card, possibly inspired by the legend of Pope Joan.

asked, according to custom, whether that was what everyone else wanted, everyone cried out 'Yes!' with extraordinary unanimity, saying that he was worthy to be pope of the universal, Apostolic See. Then the cardinal bishop of Albano proclaimed Otto pope, and said that he wished to be called 'Urban'.

Peter the Deacon *Chronicon Casinense* 4.2

In 1095, Urban II proclaimed the first crusade from the town of Clermont (*below*). With a cry of, 'God wishes it', huge numbers took the cross. From the 15th-century *Livres des Passages d'Outre Mer* (Bibliothèque Nationale, Paris).

Clement was still in effective control of Rome when Victor died and **Urban II** (1088–1099) succeeded. He was prepared to be more diplomatic in his dealings with Henry IV. But it did him no good. Clement rode high on the back of the emperor's hostility, and Urban was forced to retreat to the Campania. The stand-off lasted until 1093, with Henry in the north and Urban in the south, and it took patience and bribery to see the pope back in Rome. But he managed it in 1093, and two years later felt secure enough not only to decree fresh reforms, but also to preach a crusade for the liberation of Jerusalem. Both measures were very successful. Urban's control over the Church was tightened, and the crusade took Jerusalem two weeks before he died (see p. 106).

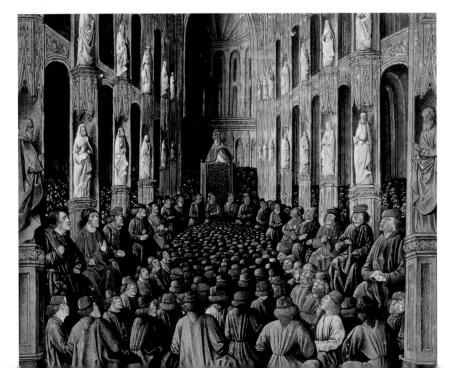

Paschal II
1099–1118

Gelasius II
1118–1119

Callistus II
1119–1124

Honorius II
1124–1130

Innocent II
1130–1143

Celestine II
1143–1144

Lucius II
1144–1145

Eugene III
1145–1153

PAPAL NAMES

PASCHAL II
Nationality
  Italian, from Bieda
  di Galeata in
  Romagna
Original name
  Rainerius
Family background
  Modest
Early career
  Abbot, cardinal
  priest
Elected pope
  13 August 1099
Died
  21 January 1118
Length of pontificate
  18 years, 5
  months, 8 days
Antipopes
  Clement III (1080;
  1084–1100),
  Theoderic
  (1100–1101),
  Adalbert (1101),
  Silvester IV
  (1105–1111)

GELASIUS II
Nationality
  Italian, from
  Gaeta
Original name
  John
Early career
  Cardinal deacon,
  chancellor
Religious status
  Gelasius was a
  monk but not yet
  a priest when
  elected
Elected pope
  24 January 1118
Age at election
  Elderly
Died
  29 January 1119,
  at Cluny
Length of pontificate
  1 year, 5 days
Antipope
  Gregory VIII
  (1118–1121)

... the Germans decided that the king must be crowned at once.... At this point, armed soldiers began to close round the pope [Paschal II] and all those who were with him, and at length it was scarcely possible for them to get to St Peter's altar to take part in celebrating mass.... After mass, the pope was forced to come down from his throne and sit below with his brethren in front of St Peter's tomb, where he was kept under guard by armed soldiers until night-fall. Then they were taken away.... A large number of people, both cleric and lay, was arrested with him.... Some were beheaded, some were robbed, some were beaten, and others held prisoner.

Peter the Deacon *Chronicon Casinense* 4.38

Urban's successor, **Paschal II** (1099–1118), had the unenviable distinction of being challenged by no fewer than four antipopes during his reign, *Clement III, Theoderic, Adalbert* and *Silvester IV*. The reasons for this were several. One lay in the continuing struggle with the Western emperor for control over ecclesiastical appointments; and when Henry IV's son staged a successful coup with papal support, Paschal, who had hoped for a change in imperial attitude, quickly discovered his mistake. Henry V was as limpet-like as his father when it came to imperial privi-

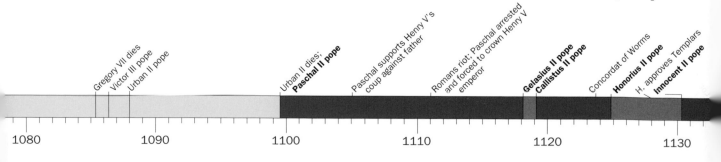

Marginal drawing from the *Chronicon Vulturnense*, 1124–1130 (Vatican Library). Paschal II gave papal approval and protection to the Knights Hospitaller of St John.

Mid-12th-century miniature from the *Cronaca di Santa Sofia* showing Pope Gelasius II (Vatican Library).

lege. Another reason was Paschal's personal weakness. Henry V was determined to be crowned emperor by the pope; Paschal tried to use this to solve the investiture problem; publication of a tentative agreement between them, however, caused a riot; Henry at once turned nasty and had Paschal arrested; Paschal capitulated and crowned Henry on the emperor's terms; violent censure followed. Poor judgment, irresolution, bad luck, ill-founded intransigence: these must be regarded as the hallmarks of Paschal's unhappy reign. **Gelasius II** (1118–1119), therefore, had a difficult task and, alas, enjoyed no more comfortable a pontificate, being forced by violence in Rome to flee to France where he fell sick and died. An antipope, *Gregory VIII*, supported by Henry V, reared his head and lasted to trouble Gelasius's successor, **Callistus II** (1119–1124). Callistus was not so timid. While still archbishop of Vienne, he had taken the offensive over the investiture question, not only declaring the imperial stance heretical but also excommunicating Henry himself. But once he became pope he looked for accommodation. Unfortunately the first attempt failed and they retreated, more or less, into their former obdurate corners. But by 1121 the situation changed once again and in 1122 they were able to sign the Concordat of Worms, which traded the spiritual side of investiture to the pope and the temporal side to the emperor. The pope, therefore, had won an important victory and assured future papal freedom from these particular imperial pretensions.

Honorius II (1124–1130) was elected and installed amid scenes of pandemonium. The aristocratic Frangipani family objected to the election of one Teobaldo as *Celestine II* – who is generally counted as an antipope – and quite literally forced the pontifical vestments upon their own man, then proclaimed as Honorius. Tumult and anarchy followed for several days. Once the uproar had died down, however, Honorius was able to pursue independent policies: for example, supporting Lothair III as successor to Henry V against his rival, Conrad, and approving the recently founded military-monastic Order of Knights Templar.

The turbulence which had attended Honorius's accession was repeated as soon as he was dead. **Innocent II** (1130–1143) was elected and enthroned by a minority of cardinals the moment Honorius breathed his last. When the majority found out, they unhesitatingly elected someone else, the antipope *Anacletus II*, and for the next eight years each man claimed to be the rightful pontiff. Because of the uproar in Rome, Innocent went to France whence he gradually convinced most of Christendom to recognize his title. In 1133, he and Lothair III marched on Rome where Lothair at last received the imperial crown; but

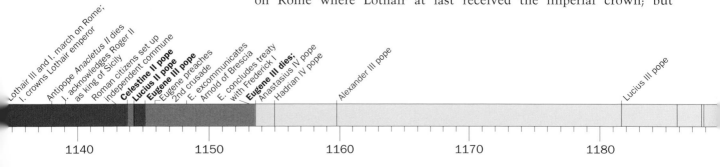

Lothair III and I. march on Rome; I. crowns Lothair emperor

Antipope *Anacletus II* dies

I. acknowledges Roger II as king of Sicily

Roman citizens set up independent commune

Celestine II pope

Lucius II pope

Eugene III pope

Eugene preaches 2nd crusade

E. excommunicates Arnold of Brescia

E. concludes treaty with Frederick I

Eugene III dies;
Anastasius IV pope

Hadrian IV pope

Alexander III pope

Lucius III pope

1140   1150   1160   1170   1180

(*Right*) Roger II became king of Sicily in 1130. He was crowned on Christmas Day in Palermo Cathedral. This 10th-century mosaic from the Chiesa della Martoraria shows him receiving his crown from Christ and wearing Byzantine robes. Roger saw himself as God's viceroy, a concept bound to bring him into conflict with the papacy.

PAPAL NAMES

CALLISTUS II
Nationality
  Burgundian
Date of birth
  c. 1050
Original name
  Guido
Family background
  Callistus was related to the royal families of Germany, France and England
Early career
  Archbishop of Vienne
Elected pope
  2 November 1119
Age at election
  c. 69
Died
  14 December 1124
Length of pontificate
  5 years, 1 month, 12 days
Antipope
  Gregory VIII (1118–1120)

HONORIUS II
Nationality
  Italian, from Imola
Original name
  Lamberto Scannabecchi
Family background
  Humble
Early career
  Cardinal bishop
Elected pope
  21 December 1124
Died
  13 February 1130
Length of pontificate
  5 years, 1 month, 24 days
Antipope(?)
  Celestine II (1124)
Notable feature
  It is arguable whether Celestine should be counted as an antipope. His election may have been valid, although he was never consecrated pope

INNOCENT II
Nationality
  Italian, from Rome
Original name
  Gregorio Papareschi
Family background
  Aristocratic
Early career
  Cardinal deacon, papal legate
Elected pope
  14 February 1130
Died
  24 September 1143
Length
  13 years, 7 months, 8 days
Antipopes
  Anacletus II (1130–1138), Victor IV (1138)

CELESTINE II
Nationality
  Italian, from Umbria
Original name
  Guido
Family background
  Aristocratic
Early career
  Cardinal priest, papal legate
Elected pope
  26 September 1143
Died
  8 March 1144
Length of pontificate
  5 months, 13 days

LUCIUS II
Nationality
  Italian, from Bologna
Original name
  Gherardo Caccianemici
Early career
  Cardinal priest, papal legate, chancellor
Elected pope
  12 March 1144
Died
  15 February 1145; Lucius was badly injured while leading an assault on the Capitol, and died of his injuries
Length of pontificate
  11 months, 3 days

Anacletus still held important parts of the city and Innocent was obliged to retreat to Pisa. When Anacletus died, his supporters elected another antipope, *Victor IV*, who resigned two months later, and thus Innocent was left in some kind of shaky command. Even so, he managed to fall into the hands of Roger II, count of Sicily, who prised out of him the title of 'king' before letting him return to Rome, a city still riven by murderous factions. It was thus a reign fraught with violence and ill omens for the future.

Celestine II (1143–1144) was old when he was elected, but survived long enough to lift an interdict which Innocent had placed on Louis VII of France, and to strike a blow at Roger's pretensions in southern Italy.

Map of Europe *c.* 1180. Note the Norman kingdom of Sicily which had been created by Roger II of Sicily in 1130 to unite his dominions in Sicily and southern Italy.

His successor, **Lucius II** (1144–1145), however, needed Roger's support against a new political secularist body in Rome, which had set itself up independently of the pope, and agreed to proceed no further against him in return for his neutrality in the coming struggle with the Roman populace. This done, the pope armed himself as a soldier and led an assault on the Capitol, during which he was badly wounded. He died not long after of the injuries he received.

At once the cardinals elected **Eugene III** (1145–1153), a Cistercian abbot, whom the political commotions of Rome kept absent from the city for much of his pontificate. He is known especially for his preaching of the second crusade which proved a failure, and for the vigour with

KNIGHTS TEMPLAR

At this time there arose in Jerusalem a new kind of soldiery, founded by the nobleman Hugh de Payns. They live as monks, take a vow of chastity, observe discipline at home and on the battle-field, eat in silence, and hold everything in common. They fight only against infidels and have spread themselves far and wide.... They are called 'Soldiers of the Temple' because they have fixed the seat of their Order in the Portico of Solomon.

Richard of Poitiers *Chronica*

The Templars were originally formed to protect pilgrims on the perilous journey from Jaffa to Jerusalem. The power of the order grew, however, so that by the 14th century it was looked on with envy and distrust.

(Above) Templar knights riding out of a fortified town, from a wall-painting in the chapel of the Templars at Charente.

(Above left) The Seal of the Templars, 'the knights of Christ'.

PAPAL NAMES	
EUGENE III	*Elected pope*
Nationality	15 February
Italian, from Pisa	1145
Original name	*Died*
Bernardo Pignatelli	8 July 1153, at
Family background	Tivoli
Humble	*Length of pontificate*
Status	8 years, 4 months,
Monk	22 days
Early career	
Abbot	

which, encouraged by Bernard of Clairvaux, he pursued reform in the Church. In 1148, he excommunicated Arnold of Brescia, a man whose zeal for reform had deviated into heresy and whose intemperate language against both Eugene and Bernard had helped to inflame the republican movement in Rome. The atmosphere was explosive. Eugene approached Frederick Barbarossa, now Western emperor (1152–1190), for assistance and the two men, after hard bargaining, formed an alliance. But Eugene died before Frederick was able to come to Rome, and the papacy reeled and slewed on a sea of troubles.

15th-century painting by Jean Fouquet showing Bernard of Clairvaux (1090–1153) preaching (Musée Condé, Chantilly). Bernard took up religion after a frivolous youth. He must have had great gifts of persuasion, for 31 of his friends and relatives went with him. The order he chose was the Cistercian Order, which observed a strict variety of the Benedictine Rule. He helped Pope Eugene III preach the disastrous second crusade, and after it failed, Bernard apologized to Pope Eugene: 'We said "Peace, and there is no peace"; we promised good things, "and behold trouble". It might seem, in fact, that we acted rashly in this affair.... These few things have been said by way of apology, so that your conscience may have something from me, whereby you can hold yourself and me excused, if not in the eyes of those who judge causes from their results, then at least in your own eyes.' (*Things to Consider* 2.1)

Anastasius IV
1153–1154

Hadrian IV
1154–1159

Alexander III
1159–1181

Lucius III
1181–1185

Urban III
1185–1187

Gregory VIII
1187

Clement III
1187–1191

16th-century woodcut of Hadrian IV, the only Englishman to sit on the papal throne. It was on the basis of a letter or bull (*Laudabiliter*), allegedly sent by Hadrian IV, that Henry II of England invaded Ireland with the intention of providing his brother William with a fief. The authenticity of the letter, however, has been questioned.

PAPAL NAMES

ANASTASIUS IV	*Date of birth*
Nationality	c. 1100
Italian, from Rome	*Original name*
Original name	Nicholas
Corrado	Breakspear
Early career	*Family background*
Cardinal bishop	Son of a clerk
Elected pope	*Early career*
8 July 1153	Abbot, cardinal
Age at election	bishop, papal
Elderly	legate
Died	*Elected pope*
3 December 1154	4 December 1154
Length of pontificate	*Age at election*
1 year, 4 months	c. 54
26 days	*Died*
	1 September 1159
HADRIAN IV	*Length of pontificate*
Nationality	4 years, 8 months,
English, from	28 days
Abbot's Langley	

At Anagni Hadrian [IV] proclaimed the emperor excommunicate and a few days later, to cool himself down [during the hot weather] he started off for a certain fountain along with his attendants. When he got there he drank deeply and at once (according to the story), a fly entered his mouth, stuck to his throat, and could not be shifted by any device of the doctors: and as a result, the pope died.

Burchard and Conrad *Uspergensium Chronicon*, 1159

Anastasius IV (1153–1154) was an old man when he became pontiff. He seems to have been chosen partly because he was a Roman and well-versed in local intricacies. Certainly the republicans accepted him with good grace, thus allowing him to adopt conciliatory measures in both Germany and England where previous popes had encountered problems over ecclesiastical appointments. He was succeeded by **Hadrian IV** (1154–1159), who allied himself with the Western emperor Barbarossa

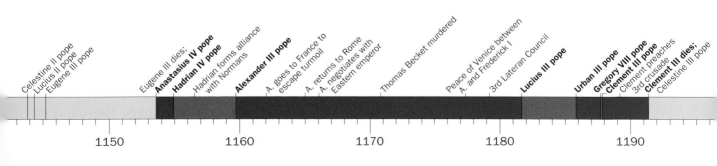

Celestine II pope
Lucius II pope
Eugene III pope
Eugene III dies; **Anastasius IV pope**
Hadrian IV pope
Hadrian forms alliance with Normans
Alexander III pope
A. goes to France to escape turmoil
A. returns to Rome
A. negotiates with Eastern emperor
Thomas Becket murdered
Peace of Venice between A. and Frederick I
3rd Lateran Council
Lucius III pope
Urban III pope
Gregory VIII pope
Clement III pope
Clement preaches 3rd crusade
Clement III dies;
Celestine III pope

1150   1160   1170   1180   1190

(*Above*) Detail from a 13th-century manuscript, the *Bible Moralisée*, showing the Albigensians seducing the faithful. The strict Albigensian heresy taught that Satan had created the material world and was a rival god to the Christian creator.

(*Right*) 16th-century woodcut from Luther's *Depiction of the Papacy* (1545) showing Pope Alexander III dishonouring Emperor Frederick Barbarossa.

PAPAL NAMES	
ALEXANDER III	*Original name*
Nationality	Ubaldo
Italian, from Siena	Allucingoli
Date of birth	*Status*
c. 1100	Monk
Original name	*Early career*
Orlando Bandinelli	Cardinal bishop
Early career	*Elected pope*
Professor of law,	1 September 1181
cardinal priest,	*Age at election*
chancellor	c. 71
Elected pope	*Died*
7 September 1159	25 November 1185
Age at election	*Length of pontificate*
c. 59	4 years, 2 months,
Died	24 days
30 August 1181	
Length of pontificate	**URBAN III**
21 years, 11	*Nationality*
months, 23 days	Italian, from Milan
Antipopes	*Original name*
Victor IV	Umberto Crivelli
(1159–1164),	*Family background*
Paschal III	Aristocratic
(1164–1168),	*Early career*
Callistus III	Archbishop of
(1168–1178),	Milan
Innocent III	*Elected pope*
(1179–1180)	25 November 1185
	Died
LUCIUS III	19/20 October
Nationality	1187, at Ferrara
Italian, from Lucca	*Length of pontificate*
Date of birth	1 year, 10 months,
c. 1110	25 or 26 days

against the Roman republicans and executed their mentor, Arnold of Brescia. But the emperor had designs of political aggrandizement which Hadrian could not brook, and in 1156 Hadrian broke with the emperor and made an alliance with the Normans of Sicily. Barbarossa responded by laying claim to imperial rights in northern Italy, and thus the pontificate ended in acrimony and suspicion.

With **Alexander III** (1159–1181) we have a succession of antipopes – *Victor IV* (not the same as the one in 1138), *Paschal III, Callistus III* and *Innocent III* – and their number alone tells us what kind of a reign Alexander had. The papacy's struggle with the Western emperor worked only to Barbarossa's advantage, as dissension spread to the rest of Christendom which was divided between support for Alexander and support for one of his rivals. Alexander did his best to maintain a relative independence, turning (unsuccessfully) to the Eastern emperor and gradually winning approval in Germany. At last, in 1177, the quarrel died down with a treaty. Meanwhile, major heresies were raising their heads: the Waldensians, who emphasized preaching and poverty; and the Cathars – or Albigensians – who identified the material world as something evil, to be abhorred and rejected – both of them promising subversion of orthodox theology. Alexander, a great canon lawyer, presided over the Third Lateran Council which, among its other decrees, condemned such heretical notions and promoted education as a means to ensure proper reform.

Alexander, then, managed to outrun the worst of the storm while

Alexander III and the Antipope Victor IV

Cardinal Rolando (Alexander) and Cardinal Octavian (antipope Victor) are involved in a brawl during the conclave:

... the whole body of the cardinals ... tried to promote the chancellor, i.e. Rolando, to the papacy by having the archdeacon clothe him ... with the red mantle which is the distinctive dress of the pope ... at last his brethren's entreaties won him over.... Octavian, however, snatched the mantle from their hands ... and it was ripped to pieces as the cardinals tried to pull it away from him. Then Octavian was clothed by his chaplain in another mantle which he had had prepared and brought from his house, after which he climbed up to a more prominent position and summoned a group of priests who were in another part of St Peter's Basilica, waiting for the conclave to finish. Octavian told them, 'I have been elected pope' and said that they should pay him due reverence. These priests ran forward, saw that Octavian was wearing a red mantle, believed he had been elected by the unanimous consent of the cardinals, and shouted their approval. The doors of the basilica were unbarred and Roman citizens, fully armed, came in. Thinking that everything had passed off peacefully, they too acclaimed Octavian's election. But the cardinals who had voted for Alexander ... locked themselves in for nine days until they obtained a safe-conduct from the Roman citizens and were conducted outside the city. There they gained their liberty, raised up their candidate, and named him 'Pope Alexander'.

Gerhoh *De Investigatione Antichristi*, Book 1 (year 1159)

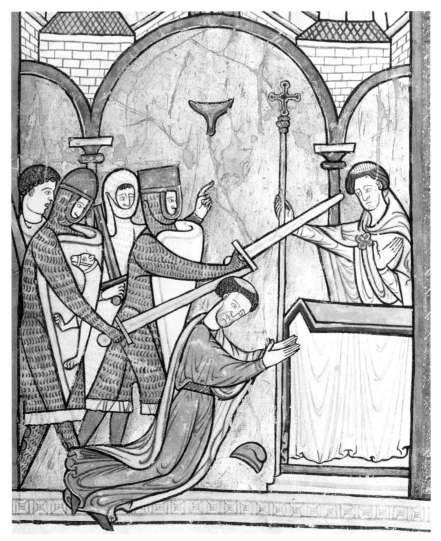

12th-century psalter depicting the murder of Thomas Becket (British Library). Pope Alexander III supported Becket in his struggles with King Henry II of England over the independence of the English crown from the Church.

asserting the authority of his office over secular rulers, as one can see, for example, in his support for Thomas Becket against Henry II of England. His successor, **Lucius III** (1181–1185), however, was too old, weak and vacillating to maintain this momentum and succeeded only in irritating the emperor who withdrew his goodwill. It was left to **Urban III** (1185–1187) to attempt to retrieve the situation, something he signally failed to do by openly quarrelling with Barbarossa. The emperor ordered his son Henry to invade the Papal States; whereupon Urban was forced to surrender and perhaps fortunately for the Church died before he could do any further damage. **Gregory VIII** (1187) enjoyed the distinct advantage of being on amicable terms with Barbarossa and Henry. In consequence, abrasion eased, aided by Gregory's personal sincerity and piety; reform of clerical morals and behaviour proceeded apace. But the pope's greatest preoccupation was a new crusade which he preached with especial fervour after receiving the news that Saladin had captured Jerusalem. Gregory was convinced that it was Christian sin which had

Late 12th-century miniature from the *Welf Chronicle* of Frederick I (Barbarossa) with his sons Henry VI and Frederick of Swabia (Landesbibliothek, Hess). Pope Clement III agreed to crown Henry VI (on the left) emperor but the pope died before he could carry out his promise, leaving his successor Celestine III to crown him. An aggressive emperor, Henry had dreams of establishing a universal empire, in pursuit of which he harrassed the kings and princes of Europe with a mixture of threats and blandishments.

PAPAL NAMES	
GREGORY VIII	1187, in Pisa
Nationality	*Length of pontificate*
Italian, from	1 month, 27 days
Benevento	
Date of birth	CLEMENT III
c. 1110	*Nationality*
Original name	Italian, from Rome
Alberto de Morra	*Original name*
Early career	Paolo Scolari
Professor of law,	*Early career*
chancellor	Cardinal bishop
Elected pope	*Elected pope*
21 October 1187	19 December 1187
Age at election	*Died*
c. 77	Late March 1191
Died	*Length of pontificate*
17 December	3 years, c. 3 months

Numerous heresies sprang up during this period which tested the beliefs of the Catholic Church. (*Right*) 15th-century painting attributed to Jean Fouquet depicting King Philip Augustus of France overseeing the burning of Amalrician heretics (Bibliothèque Nationale, Paris). These were followers of Amalric of Bène whose body was dug up and burned in 1210. Amalricians believed that God was identical with the universe, there was no difference between good and evil, all men and women were potentially divine, and religious ceremonies were entirely superfluous.

brought this disaster upon them, and therefore urged penitence on Christendom and crusaders as a means of regaining God's favour.

Suddenly, however, Gregory died and was succeeded by **Clement III** (1187–1191). Clement was a Roman, with widespread connections in the city. It was his particular advantage, therefore, to be in a position to reconcile the republicans – hostile for several decades – to the papacy. Moreover, the shift in relations with the empire continued. Treaties were signed to the apparent satisfaction of both sides, and when Barbarossa died in 1190, Clement promised to crown Henry, refusal to do so having been one of the discords of Urban III's pontificate. The third crusade proceeded and the preaching of it in Europe helped to focus attention on the papacy as both a unifying and an organizational force. The only cloud darkening this amiable weather was the appearance of a new ruler in Sicily, unacceptable to Henry. Clement, unwilling to offend the Normans to his south and the Germans to his north, was poised on the brink of embarrassment, but with political good fortune (though personal unhappiness), he was able to leave the solution to someone else by dying before Henry arrived in Italy.

Celestine III
1191–1198

Innocent III
1198–1216

13th-century fresco of Innocent III from the 'Holy Cave' at Subiaco, thought to be the hermitage of Benedict of Nursia. Innocent III came from a family, the Conti, which, over a period of some 500 years, gave the Church 13 popes, 3 antipopes, 40 cardinals and a queen.

CELESTINE III	
Nationality Italian, from Rome	*Elected pope* March/April 1191
Date of birth c. 1105	*Age at election* c. 85
Original name Giacinto Bobo	*Died* 8 January 1198
Family background Aristocratic	*Length of pontificate* 6 years, c. 8
Early career Cardinal deacon	months, c. 8 days

CELESTINE III

When we heard of your Holiness's election, we rejoiced more than others because you, of your natural goodness, have mercifully come to the help of our misery. We recognise the hand of God in your election. For He has called to the chief priesthood one who is no accepter of persons, but who regards truth and innocence, and who with all his might has up to this point cherished and loved the Church of God.

Letter of the monks of Canterbury to Pope Celestine

Clement III's successor, **Celestine III** (1191–1198), was clearly chosen to continue the recent fraternal relations between the papacy and the Roman republicans which had been initiated by his predecessor; and certainly his earlier career had been that of a peacemaker, for he had managed to smooth the Western emperor's feathers after Hadrian IV had challenged certain imperial concepts of privilege, and had negotiated Frederick out of the mess he was in with Alexander III. By the time he became pope Celestine had accumulated the patience which would be necessary to deal with the new young Western emperor, Henry VI, now champing outside Rome and waiting to be crowned.

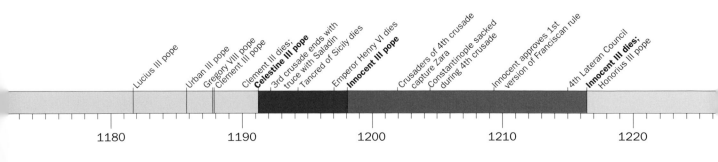

Lucius III pope · Urban III pope · Gregory VIII pope · Clement III pope · Clement III dies; **Celestine III pope** · 3rd crusade ends with truce with Saladin · Tancred of Sicily dies · Emperor Henry VI dies · **Innocent III pope** · Crusaders of 4th crusade capture Zara · Constantinople sacked during 4th crusade · Innocent approves 1st version of Franciscan rule · 4th Lateran Council · **Innocent III dies;** Honorius III pope

1180 · 1190 · 1200 · 1210 · 1220

PETER'S PENCE

This began in England, perhaps during the reign of King Alfred, as a tax upon individual households paid directly to the Holy See. After England had been conquered by the Normans, the new kings agreed to continue to levy the tax and eventually, because of problems of collection, it was changed from a hearth-tax to a specific sum raised from each diocese according to intermittent assessment. In 1213, Innocent III complained that only a part of the total sum was reaching Rome, while the English bishops were keeping the major share for themselves. His protests, however, went unheeded. After the 13th century, the value of the sum diminished, and by the time the Reformation swept it away it was worth very little. 'Peter's Pence' was revived by Pius IX in the 1860s and its modern form consists of a free offering made to the pope by a Catholic diocese.

The principal difficulty was the new ruler in Sicily, Tancred. The illegitimate grandson of Roger II, count of Sicily, Tancred had enjoyed the blessing of Clement III, but was opposed in his claim by his great-aunt Constance and her husband, Emperor Henry. Unfortunately, Tancred suffered from certain disadvantages. He was tiny, many of the Norman barons did not support him, Richard I of England was threatening to

Celestine III crowning Henry VI emperor in Rome. Miniature from a chronicle by Peter of Eboli, end of the 12th century (Burgerbibliothek, Bern). After Henry and his wife Constance had kissed the pope's foot in token of humility, the queen withdrew and the coronation service began. The pope gave Henry the kiss of peace, and the rubric notes that the emperor-elect should have shaved for this occasion.

12th-century manuscript by Peter of Eboli of the wheel of fortune (Burgerbibliothek, Bern). Tancred is crushed by the wheel of fortune as Henry VI sits enthroned on the left. It is a far cry from 1191 when Queen Constance was seized by the people of Salerno and sent as a hostage to Tancred in Sicily.

attack and Henry had captured several key cities in northern Italy. Tancred was thus isolated. Pope Celestine, faced with such intractable facts, gave way to Henry and crowned him in April 1191. Tancred, however, who was no mean soldier, established his dominance in southern Italy and had the satisfaction of getting his title recognized by the pope. But neither satisfaction nor title lasted long, for Tancred died early in 1194 and so did his son and heir a few days later. Henry swept through the south, had himself crowned, and the episode was over.

This left relations between the emperor and the pope a little strained; yet each man needed the other. In Rome, for example, the ruling senators broke out into a turmoil of inter-rivalry and were inclined to ignore the pope in their struggles for power; while in the empire, Albert of Brabant, newly elected bishop of Liège, was disregarded by Henry who had eyes on another Albert. The Brabantine bishop-elect came to Rome to appeal to the pope and successfully pleaded his case. But when he returned to Liège for his consecration, Henry had him murdered by three German knights in an outrage curiously parallel to the earlier murder of Thomas Becket by the English Henry. Europe was aghast but Henry seemed impervious, for when Richard I of England fell into his hands in March 1193, he kept him prisoner despite a papal decree that crusaders were inviolate. Celestine retorted by placing Richard's enemies under excommunication and interdict, which had the effect of bringing about a negotiated settlement and Richard's release in February 1194.

With accumulated hostility from almost every part of Christendom raging about his head, the emperor decided it was time for accommodation. Henry wanted his infant son declared emperor by the pope and decided to urge another crusade as a means of obtaining Celestine's goodwill. Celestine, however, could neither be bullied nor bribed to agree, and in a fury Henry set out for Italy where he made sure Celestine was cooped up in Rome before crossing to Sicily to deal with a plot against him. There he died in 1197, to be followed the next year by Celestine himself. Aged 97, the pope was worn out; but he had successfully out-faced a despot 60 years his junior, and the papacy had emerged the stronger for his endurance.

INNOCENT III

While his election was being celebrated, the following sign appeared. Apparently three doves were flying around in the room in which the cardinals had taken their seats, and when Innocent was elected and

INNOCENT III	
Nationality Italian, from Anagni	*Early career* Cardinal deacon
Date of birth 1160/1161	*Elected pope* 8 January 1198
Original name Lotario	*Age at election* c. 37
Family background Aristocratic	*Ordained priest* 21 February 1198
Status Innocent was not yet a priest when he was elected pope	*Died* 16 July 1216, in Perugia of fever
	Length of pontificate 18 years, 6 months, 8 days

Among the innumerable cares and worldly concerns I have, I consider my responsibility for and tenure of the kingdom of Sicily to be of especial importance; for, in addition to the duty I owe it as pastor, I have a particular concern for it as its lawful sovereign and guardian.

Innocent III *Regesta* 2.243

Painting attributed to Giotto showing Innocent III approving the Franciscan Order (Louvre). Scores of *Lives* of St Francis appeared within a few years of his death. The most popular stories, the *Fioretti*, have been extracted from a longer work, written in *c.* 1320, which is poetic, romantic and more or less untrustworthy.

had been taken apart from the rest, the whitest of the doves flew to him and settled next to his right hand.

Anon *Gesta Innocenti III Papae*, 6

Innocent III (1198–1216) was a Roman aristocrat, a nephew of Clement III. Innocent was erudite, energetic, stern in morals and diplomatic but firm in his management of others. As soon as he became pope, for example, he settled the factionalism in Rome by subordinating its political ministers to himself. He reasserted his authority over the Papal States and actually added to their number. Sicily was brought to quietude when Innocent agreed to act as regent on behalf of Henry VI's heir, Frederick II; and when the death of Henry VI in 1197 raised a whirlwind of rivalry for the imperial crown, Innocent supported and crowned Otto of Brunswick (although when Otto was rash enough to invade Sicily, Innocent at once excommunicated and deposed him). Innocent also famously excommunicated King John of England and put his kingdom under an interdict until John bowed to papal authority. To Innocent, too, fell the task of

Marginal drawing from Matthew Paris's *Cronica Maiora* (1215) of the Fourth Lateran Council (Corpus Christi College, Cambridge). Pope Innocent summoned the Fourth Lateran Council to discuss the needs of the Holy Land, the reformation of the Church, the problems raised by outbreaks of heresy and the best means of promoting international peace.

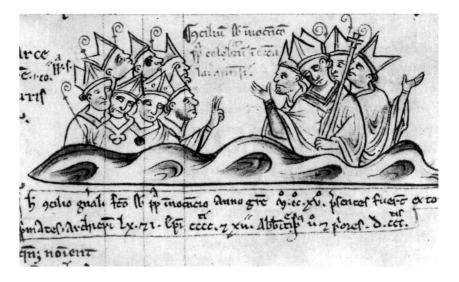

(*Below*) 14th-century Spanish wallpainting from the transept of Tarragona Cathedral showing a Jew wearing a badge. One of the principal reasons advanced for requiring Jews and Muslims to wear at least a badge denoting their religion was to prevent Christians from being deceived into marrying them.

promulgating the fourth crusade, and when that ended in squalor, he started to preach a fifth.

The list of Innocent's political accomplishments appears endless; but perhaps his most lasting achievements are to be found in other fields. While still a cardinal, he had published three treatises of which two, 'On Contempt for the World', and 'The Sacred Mystery of the Altar', give clear indications of his abiding preoccupations. For Innocent was a reformer, as one can see by his encouragement of the Order of Friars Minor newly founded by Francis of Assisi, and by the help he gave to the Spaniard Dominic Guzmán in drawing up parts of the *Constitutions* of his Order of Friars Preachers. This last, however, brings us to a dark spot in his pontificate, for one of the principal objectives of the Dominicans was to combat heresy, and in 1208 Innocent called for a special crusade against the heretic Cathars (or Albigensians) and their sympathizers in southern France. He was not the first pope to have done so, nor would he be the last; but this 'Albigensian Crusade' was conducted with ferocious slaughter and permanently changed both the religious and the political complexion of the area.

More significant, though, was his presiding over the Fourth Lateran Council in 1215. Among the many decrees which issued from this assembly were a careful definition of the Real Presence during the mass; a general condemnation of heresy and a call to the secular powers to assist the Church in eradicating it; and an insistence that Muslims and Jews in Christian societies should wear distinctive clothing to mark them out from the rest. Each of these points would have incalculable results in the future.

THE CRUSADES

The first crusade (1096–1099)

In November 1095, Urban called a Church council at Clermont and preached a sermon in which he summoned Frankish knights to march to the Holy Land to liberate the Christians from Islamic rule and also to set free the tomb of Christ. Events soon slipped out of his control. Pogroms against the Jews in France and Germany were one indication that populist passions had been aroused and were going to follow their own destructive urges. The Crusaders captured Nicaea and Antioch in 1097 and 1098 respectively, and stormed Jerusalem in 1099. Some territories became part of a new Western outpost in the Middle East, the so-called 'Crusader States', and thus Urban's call appeared to have been successful.

The second crusade (1147–1149)

Organized by Eugene III and preached by St Bernard, the second crusade was led by Louis VII of France and Barbarossa's predecessor, Conrad III. But in spite of the pious enthusiasm with which these two rulers took the cross, their military endeavours were not successful and the crusade fell to pieces in the fiasco of a failed assault on Damascus in 1178.

The crusaders' capture of Jerusalem in 1099 brought together artists and patrons from different cultures and thus stimulated a burst of distinctive building and painting. 14th-century manuscript of the capture of Jerusalem by William of Tyre (Bibliothèque Nationale, Paris).

(Below) Map showing the routes of the first four crusades. The inset shows the Crusader States set up after the first crusade.

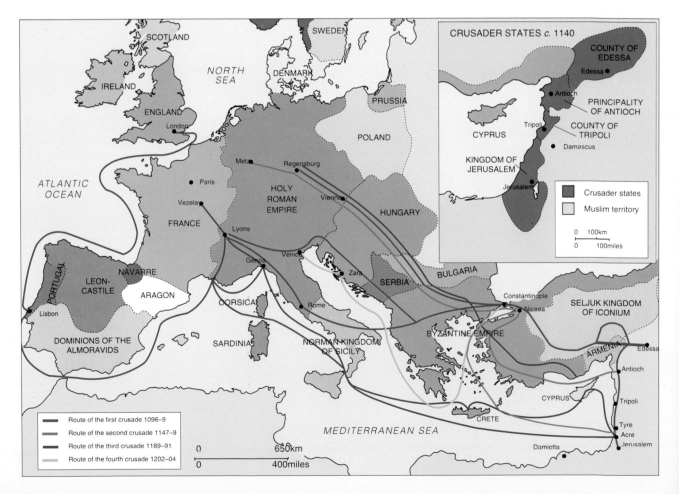

Krak des Chevaliers, perhaps the best-known crusader castle in the Levant.

The early crusading knights' distinctive weapon was a heavy lance which in battle was couched under the arm and extended well in front of the horse's head (British Library).

The third crusade (1189–1192)

Philip Augustus of France, Richard I of England, and Frederick Barbarossa were the principal leaders of the third crusade. At first all went fairly well for the German army; but on 10 June 1190, Barbarossa drowned while trying to swim across a river. His death was a serious blow and his army disintegrated. Philip Augustus and Richard, however, had greater success. First Cyprus, then Acre were captured. But at the beginning of August 1191, the French king returned home and then Richard, after slaughtering his Muslim hostages at Acre, spent the autumn and following spring in skirmishes before being obliged by domestic English politics to make peace with Saladin and leave the Holy Land.

The fourth crusade (1202–1204)

Enthusiasm for the fourth crusade took a long time to ignite. After four years of encouragement and preparation, the crusaders were ready to start. Unfortunately, however, they hired ships from Venice and when Venice discovered that payment would not be forthcoming, she took advantage of the situation: the crusading knights were used to capture the city of Zara from Hungary in 1202.

The crusaders made their way to Constantinople and in June 1203 were encamped before the city with no resources to see them through the immediate days and weeks, never mind the rest of their mission to rescue the Holy Land. So, when their nominal patron the Eastern emperor Alexius IV, was strangled and replaced by another Alexius, the crusaders panicked and, egged on by Venice who saw for herself a glittering commercial prize in the East if Constantinople fell, set about assaulting the city and looting it by way of payment and reparation. Blood-lust took over and for three days, from 12 to 15 April 1204, Constantinople was ravaged and its inhabitants raped and slaughtered. Christian savaged Christian in the name of holy war, the atrocity of which could not be concealed, although many did their best to excuse it.

French and Genoese crusaders departing by ship. Earlier crusaders went by land with many losses en route. Few actually reached the Holy Land; so by the fourth crusade, the use of ships was common.

Honorius III
1216–1227

Gregory IX
1227–1241

Celestine IV
1241

Innocent IV
1243–1254

Alexander IV
1254–1261

Urban IV
1261–1264

Clement IV
1265–1268

Gregory X
1271–1276

PAPAL NAMES	
HONORIUS III	*Date of birth*
Nationality	c. 1155
Italian, from Rome	*Original name*
Original name	Ugo
Cencio Savelli	*Family background*
Family background	Aristocratic;
Aristocratic	Gregory was a
Early career	nephew of Pope
Cardinal priest	Innocent III
Elected pope	*Early career*
18 July 1216	Cardinal bishop,
Age at election	papal legate
Elderly	*Elected pope*
Died	19 March 1227
18 March 1227	*Age at election*
Length of pontificate	c. 72
10 years, 8	*Died*
months, 1 day	22 August 1241
	Length of pontificate
GREGORY IX	14 years, 6
Nationality	months, 4 days
Italian, from Anagni	

At this time the emperor Frederick, with hysterical madness and heretical duplicity, was engaged in arrogant abuse of the Church of God, and was polluting almost the whole world by his snake-like fall from grace. Pope Innocent IV ... brandished the sword of Peter with all his might, and pronounced sentence of excommunication against the emperor; and ... the universal Church deprived Frederick of his imperial sceptre.

Continuation of *Gesta Episcoporum Virdunensium*, 12

A quick election followed the death of Innocent III. It took the conclave only two days to elect an old, frail man, **Honorius III** (1216–1227) whose waking thoughts practically began and ended with raising the fifth crusade. To this end he juggled with European politics, giving a helping hand here, exerting a little pressure there, until his dream was realized and the crusade was on its way to the Middle East. But Frederick II of Germany who should have been one of its leaders failed to join it, despite his being crowned Holy Roman emperor by the pope in 1220 by way of inducement. The new emperor turned his attention to Sicily instead, where affairs were in chaos as a result of Innocent III's absentee guardianship on Frederick's behalf while he was a child. Postponement

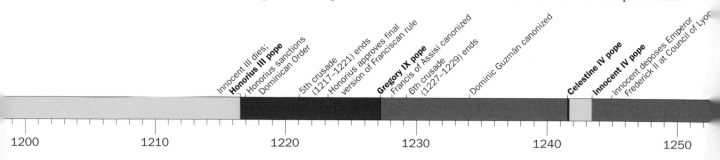

Innocent III dies; **Honorius III pope** · Honorius sanctions Dominican Order · 5th crusade (1217–1221) ends · Honorius approves final version of Franciscan rule · **Gregory IX pope** · Francis of Assisi canonized · 6th crusade (1227–1229) ends · Dominic Guzmán canonized · **Celestine IV pope** · **Innocent IV pope** · Innocent deposes Emperor Frederick II at Council of Lyon

1200 · 1210 · 1220 · 1230 · 1240 · 1250

Terracotta pulpit panel by Benedetto da Maiano of Honorius III confirming the final version of the rule of the Franciscan Order in 1223 (Victoria and Albert Museum, London). Raising money to pay for the crusades presented a problem for Honorius III and other crusading popes. They therefore devised systems of collection and transmission which resulted in the development of a highly centralized and largely efficient papal financial bureaucracy.

PAPAL NAMES

CELESTINE IV
Nationality
  Italian, from Milan
Original name
  Goffredo da
  Castiglione
Family background
  Aristocratic
Early career
  Cardinal bishop
Elected pope
  25 October 1241
Died
  10 November 1241
Length of pontificate
  16 days

INNOCENT IV
Nationality
  Italian, from Genoa
Original name
  Sinibaldo Fieschi
Family background
  Aristocratic
Early career
  Cardinal priest,
  vice-chancellor,
  governor of
  the March of
  Ancona
  (1235–1240)
Elected pope
  25 June 1243
Died
  7 December 1254
Length of pontificate
  11 years, 5
  months, 13 days

ALEXANDER IV
Nationality
  Italian

Original name
  Rinaldo
Family background
  Aristocratic;
  nephew of Gregory
  IX
Early career
  Cardinal bishop
Elected pope
  12 December 1254
Age at election
  50s/60s
Died
  25 May 1261
Length of pontificate
  6 years, 5 months,
  14 days

URBAN IV
Nationality
  French, from Troyes
Date of birth
  c. 1200
Original name
  Jacques Pantaléon
Family background
  Son of a
  shoemaker
Early career
  Patriarch of
  Jerusalem, papal
  legate
Elected pope
  29 August 1261
Age at election
  c. 61
Died
  2 October 1264, in
  Perugia
Length of pontificate
  3 years, 1 month, 5
  days

after postponement followed until in 1225 Honorius lost patience and threatened to excommunicate Frederick unless he joined the crusade by mid-1227. Honorius was well aware, however, that Frederick's fixed intention was to reinstate imperial power over Italy, and he was determined to resist it.

But Honorius did not merely pursue a crusade in the Middle East. There were other non-believers to be hunted. In 1217, he gave his approval to the Dominican Order and its mission to preach against heresy; in 1218 he directed a crusade against the Muslims in Spain; he vigorously pursued the Albigensian crusade begun by Innocent III and in 1226 invited Louis VIII of France to assume responsibility for it; and it

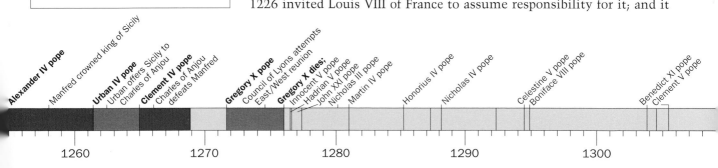

Alexander IV pope
Manfred crowned king of Sicily
Urban IV pope
Urban offers Sicily to Charles of Anjou
Clement IV pope
Charles of Anjou defeats Manfred
Gregory X pope
Council of Lyons attempts East/West reunion
Gregory X dies;
Innocent V pope
Hadrian V pope
John XXI pope
Nicholas III pope
Martin IV pope
Honorius IV pope
Nicholas IV pope
Celestine V pope
Boniface VIII pope
Benedict XI pope
Clement V pope

1260   1270   1280   1290   1300

FRANCISCANS

The Order of Friars Minor was founded by Francis of Assisi (1181/2–1226), and the first version of its rule was approved by Innocent III in April 1209. The early friars were travelling preachers and lived by whatever trade they knew. They preached simple sermons, and looked after the poor and the sick, especially those called 'lepers' at the time. The order grew rapidly and in consequence a more elaborate organization and structure were required to prevent the friars from falling into undisciplined ways. Such a necessity, however, with its inevitable concomitant – a revised rule – began to worry some brothers who were concerned that the original spirit of the order might be lost. In 1221, Francis issued a new rule which attempted to accommodate both needs and concerns; but the order split between those who were willing to accept accommodation and those who were not. The latter (called first *Zelanti* and later Spirituals) then became involved in a protracted battle with the former, and successive popes legislated against them and condemned some of their notions as heresy.

Franciscan sisters were originally called Poor Ladies and were founded as an order of contemplative nuns by Clare of Assisi in 1212. The Third Order of the Franciscans was begun by Francis in 1221 for people who continued to live in the world but wished to follow the ideals and take the same vows as the friars and nuns. The Tertiaries received papal approval from Nicholas V in 1447.

(Above) St Francis cutting out his habit, 14th-century English manuscript illumination (British Library). One day, while Francis was praying, a seraph with six flaming wings appeared to him, with Christ on the cross between the wings. Darts of flame then printed Christ's wounds on Francis's body. These are the stigmata.

(Right) 15th-century detail of a miniature from the psalter of Henry VI – the Poor Clares in choir (British Library). The foundress of the Poor Clares, the second order of the Franciscans, was born in Assisi in 1194. Under the influence of Francis she was converted to the religious life and soon gathered around her other like-minded women. Francis established them in the convent of San Damiano not far from Assisi, and here Clare remained for the rest of her life. Her order, later called the Poor Clares after her, was approved by Innocent IV in 1253, two days before she died.

(Above) After St Francis had restored a ruined chapel of Our Lady not far from Assisi, he asked Honorius to grant a plenary indulgence to those who went there each year on the anniversary of its consecration. 13th/14th-century fresco, in the Church of San Francesco in Assisi, by Giotto, of St Francis preaching before Honorius III.

DOMINICANS

The Order of Friars Preachers, to give the Dominicans their official title, was founded by the Spaniard Dominic Guzmán (1170–1221) in 1215. It sprang from the preaching mission directed against the Albigensian heretics in the south of France, and was approved by Honorius III in 1217. The order is partly contemplative, partly missionary, and has made its mark especially in teaching and preaching. From the start, the

friars carried their missions far afield, and produced outstanding scholars: Albertus Magnus and Thomas Aquinas are perhaps the most famous examples. Because

of this special interest in preaching and scholarship, Dominicans were quickly associated with the various Inquisitions established to secure orthodox faith and root out heresy, most famously in the person of Tomás de Torquemada, appointed Inquisitor General of the Spanish Inquisition by Sixtus IV in 1483. Like the Franciscans, the Dominicans have an order of nuns and a Third Order for lay people; unlike the Franciscans, however, it did not have to endure a split between adherents to the old rule and accepters of subsequent change.

(Above) El Greco's painting St Dominic in prayer *(1606); the saint looks spiritually tortured and drawn (Museo de Santa Cruz, Toledo).*

(Above) St Dominic burning the Albigensian scriptures, *painting by Pedro Berruguete (c. 1480/90) (Prado, Madrid).*

(Right) St Thomas, a famous Dominican, had been a controversial figure during his life, and not long after his death Pope John XXI condemned 19 of his propositions. But John XXII canonized him in 1323 and Pius V declared him a Doctor of the Church in 1567.

ALBERTUS MAGNUS

Albert the Great (*c.* 1200–*c.* 1280) was one of the most remarkable Western scholars of the Middle Ages. He was born in Lauingen on the Danube and, in spite of vigorous opposition from his wealthy family, became a Dominican in 1223. While he was lecturing at the University of Paris in the 1240s he began a series of works intended to present the whole of human knowledge to Western students. Part of his corpus consists of paraphrases and explanations of all the known works of Aristotle, including those bearing Aristotle's name but actually written by other anonymous hands. To these he added an immense body of his own work, ranging from theology to natural science, and so famous did he become that a good many books were attributed to him by later authors who wanted their works to bask in the glory of his name.

In 1253, Albert was elected provincial (i.e. head) of the German Dominicans and travelled throughout the German states, principally on foot, still studying and writing almost without pause. In 1256, he defended the mendicant orders before the pope at Anagni, when they came under attack, and in 1260 very reluctantly accepted appointment by Alexander IV as bishop of Regensburg. From 1262 to 1264 he was preaching Urban IV's crusade throughout Germany, but from 1269 until his death he settled in Cologne, leaving it only briefly in 1274 and 1277. His reputation was so immense that even during his lifetime he was called *Magnus* (i.e. the Great'), and in 1323 he was canonized by John XXII and is honoured by the title *Doctor Universalis*.

13th-century fresco of Gregory IX and St Francis in the Church of Santo Speco, Subiaco. So high was Gregory's regard for St Francis that he sometimes wore the Franciscan habit while he visited the poor or washed their feet.

was these three – Honorius, Frederick and Louis – who promulgated ordinances of particular severity against heretics in general. Honorius also took a particular interest in the new Franciscan Order, approving the final version of its rule in 1223; and in *c.* 1226 he authorized the issue of a collection of his decrees with the instruction that they be used as a standard text in the law courts and universities of the West.

Honorius was followed by **Gregory IX** (1227–1241). He had had a distinguished career as a canon lawyer and papal legate, and brought to his pontificate a remarkable energy and a lofty sense of his office. Like Innocent and Honorius before him, he had a high regard for Francis and Dominic, whom he canonized in 1228 and 1234 respectively. But his principal concern as pope was the ambition of Emperor Frederick II, who had outmanoeuvred Honorius and now, in 1227, abandoned yet another promise to join a crusade. This time he had a legitimate excuse: he was ill. But the pope remembered only his earlier procrastinations and

14th-century French manuscript by Jean Joinville, the *Histoire de Saint Louis,* showing the Egyptian port of Damietta being assaulted by Louis IX of France (later St Louis) in 1249 (Bibliothèque Nationale, Paris). Damietta was subject to frequent attacks by crusaders. Its longest siege lasted from May 1218 to November 1219.

PAPAL NAMES

CLEMENT IV
Nationality
  French, from Saint-Gilles-sur-Rhône
Date of birth
  c. 1195
Original name
  Guy Foulques
Status
  Widower with two daughters. He took holy orders after his wife's death
Early career
  Cardinal bishop
Elected pope
  5 February 1265
Age at election
  c. 70
Died
  29 November 1268, at Viterbo
Length of pontificate
  3 years, 9 months, 22 days

GREGORY X
Nationality
  Italian, from Piacenza
Date of birth
  c. 1210
Original name
  Tedaldo Visconti
Family background
  Aristocratic
Status
  Gregory was not yet a priest when he was elected pope
Early career
  Archdeacon of Liège
Elected pope
  1 September 1271, while he was in Acre in the Holy Land during a crusade
Age at election
  c. 62
Consecrated
  27 March 1272
Died
  10 January 1276, at Arezzo of fever
Length of pontificate
  4 years, 4 months, 10 days

assumed that this time was no different. So he excommunicated him. Frederick, however, recovered and in 1228 set out on what was by now the sixth crusade, the fifth having concentrated on capturing the port of Damietta in Egypt, which it quickly lost again to Muslim arms.

Gregory was furious; an excommunicate had no business leading a crusade. Therefore the pope proclaimed that Frederick was no longer king in Germany and that Sicily owed no further allegiance to him. Troops were also raised to attack the imperial armies in Italy and Sicily. Frederick tried to ignore the excommunication but then sent letters to everyone, declaring that he was astonished by the pope's actions, and urging all crusaders and Christian princes not to slacken in their zeal for the holy enterprise. In addition, he roused the Roman nobility against Gregory to the extent that the pope was forced to retire from Rome to Perugia. Having thus issued a counterblast to Gregory's fulminations, Frederick set sail for Jerusalem where, on 18 March 1229, he crowned himself king. When he returned to Italy in June 1230 he easily defeated the papal troops, but then he and the pope made a truce; it did Frederick no good to be excommunicate, and Gregory could not afford to have a bellicose emperor treating Italy as an imperial fief.

The truce lasted for nine years and the peace enabled Gregory to turn his attention to religious affairs. He extended the scope of legislation against heretics, directing that after condemnation by the Church they be handed over to secular tribunals for punishment; entrusted to the Dominicans the duties of inquisitors and laid down procedures for them to follow; re-opened the University of Paris which had been closed for two years because of strife between the ecclesiastical authorities and the students; founded a new university at Toulouse; and in 1234 made an unsuccessful attempt to effect an understanding between Rome and the Orthodox churches of the East.

In 1234, however, he and the emperor were once more at loggerheads. They quarrelled over Sicily and Lombardy, with Frederick openly trying to make himself master of the whole of Italy and Gregory offering valiant resistance. Once again Frederick was excommunicated. Once again an emperor called for a general council of the Church to condemn and depose a pope. Gregory, however, took the wind out of Frederick's sails by summoning a council himself and Frederick sought to ensure its failure by capturing most of the would-be participants who were travelling there by sea. His army surrounded Rome. Everyone waited to see what would happen next. Then Gregory died.

ST THOMAS AQUINAS

Thomas Aquinas (c. 1225–1274) was the most important theologian and philosopher of the Medieval Church, whose influence is still potent today. He was born into a wealthy family and was given, according to the common custom of the period, to the Benedictine abbey of Monte Cassino at the age of five or six, in the hope that he would grow up to become a monk and in due time, perhaps an abbot or bishop. In 1239, he was sent to the University of Naples, and in 1244 joined the Dominican Order there, after which he was ordered to go to Rome. At this point he was kidnapped by one of his brothers and returned to the family home where his mother made clear her opposition to his becoming a mere friar. After several months of virtual house arrest, however, Thomas was allowed to leave. At Cologne in 1248 he met Albertus Magnus and became his pupil, during which time he wrote two short books on logic. Then, in 1252, he went to Paris and studied for his doctorate. Tension between the various religious orders at the university created storms most of the time he was there. But he survived them to become professor for three years before returning to Italy. He held a second professorship in Paris between 1269 and 1272, and then came back to Naples where he died.

The range of his writings is immense. He is most famous, however, for his exposition of Church doctrine, the *Summa Theologiae*, in which he sets out theology as though it were one of the sciences. Its influence was immediate. It became the authoritative account of the Church's teaching, and popes right up to Pius XII have endorsed the work and given it their approval. Little wonder, therefore, that Thomas was canonized. This was requested as early as six months after his death, but partisan opposition from the Universities of Paris and Oxford delayed the canonization until 1323.

At once there was a crisis. Only 10 cardinals were available to form a conclave, and they were deeply divided over who should succeed as pontiff. They were locked up during the frightful heat of August in a building originally built by the Roman emperor Septimius Severus. Week followed week as the cardinals failed to produce the necessary two-thirds majority. August became September; the English cardinal died, and an Italian was brought to death's door. Finally, on 25 October, an old and infirm Milanese was elected and took the name **Celestine IV** (1241). But he, too, must have been weakened by the long and arduous conclave, for after only 17 days he died and the process had to start all over again.

There should have been 12, not 10, cardinals during the summer conclave of 1241. Two, however, were being held prisoner by Frederick and negotiations for their release helped to cause the 18-month hiatus between the death of Celestine IV and the election of **Innocent IV** (1243–1254). An excellent canon lawyer, Pope Innocent was rather more worldly than his predecessor Gregory and thus more of a match for Frederick. Frederick initially thought he had a friend in the new pope and hoped his excommunication might be lifted in return for an easing of the imperial grip upon Italy. The two men got as far as drafting an agreement, but then papal suspicion surfaced, partly because Frederick refused to relinquish imperial rights over Lombardy, and so matters came to a head. Innocent fled to Lyons and there in 1245 convened a general council of the Church.

The council's agenda was wide-ranging but its principal aim was to find Frederick guilty of several grave offences – heresy, perjury and sacrilege being but three. The verdict of the council was a foregone conclusion and the pope pronounced Frederick culpable and deposed him. Frederick challenged Innocent's power to do so. Innocent referred to the absolute authority over temporal as well as spiritual matters, transmitted by St Peter to his successors, and then sought to raise a crusade against the ex-emperor. Louis IX of France (later St Louis) dithered between the two of them, attempting to mediate; but the impasse was broken by Frederick's death in December 1250, after which Innocent returned to Italy and prepared to do battle with the new German king, Conrad, Frederick's son.

Sicily once more became a bone of contention. Innocent, determined that Conrad should not have it, offered it to several princes before conferring it on Manfred, Frederick's bastard son, who agreed to acknowledge the pope as his feudal lord. Innocent then went to live in Naples in order to keep an eye on his new estate. He did well to do so, for Manfred changed his mind and decided to revolt. With treasure handed to him by Muslim adventurers in Apulia, who did not relish the thought of strong papal rule in that area, Manfred defeated a papal army at Foggia on 2 December 1254. Innocent was already ill and it is possible that news of this calamity exacerbated his condition. He died on 7 December and was buried in the Cathedral of Santa Restituta in Naples.

His successor, **Alexander IV** (1254–1261), lacked Innocent's drive and

Innocent IV deposes Frederick II at the Council of Lyons; miniature from the 13th-century *Chronicle* by Matthew Paris (Corpus Christi College, Cambridge). Innocent IV's reputation has suffered at the hands of the chronicler Matthew Paris who did not know the pope personally and was clearly prejudiced against him.

In the year of Our Lord 1264 a remarkable comet appeared, the like of which no living person had seen before. It rose in the East with great brilliance, rose high in the sky, and then turned towards the West, trailing a very bright tail. It may have signified many things in different parts of the world, but this is certain: it was visible for three months; at its first appearance, Pope Urban [IV] was taken ill; and the very night the pope died, the comet disappeared.

Continuatio Sanblasiana Chronici Ottonis Frisingensi (year 1264)

decisiveness. In consequence he made several mistakes. At first he tried to negotiate with Manfred, but then excommunicated him, thus ensuring his enmity. Conrad of Germany, who had died in 1254, had made his young son, Conradin, a ward of the papacy; but Alexander chose to undermine the child's imperial claims to the dukedom of Swabia and the kingdom of Sicily by offering the first to Alfonso X of Castile and the second to an English prince, Edmund. The latter failed to take up the offer only because his father, Henry III, could not afford the military cost. But the offer was enough to spark Manfred into hostility and conquest, and by 1258 he controlled the whole of Sicily and proclaimed himself king. He then cut a swathe through southern Italy, made friends in the north, and even got himself elected a senator in Rome. Germany, meanwhile, was without effective government owing to Conrad's death and Conradin's minority. There were several candidates for the throne. Alexander supported a Dutchman and then, when he died, wavered between the brother of Henry III of England and Alfonso of Castile, the dispute still languishing unresolved in 1261 when Alexander died.

Only eight cardinals remained to form the conclave which elected **Urban IV** (1261–1264). As was becoming customary, the election came at the end of a long, bitter dispute. But the cardinals' choice seemed wise, for Urban was determined to solve the immediate problem of Manfred by conferring Sicily upon someone who would be a genuine dependant of the papacy, and to free Italy once and for all from any German king's control. First, then, he increased the College of Cardinals by 14, six of them Frenchmen. This, he hoped, would put an end to the kind of protracted venom which had characterized recent conclaves. Secondly, he built up a pro-papal party in Tuscany. Thirdly, he replenished the papal coffers. Fourthly, he promoted the interests of families in northern Italy hostile to Manfred.

Thus prepared, he turned his attention to Sicily. Louis IX of France did not want it, so Urban offered the crown to Louis's younger brother, Charles of Anjou. Charles was happy to accept both the kingdom and the pope's terms, which consisted of a demand for an immediate sum of money, annual tribute thereafter, freedom of action for the Church in Sicily and non-compliance with Western imperial ambitions in Italy. But things went badly wrong. Manfred began hostilities in Tuscany and the Papal States, and the pope was forced to make concessions and flee to Perugia where he died. His reign had been too short to accomplish his good intentions, although it has to be admitted that he had rescued the papacy from the weak position in which Alexander IV had left it.

Clement IV (1265–1268), like Urban a Frenchman and elected after a lengthy conclave, inherited the problem of Manfred's ambitions. Clement's election had been odd. He himself was not present with the rest of the cardinals, being papal legate to England at the time, and because of the unrest in northern Italy he was obliged to come to Perugia, disguised as a monk, to take up the papacy. One of his first acts was to urge Charles of Anjou to hurry to Italy with a French army so that

(*Right*) 13th-century French wallpainting depicting Pope Clement IV investing the kingdom of Naples and Sicily to Charles of Anjou (Pernes, Tour Ferande). A contemporary wrote of Clement IV that he was an all-round churchman, i.e. a first-rate advocate, and outstanding preacher, a really beautiful singer and an orator without equal.

One of the eight cartoons commissioned by Martin Luther in 1545 with Clement IV about to behead Conradin. The Latin title reads: 'The pope thanks the emperor for his immense benefits'.

he might capture his new kingdom and thus deal Manfred a final blow. Charles needed no urging and success attended French arms, for in February 1266 Manfred died in defeat. All was still not well, however, because Conradin of Germany had come of age and now descended upon Rome to claim what he saw as his heritage. Charles, however, retaliated at once and not only defeated Conradin in battle, but beheaded him, thus putting an end – at least for the time being – to imperial pretensions in the Italian peninsula. Clement quickly realized, however, that the papacy had merely exchanged the frying pan for the fire, since French domination of Italy was now as great as imperial German sway had ever been, and Charles might prove an unstable friend and ally.

Clement also inherited from Urban a papal attempt to reunite the Western and Eastern Churches. In 1262, the Eastern emperor Michael Palaeologus had suggested it was time to end the schism and Urban had

Cardinals leaving a conclave; miniature from the *Richental Chronicle* (Rosgartenmuseum, Constance). The well-known saying has it that he who goes into a conclave as pope comes out as cardinal – a comment on the frequent unpredictability of papal elections.

GUELPHS AND GHIBELLINES

The partisan rivalries of Italian politics during the 12th century in particular saw the creation of two loose groupings fiercely opposed to one another. Supporters of the pope were known as Guelphs; supporters of the German emperor were called Ghibellines. Both names were originally German and referred to rival Saxon and Swabian families.

Stone relief of the device of the pro-papal Guelph party (Florence, Via degli Alfani).

taken up the proposal, especially in view of the emperor's declared willingness to accept papal supremacy. Urban died, however, before their discussions came to any firm resolution, and in 1267–8 Michael renewed his offer with Clement. But Clement asked for too much – grovelling submission by Constantinople and the East – and this proved unacceptable to the emperor. The real reason for the failure, however, perhaps lies elsewhere; for Charles wanted to conquer Constantinople by force of arms and make it a Latin as opposed to a Greek city, and Clement approved the project. Whatever the truth, a *rapprochement* was no longer possible while Clement lived.

Clement died in Viterbo, and the cardinals took nearly three years to find a successor. Their delays were outrageous and at last they were locked in the papal palace, the roof of which was removed, and they were threatened with cessation of food supplies unless they produced a pope. In March 1271, the new king of France, Philip III, and Charles of Anjou came to Viterbo, hoping that their presence would force the cardinals to stop bickering and make a choice. It was not until September that they deputed six of their number to choose a compromise candidate. That decision lit upon the archdeacon of Liège, then in the Holy Land on crusade with Prince Edward of England.

The new pope, **Gregory X** (1271–1276), immediately called upon Emperor Michael Palaeologus to send delegates to a general council of the Church, which he intended to convene at Lyons. Michael consented and when the council opened in 1274, his Greek representatives agreed to accept the form of the creed used in the West and to acknowledge the supremacy of the pope over the universal Church. Thus, in July that year, the rift of over two centuries was healed. Gregory also published several decrees aimed at reforming abuses in the Church and above all, an edict which was intended to prevent any further protracted, disgraceful conclaves. Cardinals in future must meet within 10 days of the pope's death at the place where he died, and be sequestered from all other society in conditions becoming progressively more spartan, until they elected a suitable candidate. It was indeed a directive long overdue.

Gregory set about reconciling the Guelphs (pro-papal party) and the Ghibellines (pro-imperial party) whose murderous rivalry had long disrupted Italy. Moreover, a new German king – Rudolf, count of Habsburg – was elected in October 1273, and when he formally renounced all claim to papal territories and to Sicily, two major problems were solved at a stroke. First, the pope could breathe easily without fear of imperial pretensions in Italy; and secondly, the existence of an effective German king would counterbalance French influence there. Gregory now felt able to initiate a crusade. In 1275, he met Rudolf whom he intended to crown Holy Roman emperor in February the following year, but in January 1276 Gregory succumbed to a fever and died. It was an ill-timed death, for it left Rudolf, Church unity and crusade all hanging fire while Charles of Anjou could regroup his forces and prepare to exert a greater authority.

Innocent V
1276

Hadrian V
1276

John XXI
1276–1277

Nicholas III
1277–1280

Martin IV
1281–1285

Honorius IV
1285–1287

Nicholas IV
1288–1292

Celestine V
1294

Boniface VIII
1294–1303

Benedict XI
1303–1304

Clement V
1305–1314

PAPAL NAMES

INNOCENT V
Nationality
  French, from
  Tarentaise
  (Savoy)
Date of birth
  c. 1224
Original name
  Pierre
Status
  Dominican friar
Early career
  Cardinal bishop
Elected pope
  21 January 1276
Age at election
  c. 42
Died
  22 June 1276
Length of pontificate
  6 months, 2 days
Notable feature
  The first Dominican
  to become pope

HADRIAN V
Nationality
  Italian, from Genoa
Date of birth
  c. 1205
Original name
  Ottobono Fieschi
Family background
  He was the nephew
  of Pope Innocent IV
Status
  He was not yet a
  priest when he was
  elected pope
Early career
  Cardinal deacon
Elected pope
  11 July 1276
Age at election
  c. 71
Died
  18 August 1276, in
  Viterbo
Length of pontificate
  1 month, 7 days

[The dead Pope Hadrian V speaks to Dante]

I was the successor of Peter ... but when I was made Roman Shepherd, I discovered the deceitfulness of life.... I was a wretched soul, separated from God and wholly given to avarice. Now, as you see, I am punished for it.

Dante *Purgatorio*, Canto 19

Pope Gregory X's procedure for the election of a pontiff worked well the first time it was used. Only 11 days after Gregory's death, the cardinals elected **Innocent V** (1276), the first Dominican to be pope. Innocent at once showed himself favourable to Charles and, in spite of his personal interest in pursuing discussions with the Eastern emperor Michael on the subject of the new crusade and the implementation of the new Church unity, he allowed Charles to press him into using forms and expressions which would be sure to upset the emperor and undermine any accord the two men might have achieved. But Innocent died and his successor, **Hadrian V** (1276), owed his election to Charles who had

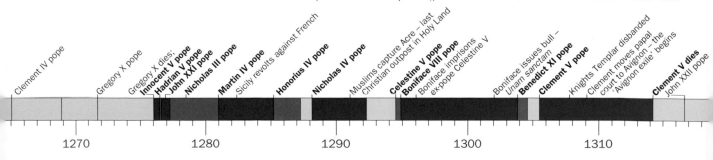

15th-century manuscript illustration showing Dante greeting Pope Hadrian V in Hell – see quote opposite (British Library). Dante's *Divine Comedy* takes the poet through Hell and Purgatory into the presence of God in Heaven. His guide through Hell is the Roman poet Virgil.

[While he was a young man, Pope John XXI wrote a medical treatise on diseases of the eye.]

I, Master Peter of Spain, the very least professor of the art of medicine, but a tracker down of truth, have put together this particular book from reason and experience at the earnest request of my pupil, Fabian of Salerno.

John XXI Preface to his *De Oculo Liber*

PAPAL NAMES

JOHN XXI
Nationality
  Portuguese, from Lisbon
Date of birth
  Between 1210 and 1220
Original name
  Pedro Julião
Family background
  Son of a physician
Early career
  Physician, cardinal bishop
Elected pope
  8 September 1276

Age at election
  Between 56 and 66
Died
  20 May 1277, of injuries received when a ceiling collapsed on him
Length of pontificate
  8 months, 13 days
Notable feature
  He is best known for a short treatise on diseases of the eye

---

forced the cardinals to decide when they gave signs of delaying. His only act was to suspend Pope Gregory's provisions for papal conclaves after which, already sick when elected, he left Rome for Viterbo and died. The resulting conclave began badly as the cardinals refused to abide by Gregory's directions, but then pulled themselves together and chose a Portuguese cardinal who took the name **John XXI** (1276–1277). This should really have been XX, since there had as yet been only 19 pontiffs called 'John', but somehow the mistake was made. John was first and foremost a scholar, not only of the arts but of medicine, too – he had actually been a practising physician – and published a good many books which ranged from commentaries on Aristotle to popular manuals on how to cure diseases. Not in the least interested in the political or administrative functions of the papacy, he retired to a small room he had built for himself in the papal palace at Viterbo and there doggedly continued his studies. The day-to-day duties of his office he left to Cardinal Orsini who had a definite political programme of his own. Orsini started by seeking a reconciliation between Charles of Anjou and Rudolf, and between Alfonso of Castile and Philip III of France, as a preliminary to launching yet another crusade against the Middle East. He also approached Emperor Michael as part of the same overall preparation, and received the emperor and his heir's full formal submission to Rome.

But suddenly the pontificate ended. The new room John had had constructed for his studies collapsed without warning while the pope was working there alone at night. Dreadfully injured by the falling beams, John lingered for six days and then died, leaving behind a reputation which slowly achieved the status of legend. It was said, for example, that he was really a magician who had been struck down in the midst of writing an heretical treatise.

The most obvious person to succeed John was Cardinal Orsini, since he had effectively been pope for the past nine months. Even so, it took the cardinals six months to elect him. As **Nicholas III** (1277–1280), his objective was to curb the power of Charles of Anjou in Italy. So when Charles's term as a Roman senator expired, Nicholas persuaded him not to re-stand and then got himself elected to that position for life. At the same time he received Rudolf's formal assurances that the empire would not seek to exert control over papal territories, or try to extend its claims to disputed areas such as Romagna. Next, he arranged a marriage between Charles's grandson, Charles Martell, and Rudolf's daughter, hoping thus to put an end to rivalry between the two ambitious crowns. Meanwhile he was busy negotiating with Alfonso of Castile and Philip III of France, each of whom was now claiming the crown of Navarre, and with Emperor Michael whose submission to John XXI was deemed not quite sufficient; while in Rome itself Nicholas undertook a major restoration both of St Peter's Basilica and of the Vatican Palace which he made his official residence.

Such fevered activity at last took its toll and in August 1280, Nicholas had a stroke and died in Soriano, not far from Viterbo. Six months of

View of Rome, showing the Vatican Palace (centre, top) and old St Peter's, both of which Nicholas III restored. Woodcut from Hartmann Schedel's *Liber Chronicarum* (1493).

PAPAL NAMES	
NICHOLAS III	his official
Nationality	residence
Italian, from Rome	
Date of birth	MARTIN IV
Between 1210 and	*Nationality*
1220	French, from Brie
Original name	*Date of birth*
Giovanni Gaetano	Between 1210 and
Family background	1220
Aristocratic	*Original name*
Early career	Simon
Cardinal deacon	*Early career*
Elected pope	Chancellor of
25 November 1277	France, cardinal
Age at election	priest, papal legate
Between 57 and 67	*Elected pope*
Died	22 February 1281
22 August 1280 at	*Age at election*
Soriano, of a stroke	Between 61 and 71
Length of pontificate	*Died*
2 years, 8 months,	28 March 1285, in
29 days	Perugia
Notable feature	*Length of pontificate*
The first pope to	4 years, 1 month, 7
make the Vatican	days

The pope [Martin IV] hated the Germans so much that he often wished he could become a stork and that the Germans were frogs in a marsh, so that he could have a chance of eating them.

Continuatio Vindobonensis (year 1284)

13th-century French manuscript showing French soldiers from the same period as the Sicilian Vespers, a riot which is said to have been sparked off by the insults of a French soldier to a Sicilian woman (Bibliothèque Nationale, Paris).

intrigue and trafficking then ensued. In February 1281, the bells of Viterbo rang as a signal for action, and the citizens, infuriated by the cardinals' delay, stormed the papal palace and carried off those two whom they deemed most to blame for the conclave's irresolution. They imprisoned both, one for three days, the other for three weeks, and yet still the conclave argued. Finally, 20 days after the attack, **Martin IV** (1281–1285) emerged as pope.

Martin was a Frenchman whose previous career had been spent largely in France and who was therefore, not surprisingly, pro-French in his policies. In consequence he was, if not a puppet, at least a servant of Charles of Anjou to whom he more or less owed his election. Pope Nicholas's attempts to mollify and conciliate all parties were thus overturned, and under the circumstances one must admire Rudolf's restraint as his coronation as Holy Roman emperor, first promised by Gregory X, faded yet again into uncertainty. Emperor Michael was excommunicated, Charles's plans to attack Constantinople approved, the reunion of the Western and Eastern Churches annulled: Pope Martin seemed to do Charles's bidding without a thought for the consequences. On 30 March 1282, he was given an opportunity to break free from this tutelage, for Sicily rose against the French, the ringing of bells for Vespers being the signal for revolt. The rebels were successful and sent messages to the pope, asking him to accept Sicily as a papal fief. But Martin not only rejected their suggestion; he promised Charles every assistance to recover the island, and, when the islanders turned to Peter III of Aragon, Martin excommunicated and then deposed him for his temerity in accepting the crown he had been offered.

Europe's teeth were on edge, but in January 1285 Charles died and, faithful to the last, Pope Martin followed him just over two months later. In only four days the cardinals chose **Honorius IV** (1285–1287) as pope. Perhaps they should have waited. The new pope had been on good

Seal of James II of Aragon. The son of Constanza of Sicily, and a grandson of James I of Aragon, the Conquistador, James II was more peaceably known as *el Justo*.

terms with Charles of Anjou and sought few, if any, modifications of his predecessor's policies. Thus, he tried to bring Sicily back under French control and then encouraged Philip III's efforts to conquer Aragon for himself, its throne, according to Pope Martin's *pronunciamenti*, being vacant. These efforts, however, proved hopeless, and late in 1285 Honorius was presented with a chance to think again. For both Philip and Peter III conveniently died, and King Peter's two sons became kings – the elder of Aragon, the younger of Sicily. Honorius, however, chose not to alter course. He excommunicated the new king, James of Sicily, and was livid when Charles of Anjou's heir, Charles II of Salerno, renounced that title in favour of James to buy his freedom – he had been imprisoned by Peter III.

Meanwhile Rudolf was still waiting to be crowned. His coronation was appointed for 2 February 1287, but was postponed yet again because Rudolf was unable to reach Rome in time, and a meeting at Würzburg, convened to arrange another date, broke up in disorder because the German delegates refused to contribute towards the cost of Rudolf's future journey to Rome.

Honorius had been 75 when he was elected. He died suddenly on 3 April 1287, perhaps of a stroke, and thereupon the papacy was vacant for 11 months while the conclave wrangled. The English chronicler, Thomas Wykes, wrote bitterly: 'Because of the cardinals' discord, at once frivolous and despicable, and due perhaps to the fact that each man wanted the papal office for himself … the Church swayed to and fro

PAPAL NAMES

HONORIUS IV
Nationality
  Italian, from Rome
Date of birth
  1210
Original name
  Giacomo Savelli
Family background
  Aristocratic;
  Honorius was the
  great-nephew of
  Pope Honorius III
Early career
  Cardinal deacon
Elected pope
  2 April 1285
Age at election
  75
Died
  3 April 1287
Length of pontificate
  2 years

NICHOLAS IV
Nationality
  Italian, from

  Lisciano
Date of birth
  30 September
  1227
Original name
  Girolamo Masci
Family background
  Son of a clerk
Status
  Franciscan friar
Early career
  Cardinal priest
Elected pope
  22 February 1288
Age at election
  60
Died
  4 April 1292
Length of pontificate
  4 years, 1 month,
  11 days
Notable feature
  Nicholas was
  the first Franciscan
  to become pope

Effigy of Honorius IV. Honorius was buried in old St Peter's near the grave of Nicholas III. Paul III, however, had his body removed to the family vault in the Church of Santa Maria di Ara Caeli.

without a Head.' Spring passed and the summer heats set in. Six cardinals died, reducing their number to nine, and this remainder decided to suspend its sittings and disperse. Only Cardinal Girolamo Masci, a Franciscan, stayed behind, burning fires in every room of the papal residence to escape infection. At length, when autumn had gone and winter was far advanced, he received his reward and was elected pope.

Nicholas IV (1288–1292) at first refused the office but was elected again and felt obliged to accept. His political policies, like those of his immediate predecessors, were somewhat perverse. He tried to restore Sicily to France and spent much time and energy towards that end. Regardless of King James, he crowned Charles II of Salerno king of Sicily (although he had at least the sense to make him do homage to the papacy for it), and used Church funds to subsidize armed resistance to James's subsequent attack on southern Italy. In August 1289, an armistice was arranged, and in June 1291, James's elder brother died and James became king of Aragon as well as of Sicily. That year Rudolf also died, still waiting for his coronation, while in the Holy Land Muslim arms triumphed over Acre, the last stronghold still in Christian hands. Nicholas called for a crusade, but no one listened. In Rome, too, his tactics came to nothing. From the start he had singled out a patrician family, the Colonnas, on which to bestow his favours, a mistake which stirred the people into faction and disorder. His pontificate thus ended in dissatisfaction. His one enthusiasm which was above criticism was his zeal for missionary work in China and his efforts to promote and preserve the Catholic faith in Serbia, Bulgaria, Armenia and Ethiopia.

Two years and three months passed after his death while the cardinals vainly endeavoured to fill the vacancy. In March 1294, Charles II of Sicily arrived at Perugia, whither the conclave had retreated, to discuss Sicilian politics and sharpen the cardinals' minds by producing a list of four suitable candidates. No one took any immediate notice, but after the king's departure there were outbreaks of violence in Rome as partisans of the absent cardinals carried familial fights as far as riot and murder. Something had to be done, and it was at this point that one of the cardinals revealed the contents of a letter he had received from a well-known Benedictine hermit, Pietro del Morrone, warning him that God would punish the conclave unless it elected a pope forthwith. By happy inspiration, the cardinal then suggested Pietro himself for the office and the conclave agreed in a burst of emotion.

It may have seemed like a good idea at the time. Pietro already had a reputation for saintliness and had founded a new monastic order (later called 'Celestines'), which devoted itself to looking after the poor and the sick. But Pietro was in despair at the news of his election and meditated flight. He was forestalled by Charles II who begged him to accept the office and then, when Pietro reluctantly gave way, escorted him to Aquila where he was consecrated. **Celestine V** (1294), as he now became, meekly handed himself over to Charles, even agreeing to reside in Naples rather than Rome. He appointed to office those whom Charles

PAPAL NAMES	
CELESTINE V	*Abdicated*
Nationality	13 December 1294
Italian, from Molise	*Died*
Date of birth	19 May 1296 in
1209 or 1210	prison in Castel
Original name	Fumone, near
Pietro del Morrone	Ferentino. Death
Family background	was caused by
Peasant	infection from an
Status	abscess, possibly
Benedictine hermit,	exacerbated by bad
priest	treatment
Early career	*Length of pontificate*
Abbot, although he	5 months, 9 days
continued to live as	*Notable features*
a hermit apart from	Celestine was
the community	famous as an
Elected pope	ascetic and
5 July 1294	miraculous
Age at election	healer
84 or 85	

Celestine V received the news of his election in his hermit's cell at Rieti, and it took the combined effort of the kings of Naples and Hungary, along with the archbishop of Lyons, to persuade him to accept the papacy and be crowned pope (*above*) 16th-century painting (Louvre).

wanted, made the king official guardian of the next electoral conclave, and without the king's instructions failed to carry out efficiently any of his administrative duties as pontiff. Saintliness, it now became clear, was not enough. To do Celestine justice, he knew it and five months after his election abdicated, leaving a conclave to choose his successor according to the procedure first introduced by Gregory X.

Boniface VIII (1294–1303), who had advised Celestine on the canonical way to abdicate, could not have presented the Church with a greater contrast. In certain ways he reminds one of later Renaissance popes. He was interested in learning and reorganized the Vatican archives and had the library catalogued; he founded the University of Rome in 1303; he was a patron of artists, Giotto in particular, and of sculptors from whom he commissioned innumerable statues of himself; he ruthlessly pursued the interests of his own family, and above all he was arrogant.

His first act as pope was to dismiss the creatures of Charles II appointed by Celestine; his second, to remove the papal court from Naples back to Rome. He did not initiate a similar retreat from Charles himself, however, for during the next seven years he endeavoured to restore Sicily to him since, in spite of Charles's title, the actual king of Sicily was still James II of Aragon who had appointed his brother Frederick as his regent. But Boniface's reign was dominated by two disastrous quarrels: one with the Colonna family, over whom he won a pyrrhic victory; the other with

PAPAL NAMES

BONIFACE VIII	Elected pope
Nationality	24 December
Italian, from Anagni	1294
Date of birth	*Age at election*
c. 1235	c. 59
Original name	*Died*
Benedetto Caetani	11 October 1303
Family background	*Length of pontificate*
Aristocratic	8 years, 9 months,
Early career	22 days
Cardinal priest	

UNAM SANCTAM

By our faith we are compelled to believe and sustain one holy Catholic and Apostolic Church. This We firmly believe, and We make simple confession that outside the Church there is no salvation or remission of sins.... Therefore, We declare, affirm and define as a truth necessary for salvation that every human being is subject to the Roman pontiff.

From Boniface's bull, *Unam sanctam*

In the bull, *Unam sanctam*, we have the clearest statement and most sweeping claim of papal supremacy. Never before had the full implication of the titles 'supreme pontiff' and 'vicar of Christ' been made so manifest. Whoever succeeded Boniface, therefore, had a formidable pronouncement at his back to defend him from enemies.

14th-century manuscript of Boniface VIII presiding over the college of cardinals.

Philip IV of France who harried him vigorously throughout his reign.

The pope's arrogance first set the Colonna family against him, but they also disapproved of his Sicilian policy and therefore raised doubts about whether Celestine's abdication was valid. Had it not been, Boniface would not legitimately be pope. Not that the Colonnas had any genuine grievance over Boniface's election; their cardinals had voted for him, and he had stayed at the Colonna stronghold of Zagarolo after his coronation. But Celestine was weak and easily influenced and, until May 1296, was still alive. So to safeguard his own position, Boniface made arrangements for him to be taken into protective custody – recapturing him after he tried to escape overseas – and locked him up in a castle about 40 miles southeast of Rome. Aged about 85, Celestine lingered for 10 months with an abscess which gave him great pain, and then quietly died. In 1297, the Colonnas turned from slander to action and stole Boniface's personal treasure while it was being transported from Anagni to Rome. It was later returned, but the family continued to issue manifestos to the tune that Boniface was not really pope, and in consequence Boniface published decrees of excommunication and summoned a 'crusade' against them. Subsequent military action brought them to their knees in 1298, but before the year was out they rebelled again and fled to France where Philip IV extended them sanctuary and used their hostility as a weapon in his own war with the pope.

The quarrel between Philip and Boniface began when the pope tried to arbitrate between France and England over lands in France held by the English king. The war which accompanied the territorial dispute was paid for in part by taxes raised on the clergy, a practice to which Boniface vigorously and publicly objected. An initial flurry of hostilities between Philip and Boniface ended briefly when Boniface canonized Philip's grandfather, Louis IX, in 1297. But in 1301, Philip sought again to exercise personal authority within the Church in France, and Boniface saw a serious threat to papal supremacy over secular powers. So he issued a bull underlining that supremacy and, when the French replied with a statement of royal independence in France, published another – *Unam sanctam* (1302) – which included his most famous dictum that salvation depended on a person's being subject to the Roman pope. Satisfied that this must end the matter, Boniface then sought reconciliation; but a new French minister, Guillaume de Nogaret, took the opposite view and proposed an outright attack on the pope. Using information supplied by the disgruntled Colonnas at the French court, de Nogaret published a list of the pope's supposed personal failings and demanded a general council of the Church to depose him.

Boniface, who in September 1303 was resident in Anagni, prepared a counter-publication; but before he could publish it, de Nogaret arrived with Sciarra, head of the Colonna family, and demanded that Boniface resign. When Boniface refused, Sciarra struck him in the face and then he and de Nogaret stripped the pope of the papal tiara and vestments. De

Nogaret's intention seems to have been to take Boniface to France and there have him deposed by a council. But Sciarra wanted to kill him and had to be restrained. The two men fell to a violent quarrel which lasted until the next day. This gave time for the pope to be rescued and, after a short but bloody skirmish, his would-be assassins and kidnappers were dispersed or dead. Boniface returned to Rome where he was received with general relief and acclaim. It may have been some comfort to know that Charles II of Naples and Frederick III of Sicily, appalled by the violence offered to the pope, were preparing to come to his aid.

Boniface, however, who was probably in his 80s, had been badly rocked by the experience, and on 11 October he unexpectedly died. Europe was shaken to the core by what had happened, and the Swiss bishop of Sion prophesied that calamity would overtake Philip and that he and his sons would lose the crown of France, a prophecy which soon came true, for by 1328 the last of Philip's sons was dead and the French crown passed across to the House of Valois.

Benedict XI (1303–1304) was a Dominican, supported during the election by Charles II of Naples who was in Rome at the time, and opposed by the two Colonna cardinals who denounced the result as invalid. In an effort to appease them, Benedict released them from the sentence of excommunication imposed by Boniface in 1297; but this annoyed his own supporters and caused uproar in the city. So he retired to Perugia in April 1304 where he grappled with the problem of what to do about Philip IV of France. His resolution was to absolve the king and everyone else except de Nogaret from any retribution due to their actions against Boniface. De Nogaret was summoned to Perugia to answer accusations of sacrilege. Dysentery, however, carried the pope away before anything more could be done, and 11 months of dissension followed as pro-French and anti-French cardinals battled inside the conclave.

Eventually they chose a Frenchman, the archbishop of Bordeaux, who took the papacy to France and left it there in what has become known as the 'Avignon exile' or the 'Babylonian captivity'. **Clement V** (1305–1314) in fact never set foot in Rome. Instead, after a peripatetic search round France for suitable accommodation, he eventually settled as a permanent guest in the Dominican monastery at Avignon, and there nursed the cancer which tormented him throughout his pontificate. King Philip IV insisted that the new pope be crowned at Lyons, and Clement's yielding to this insistence set the tone for the rest of the reign. Despite a painfully drawn-out demur, he eventually agreed to

Fresco of Benedict XI by Fra. Angelico (1400–1455) (San Marco, Florence). Benedict XI was beatified by Clement XII in 1736. He took as his papal motto, 'Make thy face shine upon thy servant' (*Psalm* 30.17).

PAPAL NAMES	
BENEDICT XI	Villandraut
Nationality	*Date of birth*
Italian, from Treviso	c. 1260
Date of birth	*Original name*
1240	Bertrand de Got
Original name	*Early career*
Niccolò Boccasino	Archbishop of
Family background	Bordeaux
Son of a notary	*Elected pope*
Status	5 June 1305
Dominican friar	*Age at election*
Early career	c. 45
Cardinal bishop	*Died*
Elected pope	20 April 1314 at
22 October 1303	Roquemaure
Age at election	*Length of pontificate*
63	8 years, 10
Died	months, 14 days
7 July 1304, at	*Notable features*
Perugia of	Clement was
dysentery	the first of the
Length of pontificate	popes to reside in
8 months, 16 days	Avignon at the
	beginning of a
CLEMENT V	long papal exile
Nationality	from Rome
French, from	

Clement V leaving a grieving Ecclesia, symbolic of the papacy leaving Rome for Avignon; from a 15th-century manuscript of the pseudo-Joachite prophecies on the papacy (British Library). Clement was crowned pope in the presence of Philip IV of France by whose manoeuvres he had been elected in the first place. He quickly created nine French cardinals, a precedent which later Avignon popes were content to follow.

summon a general council which would have as its sole purpose full rehabilitation of King Philip and Guillaume de Nogaret after their attack on Pope Boniface, and the annulment of all Boniface's decrees hostile to French interests. Clement even published a bull praising Philip for his fervour in hostility toward that unfortunate pope.

But more craven still was Clement's acquiescence in the downfall of the Order of the Knights Templar in France. With an eye to seizing their considerable wealth, Philip had them all arrested on 13 October 1307 and, by dint of atrocious torture, had them presented to the pope and general public as heretics who worshipped an idol called Baphomet and sodomized one another during secret and blasphemous initiation ceremonies. A Church council was called to Vienne and there Clement dissolved the order and assigned their French property to the Order of the Knights Hospitaller, although they did not actually enjoy the spoils, which fell to Philip himself.

French influence also dominated the college of cardinals. Between 1305 and 1312 Clement created a large number of new cardinals, most of them were French, and five of them were even members of his own family whom he so enriched by lavish legacies after his death that the papal treasury was exhausted. Nevertheless, Clement did touch upon matters beyond those which were purely in the interests of France. In Scotland he is remembered for excommunicating Robert the Bruce who had engineered the murder of a personal enemy, John Comyn, in church during mass. With regard to German affairs, Clement nominated Henry of Luxemburg to the imperial crown after the assassination of Albert I of Habsburg; and by his bull, *Pastoralis cura*, he declared the supremacy of the pope over the empire, and thus the papal right to nominate a papal vicar (or regent) should a vacancy occur on the throne. Nor should it be forgotten that he founded the universities of Orléans and Perugia, and established chairs of Oriental languages at Paris, Bologna, Oxford and Salamanca.

But it cannot be overlooked, either, that it was Clement's innate weakness which removed the papacy to France and tied it to the desires of a vicious monarch, thus creating a scandal in the Church, which was to last for over a century and breed schism and antipopes to the impairment of the whole of Christendom. It is therefore not surprising that when disease carried Clement off, the conclave in 1314 took two years, three months and 17 days to find a replacement. Clement may have left earthly treasure to his 'nephews', but to the Church his bequests were acrimony, hatred and strife.

THE FALL OF THE KNIGHTS TEMPLAR

Your Beatitude is aware that I have been informed by trustworthy people of the results of inquiries into the brethren and Order of Knights Templar. These revealed that they committed such great heresies and other dreadful, detestable crimes that for this reason the order should justifiably be suppressed. In consequence, burning with zeal for the true faith, and lest so great an injury done to Christ remain unpunished, I lovingly, devotedly, and humbly beg Your Holiness to be pleased to suppress the aforesaid order.

A letter to Pope Clement V from King Philip, dated 2 March 1312

The Templars before Clement and King Philip; 14th century (British Library). Jacques de Molay, the last Grand Master of the Templars, was burned alive in 1314. As he died, he asked Clement and Philip to appear with him before the throne of God. Clement died a month later, and Philip in November the same year.

John XXII
1316–1334

Benedict XII
1334–1342

Clement VI
1342–1352

Innocent VI
1352–1362

Urban V
1362–1370

Gregory XI
1370–1378

15th-century manuscript showing John XXII (British Library). He had had an academic career in Paris, Orléans, Cahors and Toulouse before becoming chancellor to Charles II of Naples in 1309.

PAPAL NAMES	
JOHN XXII	Elected pope
Nationality	7 August 1316
French, from	*Age at election*
Cahors	c. 72
Date of birth	*Died*
c. 1244	4 December 1334
Original name	*Length of pontificate*
Jacques Duèse	18 years, 3
Family background	months, 29 days
Wealthy bourgeois	*Antipope*
Early career	Nicholas V
Cardinal priest	(1328–1330)

In the year of Our Lord 1334, on Easter Eve, Pope John was celebrating mass and had made his communion, and wanted Giovanni Gaetano, a cardinal deacon who had served the mass with him, to make his communion too. But when John offered him part of the host, thinking he would put it in his mouth, the cardinal said he saw nothing there. So for an hour they looked for it all over the place where the pope had been standing. At last it was found in a fold of the pope's chasuble, and then given to the cardinal. When mass was over, the pope said he has seen with his own eyes the body of God slip away and fall out of his hands, and he could not see where it was hiding until they had made a careful search and discovered it in a fold of his chasuble. This incident the pope regarded as a miracle.

Heinrich the Seneschal of Dissenhoven *Vita Joannis XXII*

John XXII (1316–1334), despite his advanced years and his clear intention to settle the papacy at Avignon, initially appeared to have been a good choice. With remarkable vigour he set about restoring papal finances, instituted administrative reforms which made for better gov-

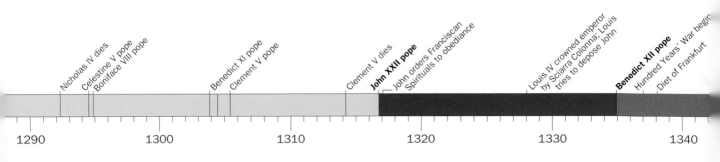

Nicholas IV dies
Celestine V pope
Boniface VIII pope
Benedict XI pope
Clement V pope
Clement V dies
John XXII pope
John orders Franciscan Spirituals to obediance
Louis IV crowned emperor by Sciarra Colonna; Louis tries to depose John
Benedict XII pope
Hundred Years' War begins
Diet of Frankfurt

1290　　1300　　1310　　1320　　1330　　1340

(*Right*) 14th-century miniature from an *Address* by the town of Prato to Robert of Anjou, king of Naples (British Library). Robert had been crowned by Clement V at Avignon and was rapidly recognized as the leader of the Guelph party. Dante, however, dismisses him as 'a king of words' only. Before being made pope, John XXII had served as Robert's chancellor prior to being made bishop of Avignon in 1310.

DECRETALS

A decretal is a papal letter which contains a pope's ruling on some specific matter, usually of Church discipline. It is thus different from a bull which bestows or corroborates rights, and deals with matters of lesser importance. Dating from the fourth century, decretals became important expressions of papal authority in succeeding centuries since when they were collected together they influenced the development of canon law by providing precedents, definitions and classifications upon which subsequent popes and canonists could build. Forged decretals were also collected and they, no less than the genuine, played their part in stressing papal authority and clerical privilege.

ernment and published decrees by Clement V and himself, dealing with points of doctrine or ecclesiastical law (decretals). Pope John also encouraged missionary work in Asia; launched the papal library at Avignon; and founded a university at Cahors.

But John soon came into conflict with the Franciscans. Soon after the foundation of the order, certain brothers – first called *Zelanti* and later Spirituals – insisted upon undeviating adherence to the original rule, and upon the concept and observance of absolute poverty; successive popes

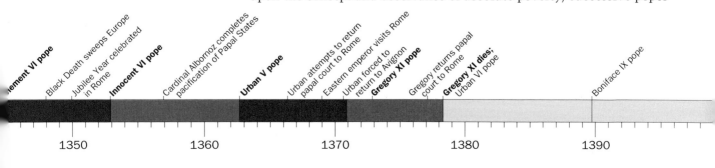

Clement VI pope
Black Death sweeps Europe
Jubilee Year celebrated in Rome
Innocent VI pope
Cardinal Albornoz completes pacification of Papal States
Urban V pope
Urban attempts to return papal court to Rome
Eastern emperor visits Rome
Urban forced to return to Avignon
Gregory XI pope
Gregory returns papal court to Rome
Gregory XI dies; Urban VI pope
Boniface IX pope

1350   1360   1370   1380   1390

PAPAL NAMES

BENEDICT XII	CLEMENT VI
Nationality French, from Saverdun, near Toulouse	*Nationality* French, from Maumont, Limousin
Date of birth c. 1280–1285	*Date of birth* 1291
Original name Jacques Fournier	*Original name* Pierre
Family background Humble	*Family background* Second son of a minor lord
Status Cistercian monk	*Status* Benedictine monk, doctor of theology
Early career Abbot, cardinal priest	*Early career* Abbot, archbishop of Rouen, chancellor of France
Elected pope 20 December 1334	*Elected pope* 7 May 1342
Age at election c. 49–54	*Age at election* 51
Died 25 April 1342	*Died* 6 December 1352, in Avignon
Length of pontificate 7 years, 4 months, 5 days	*Length of pontificate* 10 years, 7 months

Monument to Benedict XII by Paolo da Siena (Vatican Grottos). Before his election, Benedict XII had been an energetic and efficient inquisitor, sweeping away heretic Waldenses and Albigensians from his dioceses of Pamiers and Mirepoix. He was also a skilled debater and wrote about and against some of the well-known controversialists of the 12th and 13th centuries.

were asked to arbitrate in this dispute. No pope supported the extreme Spiritual position, so Spirituals demanded separation from the rest of the order and were, in turn, subject to increasing persecution. In 1317, Pope John ordered the renegades to return to full obedience to their superiors. Those who did not comply were handed over to the Inquisition and four were burned. All remained quiet for a while, but in 1322 a general chapter of the order announced that it was a valid theological opinion that Christ and his Apostles had owned nothing of their own, a notion very close to that of the Spirituals. John denounced this as heresy and the order was immediately split between those who submitted to the pope and those who did not. John reinforced his decision by issuing a bull affirming the right to hold property and the teaching that the Apostles had indeed had personal possessions.

John's enemies then turned to the German king, Louis IV. John had alienated King Louis by not supporting his claim to the imperial crown. Louis took what was rapidly becoming a familiar step among royal opponents of the papacy, that of calling for a general council to have the pope deposed. But Louis relied on more than simple words; for in January 1328 he entered Rome, had himself crowned emperor by the villainous Sciarra Colonna, declared John deposed, and had a Spiritual elected pope in his stead. But it was all too extreme to last. Louis left Rome a year later and his antipope, *Nicholas V*, fled to Avignon and there submitted himself to John. The pope was not vindictive and allowed Nicholas to live out his life in comfortable seclusion in the papal palace.

Controversy, however, clouded the pope's last days. In the winter of 1331 he preached certain novel opinions of his own about the exact condition of the blessed in heaven, and was soon condemned as a heretic by the University of Paris and many individual theologians. All those whom he had offended rushed to declare him and his notions anathema, and he was saved from serious difficulty only by a deathbed repentance although, true to form, he made this partial rather than complete.

Benedict XII (1334–1342) was a Cistercian whose theology was perhaps more sound than that of his predecessor, and he quickly settled the theological point which John had handled so badly during his final years. In accordance with his strong reformist views, Benedict set about excising undesirable practices among the clergy, such as not residing in their benefices, holding more than one ecclesiastical office at once, and charging extortionate sums for drawing up documents; and among the religious orders by insisting

THE POPES AT AVIGNON

Originally driven to Avignon by the turbulence of Italian, and particularly Roman, politics, the popes came to appreciate certain advantages which Avignon offered them. It was more peaceful, so the pope could disentangle himself to a large extent from parochial concerns and direct his attention to the larger questions of Church government. The curia thus became more efficient, and so the pope's authority grew in the sense that his decrees were more efficiently carried out. More taxes flowed into papal coffers, and as the papacy became richer, so the pope's opportunities for exercising patronage multiplied. The pope became, in effect, more like a temporal monarch and hence more threatening to temporal kings, especially the king of France at whose threshold Avignon lay.

But coincidental with this growing papal control over the Church's administration and the evident increase in worldliness which accompanied it, was a growing dissatisfaction with papal nepotism, luxuriousness, corruption and love of Mammon. Spiritual growth did not keep pace with material expansion, and in consequence, the world beyond Avignon was first suspicious and then scandalized.

that monks and nuns observe their rules strictly. As far as residence in Avignon was concerned, Benedict seems to have wondered about a return to Rome; but the chaotic state of the city and of Italy as a whole dissuaded him, and he began construction of the papal palace at Avignon. In politics he must be accounted a failure. Papal authority in Italy was disregarded in secular affairs; and when Emperor Louis IV tried to effect a reconciliation between himself and the papacy, Benedict weakly gave in to King Philip VI of France's objections to it and thus alienated Louis even further – so much so that in 1338 a meeting of the German states (the Diet of Frankfurt) announced that imperial authority came from God, and that papal approval of a newly elected emperor was not required.

After Benedict's death, the cardinals chose as pope the chancellor of France who became **Clement VI** (1342–1352). In contrast to the austerity of Benedict, Clement lived like a secular prince and settled the papal court sumptuously in a much-enlarged palace. Clement was surrounded by armed conflicts. The Hundred Years' War (1337–1453) between France and England was well under way; and his efforts to intervene militarily in the complex struggles which were rending Italy came to nothing. He had greater success, however, in his inherited quarrel with Emperor Louis IV. In 1342 and 1343 he renewed John XXII's decrees against him and called on him to resign the imperial crown. Louis, despite the bravado of the Diet of Frankfurt, was prepared to make some concessions, but Clement was not interested; in 1346 he declared Louis deposed and excommunicated, and Clement's protégé, Charles IV of

Anti-papal caricature of Clement VI from a 15th-century manuscript illustrating the prophecies of Joachim of Fiore about the popes (National Library, Vienna). Clement VI has long been called 'a tragic actor in the tattered purple of antiquity'. By creating a large number of French cardinals, he made the Church even more dependent on the goodwill of France.

Bohemia, was elected in Louis's stead. Louis's objections were stilled by his sudden death in a hunting accident in 1347, and Clement had the satisfaction of crowning Charles king in November that same year.

When he died, Clement left behind a reputation which went a long way to redeeming his political failures and luxurious living. He was famous as a preacher and was noted for personal benevolence and generosity. In 1348, when the Black Death swept through Europe and three-quarters of the population of Avignon are said to have died, Clement personally protected the Jews who were being blamed for initiating and spreading the plague, and issued bulls to command that others protect them too.

Innocent VI (1352–1362) experienced difficulties the moment he was elected. An austere reformer by inclination, Innocent faced cardinals who wanted to restrict the power of the pope and increase their own. Although he had given his assent to this in conclave, as soon as he was pope he repudiated all such agreements and set about an extensive programme of reform. This included the monastic orders and while it is noticeable that Innocent supported the Dominicans, he was particularly severe towards the Franciscan Spirituals.

Like Clement VI, Pope Innocent tried to return the Papal States to order and obedience. For this he used the talents of a Spanish cardinal, Gil de Albornoz, and by 1357 many of the states had been restrained and rendered tractable.

A pope, probably Clement VI, in the centre of a group symbolizing Christian society. On his left are the emperor, a king, a baron and laypeople – the civil administration; on his right are a cardinal, a bishop, and other religious entities – the ecclesiastical administration. At the feet of the pope and emperor are sheep symbolizing the ordinary citizens, guarded by dogs, *Domini canes*, which symbolize the Dominicans looking after the people. A detail from the *Triumph of St Thomas* by Andrea da Firenze (1355) a fresco in the Church of Santa Maria Novella, Florence.

The Black Death ravaged Europe between 1347 and 1351, killing between 25% and 45% of the entire population. In some places, Jews were blamed for the outbreak and massacred (*above*).

PAPAL NAMES

INNOCENT VI
Nationality
  French, from Monts, Limousin
Date of birth
  1282
Original name
  Étienne Aubert
Early career
  Professor of law, chief judge of Toulouse, cardinal bishop
Elected pope
  18 December 1352
Age at election
  64
Died
  12 September 1362
Length of pontificate
  9 years, 8 months, 26 days

URBAN V
Nationality
  French, from Lozère
Date of birth
  1310
Original name
  Guillaume de Grimoard
Family background
  Aristocratic
Status
  Benedictine monk, doctor of canon law
Early career
  Abbot, papal legate
Elected pope
  28 September 1362, during his absence in Naples
Age at election
  52
Died
  19 December 1370, buried in Marseilles
Length of pontificate
  8 years, 2 months, 23 days
Notable feature
  After his election, Urban continued to live and dress as a Benedictine monk

Cardinal Gil de Albornoz receiving homage from the Papal States which he pacified for Pope Innocent VI in 1357. Albornoz also aided Pope Urban V by placating Bernabò Visconti of Milan who was occupying Bologna against papal orders; 14th-century manuscript (Vatican Library).

Elsewhere, however, he was not so successful. His relations with Charles IV of Bohemia, crowned Holy Roman emperor in 1355, were amicable and yet Charles made public a pronouncement – called the Golden Bull – which reiterated the earlier decree of Louis IV, that papal approval was not required after the election of an imperial candidate. Nor did Innocent manage to prevent a resumption of the Hundred Years' War, although he did succeed in arranging a truce in 1360 which halted hostilities for 10 years; and his attempts to revive interest in a crusade and blow upon the cold embers of reunification between Eastern and Western Churches came to nothing. At home in Avignon, the city came under frequent assault from marauding soldiery and the pope had to spend vast sums in fortifying the city and palace, and in buying the free-booters' temporary departures. All this, and the weakness of France caused by the long war with England, made Avignon a much less attractive place to live. Even Italy's internal struggles did not look quite so bad by comparison, and by the time of his death Innocent was giving serious consideration to a restoration of the papacy to Rome.

Innocent's successor, **Urban V** (1362–1370) sent word to the Romans in May 1363 that he wished to return, despite the news that both the Vatican and Lateran palaces were uninhabitable and Rome itself dilapidated and dangerous. In October 1367, he was able to take up residence in the restored Vatican, much to the intense opposition of the French cardinals who formed a majority of the curia. It was a brave move, but Cardinal de Albornoz had effected wonders against a particularly dangerous enemy, Bernabò Visconti of Milan, who was occupying Bologna in defiance of papal strictures, and the omens were good for a successful end to the Avignon exile.

Yet the omens were deceptive. In spite of the cardinal's military successes, Urban decided to bribe Visconti to leave Bologna, a decision

14th-century manuscript of Urban V returning to Rome from Avignon in 1317 (Musée Calvet, Avigon). When Urban died, his body was buried first in Avignon but was then translated to Marseilles in 1372. He was beatified in 1870.

THE BENEVOLENT BENEDICTINE

Urban had been another of those popes somewhat too saintly for the political part of their office. He was a Benedictine monk and after his election continued to live as such. Personally frugal, he cut down papal expenses and spent the money on supporting poor students – a thousand of them, according to one account. He founded universities at Orange, Vienne and Cracow; endowed colleges at Montpellier, and spent lavishly on the restoration of churches in Rome, especially St John Lateran which had to be more or less rebuilt. In consequence, of course, he left to his successor as little money as a prince such as Clement VI had left to his: but the objects of his generosity were perhaps somewhat more commendable.

PAPAL NAMES	
GREGORY XI	*Early career*
Nationality	Cardinal deacon at
French, from	the age of 19
Maumont, Limousin	*Elected pope*
Date of birth	30 December 1370
1329	*Age at election*
Original name	42
Pierre Roger de	*Died*
Beaufort	27 March 1378
Family background	*Length of pontificate*
Aristocratic; Gregory	7 years, 2 months,
was the nephew of	29 days
Pope Clement VI	

My sweet, my sweetest Babbo.
Catherine of Siena to Gregory XI in several of her letters

which Visconti milked for immense sums of money. Urban's reasons were not due to cowardice. One of his major preoccupations was the advancement of a crusade against the Turks, and if this was to be successful he needed peace at home and harmony abroad. Hence his desire to seek reunion between Rome and Constantinople. But the crusade evoked little interest and by the end of 1365 was effectively dead. Nevertheless, Urban pressed on and in 1369 was gratified not only by the visit of the Eastern emperor, John V Palaeologus, to Rome but also by John's submission to Latin Catholicism and the pope. The emperor's motives were not entirely altruistic; he wanted Western support against Turkish menaces to Constantinople. But subordination of the Eastern emperor to the Latin faith was the acme of Urban's pontificate. Soon after, a revolt in Perugia was joined by Rome; Visconti again turned hostile, and Urban was obliged to retreat first to Viterbo and then to Montefiascone. Such unrest made Urban decide to return to Avignon in August 1370. The Holy Roman emperor, Charles IV, who had supported his move from France and had visited him in Rome in October 1368, must have been very disappointed. Once again the pope would come under French control.

But Urban scarcely had time to enjoy his return. He died on 19 December in front of the high altar of the cathedral while mass was being sung.

Gregory XI (1370–1378) was the last of the French popes. As the nephew of Clement VI, he had received both an excellent education and encouragement in his career. Like Urban V, he was deeply religious, felt guilty about residing in Avignon, hoped to unify the Latin and Orthodox Churches, and looked forward to a crusade. Not one of his hopes was fulfilled according to his wishes. Italy was in a state of upheaval, and in spite of a valiant military attempt to crush Visconti, lack of sufficient money and the weakness of allies on whom he was relying meant that Gregory had to seek accommodation with his enemy. Then Florence turned against him and roused the Papal States to revolt, a fresh misfortune which was crushed only by mercenaries and a papal interdict which brought everyday life to a halt and threatened to cripple commercial activity throughout the region.

But in 1376 Gregory felt able to return to Rome and in October set out on a sea voyage which was so wracked by storms that it took him over two months to get from Marseilles to (modern) Tarquinia. His resolution, however, was strengthened by Catherine of Siena, a mystic and visionary attached to the Dominican Order. In February 1377 there was a massacre in Cesena, ordered by the papal representative, and consequent fury in Rome against the pope was so great that he had to retire to Anagni. During the next few months exhaustion set in and all sides were willing to seek a peace settlement. A conference was called in March 1378, with Bernabò Visconti as chairman; but while negotiations were in progress Gregory fell ill and died painfully with stones in the bladder, a saddened man come to a pitiful end.

His pontificate had not been altogether unsuccessful. He had been instrumental in reforming the Order of the Knights Hospitaller who had fallen into laxity; and he ruthlessly used the Inquisition to suppress heresy in France, Germany and Spain, while he vigorously condemned the errors of the would-be reformer John Wycliffe in England. But such bright spots were few. It is said that on his deathbed he foresaw disaster for the Church, even to the point of schism. He was quite right.

CATHERINE OF SIENA

I have heard here that you have appointed cardinals. I believe it would honour God and profit us more if you would take care always to appoint virtuous men. If the contrary is done, it will be a great insult to God and disaster to Holy Church.

Catherine of Siena, Letter to Pope Gregory XI

Catherine of Siena (1347–1380) was a celebrated Dominican mystic. During her life she had great influence on the political affairs of the Church, writing numerous letters to the rulers of Europe and attempting to end the Great Schism. Her spiritual doctrine is set forth in her *Letters* and *Dialogue*.

JOHN WYCLIFFE

John Wycliffe (c. 1330–1384), an English priest and a graduate of Oxford, was a voluminous writer whose final years were clouded with charges of unorthodoxy. He attacked transubstantiation, the central doctrine of the mass, which says that the bread and wine miraculously change into the real flesh and blood of Christ while maintaining their outward appearance. Wycliffe's position was complex. He seems to have thought that the bread and wine and flesh and blood somehow coexisted simultaneously, side by side. He also attacked papal authority, the vows taken by monks and nuns, indulgences, the sacramental system of the Church and the wealth of its clergy. In some ways, therefore, he can be seen as a pale forerunner of Luther (see p. 174).

Gregory returns to Rome from Avignon; fresco by Vasari (1511–1574), in the Sala Regia, Vatican. On the same day Gregory left Avignon to return to Rome, Catherine of Siena left also, and the two parties met one another in Genoa.

THE PALAIS DES PAPES AT AVIGNON

The Palais des Papes at Avignon was built on the remains of the bishop's residence which Benedict XII was happy to pull down and redevelop, constructing in its place a cross between a monastery and a fortress. It had to be large, for it was designed to house not only the pope, but his household and the curia as well, not to mention the papal archives which had been brought there from Assisi in 1339. When Clement VI settled there, he was eager that the papal court should mirror the brilliance of the court of France, and in consequence he began a second palace next to Benedict's, much larger, much grander and much more opulent. Gradually the palace filled with *objets d'art*, plants, animals, jewels, gold and silver work, books and manuscripts. As the papal court took root there, a formal bureaucracy evolved – the pope's household, the college of cardinals, the financial department (*Camera Apostolica*), the chancery, the papal tribunals which dealt with clerical discipline and the almonry from which alms were distributed. Then one must take into account the downstairs world – the kitchen, pantry, buttery, stables and guardrooms. The list resembles that of a royal or imperial court. About 500 people could claim to be papal officials (most of them by this stage had to lodge in Avignon itself) to whom one must add about 1,000 attached to the 23 cardinals. Despite Clement's efforts, the side-by-side palaces could not cope with the crowd, and one senses a certain chaos underlying the apparent order.

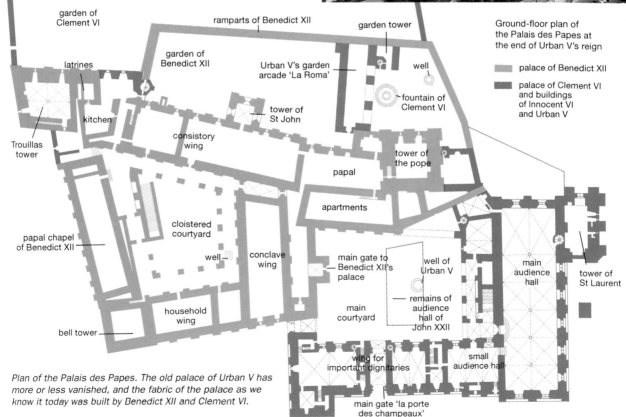

Ground-floor plan of the Palais des Papes at the end of Urban V's reign

- palace of Benedict XII
- palace of Clement VI and buildings of Innocent VI and Urban V

Plan of the Palais des Papes. The old palace of Urban V has more or less vanished, and the fabric of the palace as we know it today was built by Benedict XII and Clement VI.

(Below) Aerial view of the Palais des Papes. In 1564, Charles IX of France and the queen mother, Catherine dei' Medici, stayed in the papal palace for three weeks.

(Right) A fresco by Simone Martini. Christ as ruler of the world with the orb in his hand, from the 12th-century porch of Notre-Dame-des-Doms, housed in the consistory.

(Above) The walls in the Chambre du Cerf (Room of the Stags) in the Tower of the Popes are covered with beautiful 14th-century frescoes of hunting and fishing scenes.

(Above) Vault of the St Martial Chapel in the Tower of St John. 16 pounds of fine azure were used to decorate the chapel.

success. The schism dragged on and Boniface did nothing to end it. In 1394, France grew tired of supporting the Avignon papacy and the University of Paris proposed three ways of ending the schism: (1) both popes should resign and a new pope be elected; (2) the problem should be resolved by arbitration; (3) a general council should decide who was the genuine pope. When Clement received news of these proposals, he threw a violent fit of temper and was felled by a stroke. Not long after, he died and the cardinals at Avignon elected a new antipope, *Benedict XIII*, with whom Boniface refused to deal at all. Meanwhile he did manage to restore full papal control over Naples, but it took 10 years and a great deal of blood and money to do so. He demonstrated further his growing authoritarian tendencies in 1398 by abolishing Rome's republican government and assigning it to senators chosen by himself.

His support in Europe wavered. France appeared to be coming over to Rome, but Sicily and Genoa defected and Boniface had a great deal of trouble maintaining good relations with Germany. When the German king Wenceslas was deposed for debauchery and incapacity in 1400, his elected successor, Rupert, had to wait for nearly four years before Boniface published his approval, and even then needlessly claimed that he himself had been instrumental in Wenceslas's deposition. Boniface's worst fault, however, was simony. Because he needed cash, he sold

SIMONY

The New Testament *Acts* (8.18–24) tells the story of an attempt by Simon the Magician to buy from the Apostles their power to work miracles. From his name comes the word 'simony'. Modern usage, however, extends the meaning from a bid to purchase spiritual powers to the practice of buying and selling ecclesiastical offices and preferments, along with indulgences and emoluments. At first the sin was uncommon, but once the Church started to acquire wealth it grew and spread until by the 11th century it was rampant. Several popes issued decrees against it, but the practice was too tempting and too lucrative for people to take much notice until the second half of the 16th century when a marked renewal of the Church's spiritual life led to its elimination.

Dante and Virgil greet the simoniac popes who are trapped upside down in holes in the ground with their soles on fire; 15th-century manuscript (British Library).

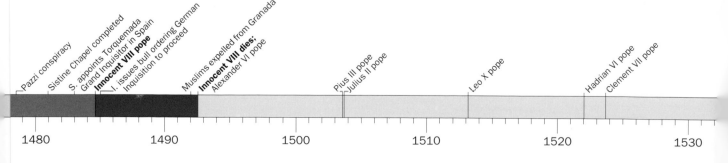

Pazzi conspiracy
Sistine Chapel completed
S. appoints Torquemada Grand Inquisitor in Spain
Innocent VIII pope
I. issues bull ordering German Inquisition to proceed
Muslims expelled from Granada
Innocent VIII dies; Alexander VI pope
Pius III pope
Julius II pope
Leo X pope
Hadrian VI pope
Clement VII pope

1480   1490   1500   1510   1520   1530

THE ANTIPOPES OF THE GREAT SCHISM

CLEMENT VII (1378–1394)

Clement (originally Robert) become a cardinal at the age of 29. When Gregory XI died, Cardinal Robert voted for Urban VI but grew disillusioned with him and led a revolt against him. Thirteen French cardinals agreed that Urban's election had been a mistake, and elected Robert in Urban's place as Clement VII. At first Clement enjoyed success. Scotland, France, Sicily, Castile, Aragon, Navarre, Portugal, Cyprus, Savoy and most of Ireland declared for Clement. Urban retained Flanders, Poland, Hungary, Germany, central and northern Italy, England and a small part of Ireland. With Urban firmly installed in Rome, Clement was obliged to go to Avignon and settle there 10 months after his 'election'. When Urban died in October 1389, Clement thought that his return to Rome was assured. But the opulence of his court and the costs of his single-minded diplomacy meant that he had turned into a harsh tax collector, and this undermined his support. What is more, the schism caused by his election in 1378 and continued by that of Pope Boniface IX in 1389 was increasingly unpopular. Led by France, pressure mounted for him to resign, and he was saved from having to do so only by having a fatal apoplectic fit.

The Italian cardinals attended the election of 'Clement VII' but did not participate in it; 14th-century manuscript, the Chroniques de France ou de St Denis *(British Library).*

BENEDICT XIII (1394–1417)

After Clement VII's death, the Church could have ended the schism, but the Avignon cardinals elected Pedro de Luna who took the title 'Benedict XIII'. He had the wit to learn from some of Clement's mistakes and did not bend every sinew to recover Rome. Instead, with a deep belief in the validity of his election, he sought to negotiate with Boniface IX. France, however, which had withdrawn her support from Clement, now withdrew her complaisance from Benedict and thus deprived him of most of his revenues and cardinals. Benedict shut himself up in the papal palace and prepared to resist. In fact he became a virtual prisoner until he escaped in 1403. Attempts to negotiate with Innocent VII and then with Gregory XII broke down, and Benedict retreated to Perpignan where, in answer to Gregory's call for a Church council, he summoned one of his own. Gregory's council not only condemned and deposed Benedict, it did the same for Gregory and elected a new 'antipope', Alexander V (1409–1410). The German king, Sigismund, tried to persuade Benedict to resign, but he refused, and was still refusing in 1417 when the Council of Constance again declared him deposed. Benedict continued his defiance for nearly six more years until he died in 1423.

ALEXANDER V (1409–1410)

Cardinal Pietro Philarghi was one of the chief organizers of the Council of Pisa, which elected him 'pope' as Alexander V in an attempt to end the schism. He had the support of France, England, Bohemia, Prussia and northern and central Italy, but both Gregory XII and Benedict XIII clung to their diminishing power. Alexander conferred bishoprics and other favours to his friends, dashing the hopes of the cardinals that this reign would cure the breach. Rome was occupied by King Ladislas of Naples, who supported Gregory XII. Alexander attempted to liberate Rome by excommunicating Ladislas and giving Louis II of Anjou the kingdom of Naples. Louis besieged the city and in January 1410 captured it. Alexander delayed taking up residence in the city, preferring to stay in Bologna where he died suddenly on 3 May 1410 leaving the Church still in schism.

JOHN XXIII (1410–1415)

Cardinal Baldassare had begun his varied career as a pirate. With Cardinal Pietro Philarghi, he arranged the Council of Pisa, and on Alexander V's death, Baldassare was elected as John XXIII. The conclave hoped that John's previous military experience would be an asset in recovering Rome from Ladislas, which he did in May 1411 with the army of Louis II. Ladislas still threatened, however, and John was forced to come to terms with him, offering him the kingdom of Naples in return for Ladislas dropping his support for Gregory XII. Ladislas went back on the bargain, however, and John was forced to seek help from Sigismund, who persuaded John to call the Council of Constance to settle the schism once and for all. The council called for the abdication of John, Benedict and Gregory, electing Martin V as the new legitimate pope. Some years later John mangaed to salvage part of his career when Martin V appointed him cardinal bishop of Tusculum, an office he held until his death a few months later.

'John XXIII's' tomb in the baptistery in Florence, by Donatello and Michelozzo, carries the papal insignia.

benefices and offices on a scale which was iniquitous even by the standards of the day; and to this he added a sale of indulgences and an increase of Church taxes, which threatened to become legendary.

In September 1404, antipope Benedict sent a deputation to Rome to sound out Boniface's reaction to proposals to end the damaging schism. Boniface received them with arrogance which was answered by the barbed observation that even if Boniface did think Benedict was an antipope, at least Benedict could not be accused of simony. Boniface reacted violently and collapsed. Two days later he was dead and Benedict's envoys found themselves in prison until they paid an enormous ransom and were allowed to go free.

It was then left to **Innocent VII** (1404–1406) to pick up or reject Benedict's suggestions. Innocent had been elected by a conclave of only eight cardinals. He, like each of the others, had previously taken an oath to abdicate, provided Benedict would do the same, if this would help to end the schism. Once elected, however, he ignored this possibility and spurned Benedict's plea for a personal meeting.

But the Romans were unhappy with Innocent's election, so he had to call upon the king of Naples, Ladislas – son of Charles of Durazzo – to help him. Ladislas agreed on condition that Innocent promise not to do a deal with Avignon which would endanger his claim to Naples, and a treaty between the pope and the people of Rome, engineered by Ladislas, brought peace for a while. The Romans grew restive, however, and in August 1405 confrontation broke into violent abuse of the pope to his face. Innocent's nephew, Ludovico Migliorati, tried to settle matters by waylaying the leaders of the Roman deputation, murdering 11 of them, and throwing the bodies contemptuously into the street. A mob blamed Innocent, attacked the Vatican, and the pope fled to Viterbo.

After only seven months, however, he returned by general invitation. Ladislas's period of authority over Rome had been so unpleasant that the citizens decided they preferred the rule of the pope. But once again a pontiff fell victim to a stroke, and the cardinals were called on to elect a suitable replacement. Again everyone in the conclave took an oath that, if elected, he would abdicate if necessary and seek a meeting with Antipope Benedict (who must likewise resign). The cardinals' choice fell on an 80-year-old Venetian who became **Gregory XII** (1406–1415) and immediately announced that he was ready to fulfil the conditions of his oath. Unfortunately things did not turn out so promisingly. At first there were quarrels about where the two men should meet. These turned into doubts whether they should meet at all; and finally the doubts hardened into outright refusal. Negotiations, however, continued even though it was clear that Benedict had no intention of resigning. In the spring of 1408 two unconnected events triggered calamity: King Ladislas once again became master of Rome, and Gregory made the mistake of creating four new cardinals, two of whom were his nephews. He had earlier sworn to maintain parity of numbers with the Avignon college, and these creations breached his solemn word. The other cardinals were

Gregory XII from the cover of a record of the developments of the consistory – 1407 Sept/Oct (State Archives, Siena). Gregory died at Recanati and was buried there. In 1623, during repairs to the cathedral, his tomb was opened and his body was found in a good state of preservation, clad in full pontificals.

Not only did the Council of Constance (*above*) seek to end the papal schism, it dealt with the heresies of Hus and Wycliffe, which had been troubling the Church for some years.

PAPAL NAMES	
MARTIN V	11 November 1417
Nationality	*Age at election*
Italian, from	49
Gennazano	*Died*
Date of birth	20 February 1431,
1368	of apoplexy
Original name	*Length of pontificate*
Oddo Colonna	13 years, 3
Family background	months, 9 days
Aristocratic	*Antipopes*
Early career	Clement VIII
Cardinal deacon	(1423–1429),
Elected pope	Benedict XIV (1425)

Martin V (*above*) was careful to oppose any suggestion that papal power should be restricted by the pretensions of Church councils (British Museum).

incensed and seven left him, entering into correspondence with Benedict about the possibility of convening a general council to settle affairs.

In June 1408, the University of Paris declared against Benedict who ignored their opinion. But he had lost the support of France. Both pope and antipope were then summoned by a majority of the college of cardinals to a council at Pisa in March 1409. Neither attended, and after protracted discussion the council proclaimed on 5 June that both men were deposed on the grounds of schism, heresy and perjury. Three weeks later the council elected a Franciscan as *Alexander V*. Gregory, however, had convened his own council not far from Aquileia. There were not many cardinals present, but Gregory had the political advantage of support from King Ladislas and the German king, Rupert. The support proved a weak reed. The king of Naples could not be trusted, and when Alexander died suddenly and the Pisan council elected *John XXIII*, Ladislas made an agreement with the antipope John. Gregory fled from Naples to Rimini. Then Rupert died and his successor, Sigismund, supported John.

Meanwhile Benedict continued to function as though he were pope. Although France had abandoned him, he was still supported by several countries, including Scotland whose oldest university at St Andrews had its foundation charter confirmed under his seal. But the spectacle of three 'popes' was too much for Christendom to bear, and a council was called to Constance to end the schism once and for all. It met between 1414 and 1417, and finally managed to force a general solution. Gregory abdicated and retired with honourable appointments and died in October 1417. Benedict retreated to Spain, still obdurate in his refusal to surrender office, and died there in 1423 at the age of 90. After his death, three of his four remaining cardinals elected an antipope, *Clement VIII*; but even here there was disagreement, and the fourth cardinal promoted another who took the name *Benedict XIV* and then disappeared. John tried to flee to Germany, but was captured and formally deposed. He died in 1419 in Florence and was buried there in splendour.

Thus the great schism ended. The low point to which the Church had descended was a scandal to the whole of Europe, but the Council of Constance now had the opportunity to set it on an upward path. The council chose a member of the Colonna family, who took the name **Martin V** (1417–1431) and immediately proclaimed that no one can appeal from the pope to any other body or question his authority on matters of faith. It was a vigorous reminder to everyone that the Roman pontiff is superior to a general council. Martin then set about reforming papal taxation, and then dissolved the council in April 1418.

For the next two years Martin resided in Mantua and Florence before entering Rome in September 1420. A combination of diplomacy and force of arms re-established his control over the Papal States, thus ending the brigandage and desolation which had attended them during the schism. His attempts to reach amity with Constantinople, however, foundered on the intransigence of the Eastern emperor, and he was

PAPAL NAMES

EUGENE IV	governor of the
Nationality	March of Ancona
Italian, from Venice	and Bologna
Date of birth	*Elected pope*
c. 1383	3 March 1431
Original name	*Age at election*
Gabriele	*c.* 48
Condulmaro	*Died*
Family background	23 February 1447
Bourgeois; related	*Length of pontificate*
to Pope Gregory XII	15 years, 11
Status	months, 20 days
Augustinian monk	*Antipope*
Early career	Felix V
Cardinal priest,	(1439–1449)

Detail of Benozzo Gozzoli's fresco in the Palazzo Medici-Riccardi, Florence, showing John VIII Palaeologus on his way to Florence to seek papal help against the Turks in 1439. John became effective Eastern emperor in 1421 when his father suffered a stroke, and then assumed complete rule in 1425 when Manuel I died.

unable to suppress the followers of John Hus, a Czech reformer condemned and burned as a heretic by the Council of Constance. On the other hand, he twice denounced anti-semitic preaching (in 1422 and 1429), and in Rome itself undertook a large-scale restoration of public buildings, including St Peter's Basilica and the Lateran Palace.

In 1423, he summoned a council at Pavia, but due to the outbreak of plague in Italy the venue was shifted to Siena and then prorogued for seven years, at which time delegates met at Basel. Before the council could get under way, however, Martin died and a conclave was summoned to Rome. The cardinals determined to elect someone who would agree to regard them as partners rather than servants of the papacy. They chose a handsome nephew of Gregory XII, an Augustinian monk who became **Eugene IV** (1431–1447), and almost at once a swarm of problems buzzed angrily round his head. Many of them were exacerbated by his naivety. Eugene forced the Colonna family to surrender the wealth and territories Pope Martin had lavished upon them and thus created a host of enemies. In 1434, when the Papal States were suffering the attentions of *condottieri*, the Colonnas stoked up the fires of revolution in Rome to such effect that the pope had to flee to Florence.

Eugene had also impulsively dismissed the Council of Basel to the general shock of everyone taking part, only to be greeted by defiance and a refusal to disperse. The conciliar members were standing by their doc-

Nicholas V crowning Frederick III (Germanisches Nationalmuseum, Nuremberg). The emperor was described as indolent and incapable, although he had a love of learning and a firm belief in the future greatness of his family.

CONDOTTIERI

The word *condottieri* derives from the Italian word *condotta*, meaning a contract between a commander and a government. A *condottiere* was, therefore, a commander of mercenaries or soldiers of fortune. These commanders were often in a position to hire out military bodies several thousand strong, and thus played a conspicuous role in the troubled history of the Italian states for at least 200 years (*c.* 1250– *c.* 1450). The soldiers came from every part of Europe and were welded into efficient armies by their commanders, although they could also be unreliable, rapacious and disorderly. During Pope Eugenius IV's reign, one of the most powerful *condottiere* was active – Francesco Sforza. He was a formidable commander and was, at different times, in the pay of both the pope and the pope's enemies. He went on to become the powerful duke of Milan.

trine that a council is superior to a pope. Fresh schism was narrowly averted through the efforts of the German king Sigismund whom Eugene crowned Holy Roman emperor in 1433. Even so, the council continued to sit and issue reforming decrees aimed largely at the financial and administrative power of the pope and the curia. A further source of trouble came from the East. Emperor John VIII Palaeologus was being threatened by Turkish invasion and decided to revive the vision of Church unity as a means to induce Eugene to call a crusade. Eugene transferred the meeting-place of the council to Ferrara and in January 1438 declared it in session. The following year, however, he moved it to Florence, and in July 1439 an act of union between the two Churches was published, an act destined to be as ephemeral as those which had preceded it.

A rump of cardinals had stubbornly stayed in Basel. These now seized the opportunity to summon Eugene to explain himself before them, and when he did not appear, declared him deposed and proceeded to elect an antipope, *Felix V*. The Basel cardinals had been encouraged by the action of France which had produced a document, the Pragmatic Sanction of Bourges, based upon Basel's anti-papal stance. This sanction announced that the pope's authority was limited and that the French Church had full control over its own temporal holdings. But Eugene managed to disengage Alfonso V of Aragon from his support of Basel by recognizing his claim to the throne of Naples and both this, and the declaration of Germany for the pope, left the cardinals at Basel more or less isolated.

During the autumn of 1446, the bishop of Bologna had been sent by Eugene to Germany and had been successful in generating support for Eugene there. In the conclave which followed Eugene's death, he received his reward, for he was elected pope and took the name **Nicholas V** (1447–1455). No less devoted to the notion of papal supremacy than Eugene, he was politically more adroit and quickly managed to bring the Papal States under his control. The new German king, Frederick III, conceded papal authority over annates (the first year's revenue of a benefice, paid to the pope), which provided a large part of the papal income, and over appointments within the German Church. This German support caused the Basel cardinals to give way to reality, and with the help of Charles VII of France, they agreed to 'elect' Nicholas pope and then to dissolve themselves. Felix abdicated and in 1449 peace was restored, in recognition of which Nicholas proclaimed 1450 a Jubilee Year.

In 1451, King Frederick III came to Italy and in the following year was crowned emperor in St Peter's, the last occasion on which such a coronation took place there. Meanwhile Nicholas, a profound scholar and lover of letters, worked to make Rome the literary and artistic capital of Christendom. He had Greek books translated into Latin, collected hundreds of manuscripts, and effectively founded the Vatican Library by the bequests he made to it. In addition, he encouraged architects and artists – Fra Angelico in particular – and conceived grandiose plans for rebuilding the centre of Rome, which were cut short by his death.

It seemed as though things might be going well at last. But 1453 brought two disasters. In January, a plot against the pope's life was uncovered, and although the conspirators were arrested and executed and then a series of negotiations between the warring Italian states produced a kind of truce to their quarrels, the mere fact that an outward tranquillity could conceal murderous intent was enough to fray Nicholas's nerves and make him wonder if peace could last. Then June saw the sack of Constantinople by Turkish armies. The horror of that fall attended by so much bloodshed filled Christendom with dismay. Nicholas sent 29 galleys to aid the Christians of the city, but they arrived too late; and his call for a crusade fell on ears which fright or indifference had closed.

Callistus III (1455–1458) was a Borgia, the first of the Spanish popes. He was 78 when the conclave elected him and people assumed he would not be pope for long. Moreover, he suffered from gout and spent much of

Sano di Pietro's portrait of Pope Callistus III as the protector of the city of Siena (Pinacoteca, Siena). The conclave which elected Callistus III seriously considered electing a Greek cardinal, John Bessarion, but a violent outburst from the archbishop of Avignon put an end to that notion. The cardinals then chose a caretaker pope instead – the first of the Borgia popes.

his pontificate in bed. His principal interest upon becoming pontiff was to raise a crusade against the Turks and in this, like Nicholas V, he failed, although in 1456 he did send a small papal fleet at great expense, which sailed up and down the coast of Asia for three years and captured a few islands. To be sure, the governor of Hungary, John Hunyadi, won a great victory over the Turks at the battle of Belgrade in July 1456; but this and the rout of the Turkish fleet off Lesbos in 1457 were the only major successes enjoyed by Christian arms. They also cost a great deal of money and Callistus's special taxes caused widespread resentment, especially in Germany which started asking for freedom of action over its own Church affairs. Callistus also quarrelled with Alfonso, king of Aragon and Naples, and when Alfonso died, planned to secure the Neapolitan throne for one of his nephews, thereby passing over Alfonso's son, Ferdinand I.

This concern for his nephews' advancement was typical of Callistus. One of them, the duke of Spoleto, he made prefect of Rome; two others he created cardinals, and one of these, Rodrigo, rapidly became vice-chancellor of the curia as well. Everywhere Spanish relatives of the pope, or simply compatriots, were favoured, much to the resentment of others who stored up their jealousy for the future. So when the pope fell ill in August 1458, Rome blazed into insurrection and the prefect, his nephew, was forced to flee for his life.

A few days later, Callistus died. It had been a short reign but not without incident, for during it he had reversed the condemnation of Joan of Arc and declared her innocent; canonized two saints; survived a red, hairy comet which appeared in 1457 and clearly foretold disaster; and died on the Feast of the Transfiguration, which he himself had instituted to commemorate the victory at Belgrade. In the 15th century, such things were not without significance.

Pius II (1458–1464) had worked for the antipope Felix V and then transferred his allegiance to Eugene IV for whom he had carried out successful negotiations in Germany, and then for both Nicholas V and Callistus III who made him a cardinal. Pius is unusual among the popes in that he was a popular *littérateur* having written, among other things, a novel (*The Story of Two Lovers*) and an erotic comedy (*Chrysis*).

His pontificate is notable for the enthusiasm with which he pressed for a crusade against the Turks. It was his vision of a united Christendom which moved him to urge such an expedition on the rulers of Europe. Pius first called for a crusade in October 1458, but his decision to favour the House of Aragon over the House of Anjou in a contest over the throne of Naples meant that France refused to give any assistance to the crusade, and, indeed, went to war with Spain on southern Italian soil in an effort to settle its claim. Nor was Pius much more successful with Germany. At first the Germans reluctantly agreed to pro-

While she was pregnant, Enea's (Pius II's) mother dreamed she would give birth to a son crowned with a mitre, and when Enea was seven, the boys with whom he was playing crowned him with a mitre of green leaves and then kissed his foot. These incidents were taken as prognostications that he would become Roman pontiff. (*Below*) Pinturicchio's fresco (1502–1505) of Pius II in Ancona during his attempt to raise a crusade against the Turk. The pope unfortunately died before a crusade could get under way (Piccolomini Library, Siena Cathedral).

A LITERARY POPE

Before he became pope, Pius had been a prolific and eclectic author, writing, among other things, a novel (*The Story of Two Lovers*); an erotic comedy (*Chrysis*); essays on the nature and care of horses, the miseries of courtiers, famous men of his time, and the education of children; histories of the Goths and Bohemia; a biography of Emperor Frederick; and descriptions of Germany, Europe and Asia which contain some wonderful thumbnail sketches of people and places. There are 24 principal works, as well as collected speeches, commentaries and letters: all in all an output impressive in quality as in quantity.

After the fall of Constantinople in 1453, Sultan Mehmet II gathered both Italian and Greek scholars at his court, and commissioned the Venetian artist Bellini to paint his portrait (National Gallery, London). The sultan did not respond, however, to Pius II's plea for him to convert to Christianity.

vide troops for a three-year period; then such feeble action as there was petered out, and in 1460 it was clear that the pope's initiative had failed.

In 1461, the new French king, Louis XI, made conciliatory moves towards the pope, hoping to change his decision over Naples. But when the pope remained firm, Louis reverted to what was rapidly becoming a traditional French position: hostility to papal intervention in the affairs of the French Church. Quarrels in Germany, too, soured relations with the pope: disagreement over a programme of Church reform there, led by Nicholas of Cusa – one of the most remarkable scholars and theologians of the period; intervention in an attempt by the king of Bohemia to replace Emperor Frederick as king of the Romans; and a direct clash with the Bohemian king over religious arrangements in Hungary. It was all very petty in comparison with Pius's grand design of reforming the Church and uniting Christian Europe.

Pius pressed ahead with his crusade and in 1460 or 1461 tried a different tack altogether. In a letter to Sultan Mehmet II, he urged him to reconsider his adherence to Islam, embrace Christianity, and become Christian emperor of the East. This was no condescending or hectoring epistle. It was meant to be the argument of one reasonable man addressed to another. Actually, the sultan may never have received the letter, but it circulated throughout Europe and had a profound effect there, emphasizing the pope's dream of uniting the world in a single, peaceful creed, and suggesting subliminally that there should be no limits to the power of persuasion, a power preferable by far to that of war.

Nevertheless, this did not stop the pope looking to war to achieve his end, and in 1463 he called again for a crusade, taking the cross himself in June 1464 in St Peter's before setting out to lead the crusade in person. But at Ancona, where he hoped to find an armada waiting, he contracted fever and died, disappointed to find that so few had heeded his final call.

The man who succeeded Pius, **Paul II** (1464–1471), was immensely vain and loved public show and ceremony. Eugene IV was his uncle and, like so many papal nephews, Paul benefited from the connection and his career blossomed under Nicholas V and Callistus III. An attempt by the college of cardinals to put a break on papal independence and wean it away from absolute to constitutional monarchy failed, however, when Paul became pope. He had no intention of being subject to regular scrutiny by general councils.

From the start of his pontificate Paul had an individual relationship with the world of learning. He abolished the college of secretaries attached to the vice-chancellery and when the papal historian Bartolomeo Platina protested, had him thrown into prison and subjected to brutal treatment – an action which caused Platina to blacken the pope's reputation in his *Lives of the Popes*. Paul also suppressed the Roman Academy, on the grounds that it leaned too far towards toleration of pagan ideas, and forbade Roman children to study the pagan poets – their own Classical heritage – for fear that they might be similarly corrupted. Yet he cannot, by any stretch of the word, be called a philistine.

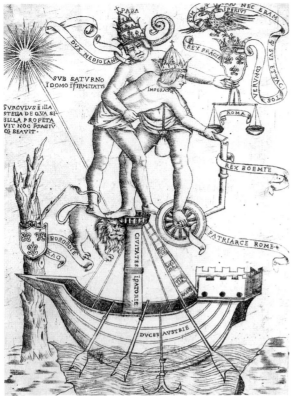

A 15th-century allegorical engraving of the struggle between Pope Paul II and Emperor Frederick III. Paul II had originally wanted to call himself 'Formosus' and then 'Mark', but was dissuaded by the cardinals who thought the first too vain and the latter too Venetian.

PAPAL NAMES	
PAUL II	**SIXTUS IV**
Nationality	*Nationality*
Italian, from Venice	Italian, from Celle
Date of birth	*Date of birth*
23 February 1417	21 July 1414
Original name	*Original name*
Pietro Barbo	Francesco della Rovere
Family background	*Family background*
Merchants; Paul's uncle was Pope Eugene IV	Humble
Early career	*Status*
Cardinal priest	Franciscan friar
Elected pope	*Early career*
30 August 1464	General of the Franciscans, cardinal priest
Age at election	*Elected pope*
46	9 August 1471
Died	*Age at election*
26 July 1471	56
Length of pontificate	*Died*
6 years, 10 months, 28 days	12 August 1484
	Length of pontificate
	13 years, 3 days

He spent vast sums on collecting silk clothes and hangings, jewels, bronzes, cameos and other *objets d'art*; built the magnificent Palazzo di Venezia in Rome, where he lived from 1466; and in 1470 decreed that jubilee years should be held four times instead of twice in a century, a change which, among other things, would gratify his love of lavish spectacle. He had, indeed, what amounted to a mania for beautiful objects and it was rumoured he even took sapphires and rubies to bed with him.

Pius II had left him a legacy of problems and Paul did his best to cope. The crusade against the Turks, which Pius had started, came to nothing. But the Turks were pressing hard on Hungary and Albania, and in 1466 Paul wondered if he could pacify the king of Bohemia who had quarrelled with Pius, and persuade him to lead a campaign against them. It was a vain hope. The attempt at reconciliation failed dismally and Paul not only ended by excommunicating the king, but even encouraged the king of Hungary to go to war with him. Meanwhile the Turks continued to menace. In 1468, Emperor Frederick III suggested that the pope call a general council to help him with these difficulties, but the proposal fell on deaf ears. In 1470, the Turks overran Euboea, the last remaining enclave of the Venetians in Greece, and Paul summoned the Christian nations to a crusade. His summons resulted in nothing more than an agreement among the Italian states to look to their own defence.

Indeed, disappointment continued to dog his footsteps. In 1471, he persuaded the Turcoman prince, Uzun-hassan, to cooperate with Rome against Sultan Mehmet; and he tried to arrange a marriage between Ivan III of Russia and Zoë Palaeologus, niece of the last Christian emperor of the East, as a preliminary to uniting the Russian Church with Rome. But during the night of 26 July, having been perfectly well all day, he felt ill and retired to bed. After an hour, his chamberlain came in to find the pope foaming at the mouth. He rushed for help, but by the time he returned, the pope was dead, apparently from a stroke. It had been a strange reign: a magnificent, theatrical performance in public but hollow below the surface, rather like a chryselephantine statue which is covered in plates of gold and ivory but has merely wood at its core.

Paul's successor, **Sixtus IV** (1471–1484), was a Franciscan who was elected partly for his personal gifts of scholarship and partly because of generous bribery to certain key individuals. Three general points can be made about him: he transformed the face of Rome, he shamelessly promoted the interests of his own family, he was involved in a murderous conspiracy against the Medici family in Florence. The improvement and beautification of Rome proceeded throughout the pontificate.

Less happy are the other aspects of his reign. He renewed Paul II's attempt to raise a crusade and spent a good deal of money on a fleet for

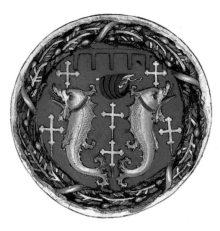

Enamelled terracotta coat of arms of the Pazzi, who had been a noble Florentine family from at least the 13th century when Jacopo de' Pazzi had distinguished himself at the battle of Montaperti.

that purpose. But as usual, the rest of Europe was disinclined to lend support and after a small naval success in 1472 the expedition, such as it was, foundered. The marriage between Ivan III of Russia and Zoë Palaeologus took place but did not bring the desired union of Russia with Rome; and relations with France, never easy since the accession of Louis XI, continued to be strained as the king insisted on maintaining control over the Church in France and the pope resisted any such notion.

But it was in Italy that Sixtus's pontificate showed itself to be disreputable rather than merely ineffective. No sooner had he become pope than he elevated two of his young nephews, Pietro Riario and Giuliano della Rovere, to the purple (soon to be followed by another four), and poured money and preferment into the laps of relatives. Cardinal Riario quickly devoted himself to dissipation and died of excess in 1474 at the age of 28. Then his brother, Girolamo, dragged the pope into the mire of factional Italian politics and ruined his reputation almost completely. For in 1477, Girolamo and a friend, Francesco de' Pazzi, formed a conspiracy against Lorenzo and Giuliano de' Medici, the virtual rulers of

SIXTUS IV AND ROME

Sixtus IV continued the building and improvements in Rome that his predecessors, particularly Nicholas V, had started. Streets were widened and paved, old houses demolished, sewers cleaned, new roadways constructed, a new bridge (still bearing his name, the Ponte Sisto) thrown over the Tiber, a hospital for foundling children restructured, a new library in the Vatican and new chapels built, the most famous of these being that called after him, the Sistine Chapel, decorated with paintings by Perugino. Sixtus also gave patronage to Botticelli, Pinturicchio, Ghirlandaio, Signorelli and Melozzo da Forli; founded the Sistine choir; established the Vatican archives; and effectively re-founded the Vatican Library, collecting books from all over Europe, and giving money for their upkeep and the salaries of the librarians. Perhaps of all his works designed to promote beauty and learning, this lavish care for the library is his greatest monument.

Melozzo da Forli's fresco Sixtus IV naming Platina Prefect of the Library *(1477). Platina was the second librarian of the Vatican Library under Sixtus IV. He dedicated his* Lives of the Popes *to Sixtus IV.*

The Spanish Inquisition

The word Inquisition simply means 'inquiry'. The institution was started by Gregory IX in 1231 to combat heresy and was originally confined to Germany before being extended further afield. It was closely associated with the Dominicans and the Franciscans. The tribunal had the right to summon persons suspected of heresy, and quickly developed procedures which differed from those commonly used under Roman law. Prosecution of an individual was in the hands of the judge himself; the accused was required by oath to tell the truth; he was not informed of the names of those who had denounced him (to protect witnesses from intimidation by relatives or friends of the accused);

testimony was accepted even from those whom the law might otherwise regard as undesirable, e.g. criminals or excommunicated persons. Meticulous records were kept of all interrogations, and these reveal that for the most part the Inquisitors were actually concerned to elicit the truth. Torture might be used, but there were strict regulations surrounding its application. No Inquisition could inflict the death penalty. Death sentences were the responsibility of the secular authorities to whom obdurate heretics might be handed over so that death might be pronounced and carried out. Penances such as wearing crosses or going on pilgrimage were common, as was confiscation of property. The various Inquisitions were most active during the 13th century. The Spanish

Inquisition, which has attracted an unpleasant reputation, partly through successful adverse propaganda, was created at the end of the 15th century by Sixtus IV, at the request of King Ferdinand of Aragon and Queen Isabella of Castile, to counter the perceived danger to Spanish Catholicism posed by Marranos (converts from Judaism) and Moriscos (converts from Islam). Sixtus IV was later obliged to issue a papal brief (letter) reprimanding the Spanish Inquisitors for abusing official procedures and being over-zealous in their treatment of supposed heretics.

A detail of a 16th-century Spanish painting showing two heretics being tortured and burned, while other heretics, wearing white hats and robes, await their fate.

Florence. Their motives were mixed. Lorenzo in particular was very unpopular in Florence at the time and the Pazzi family had come to the conclusion that he was planning their downfall, whereas Girolamo Riario may simply have had his eye on the Medicis' Tuscan and Florentine estates. The loss of an important ally – Galeazzo Sforza, duke of Milan, stabbed to death as he entered church on 26 December 1476 – made Lorenzo de' Medici somewhat vulnerable, and the murder set a disturbing precedent. Sixtus appears to have turned a blind eye to the machinations of Girolamo, his nephew; and then on 26 April 1478, murderers struck at the Medici brothers while they were hearing mass in the cathedral of Florence. Giuliano was killed; Lorenzo escaped, slightly wounded. How much did the pope really know in advance? Opinion is divided, but it is difficult to believe he was entirely innocent.

The result was war for the rest of his reign: at first with Florence and then, at Girolamo's baneful urgings, with Venice. No advantage came of these hostilities, only revolts in Rome and in the surrounding region. What is more, the constant drain on the treasury raised the spectre of penury for the pope who would follow him. But in 1480 there was a further call to spend, as the Turks invaded and captured Otranto on the Italian mainland. Indulgences were proclaimed throughout Italy and a special war-tax levied. In May 1482, Sultan Mehmet died and by the end of September the Turks had quietly withdrawn. It was a welcome but expensive reprieve.

In the middle of June 1484, Sixtus contracted a fever and in August he was crippled by gout. A peace treaty signed between the various Italian combatants enraged him, as it appeared they had ignored his authority, and full of resentment he died in the evening of 12 August. Certain decisions he took during his pontificate have a lasting resonance. He approved the Feast of the Immaculate Conception of the Virgin, established the Spanish Inquisition and appointed Tomás de Torquemada as its Grand Inquisitor, and increased the privileges of the mendicant orders, particularly the Franciscans and the Dominicans.

Such a reign, dominated by discord, could scarcely have been followed by a peaceful conclave. For a start, Sixtus had increased the number of cardinals by 34, almost all of them worldly-minded individuals who were little suited to their office. First, however, the people of Rome invaded Girolamo's palace and destroyed it. Only the bare walls were left; even the garden was ripped apart. Girolamo's wife rushed to Castel Sant' Angelo, deposed its commanding officer, and proposed holding the fortification until a new pope was elected. The Colonna family stimulated uproar in the city; another leading family, the Orsini, prepared for attack; and civil war loomed while the cardinals assembled and fell to violent dispute. Foremost among the intriguers were the Cardinals Rodrigo Borgia and Giuliano della Rovere, and it took a long time and a plenitude of offers before **Innocent VIII** (1484–1492) emerged as Della

PAPAL NAMES	
INNOCENT VIII	*Elected pope*
Nationality	29 August 1484
Italian, from Genoa	*Age at election*
Date of birth	52
1432	*Died*
Original name	25 July 1492
Giovanni Battista	*Length of pontificate*
Cibò	7 years, 10
Family background	months, 28 days
Son of a Roman	*Notable feature*
senator	His son
Status	Franceschetto
Innocent was the	was married to
father of several	the daughter of
illegitimate children	Lorenzo de' Medici.
before he was	Innocent made
ordained priest	his 13-year-old
Early career	grandson a
Cardinal priest	cardinal

Detail of the monument of Innocent VIII by Pollaiuolo in St Peter's, Rome. Innocent VIII was in such desperate need of money that he had to pawn the papal tiara to a Roman merchant.

16th-century woodcut of a friar preaching to the moors; title-page of *Improbatio Alcorani* (Disproving the Koran). The Muslims were expelled from Granada in 1492. The word 'morisca' quickly became a Spanish technical term for a Muslim who had converted to Christianity.

Rovere's candidate.

Weak, charming and ineffectual, this father of several illegitimate children whom he openly acknowledged once he was pope, allowed himself to be guided by the strong-minded, bellicose della Rovere who had promoted his election only because he himself could not command sufficient votes. Since Innocent had no money, but continued to live as a great prince; and as Rome was riven by the quarrels of the Colonna and Orsini whose supporters daily murdered each other in the street, insolvency and violence were the immediate problems requiring attention. It cannot be said that either received it.

An attempt to raise papal dues from Naples was fiercely resisted there on the grounds that Sixtus IV had released the kingdom from its obligation to pay them. Innocent, prompted by della Rovere, then invited Duke René of Lorraine to come to Naples and assume the crown, and aided those Neapolitan nobles who rebelled against King Ferdinand I of Naples. Della Rovere was despatched to France to arrange an alliance and escort the duke to Italy, but during his absence Innocent impulsively made a bad-tempered peace treaty with Ferdinand of Naples – a meaningless agreement, as the two men were to fall out and be reconciled yet again before the pope's reign was over – and in doing so lost the cardinal's support. Innocent turned to Lorenzo de' Medici, cementing their new friendship with a marriage between one of his bastards and Lorenzo's daughter, and a cardinal's hat for Giovanni, Lorenzo's 14-year-old son.

In this same year, 1489, Innocent tried to address the Turkish problem by entering into negotiations with the sultan, Bayezid II. In return for holding the sultan's brother captive in Rome, Innocent received a large annuity and the gift of a major relic, the lance which was said to have pierced the side of Christ at the crucifixion. In 1490, the pope fell ill, and the vultures, especially one of his sons, gathered to fight for the spoils. The pope managed to throw off his fever, but in 1491 the illness returned and Innocent lingered upon his death-bed for over a year. While he was ill he received the news that in January 1492 the Spanish sovereigns, Ferdinand of Aragon and Isabella of Castile, had expelled their Muslim neighbours from Granada, thereby absorbing that kingdom into their own and ending an episode in Spanish history which had begun in the 8th century, more than 700 years before.

Throughout June and July the pope's health fluctuated. On 25 July, however, after a long and painful struggle, he finally died late in the evening, just a week before Columbus set sail on his voyage to the west.

Alexander VI
1492–1503

Pius III
1503

Julius II
1503–1513

Leo X
1513–1521

Hadrian VI
1522–1523

Clement VII
1523–1534

Paul III
1534–1549

Julius III
1550–1555

Marcellus II
1555

Paul IV
1555–1559

Pius IV
1559–1565

Pius V
1566–1572

Gregory XIII
1572–1585

Sixtus V
1585–1590

Urban VII
1590

Gregory XIV
1590–1591

Innocent IX
1591

Clement VIII
1592–1605

Leo XI
1605

Paul V
1605–1621

Gregory XV
1621–1623

Urban VIII
1623–1644

Innocent X
1644–1655

Alexander VII
1655–1667

Clement IX
1667–1669

Clement X
1670–1676

Innocent XI
1676–1689

Alexander VIII
1689–1691

Innocent XII
1691–1700

Clement XI
1700–1721

Innocent XIII
1721–1724

Benedict XIII
1724–1730

Clement XII
1730–1740

Benedict XIV
1740–1758

Clement XIII
1758–1769

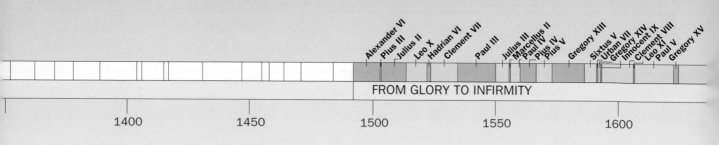

FROM GLORY TO INFIRMITY

1400   1450   1500   1550   1600

Julius II

Paul III

Gregory XV

Innocent X

FROM GLORY TO INFIRMITY
AD 1492–1769

The high point of the Church's temporal power in the 16th century coincided, unsurprisingly, with its lowest point of spiritual prestige. Excess – whether in personal behaviour at the papal court, or in the avid search for secular sway, or in the disbursement of ecclesiastical treasure upon grandiose artistic endeavours – was the watchword. Even without the challenge thrown down by Protestant reformers, the popes knew that sweeping amendment must be made. Stunned at first by the outbreak of retreat from traditional teaching and practice, the Church quickly rallied and produced its Counter-Reformation, renewing itself in the process. Teresa of Avila, reformer of the Carmelites, and Ignatius of Loyola, founder of the Society of Jesus (Jesuits), are the foremost examples of this transforming adjustment in the Church.

Not that popes forswore politics. As major figures in the rapidly expanding world, they could scarcely have avoided them. Nor did the vicious religious wars of 17th-century Europe allow them to retire from worldly fray. But, as that century wore on, the newly enlarged and ambitious France of Louis XIV emerged to dominate the Western continent, and the popes gradually faded from view. This process continued. There hangs about the popes of the 18th century a sense of growing impotence. As the world and the Church diverged to go their increasingly separate ways, the papacy seemed hesitant, unwilling quite to relinquish its hold on secular affairs, but unable any longer to behave as a purely temporal power.

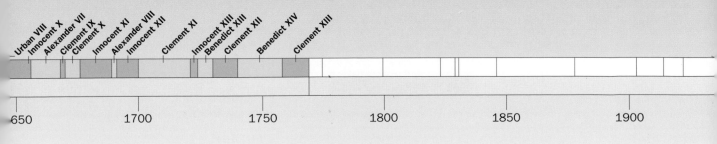

Urban VIII Innocent X Alexander VII Clement IX Clement X Innocent XI Alexander VIII Innocent XII Clement XI Innocent XIII Benedict XIII Clement XII Benedict XIV Clement XIII

650   1700   1750   1800   1850   1900

Alexander VI
1492–1503

Pius III
1503

(*Right*) Detail of a stucco relief showing bulls adoring Alexander VI, in the Borgia Apartments of the Vatican. This portrait of the new pope by Bernardino Pinturicchio (*c.* 1454–1513) may be compared with the same artist's painted depiction in *The Resurrection*, shown on p. 162.

ALEXANDER VI	
Nationality Spanish, from Játiva	perhaps of malaria, perhaps of poison
Date of birth 1 January 1431	*Length of pontificate* 11 years, 7 days
Original name Rodrigo de Borja y Borja	*Notable features* Alexander had two known mistresses, Vanozza dei Catanei and Giulia Farnese, as well as other unnamed women. He fathered nine children: Pedro Luis, Isabella, Girolama, Giovanni, Rodrigo, Cesare, Juan, Lucrezia and Jofré
Family background Alexander was the nephew of Pope Callistus III	
Early career Cardinal bishop, papal legate	
Elected pope 11 August 1492	
Age at election 61	
Died 18 August 1503,	

ALEXANDER VI

He [Alexander VI] is tall, in complexion neither fair nor dark; his eyes are black, his mouth somewhat full. His health is splendid and he has a marvellous power of enduring all sorts of fatigue. He is singularly eloquent and is gifted with an innate good breeding which never forsakes him.

F. Gregorovius *Lucrezia Borgia, 8*

In the year which is inextricably associated with Columbus, Rodrigo de Borja (Borgia) was elected pope and took the symbolically triumphalist name **Alexander VI** (1492–1503). He was 61 when he became pontiff and had had a long and distinguished career in the Church – not, perhaps, surprising when one considers that one of his uncles was Pope Callistus III. At the age of 25, Rodrigo became a cardinal and the following year, vice-chancellor of the Holy See, an office which enabled him to amass extraordinary wealth by accumulating bishoprics and other benefices, but which also kept him in close touch with those people in Rome who were and would be of most use in furthering his ambitions. Rodrigo was vice-chancellor for 35 years and scarcely missed a meeting of the curia,

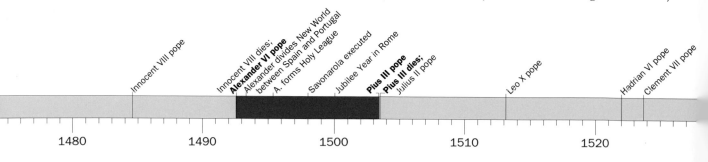

Innocent VIII pope

Innocent VIII dies; **Alexander VI pope**
Alexander divides New World between Spain and Portugal
A. forms Holy League

Savonarola executed

Jubilee Year in Rome

Pius III pope
Pius III dies;
Julius II pope

Leo X pope

Hadrian VI pope
Clement VII pope

1480   1490   1500   1510   1520

the consistory (the papal senate), during that time.

But he did not owe his success merely to family patronage and his network of connections. He was a man of remarkable abilities, and when Callistus died the next four popes also recognized his qualities and used him on several important affairs of ecclesiastical state.

The situation on the eve of the conclave which elected him pope was as follows. Cardinal della Rovere (later Julius II), a nephew of Pope Sixtus IV, was a possible candidate. He enjoyed the support of Charles VIII of France who paid large sums of money to draw cardinals to della Rovere's cause. Cardinal della Porta and Cardinal Sforza were two other candidates, favoured by Milan, and initially benefited from the determination of many Italian cardinals not to elect a foreigner – Rodrigo, the fourth candidate, had been born in Spain. But Rodrigo was very rich and had not accumulated experience for nothing. Money fell like rain and on the fourth day of the conclave Rodrigo needed just a single vote to make him pope. He got it from the 96-year-old patriarch of Venice, whose clouded faculties were pierced at just the right moment to swing the election. The papacy had been bought by the Borgia candidate.

Nevertheless, the election proved to be popular both in Rome and abroad and the coronation on 26 August 1492 was unusually splendid although, because of the heat and fatigue, the new pope fainted twice.

The first two years of his reign were full of diplomatic difficulties. The Papal States were seething with intrigue; the Spanish king of Naples, Ferdinand I, was at odds with the pope because Alexander had begun to draw closer to Charles VIII of France, who was himself raising a family claim to the throne of Naples; the menace of a growing Turkish empire was felt more nervously year by year; and in Rome Cardinals della Rovere and Sforza were locked in virulent hatred. Alexander tried to cope with these problems by forming a 'League of St Mark' which bound Milan and Venice to the papacy; by marrying two of his sons, one to Spain and the other to Naples; by receiving the Turkish ambassador in great state and forming what appeared to be a tacit alliance with the sultan; and by allowing himself to be bribed into amity with Cardinal della Rovere. The pontificate had thus begun well. Indeed, Alexander even managed to intervene in the discovery of the New World; for following the voyage of Columbus, Spanish and Portuguese navigators were eager to exert their claims to the new lands and Alexander was asked to arbitrate. He drew a line on the map which distinctly favoured Spain, and thus

The 'Cantino' planisphere (1502), an early sea chart showing the Tordesillas line which divided the New World between the Portugese – to the east of the line – and the Spanish – to the west of the line (Biblioteca Estense, Modena). After Columbus returned from his famous voyage to the New World in 1492, Portugal and Spain had quarrelled over the new lands and had appealed to Alexander VI to arbitrate their claims. In 1493, the pope divided the new-found lands by drawing a line on the map. In 1494, however, in the Treaty of Tordesillas, this line was moved a further 270 leagues to the west. Knowledge of the shape of the New World was limited at this time, hence the somewhat strange coastline of the South American landmass.

THE CHILDREN AND MISTRESSES OF ALEXANDER VI

Alexander had six sons and three daughters, the offspring of several women. The mothers of Pedro Luis (c.1462–1488), Isabella (c. 1467–1541), Girolama (c. 1469–1483), Giovanni (1498–c. 1548) and Rodrigo (born 1503) are unknown, but the children were all awarded positions of power or advantageous marriages thanks to their father's prominent status. His two most famous children, Cesare and Lucrezia, were the offspring of Vanozza dei Catanei. She and Alexander began their affair in 1473, a comfortable arrangement which

(Above) The Borgia family emblem from the ceiling of the Borgia Apartments in the Vatican.

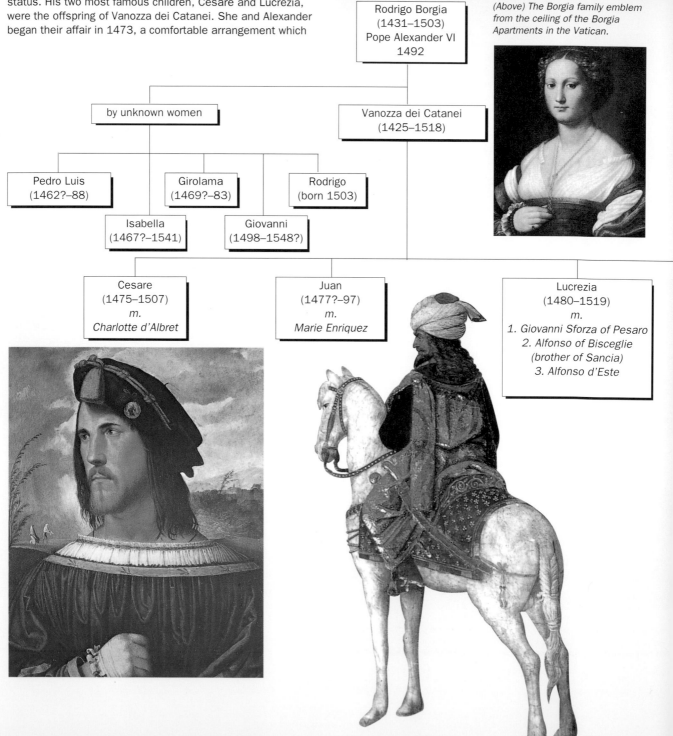

Rodrigo Borgia
(1431–1503)
Pope Alexander VI
1492

by unknown women

Vanozza dei Catanei
(1425–1518)

Pedro Luis
(1462?–88)

Girolama
(1469?–83)

Rodrigo
(born 1503)

Isabella
(1467?–1541)

Giovanni
(1498–1548?)

Cesare
(1475–1507)
m.
Charlotte d'Albret

Juan
(1477?–97)
m.
Marie Enriquez

Lucrezia
(1480–1519)
m.
1. *Giovanni Sforza of Pesaro*
2. *Alfonso of Bisceglie (brother of Sancia)*
3. *Alfonso d'Este*

lasted for about 10 years. Cesare was born in 1475 and Lucrezia in 1480. There were two other children of the union, both boys, Juan – who became the duke of Gandia and captain-general of the papal armies – and Jofré – who became Prince of Squillace.

Cesare benefited immensely from his father's position. At 18 he was invested with several bishoprics and at 19 became a cardinal. In 1498, however, the pope released him from this pseudo-priestly status in order that he might take more freely to war and diplomacy, not to mention marriage. Cesare then became in succession duke of Valentinois and duke of Romagna, and also married one of the most beautiful princesses in France, Charlotte d'Albret, the French king's cousin, only to abandon her four months later. Cesare's career was brilliant but unsavoury. He was master of the Papal States and virtual ruler of the Church after his father. He was a great Renaissance prince, with all that that suggests, and Machiavelli praised him to the skies for his abilities and attainments. But these were accompanied by ruthlessness, cruelty and the strong suspicion of murder. He was rumoured, for example, to have had his brother Juan's throat cut, and the mystery of this murder has never been solved. Certainly the duke of Bisceglie was strangled on Cesare's instructions, and it was well known that he employed a chemist, Sebastian Pinzon, who was an expert in all kinds of poison.

Lucrezia was described by contemporaries as being of medium height and graceful carriage, with a long face, long golden hair, a rather large mouth, wonderfully white teeth, and a disposition both charming and invariably cheerful. Her reputation has suffered by association with those of her father and brother, and legend has it that she was a murderous poisoner, and involved in incestuous affairs with Cesare and her father, but in fact she was quite unlike either. She was married three times and each time unhappily. Pope Alexander forcibly and fraudulently divorced her from her first husband; Cesare had her second one murdered, and from her third, the duke of Ferrara, she was periodically and miserably estranged.

But the people of Ferrara grew to love her for her piety and good works, and when she died in 1519 she had managed to win her husband's affection and the esteem of all those who knew her.

(Right) The most beautiful of Alexander's mistresses was Giulia Farnese, only 15 when she yielded to Alexander's passion (Pinacoteca Vaticana).

```
        Jofré
     (1481?–1518?)
          m.
   1. Sancia of Aragon
   2. Maria de Mila
```

(Above) Portrait possibly of Lucrezia Borgia (Städelsches Kunstinstitut, Frankfurt). She certainly looks similar to a later portrait by the same artist, Bartolomeo Veneto, which is said to show a plumper Lucrezia as duchess of Ferrara.

(Opposite, centre) A portrait of a woman presumed to be Vanozza dei Catanei, one of Alexander VI's long-standing mistresses. She was already married to a lawyer when Alexander (still Rodrigo Borgia) met her (Galleria Borghese, Rome).

(Opposite, far left) Portrait by Giorgione of Cesare Borgia (Galleria Carrara, Bergamo), Alexander's most famous and ruthless son, who was described by the Venetian ambassador as a remarkably handsome man, tall and well built.

(Opposite, left) Detail of Pinturicchio's fresco Disputation of St Catherine from the Borgia Apartments thought to show Alexander's son, Juan, who gained an unfortunate reputation in Spain for licentiousness and arrogance.

(This page, left) Sancia and Jofré are thought to have been the models for this couple in Pinturicchio's Disputation of St Catherine.

Relief showing the Holy Roman emperor, Maximilian I (Tyroler Landesmuseum, Innsbruck). Maximilian formed a Holy League with Venice, Spain and the pope in 1495, ostensibly to defend Christendom from the menace of the Turk, but in reality to curb King Charles VIII of France's ever-encroaching territorial ambitions.

pointed the way for subsequent papal interest in the Americas and the missionary activities there of succeeding monks and friars.

In January 1494, however, the king of Naples died. He had a son, Alfonso, who was recognized and then crowned by the pope in the face of opposition from Cardinal della Rovere and other cardinals who supported Charles VIII. With their encouragement, Charles invaded Italy, threatening to summon a general council of the Church and have the pope deposed. Alexander, for his part, contacted the Turkish sultan and brandished him as a potent threat of his own. Much of all this, it has to be said, was theatrical bellicosity rather than a genuine attempt to overthrow the pope. What, after all, would Charles gain from substituting the formidable della Rovere or the devious Sforza for a vulnerable Borgia? The aim of the invasion was to play upon Alexander's fears and so squeeze concessions from him. The bullying worked to a certain extent. Nevertheless, in March 1495 a treaty was concluded between Venice, Spain, the Holy Roman emperor and the pope, ostensibly for the defence of Christendom against the Turks, but partly to menace Charles from the rear. Charles took the point and withdrew and Alexander could breathe again.

Such external rancour, however, was not the pope's only problem. In Florence he faced a violent Dominican friar filled with reforming passion, Girolamo Savonarola (1452–1498). Savonarola had quickly gained ascendancy from his pulpit whence he prophesied doom for the Church, which he denounced as corrupt, and for the Florentine government, which he disparaged as self-seeking and venal. When Charles VIII invaded Italy Savonarola hailed him as 'the Sword of God' come to cleanse the Church and fulfil his own prophecies; and when Savonarola prevented Florence from joining Alexander's defensive league, it was clear that he

Italian woodcut from the *Compendio di Revelatione* (1495) showing Girolamo Savonarola preaching to the masses in Florence. His preaching was so powerful that a contemporary who was present duing one of his sermons says he felt his hair stand on end. The congregation wept and left the cathedral in silence. Savonarola denounced the immorality of Italy and welcomed the French as a means of delivering Italy from her sins.

16th-century painting showing the execution of Savonarola and his companions in the Piazza della Signoria (Museo di San Marco, Florence). When the pyre was lit, a wind blew the flames aside and people cried out, 'Miracles, miracles!' Then youths started throwing stones.

and the pope were going to come into conflict.

Alexander began in July 1495 by inviting Savonarola to come to Rome to explain how it was he claimed to be receiving revelations from God. Savonarola politely refused on the spurious grounds of ill health and Florence's need of his continued presence. But by November the French army had retreated. The pope then openly denounced Savonarola's claims to divine revelation and suspended him from preaching. Savonarola replied with a letter of submission. Nevertheless, after a few months of silence he started to preach again, his language against Rome and the curia increasingly violent. The pope was unwilling to offend Florence by further precipitate action, as he still wanted to draw her into his international treaty, and so matters continued in this unsatisfactory state until November 1496 when a change in the organization of the Dominican friaries in Tuscany, ordered by the pope, brought protests

(*Right*) A Lutheran woodcut with a fold-up caricature of Alexander VI. The one half says 'Alexander VI, supreme pontiff', and the other shows him as the Devil saying 'I am the pope'.

(*Left*) Alexander VI, a detail of *The Resurrection* by Pinturicchio, in the Borgia Apartments in the Vatican. It was painted in 1492/5 and shows the pope aged 61 at the beginning of his pontificate.

and disobedience from the community in Florence. Defiance of papal authority could have only one result, of course, and Savonarola was duly excommunicated on 18 June 1497. Plague in the city then kept him quiet all summer. Florentine politicians, made nervous by papal wrath, restrained him for the rest of the year.

In February 1498, however, Savonarola began to preach again. The city, fearful that Alexander would turn the full power of papal authority against it, begged Savonarola to cease, and he did so. Nevertheless, he wrote letters to the ruling kings and princes of Europe, urging them to summon a general council and have the pope deposed. But then one of his closest disciples accepted a challenge from a Franciscan that they should enter a blazing pyre to see which of them God would protect. The ordeal was arranged, a huge crowd gathered to witness the miracle, and the disciple's courage failed. At once there was a riot, and Savonarola's hold over the Florentines disappeared. In consequence it was easy to arrest him. He was tortured, put on trial, condemned to death, hanged and his body was afterwards burned in a public square.

One of the things to which Savonarola had particularly objected was art, or rather the introduction of secular themes and sensuality into religious pictures. 'You trick out the Mother of God in the frippery of a prostitute', he thundered, 'and fill the churches with vanities.' Another was luxuriousness and immodesty of dress and behaviour. He wanted gam-

17th-century painting of the fortress of Imola (Vatican Library). Cesare attacked it in 1499 because it was controlled by the Sforza family – enemies of Louis XII of France now related to Cesare through marriage. The twin town of Forlì was defended by Caterina Sforza who put on armour to give heart to the town's inhabitants. Cesare's many military conquests were partly funded by Alexander's holding of a Jubilee Year in 1500 which brought a massive influx of pilgrims and income to Rome.

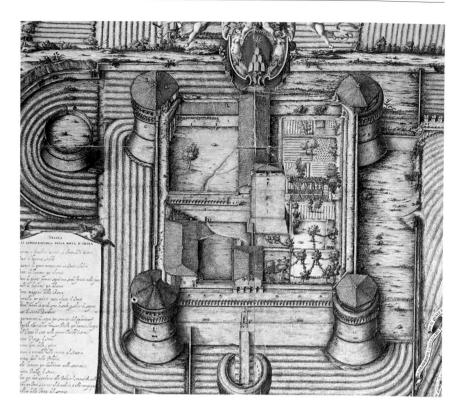

THE DEATH OF ALEXANDER VI

A legend about Alexander's death:

Cardinal Arian da Corneto received notice that the pope ... wished to come and dine with him at his vineyard and that His Holiness would bring dinner with him. The cardinal suspected that this invitation had been extended for the purpose of ending his life by poison ...

So the cardinal bribed the pope's personal servant to save him. The pope's plan had been to offer the cardinal a box of poisoned confectionary, while he himself ate safe sweetmeats from another box. The servant agreed to switch boxes.

Then His Holiness, trusting his servant, concluded there was no poison in his and ate from it heartily, while the cardinal ate from the other which the pope thought was poisoned, but which was not. At the time the poison usually started to work, His Holiness started to feel its effects, and in consequence died.

Marino Sanuto *I Diarii*

Another source described Alexander's body:

The face was very dark, the colour of a dirty rag or a mulberry, and was covered all over with bruise-coloured marks. The nose was swollen; the tongue had bent over in the mouth, completely double, and was pushing out the lips which were, themselves, swollen. The mouth was open and so ghastly that people who saw it said they had never seen anything like it before.

Johann Burchard *Liber Notarum*

blers in Florence to be tortured and blasphemers to have their tongues run through with skewers. Everyone was to spy on everyone else, and his inquisitors did not hesitate to raid private houses and seize any objects of which they disapproved – cards, perfumes, mirrors, copies of poems – which were then taken away and burned. It is scarcely surprising, therefore, that he and Pope Alexander engaged in bitter contest. For Alexander is perhaps the most notorious example of corruption among the Renaissance popes, as his numerous mistresses and illegitimate offspring attest.

For Pope Alexander, 1500 was a significant year. He had proclaimed it a Jubilee or Holy Year, during which an enormous influx of pilgrims could be expected to come to Rome, seeking the extra indulgences attached to their visit during such a period, and offering large sums of money to swell the papal coffers. Alexander VI was the first pope to create a special 'Holy Door' in St Peter's, which would be opened at the start of the Jubilee and closed at its end, a custom which is still observed. The Jubilee of 1500 was certainly a success in one way, for it helped to finance the military requirements of Alexander's son, Cesare; but it also had the unfortunate effect of letting large numbers of people see at first hand the gross wealth and corruption which was corroding the Holy City, and this in turn fed disillusion and discontent when the pilgrims returned to their native cities and villages.

On 11 August 1503, the anniversary of his election as pope, Alexander missed the usual celebration in St Peter's. He had a fever, and despite –

PIUS III	
Nationality Italian, from Siena	Cardinal deacon, papal legate
Date of birth 1439	*Elected pope* 22 September 1503
Original name Francesco Todeschini	*Age at election* 72
Family background Pius was a nephew of Pope Pius II	*Died* 18 October 1503
Early career	*Length of pontificate* 27 days

actually it would be truer to say because of – the attentions of his doctors, within a week he was dead. The weather was very hot and his body quickly decayed. While it lay in the Sistine Chapel, the face turned a mulberry colour and broke out in blackish-blue spots, and the lips swelled to grotesque proportions. When at last it was removed for burial, the officials discovered that the coffin had been made too small. So the pope's body was rolled up in an old carpet, and shoved and pushed and punched until it fitted. It was a repulsive but symbolic end to a reign which had been both shocking and arrogant.

PIUS III

The disasters of the recent times, the ravaged face of our mother the Church ... are still in front of my eyes.... The compassion of God and the kindness of our Saviour gave you to us as an unexpected pontiff whose very great abilities, learning, culture, religious nurture and life lived in every virtue right up to the present day.

Letter from the bishop of Arezzo to Pius III, 28 September 1503

Another papal nephew succeeded Alexander, this time a relative of Pius II, who probably for that reason took the name **Pius III** (1503). He had had, as one might expect, a dazzling career – archbishop of Siena and cardinal at the age of 21, papal legate to Germany under Paul II and to France under Alexander VI – but in contrast with many high-placed clerics of his day, he was a man of personal integrity. He had, for example, refused to be bribed to vote for Rodrigo Borgia at the conclave of 1492.

So in September 1503 he was the ideal compromise candidate. For as usual the cardinals were torn by conflicting national interests. King Ferdinand of Spain was keen to have another Spanish pope, but reaction against Alexander had been very strong, so the Spanish cause was doomed from the start. Cardinal della Rovere was regarded as a partisan of France: a Frenchman or a French candidate, it was thought, might well transfer the papacy to France again and nobody wanted a repetition of Avignon. Nevertheless, della Rovere fully expected to be elected. The Italian cardinals were divided amongst themselves; so that pointed the way to eventual compromise. The floating Spanish votes, of course, could have settled the matter, but in fact initially there was stalemate and the conclave took a week to make up its mind. In the end, however, a 64-year-old invalid broke the deadlock.

Pius III was eager to reform the manifest abuses of the Church and indeed seemed to be the very man for the task. He began by seeking to convene a general council of the Church, drew up regulations for the Church's better administration, and reduced considerably his own expenditure. But his health, not good for many years, began rapidly to decline and by 18 October 1503 he was dead. Everyone lamented his passing. He had provided a temperate interval between the recent unwholesome dog-days and the storms which were about to burst.

The tomb of Pius III. His was the last tomb to be erected in old St Peter's, and when Julius II demolished the basilica , it was removed to Sant' Andrea della Valle where it now stands opposite that of his uncle, Pius II. A somewhat overelaborate structure, it was designed by Nicolo della Guardia and Pietro da Todi.

Julius II
1503–1513

Raphael may have painted his portrait of Julius II from a death mask. Certainly, he shows the pope old, sick and near his end. The handkerchief in his hand is an ancient Roman symbol of authority. His beard, grown in 1510 in fulfilment of a vow that he would not shave until the French left Italy, represents a deep and bitter disappointment of the pontificate. The image thus presented is a far cry from the arrogant warrior-pope of his early years (Uffizi Gallery, Florence).

Pope Julius II's tiara. The papal headdress began with only one coronet. Boniface VIII added a second, and a third was added some time later. It was Julius II who turned the tiara into a richly jewelled work of art (British Museum).

[Julius arrives at the gates of Heaven and is accosted by St Peter who pretends not to recognize him.]

Peter: *The silver key is vaguely familiar, but it is very different from those which Christ, the true shepherd of the Church, entrusted to me long ago. As for that sumptuous crown of yours, why on earth should I recognize it? No barbarian tyrant ever dared wear such a thing as that, let alone anyone trying to get in here. I am certainly not impressed by the robe, because I always scorned gold and jewels …*

Julius: *Stop this nonsense, if you know what is good for you. For your information, I am Julius … Pontifex Maximus [supreme pontiff].*

From *Julius Exclusus* (1517/18), probably by Erasmus

Giuliano della Rovere, who had been aching for the papacy, now finally achieved it. There is a saying that 'he who enters a conclave as pope comes out as cardinal', a warning to the over-confident. Della Rovere seemed to have no doubts, however, that this time he would win. It was remarkable bravado by someone who knew he was both hated and feared by most of the electors, but after the shortest conclave

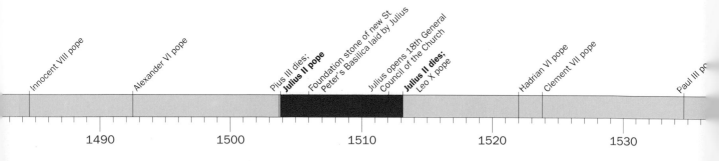

Innocent VIII pope
Alexander VI pope
Pius III dies; **Julius II pope**
Foundation stone of new St Peter's Basilica laid by Julius
Julius opens 18th General Council of the Church
Julius II dies; Leo X pope
Hadrian VI pope
Clement VII pope
Paul III po

1490   1500   1510   1520   1530

JULIUS II

Nationality	*Age at election*
Italian, from	50
Albissola	*Died*
Date of birth	21 February 1513
5 December 1453	*Length of pontificate*
Original name	9 years, 3 months,
Giuliano della	20 days
Rovere	*Notable feature*
Family background	Julius had an
Humble, but he was	acknowledged
the nephew of	daughter, Felice,
Sixtus IV	and may have had
Early career	other children. He
Cardinal priest,	was the patron of
papal legate	Michelangelo,
Elected pope	Bramante, and
1 November 1503	Raphael

One of Raphael's frescoes for the Stanza della Segnatura in the Vatican, *c.* 1510; the triumph of Christianity over pagan thought. The figure in the papal tiara left of the altar is probably Gregory the Great, while on the right Innocent III is seated and Sixtus IV, Julius II's uncle, stands nearer the foreground.

hitherto convened – it lasted a few hours only – his papacy was announced.

Julius II (1503–1513) was the third papal nephew in succession to become supreme pontiff, his uncle being Sixtus IV. Julius was a Franciscan and his uncle had appointed him cardinal at the age of only 18. Another nephew, Pietro Riario, was made a cardinal at the same time and the two men grew up to be rivals and enemies. But perhaps fortunately for della Rovere, Cardinal Riario was exceptionally dissipated and his excesses killed him before he could do much damage to his cousin's career. That career included a period of being papal legate in France for Sixtus IV, and during Innocent VIII's pontificate della Rovere played a major role in papal government. Alexander VI, however, hated him and the cardinal thought it prudent to seek refuge in France. There he encouraged Charles VIII to pursue his claim to the throne of Naples, and actually accompanied the king during his invasion of Italy. But his contacts and alliances with many of the most powerful Italian families made della Rovere too significant to keep at arm's length, and so Pope

In 1505, Julius II commissioned Bramante to build the Belvedere courtyard (*right*). It was supposed to connect the Vatican with the Belvedere, a villa built by Innocent VIII. The original plan was on a grandiose scale and was much altered later on.

He [Julius II] has been informed that Princess Catherine of Spain had contracted a marriage with Arthur, late prince of Wales, and that this marriage has, perhaps, been consummated. Notwithstanding this, he authorizes, in his quality of the head of the Church, Henry, prince of Wales, and Princess Catherine, to contract a lawful marriage. Given at Rome on 26 December 1503.

Papal dispensation for the marriage of Catherine of Aragon and Henry, later Henry VIII of England

Alexander permitted himself to enter a formal reconciliation with the cardinal. A sign of this apparent truce was della Rovere's appointment to negotiate Cesare Borgia's marriage to a French princess.

Alexander left Julius a difficult legacy. Italy had been wracked by the dissension over who was the rightful heir to the throne of Naples, and Alexander's attempts to pacify France after her invasion scarcely improved matters. His ambition to turn the Papal States into a private fiefdom of the Borgia family set the rest of Italy at odds with the papacy, and his cynical sale of offices to raise cash for Cesare's armies did the Church's reputation immense harm. Pope Julius's response to these problems was largely to go to war. Cesare was driven out of Italy; France and Germany became allies; whole states and cities were restored to papal control, Julius himself in full armour leading the troops; and Venice was forced to bow to the papal will. Then Julius, deciding that France was too dangerous to be allowed to remain in control of northern Italy, did a volte-face. He made peace with Venice, wooed Spain by giving Naples to the Spanish candidate, and attacked cities friendly to the French king, Louis XII. Louis responded by holding a Church synod and calling for Julius's deposition. Julius, in turn, summoned a general council and formed another Holy League to defend the papacy. Meanwhile, Fortune smiled on papal arms and the French were obliged to leave Italy altogether. All this cost money, of course, and Julius pared and saved and cut corners in an effort to pay his way. He was very successful and actually left a full treasury after inheriting an empty one. Nevertheless, corruption had not been banished.

Julius was a great patron of the arts. Michelangelo, Bramante and Raphael all benefited from his interest and commissions: Michelangelo most famously with the decoration of the Sistine chapel, the dome of the new St Peter's and Pope Julius's sepulchral monument; Bramante with the design for St Peter's and the Belvedere courtyard in the Vatican; and Raphael with his frescoes for the pope's new apart-

INDULGENCES

After confessing your sins to a priest and receiving absolution and advice, you are given a punishment which may vary considerably in its severity. But you may be let off this punishment, should the Church through the pope or some other priest decide that this is appropriate. Such a remission of punishment is known as an indulgence. The indulgence may be in whole (plenary) or in part (partial). The practice of granting indulgences goes back to the earliest days of the Church. From the 9th century onwards, indulgences were often granted in the form of a written formula: hence the word indulgence can also refer to the document which contains the words of remission. These indulgences can be applied to the dead as well as to the living, and the first authentic example of this comes from the reign of Sixtus IV in 1476. Abuse of indulgences consists of selling them. This became a common practice despite regular condemnation by councils of the Church, and provided Luther with the occasion to condemn not only the abuse but also the doctrine itself. The right of the Church to grant indulgences, however, was reaffirmed by the Council of Trent in 1567.

Indulgences are still bestowed by the Church today, and at the beginning of each pontificate the new pope publishes a list of the Apostolic indulgences that he intends to grant.

ments, especially the room which may have served as Julius's library. To pay for the rebuilding of St Peter's in particular, the pope arranged for a massive sale of indulgences, a marketing of spiritual goods which subsequently provided ample fuel for the fiery censures of the Protestant reformers.

In May 1512, Julius opened the 18th General Council of the Church. It had a limited agenda, but its protracted sessions went on well into the following pontificate, closing only a matter of months before Luther threw down his challenge to the Church's teaching on indulgences. By early January 1513, Pope Julius's health began to wane. He was feverish. On 16 February, the general council agreed to renew one of his earlier decrees against simony in papal elections. On 21 February, he died. People's opinions about him proved to be divided. On the one hand they nicknamed him Julius the Terrible, remembering his short temper, his impetuousness, his eagerness for war. On the other, he was acknowledged to be a man of a prudent and serious-minded disposition, a great patron of the arts, and the prince who delivered Italy from foreign domination. All in all the balance swung in his favour.

Michelangelo was commissioned by Julius II to design his tomb in March 1505. After many vicissitudes, it was not completed until 1545 – 32 years after Julius's death – only the figure of Moses (centre foreground) being by Michelangelo. The pope can be seen reclining in the centre of the picture. The monument was finally erected, not in St Peter's, but in San Pietro in Vincoli of which Julius had been cardinal-priest.

THE NEW ST PETER'S BASILICA

He built this absolutely splendid church which may be considered the equal, not of the lesser stars, but of the sun itself. He places it, he said, over the very tomb of St Peter, the Apostle who described the glory of God. Bramante, the principal architect of the period employed by Julius ... tried to persuade [the pope] to move the Apostle's tomb to a more convenient part of the church.... Julius told him he could not and said repeatedly that the shrines must remain where they were, and forbade him to move what should not be moved.

Egidio de Viterbo *History*, folio 245

Donato Bramante was one of the leading architects of the Renaissance in Italy. From *c.* 1480 he worked in Milan, and used a close study of Roman ruins to improve his building techniques. In 1499, he came to Rome where the patronage of Julius II put him in command of the greatest and most daring commission of the age – the rebuilding of St Peter's Basilica. Like Leonardo da Vinci, Bramante was fascinated by the power of geometrical shapes to generate other geometrical shapes, and this can be seen in his scheme for St Peter's which is basically that of a large Greek cross, each arm of which ends in an apse containing a chapel. Within the inside angles formed by the cross are other smaller Greek crosses containing further, smaller chapels, and so forth. Thus we can see in his work the techniques of ancient Rome renewed but transformed by his own personal vision – a pattern of the Renaissance as a whole. He was working on St Peter's from 1505 until his death in 1514 when Raphael, perhaps more famous as a painter, was appointed official architect. Bramante died well before his design had been realized and Raphael planned several crucial modifications. Then when he died, more changes were made by Sangallo, the next architect, until at last the building was ready for its famous dome designed by Michelangelo.

(Above) Maarten van Heemskerck came to Rome probably in the summer of 1532 and stayed there for about three years, compiling a portfolio of paintings and pen drawings of things in the city. Here we see the new basilica under construction according to Bramante's second, modified design. On the right is the choir of Nicholas V and, on the far left, part of the nave of old St Peter's awaiting demolition (Gabinetto dei Disegni e delle Stampe, Florence).

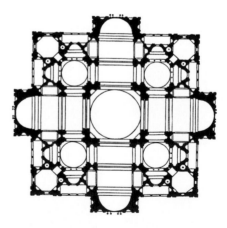

(Above) Cristoforo Caradosso (1452–1527) produced this foundation medal for St Peter's in 1506. Twelve of them were buried, along with the foundation stone, in the base of the first pier on 18 April. The reverse here shows what is almost certainly the exterior of St Peter's according to Bramante's first design. Urged on by Julius II's impatience to see tangible results, Bramante made 'an infinite number of drawings', as Vasari says, and modified his first conception. It was his second general plan which he started to build and which received later amendments from those architects who followed him. Caradosso's medal, therefore, is important and rare evidence of Bramante's original intentions.

(Above) One of Bramante's early plans for the design of the new basilica. Bramante frequently altered his design. His first project was rejected by Julius II, and a second plan also fell by the wayside.

Michelangelo was over 70 when he was appointed to supervise the work on St Peter's by Paul III at the beginning of 1547. He made numerous changes to Raphael's design, basically returning to Bramante's original intention, and constructed a plan for an immense hemispherical dome to crown the whole structure. Giacomo della Porta, his assistant and successor, then altered the profile into an ellipsoid shape which is the one we see today (right).

Leo X
1513–1521

Hadrian VI
1522–1523

Clement VII
1523–1534

Paul III
1534–1549

Julius III
1550–1555

Marcellus II
1555

Paul IV
1555–1559

Pius IV
1559–1565

Pius V
1566–1572

Gregory XIII
1572–1585

Sixtus V
1585–1590

Urban VII
1590

Gregory XIV
1590–1591

Innocent IX
1591

Clement VIII
1592–1605

PAPAL NAMES

LEO X
Nationality
  Italian, from
  Florence
Date of birth
  11 December
  1475
Original name
  Giovanni de' Medici
Family background
  Aristocratic; second
  son of Lorenzo de'
  Medici
Early career
  Cardinal deacon at
  the age of 13

Elected pope
  11 March 1513
Age at election
  37
Died
  1 December 1521
Length of pontificate
  8 years, 8 months,
  22 days
Notable features
  Leo was very well
  educated by leading
  scholars of the day.
  After 1512 he was
  the effective ruler of
  Florence

He [Leo X] was taller than average and bloated rather than fat, although his limbs were attractively proportioned and his legs rounded and straight. His hands were white, well shaped, and exceptionally beautiful. But his head was very large and out of proportion with the rest of his body, although he carried this off with dignity.... His fat cheeks and protruding, rolling eyes deprived his face of charm. They were weak, too, and he had to hold things up quite close to them if he wanted to see properly.

Paolo Giovio *Vita Leonis X*, Book 4

Following such a pope as Julius II might have been a daunting task for anyone except **Leo X** (1513–1521). He was the second son of Lorenzo de' Medici known as 'The Magnificent', virtual ruler of Florence during its most dazzling Renaissance years, and his parentage thus guaranteed he would be given a remarkable education. Marsilio Ficino, Angelo Poliziano and Pico della Mirandola were his tutors, a group which, according to Voltaire, 'was perhaps superior to that of the boasted sages of Greece'. During his youth, Leo travelled widely in France, Germany and Holland and on his return to Rome in 1500 drank deeply of literature, music and the arts. The Medici had lost control of Florence in 1494,

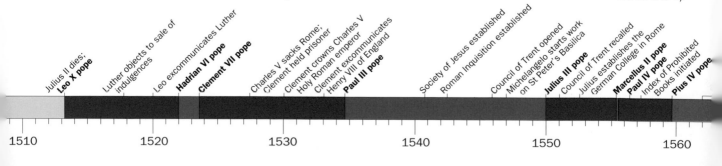

Julius II dies; **Leo X pope** | Luther objects to sale of indulgences | Leo excommunicates Luther **Hadrian VI pope** **Clement VII pope** | Charles V sacks Rome; Clement held prisoner Clement crowns Charles V Holy Roman emperor Clement excommunicates Henry VIII of England **Paul III pope** | Society of Jesus established Roman Inquisition established | Council of Trent opened Michelangelo starts work on St Peter's Basilica **Julius III pope** Council of Trent recalled Julius establishes the German College in Rome **Marcellus II pope** **Paul IV pope** Index of Prohibited Books initiated **Pius IV pope**

1510   1520   1530   1540   1550   1560

PAPAL NAMES

HADRIAN VI
Nationality
 Dutch, from
 Utrecht
Date of birth
 2 March 1459
Original name
 Adrian Florensz
 Dedal
Family background
 Son of a carpenter
Early career
 Chancellor of
 Louvain University,
 Inquisitor in Spain,
 regent of Aragon,
 cardinal priest
Elected pope
 9 January 1522
Age at election
 62
Died
 14 September
 1523
Length of pontificate
 1 year, 8 months,
 5 days

CLEMENT VII
Nationality
 Italian, from
 Florence
Date of birth
 24 May 1479
Original name
 Giulio de' Medici
Family background
 Aristocratic;
 Clement was the
 illegitimate son of
 Giuliano de' Medici,
 and a cousin of
 Pope Leo X
Early career
 Cardinal priest,
 vice-chancellor
Elected pope
 19 November 1523
Age at election
 44
Died
 25 September
 1534
Length of pontificate
 10 years, 10
 months, 5 days

Portrait of Leo X by Angelo Bronzino, a partial copy of Raphael's painting of Leo X and his nephews – see p. 7 (Museo Mediceo, Florence).

a loss which precipitated Leo's travels, but in 1512 he re-established the family there and was himself, to all intents and purposes, its ruler for the rest of his life.

He arrived late for the conclave in 1513, suffering agonies from an anal fistula. Six days after the conclave opened, Leo had his abscess lanced and then seems to have done a deal with Cardinal Raffaello Riario which involved a double bluff. Pretending to be much more ill than he actually was, Leo persuaded Riario to swing the ballot his way and Riario agreed, presumably hoping that Leo would die soon and leave the way clear for his own election. In later years when he realized how completely he had been tricked, Riario tried to poison the pope and thus settle both score and bargain.

Leo was only 37 when he became pope and had to be ordained priest, because he was merely a deacon. He spent an enormous sum on his first sacred procession to the Church of St John Lateran – nearly a quarter of Julius II's legacy – an extravagance which was to become typical of his pontificate and provides an illustration of the remark attributed to him by a Venetian writer, 'God has given us the papacy. Now let us enjoy it'. Reckless prodigality with papal funds, however, was continually followed by penury which left him open to justifiable charges of seeking to resolve his financial problems by simony and corruption. The sale of cardinals' hats and indulgences raised enormous sums of money, but Leo not only pursued personal pleasure, patronized the arts, and continued the lavish rebuilding of St Peter's; he threw himself into the most expensive pursuits of all, war and a fresh crusade.

Between 1513 and 1515, relations between the papacy and France were difficult. France and Venice joined forces to gain control of Milan and Naples; France under Louis XII was defeated in battle and compelled to an understanding. A new French king, Francis I, however, renewed hostilities and regained effective suzerainty over Milan; Leo then went to meet him at Bologna and agreed to arrangements not altogether favourable to the papacy, especially those which allowed the French king to nominate candidates for all the higher offices in the French Church. Later political manoeuvres attendant upon the succession of Charles V as Holy Roman emperor in 1519 showed Leo to be machiavellian or indecisive (depending on one's view of his character), with a preference for tortuous dealing, which might not have been so important had his reign not coincided with a religious revolution.

The year 1517 was significant for Leo personally and for the Church. In May and June that year, the pope held interviews with each member

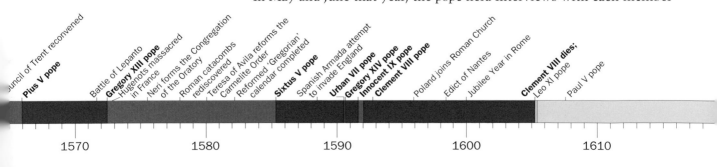

MARTIN LUTHER AND THE REFORMATION

Indulgence is allowed for the sake of imperfect and slothful Christians, who will not exercise themselves industriously in good works or are impatient. For indulgence improves no man, but only tolerates and allows his imperfection. So men should not speak against indulgence, but neither should they persuade any one to take it.

Part of a sermon by Martin Luther

Portrait of Martin Luther by Lucas Cranach the Elder.

Martin Luther was born in Eisleben in 1483. His family was poor, but its finances improved and Luther was able to receive a university education. He studied law for a while, but in 1505 decided to enter the strict Augustinian monastery in Erfurt, and in 1507 was ordained a priest. Soon after his ordination he was sent to Wittenberg as professor of moral philosophy. In 1510, he visited Rome for the first time and was not edified by the carelessness and irreverence he observed in its ecclesiastics. In 1512, he received from Wittenberg a doctorate in theology and for the next five years he lectured as professor of scripture.

His growing dissatisfaction with aspects of Catholic doctrine and practice came to a head when the Dominican John Tetzel came to Germany to raise money for the rebuilding of St Peter's by the sale of special indulgences. In October 1517, Luther posted 95 theses – or topics for debate – on the subject of indulgences, to the door of the castle church in Wittenberg, and thence developed his program of reform of the Church. Luther believed that a Christian could enter Heaven by his faith alone, he insisted that man was free from any earthly authority, such as the pope, and was answerable only to God. Eventually denounced by Rome as a heretic, and excommunicated in 1520, he was protected in Germany and began voluminous writings intended to elucidate his aims for reformation.

From 1521, the results of his publications could be seen in the spread of Protestantism in many German states. Luther had also paved the way for other reformers of the Church, such as John Calvin and John Knox, to take Protestantism (not always Lutheran) across Europe and beyond.

In 1525, Luther married an ex-nun, Katherina von Bora, by whom he had six children. In 1530, a diet – or legislative assembly – was held in Augsburg, which produced a document, the Confession of Augsburg, seeking to formalize the principle points of Lutheran teaching.

Luther died of a stroke in 1546 in his home town of Eisleben, chalking on the wall of the room where he died the words: 'In life I was a plague to you pope, and in death I shall be the death of you.'

Lutheran woodcut by Lucas Cranach the Younger. Propaganda poured from Europe's presses during the 16th century. Polemicists knew how effective visual images could be, and hundreds of woodcuts ranging from the complex to the scabrous became weapons in the religious publishing wars. On the right, the corrupt pope sells indulgences to his debauched Catholic congregation, and the devil blows into a monk's ear as he preaches, while, on the left, the devout Lutherans follow the 'true' path to God (Staatliche Museum, Berlin).

(*Above*) Title-page of Henry VIII of England's book *Defence of the Seven Sacraments* issued in 1521 (Vatican Library). The book was probably written by the king himself.

Tetzel's reputation suffered at the hands of polemical writers. He died in 1519, shortly after the furore over indulgences.

of the college of cardinals. His question was simple: had the cardinal been a member of the recent conspiracy to poison him? Several confessed they had. Cardinal Petrucci, the ringleader, had arranged to have a surgeon treat the pope's anal fistula with poisoned bandages, only to find that Leo preferred the services of his personal doctor. Petrucci was arrested and imprisoned. So were other cardinals, including Riario, evidence against them being obtained from subordinates via the rack, and Leo decided to protect himself in the future by packing the college with dependants: 31 replacements were created cardinals in July.

The principal shock of 1517, however, came as a result of the general council which had been summoned in 1512 by Julius II. Sessions had continued throughout 1513 and 1514 considering, among other things, measures for much-needed reform. Leo then closed the council on 16 March 1517 with a call for a crusade against the Turks, and an announcement of extra taxes to provide the finance. Since January that year, a Dominican, John Tetzel, had been promoting the sale of a special indulgence in parts of Germany, aimed at raising money towards the building of St Peter's. To this an Augustinian monk, Martin Luther, replied at the end of October by inviting public debate on the Church's whole teaching on indulgences. He listed 95 points of argument (theses) and nailed them to the door of Wittenberg Cathedral. Luther was soon condemned as a heretic. Pope Leo issued a bull against him in 1520, whereupon Luther burned a copy of it, proclaiming, 'Antichrist sits in the temple of God and the Roman court is the synagogue of Satan.' Leo riposted in 1521 with a second bull excommunicating Luther; and when Henry VIII of England raced to the Church's aid with an anti-Lutheran book entitled *A Defence of the Seven Sacraments*, Leo rewarded his devotion to Catholic teaching with a title, 'Defender of the Faith', which, illogically, his Protestant regal successors have maintained for themselves ever since.

On 25 October 1521 the pope was taken ill. He recovered for a few weeks but relapsed in late November, and on 1 December, after seeming to feel better, fell unconscious and died at midnight. His sudden death and the discoloration and swelling of his body gave rise to whispers of poison. It is more likely, however, that he was carried off by malaria. Leo's achievements, if one concentrates on learning and the arts, were significant. He was the patron of Raphael who, among other commissions, painted his portrait, decorated papal rooms in the Vatican, and designed tapestries to hang on the walls of the Sistine Chapel during Church festivals. Leo also gave Michelangelo his patronage, but because of his partiality for Raphael lost the opportunity to attach Leonardo da

Title-page of the bull *Exsurge, Domine* (Rise up, O Lord), dated 15 June 1520, excommunicating Luther on 41 separate counts of heresy.

16th-century portrait by Nigari of Suleiman the Magnificent (1497–1566) who reigned for 46 years and plagued a number of popes' reigns (Topkapi Saray, Istanbul). Turkish victories in Hungary in 1526 terrified Europe, and then in 1529 the sultan besieged Vienna, retiring only at the approach of winter.

Vinci to the papal service. He encouraged music: the most distinguished musicians from Italy, France and Spain were drawn to the papal court, and the papal choir was famous. Rome was beautified by many new buildings; history and literature – especially poetry – flourished, although two of the finest authors of the day, Bembo and Ariosto, were ultimately disappointed in their ambitions because they did not receive direct papal patronage; Erasmus dedicated his edition of the Greek New Testament to Leo; Aldo Manuzio, the greatest printer of the period, published editions of the Greek and Roman classics; the study of Greek received Leo's blessing, as did the study of Oriental languages; and his pontificate saw an interest in Egyptian antiquities and the supposed symbolism of their hieroglyphics.

So the Renaissance flourished, but so did the Reformation. Leo was not inclined temperamentally to appreciate how strong was the current of religious change, especially in northern Europe. Moreover, his lavish extravagance had exhausted the papal treasury and his efforts to replenish it had resulted only in increasing those scandals which had helped to precipitate the Reformation in the first place. '*Après nous le déluge*' was actually said by Madame de Pompadour, but it could equally well serve as Leo X's epitaph.

Hadrian VI (1522–1523), a Dutchman, had been tutor to Emperor Charles V and had spent several years in Spain, acting as regent until Charles V, king of Spain as well as Holy Roman emperor, was old enough to assume rule there for himself. Learned and high in favour with the imperial court, Hadrian was therefore an understandable choice to succeed Pope Leo. Nevertheless, he did not understand how to pick up the reins. Hobbled by debt, disliked by the Romans who did not accept him as one of their own, and then cold-shouldered by many of the cardinals who resented his failure to broadcast benefices with a liberal hand, Hadrian was faced by growing Lutheran defiance in the north, and by encroaching Muslim bellicosity under Suleiman the Magnificent to the east and to the south. His answers were to demand that Luther be punished and his teachings prohibited throughout Christendom, a demand which he was unable to implement; and that Europe should unite against the Turks. This last he mismanaged through political gaucherie, and thus irritated his erstwhile ally, Charles V.

Hadrian died suddenly in the summer of 1523, aged 64, and was succeeded by another Medici, **Clement VII** (1523–1534), a bastard grandson of the famous Lorenzo. Clement had been Leo X's vice-chancellor and had played a major part in the policies of his reign. Under Hadrian, he sought to preserve an alliance between Charles V and the papacy when the empire and its diplomatic league fell out with the French king, Francis I. But both emperor and French king were seeking to dominate Italy, and Clement was trapped between these ruthless and self-interested men. Francis captured Milan in 1524, so Clement thought it prudent to show himself friendly towards him. Charles was annoyed. In February 1525, Charles defeated Francis at the Battle of Pavia and took him pris-

Pope Clement having declared war against Florence, that city prepared to make a defence; orders were therefore given that the militia should muster in every quarter, and I was commanded to take arms myself. I got ready in the best manner I could, and exercised with the first nobility in Florence.... It happened one day ... [that] a letter was brought to me from ... Jacopino della Barca.... [He] was now in high favour with Pope Clement, who took great delight in his conversation. As they happened, at a particular time, to be conversing on various topics, the sack of Rome was mentioned.... In the course of this conversation, the Pope, recollecting my services, spoke of my conduct on that occasion in the most favourable terms imaginable; adding, that if he knew where I was, he should be glad to have me again in his service. Master Jacopino thereupon telling him that I resided in Florence, the Pope desired him to invite me to return. The purport of this invitation was, that I should enter into the service of Pope Clement, which would turn out considerably to my advantage.

Benvenuto Cellini *Autobiography*

oner. Clement veered to the side of Charles and sought his protection. By May 1526, he had grown afraid of Charles's power, and joined an alliance against him. These shifts of allegiance gave the impression of weakness, an impression fatal to papal safety once the jackals had gathered. Thus in May 1527, Charles invaded Italy and his troops sacked Rome, while Clement sat paralyzed in Castel Sant' Angelo. The horror of Rome's spoliation was perhaps equalled only by the sack of Constantinople by crusaders 300 years before. Clement surrendered in June but was made to undergo a further six months of suspense and humiliation before the declining vigilance of his guards allowed him to escape one night, disguised as a gardener. The settlement he had been forced to make with Charles was expensive in money, land and political prestige. During the next three years, to be sure, the situation improved with the restoration of much of Clement's secular authority; but he was actually, and evidently, under the control of the emperor, a consideration which led him in 1531 to seek a *rapprochement* with France as some kind of counterbalance. Papal dithering and the lengthy quarrel with Charles had the effect of aiding the Reformation to extend its influence throughout Germany. With pope and emperor at odds, any attempt to deal with the religious revolution was sterile from the beginning, and Clement's procrastination drove England into schism and prevented the summoning of a general council which might have done much to counter Protestant reform. The *déluge*, it seemed, had arrived and was wreaking havoc.

Unfortunately, Clement's strengths were not those required of a pope at the time he was actually pontiff. Like Leo X, he was a scholar, an Italian prince, a patron of the arts, and here he can perhaps be seen at his best. For example, he gave papal support to the great jeweller and sculptor, Benvenuto Cellini, whose autobiography gives a vivid (if biased)

16th-century engraving by Heemskerck showing Clement VII taking refuge in Castel Sant' Angelo while Charles V's troops sacked Rome in May 1527. The pope managed to escape to Orvieto in December. Papal medals struck later illustrate his deliverance.

IMAGO · ERASMI · ROTERODA
MI · AB · ALBERTO · DVRERO · AD
VIVAM · EFFIGIEM · DELINIATA ·

ΤΗΝ · ΚΡΕΙΤΤΩ · ΤΑ · ΣΥΓΓΡΑΜ
ΜΑΤΑ · ΔΕΙΞΕΙ

· MDXXVI ·

Erasmus, an engraving by Albrecht
Dürer, 1526. The inscription tells us
that Dürer took the likeness from life.
Pope Clement VII was on friendly terms
with this great Renaissance scholar and
thinker, one of the most influential
critics of medieval Catholicism.

PAPAL NAMES	
PAUL III *Nationality* Italian, from Canino *Date of birth* 29 February 1468 *Original name* Alessandro Farnese *Family background* Condottiere *Status* Before he was ordained, Paul had four illegitimate children. In 1513 he abandoned his dissolute life and in 1519 was ordained priest *Early career* Cardinal bishop, dean of the college of cardinals *Elected pope* 13 October 1534 *Age at election* 66 *Died* 10 November 1549, of fever *Length of pontificate* 15 years, 29 days *Notable features* Paul commissioned Michelangelo to	finish the painting, *Last Judgment*, in the Sistine Chapel. He promoted his teenage grandsons to be cardinals **JULIUS III** *Nationality* Italian, from Rome *Date of birth* 10 September 1487 *Original name* Giovanni Maria Ciocchi del Monte *Family background* Son of a jurist; nephew of the archbishop of Siponto *Early career* Cardinal bishop, co-president of the Council of Trent *Elected pope* 8 February 1550 *Age at election* 62 *Died* 23 March 1555 *Length of pontificate* 5 years, 1 month, 13 days

impression of the period, and to Michelangelo, from whom he commissioned the *Last Judgment* on the east wall of the Sistine Chapel. He was on friendly terms with the great Renaissance scholar and thinker, Erasmus, offered patronage to the historians Guicciardini and Machiavelli, and increased the treasures of the Vatican Library. Churches and other buildings were rebuilt or restored; practical work on fortifications in Rome and elsewhere was undertaken. Statues and sepulchral monuments rose in profusion.

Most promisingly, however, the reign witnessed the start of Catholic recovery from the shock of the Reformation. This can be seen principally in the religious orders which were notoriously corrupt at this time and needed cleansing. As early as 1517 the Oratory of the Divine Love had united clerics and lay people in a confraternity devoted to holiness of personal behaviour. In 1524, Pope Clement approved a new order, the Theatines, founded by Gaetano di Thiene (or Cajetan), which united devout priests in the administration of the sacraments and the example of a blameless life. In 1528, the Franciscans gave rise to an organization of hermits, the Capuchins, whose life was deliberately bare, simple, poor and mortified; while in 1533, Antonio Maria Zaccharia founded the Barnabites, whose aim was similar to that of the Theatines, but who made a virtue of public exercises of penance, as well as those of caring for souls and looking after the sick. Finally, in August 1534, Ignatius of Loyola revealed to six close friends his intention of organizing a spiritual army to fight heresy and ignorance of the Faith wherever the pope might choose to send it: and thus the Society of Jesus (the Jesuits) was born.

Clement VII died in September 1534. He had succumbed to a fever, and was succeeded by **Paul III** (1534–1549), another Renaissance prince and patron of the arts. His sister, the beautiful Giulia Farnese, had been Pope Alexander VI's mistress. Various political decisions he made are noteworthy: the excommunication of Henry VIII of England – over the king's divorce from Catherine of Aragon – which ensured that country's continued schism from the Church; and the pope's support for Charles V in the emperor's war against the Schmalkaldic League, an offensive alliance of German Protestants. But by far Paul's greatest contribution to Catholic history was his decision to call a general council, now known as the Council of Trent, which first met in December 1545 and continued to meet at long intervals, and under a variety of trying circumstances, until 1563. The 25 sessions of the council, intermittent though they were, produced a reformed Church which not only survived the Reformation, but went on to reaffirm itself and its body of teachings in a Counter-Reformation which proved remarkably effective.

Nor was Clement VII's encouragement of the reform of the religious orders diminished under Paul; for the Theatines and Barnabites flourished, a new order of teaching nuns, the Ursulines, was founded in 1535 by Angela Merici; and in 1540 the Society of Jesus received the pope's formal recognition in his bull *Regimini militantis ecclesiae*. Paul also established the Roman Inquisition, better known as the Holy Office, to which he gave extensive powers of censorship and prosecution.

Nevertheless, rampant nepotism still ruled the papal roost. In 1534, Paul created two of his grandsons cardinals at the ages of 14 and 16, in spite of his having declared only a month before that the college of cardinals needed thorough reform, and continued to promote members of the Farnese family whenever he could. He died aged 81. Relations with Charles V were still poor and the Turks were pounding at the gates of Christendom, so **Julius III** (1550–1555) had a difficult reign in prospect. Julius managed to surmount Charles V's hostility to his election, however, and in November 1550 actually pleased the emperor by recalling the Council of Trent, whose sittings had been suspended in 1548. There were six sessions on this occasion, attended by a number of Protestant theologians, but matters rapidly declined. France, under Henry II, refused to participate, and Julius's ill-judged attempt to remove his predecessor's grandson, Ottavio Farnese, from the governorship of Parma precipitated war – because Charles V was Ottavio's father-in-law and regarded Parma as part of the empire, which incurred the hostility of the French. Charles failed to defeat Henry and a number of German princes revolted against him in 1552, thus adding to his distraction, and in the midst of the turmoil Julius was forced to suspend the council. A treaty with France, prejudicial to papal interests, followed.

In religious affairs Julius was attended by greater success. He favoured the Society of Jesus, confirming its constitution in 1550; founded the Collegium Germanicum whose purpose was to train German priests for the restoration of Catholicism in Protestant Germany; and on 6 July 1553, through Cardinal Pole, welcomed England back into the Church. Like his immediate predecessors, Julius was a patron of learning and the arts, although many poets, including Pietro Aretino, had their initial hopes dashed by Julius's failure to grant them pensions. Architecture and music, however, fared better for it was Julius who appointed Michelangelo principal architect of St Peter's, asked Vasari to draw up plans for a new country house, the Villa Giulia, and made Palestrina master of the papal choir.

Scandal, however, blighted his pontificate in the person of a teenage boy whom he plucked from the street and made keeper of his pet monkey. The boy was then adopted by Julius's brother under the name Innocenzo del Monte, and in 1550 created a cardinal, to widespread condemnation. Nor did the new cardinal's life justify the hopes Julius may have had for him, for he was both insolent and dissolute, and incapable of fulfilling the responsibilities which Julius gave him.

Clearly, then, the conclave which elected Julius's successor was hoping for an improvement. The cardinals chose a man who seemed to have

Titian's portrait of Paul III with his nephews (Museo di Capolimonte, Naples). Paul was a rampant nepotist.

Palestrina, presenting his masses to Julius III, 1554. Although Palestrina was one of the greatest Renaissance composers, he did not fare well at the hands of the next two popes who failed to give him their patronage.

16th-century engraving by Martin Rota of Ferdinand I, the Holy Roman emperor (1558–1564). He incurred the wrath of Pope Paul IV as the pope was not consulted about his election.

every desirable qualification – ability, experience, personal integrity and a commitment to reform – all of which he began to demonstrate as soon as he became pope. But **Marcellus II** (1555) had one weakness – his health. After a pontificate of only 22 days he died, leaving the cardinals to choose **Paul IV** (1555–1559) whom they hoped would prove to be a reforming pope out of the same mould. To a certain extent they were right. The word one associates with Paul IV is 'No'. In September 1555, for example, there was an agreement worked out at Augsburg that Catholics and Protestants should coexist in Germany on the principle of *cuius regio, eius religio*, 'the ruler of a state will determine its religion'. The pope denounced this arrangement, pained by the injury (as he saw it) which it inflicted on the Church. Charles V, worn out by illness and the long endeavour to manage his turbulent times, abdicated in 1556 and the imperial electors chose his brother Ferdinand to succeed him in 1558. Pope Paul objected to both abdication and election on the grounds he had not been consulted about either. In September 1557, the Inquisition prepared a very long list of books which were to be burned – including all the works of Erasmus – and by the end of 1558 this had become the papally approved Index of Prohibited Books, 'a list', according to the official description, 'of authors and books against which the Roman and universal Inquisition orders all Christians to be on their guard, under the threat of censure and punishment'.

This tendency to say 'no' sprang partly from Paul's ascetic character, partly from his zeal for reform and aggression against Protestant heresy, and partly perhaps from an authoritarian streak which old age (he was 79 when he became pope) could not mellow. It can be illustrated by his treatment of Cardinal Morone, one of the most respected and virtuous members of the administration, and a man most eager for reform. On 31 May 1557, he was arrested, charged with heresy and thrown into prison. The cause was nothing more than Pope Paul's extraordinarily suspicious nature – made more acute, perhaps, by his years at the head of the Inquisition – and Morone was not released until the beginning of the next pontificate. Nor, unfortunately, was Paul's political judgment any more rational, since it was clouded by an unreasoning hatred of Charles V in particular and of Spain in general. In consequence, he quickly allied himself with France, hoping thereby to drive the Spanish out of Italy, and was soundly defeated in battle in 1557. The pope was not altogether free from nepotism, either. In a consistory of June 1555, he had created his nephew Carlo Carafa cardinal and promoted him to high office. Other relatives, too, were liberally rewarded and advanced. The new cardinal was able, but perhaps better suited to being a soldier than a cleric, and it was at his urging that the pope had undertaken his disastrous adventure against Spain. Finally in 1559 a Theatine priest alerted the pope to the despotic behaviour of Carafa and other relatives, and Paul was filled with horror and disgust. The cardinal and the other nephews were dismissed from their offices and exiled, a fitting end to their unprincipled history and a noteworthy comment on Paul's genuine reverence for virtue and hatred of corruption.

Nevertheless, the Carafa years had done much damage to the pope's reputation, since it was assumed his relatives acted with his consent, and when he died, perhaps of dropsy and old age, an outburst of vandalism in Rome expressed the hatred the people felt for him and his family. It took the cardinals nearly four months to elect a successor, **Pius IV** (1559–1565). At once the new pope put much of Paul's policy into reverse. Cardinal Morone was released from prison, Cardinal Carafa was executed, the Index was revised, the Inquisition reined in and amicable relations established with Emperor Ferdinand and Philip II of Spain. Pius most importantly reconvened the Council of Trent on 18 January 1562 and, with the help of Cardinal Morone, saw it safely through to its conclusion in 1563. His next major task was to make sure that Catholic countries adopted the decrees of the council – many of which

(*Right*) 16th-century engraving of Pius IV. Pius was the uncle of Charles Borromeo whom he made a cardinal at the age of 22. Charles was canonized by Paul V in 1610.

Pius reconvened the Council of Trent (*below*) in 1562. Sessions of the council were held in the Romanesque cathedral and in the Church of Santa Maria Maggiore. Many of the reforms and doctrinal formulations of the council remained the framework of Catholicism until the 1960s. 16th-century engraving.

PAPAL NAMES	
PIUS IV	cardinal priest
Nationality	*Elected pope*
Italian, from Milan	25 December 1559
Date of birth	*Age at election*
31 March 1499	60
Original name	*Died*
Giovanni Angelo	9 December 1565
Medici	*Length of pontificate*
Family background	5 years, 11
Son of a notary	months, 15 days
Early career	*Notable feature*
Commissioner with	Earlier in his life,
the papal armies in	Pius had fathered
Hungary and	three illegitimate
Transylvania, vice-	children
legate of Bologna,	

represented substantial changes in Church practice and behaviour – and in this he was greatly assisted by his secretary, Cardinal Borromeo, who was to prove an influence for good on the next two popes as well.

But heresy, in the forms of Lutheranism and Calvinism, was spreading fast. Even France was not immune; and so when Pius died of fever in December 1565 his successor, **Pius V** (1566–1572), had a great deal of work to do. The new pope was a Dominican and had long experience as an Inquisitor. Severe, ascetic, devout – he visited hospitals to comfort the dying and daily washed the feet of the poor who sought alms – and ruthless in seeking to excise all immorality and worldliness not only from the papal court, but from the Church as a whole, he set about implementing in full the decisions of the Council of Trent. Thus, he published a catechism, revised the breviary (the book of Church services which all priests, monks and nuns were to recite every day), and established the form of the mass, which lasted until recent times. Priests had to be resident in their parishes; religious orders came under scrutiny and one or two which had become degraded he abolished. The wholesale scattering of indulgences and dispensations was brought under control. Blasphemy and disregard for holy days were punished severely. To these ends, the Inquisition was given free rein and proved so successful that by the time Pius died, heresy had virtually disappeared from Italy. After 1572, the heretics appearing before the Roman tribunal were largely foreigners. Use of the Index increased and was made more systematic. Such

A group of leading Protestant reformers including Luther, Calvin, Melanchthon, Zwingli and Knox (Perth Museum and Art Gallery, Scotland). Note the disembodied pope's head (centre, bottom).

zeal for the Faith left a deep imprint on the Church and led 150 years later to Pius's canonization.

When it came to politics, however, Pius's style was somewhat abrasive. It was a mistake to rehabilitate the Carafa family so soon after its well-deserved disgrace. It was another error to underline his opposition to the control of the Church by the State in such a way as to emphasize papal supremacy at the expense of the various nationalistic regal dignities. His excommunication of Queen Elizabeth I in 1570 alienated England completely and stimulated a vicious persecution of English Catholics; and he bickered constantly with Philip II of Spain over relations between Church and State. A major success, however, was his support of a league against the Turks, which resulted in a major Catholic

PAPAL NAMES	
PIUS V	cardinal priest
Nationality	*Elected pope*
Italian, from Bosco	7 January 1566
Date of birth	*Age at election*
17 January 1504	61
Original name	*Died*
Michele Ghislieri	1 May 1572
Family background	*Length of pontificate*
Humble	6 years, 3 months,
Early career	25 days
Inquisitor General,	

(*Above*) Painting of Pius V ascribed to Zuccarelli (Stonyhurst College, England). Paul was canonized by Clement XI in 1712. His body, originally buried in St Peter's, was transferred to Santa Maria Maggiore where a splendid tomb had been built for him.

(*Right*) Engraving showing the two naval formations, Christian and Turkish, before the Battle of Lepanto on 5 October 1571 (Museo Storico Navale di Venezia). Contemporary statistics tell us that at the Battle of Lepanto 30,000 Turks were killed, 10,000 taken prisoner, 90 triremes were sunk, 180 captured and 15,000 Christian slaves set free.

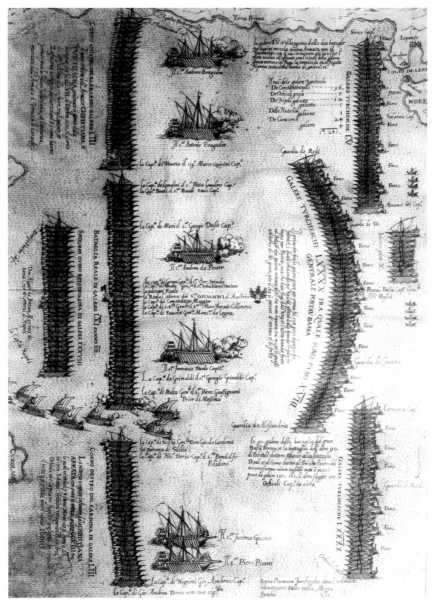

16th-century painting showing the commission for the reform of the calendar before Pope Gregory XIII in 1582 (State Archives, Siena). Gregory founded the Vatican Observatory to help provide the information necessary to reform the calendar. Non-Catholic countries refused at first to adopt the new calendar. Great Britain waited until 1752, Russia till 1918 and Turkey until 1927.

CALVINISM

The reformer John Calvin was born in Noyon, France, in 1509. Influenced by, but not fully in agreement with, the ideas of Martin Luther, and also by Ulrich Zwingli (1484–1531) – an early Swiss reformer – Calvin developed his own form of Protestantism in Geneva. Calvin's theological system can be found mainly in his *Institutes of the Christian Religion* (1536–1559). Relying upon a thorough and detailed knowledge of the Bible, Calvin produced certain doctrines which may be regarded as typically his : 1) predestination, a premise which states that eternal life is foreordained for some people, and eternal damnation for others; 2) God is absolute sovereign, and a knowledge of him and of his will can be obtained through a correct and inspired reading of the Holy Scripture; 3) human beings are in thrall to sin and can be regenerated only through belief in Christ, who acts as a kind of witness for the individual in God's tribunal; 4) the Church consists of those who preach and who in purity of intention hear God's word and receive the sacraments, of which there are only two, baptism and communion.

In Scotland, thanks to John Knox, Calvinism took root, as it did briefly in England and in the New World. In France and Hungary, Calvinists were a significant minority (the French Huguenots were Calvinists), while in Holland and parts of Germany Calvinists were soon the dominant Protestant group.

victory at the Battle of Lepanto in 1571, for thereafter, the Turks ceased to be an effective threat in the Mediterranean. A near success attended his support of the French regent, Catherine de Médicis in her struggle with French Protestants (Huguenots) – 'near' because the peace treaty of 1570 between the Huguenots and the crown granted the Protestants amnesty, liberty of conscience and free exercise of their religion. Pius was grieved and indignant, and was certain that even worse disturbances would follow, a belief which turned out in time to be perfectly correct.

March 1572 saw the pope's health start to decline. He was able to give a solemn blessing to the Roman people gathered in front of St Peter's on 6 April, but three weeks later he was very ill indeed, and on 1 May he died. His had been a remarkable reign, and it was his successors who reaped the harvest which he had sown.

The next pope, **Gregory XIII** (1572–1585), continued Pius's work of promoting Tridentine reform (the reforms of the Council of Trent) and added to the Counter-Reformation a force militant to assist the force spiritual. He welcomed, for example, the massacre of Huguenots in France on 23 and 24 August 1572 (St Bartholomew's Eve and Day) with a service of thanksgiving in St Peter's, and actively supported Catholic arms against Protestants in France and the Netherlands. In the fight against heretics and unbelievers, he was helped by cardinals in Germany, and overseas by Jesuits who were working as missionaries in India, Japan, China and Brazil. He also sanctioned a new religious order, the Congregation of the Oratory, founded by Philip Neri (1575), and reform of the Carmelites by Teresa of Avila (1580); and his reforming impulse was carried as far as the calendar which had strayed badly awry since the days of its last major reformer, Julius Caesar. Ten days, 5–14 October 1582, were consigned to oblivion so that the vernal equinox might be adjusted to coincide with Caesar's computation, and this 'Gregorian Calendar' was then promulgated throughout Christendom. Catholic states accepted it; Protestant states refused to do so until much

17th-century engraving showing the massacre of the Protestant Huguenots in France on 23 and 24 August 1572. The historian Brantôme said that Charles IX took great pleasure in seeing more than 4,000 bodies float down the River Seine.

(*Right*) Papal medal of Gregory XIII, 1572 (Staatliche Museum, Berlin). He was quite tall, with blue eyes, an aquiline nose and a thick beard.

PAPAL NAMES	
GREGORY XIII	*Age at election*
Nationality	70
Italian, from	*Died*
Bologna	10 April 1585
Date of birth	*Length of pontificate*
1 January 1502	12 years 10
Original name	months 27 days
Ugo Boncompagni	*Notable feature*
Family background	In his youth,
Son of a merchant	Gregory had an
Early career	illegitimate son; in
Cardinal priest	c. 1542, Gregory
Elected pope	was ordained priest
14 May 1572	

later; for example, it was not adopted in Britain until 1752.

Gregory favoured the Jesuits. To them, very largely, he entrusted the running of more than 20 new colleges in different countries for the training of a Counter-Reformation priesthood – the college in Rome later being named after him, the Gregorian University – and for them he built their mother church in Rome, the Gesù.

Unfortunately, all this cost money, as did the building of the Gregorian Chapel in St Peter's and a new summer palace on the Quirinal hill in Rome. To raise the necessary funds Gregory, using a variety of legalistic devices, resorted to confiscation of lands and property, which had several unforeseen and unwanted results. Nobles armed themselves to defend their interests; old feuds were resurrected; gradually the whole country became infested with outlaws and bandits; and in the midst of this confusion, Gregory died. His successor, therefore, would be confronted with immediate difficulties.

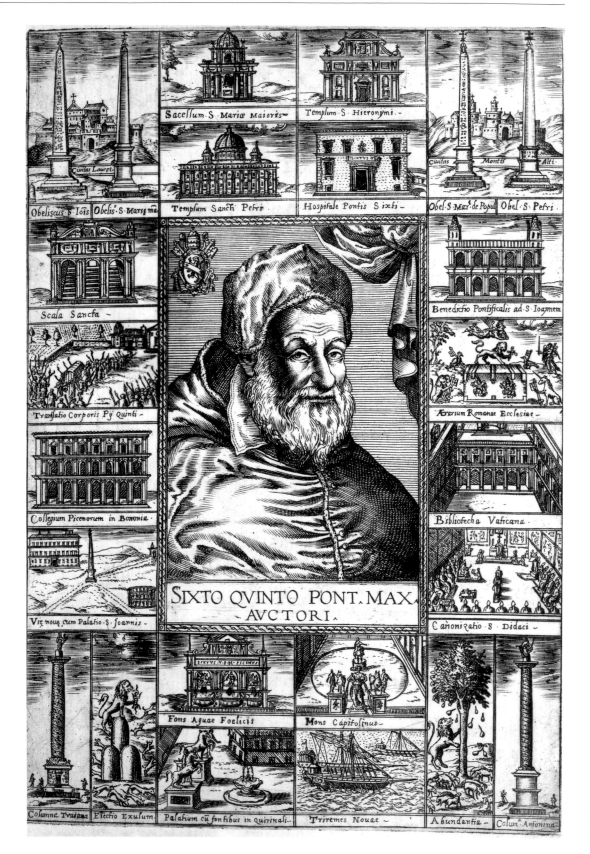

PAPAL NAMES

SIXTUS V
Nationality
  Italian, from
  Grottammare
Date of birth
  13 December 1520
Original name
  Felice Peretti
Family background
  Son of a farm
  worker
Status
  Franciscan friar
Early career
  Inquisitor for
  Venice, cardinal
  priest
Elected pope
  24 April 1585
Age at election
  64
Died
  27 August 1590
Length of pontificate
  5 years, 4 months,
  3 days
Notable features
  Sixtus rebuilt the
  Lateran Palace and
  completed the
  dome of St Peter's
  Basilica. He
  established the
  Vatican Press

URBAN VII
Nationality
  Italian, from Rome
Date of birth
  4 August 1521
Original name
  Giambattista
  Castagna
Family background
  Aristocratic
Early career
  Papal nuncio to
  Venice, governor of
  Bologna, cardinal
  priest
Elected pope
  15 September
  1590
Age at election
  69
Died
  27 September
  1590, of malaria
Length of pontificate
  13 days

GREGORY XIV
Nationality
  Italian, from
  Somma

Date of birth
  11 February 1535
Original name
  Niccolò Sfondrati
Early career
  Cardinal priest
Elected pope
  5 December 1590
Age at election
  65
Died
  16 October 1591
Length of pontificate
  11 months, 12 days

INNOCENT IX
Nationality
  Italian, from
  Bologna
Date of birth
  20 July 1519
Original name
  Giovanni Antonio
  Fachinetti
Early career
  Papal nuncio in
  Venice, patriarch of
  Jerusalem, cardinal
  priest
Elected pope
  29 October 1591
Age at election
  72
Died
  30 December 1591
Length of pontificate
  2 months, 2 days

CLEMENT VIII
Nationality
  Italian, from Fano
Date of birth
  24 February 1536
Original name
  Ippolito
  Aldobrandini
Family background
  Son of an advocate
Early career
  Cardinal priest,
  papal legate
Elected pope
  30 January 1592
Age at election
  55
Died
  5 March 1605
Length of pontificate
  13 years, 1 month,
  6 days
Notable feature
  Clement made his
  teenage grand-
  nephew a cardinal

16th-century engraving showing Pope
Sixtus V and the magnificent
achievements of his reign.

Like Pius V, **Sixtus V** (1585–1590) was a friar, a Franciscan. Far from being a gentle soul, however, he had no hesitation in exercising the papacy like a claymore, executing brigands by the thousand, along with their patrons. He then vigorously tackled a host of other problems. Finance, economy, industry, Church administration, enforcement of Tridentine decrees – one thorny task after another received his close and tireless attention. The results were impressive. Italy became much safer, new jobs appeared, the papal finances improved to such an extent that Sixtus became very rich, and his remodelled secretariat proved so effective that its constitution was not changed until 1962–65. Papal assistance advanced the Catholic faith in Poland, and in 1587–88 nearly achieved the same in England through the Armada sent thither by Spain. At home, Sixtus reconstructed the layout of Rome, rebuilt the Lateran Palace, and completed the dome of St Peter's Basilica. All in all, it was a whirlwind of a pontificate, which must be accounted one of the great periods of the papacy. A measure of his attitude towards the office can be gauged from his frequently quoted saying (borrowed from the Roman emperor Vespasian), that a prince ought to die on his feet in the midst of action.

Sixtus's death saw the election of three short-lived popes: **Urban VII** (1590), who fell ill on the night after his election and died 11 days later; **Gregory XIV** (1590–1591), who was an invalid from the start and destined to die of a large gallstone, which weighed 70 grams (2.5 ounces); and **Innocent IX** (1591), whose age – 82 years – and fragile health combined to carry him off after a reign of only two months; although his firm views on the role of the papacy during his short reign were evident in this tale: 'He was once solicited to grant a certain favour, the petitioner at the time presenting him with a considerable sum of money to defray the expenses of the papal treasury during a time of famine in the Roman states. The pope indignantly spurned the riches offered to him and said: "I am not asking for money, but for obedience."'

These three popes had tried to forward the work set in motion by Pius, Gregory and Sixtus, and each tended to favour Spain over France during the war for the French throne then being fought to prevent the Huguenot Henry of Navarre from succeeding to it. This French dilemma was solved when Henry became a Catholic in 1593. His conversion came as a relief to **Clement VIII** (1592–1605) who was, nevertheless, compelled to accept the subsequent Edict of Nantes (1598) which confirmed the Huguenots' right to freedom of conscience and worship, as well as other civil benefits.

Clement had been a serious candidate for the papacy during the three previous conclaves, and when he was finally elected he proved to be a devout and indefatigable reformer from the Counter-Reformation mould. In December 1595, he had the satisfaction of knowing that much of Poland was about to turn from Orthodox to Roman Catholic Christianity, while in 1599 his appointment of Francis de Sales (canonized in 1665) as bishop of Geneva did much to advance the cause of the Faith in Switzerland. Saints, indeed, seemed to play quite a large part in

THE COUNTER-REFORMATION

From the end of the 15th century to the beginning of the 16th century, the Catholic Church saw several movements aimed at reform and spiritual renewal. The Oratory of Divine Love was followed by Philip Neri's Congregation of the Oratory, Cajetans's Theatine Order, Antonio Zaccharia's Barnabites, Angela Merici's Ursulines, Teresa of Avila's reformed Carmelites and Ignatius of Loyola's foundation of the Society of Jesus (Jesuits). Several popes, too, actively sought reform – Hadrian VI, Paul III, Paul IV, Pius IV and Pius V – all taking steps to mitigate the effects of the Reformation and remove the Churches most scandalous abuses, and to harness the renewal of the religious orders and the missionary zeal of the Jesuits in a Counter-Reformation (or Catholic Reformation as it is known today).

The Council of Trent embodied the Catholic urge to cleanse and renovate. It held three sessions: 1) 1545–1548, 2) 1551–1552, and 3) 1562–1563, and in spite of the council being interrupted by political crises, it succeeded in producing a revival of Catholic Christianity which could and did counter the teachings and advances of the various Protestant churches. This intensified zeal also stimulated missionary work, which can be seen especially in the work of the Jesuits in India and the Far East, and in the continental seminaries which trained priests for missions in England and Sweden. Painters, sculptors, writers, musicians and architects played their part in embodying this revitalization of the Catholic Church and the subsequent spiritual dynamism which flowed strongly from it.

Battista's painting of the Madonna and St Philip Neri (1515–1595), who developed the Oratory out of a fellowship of priests.

(Above) Title-page of the Jesuits' canons (1574). The Jesuit motto is, 'To the greater glory of God'.

(Below) Ignatius of Loyola (1491–1556) before Paul III (Jesuit Church, Rome). Ignatius came from a noble Spanish family and was a soldier before his spiritual conversion. While he prayed and performed penance, he wrote his most influential work, Spiritual Exercises.

(Above) St Teresa of Avila (1515–1582) was proclaimed patroness of Spain by the Spanish parliament in 1617.

St Francis de Sales (1567–1622) came from a noble Savoyard family and was the oldest of 13 children. He became a priest, with his father's reluctant agreement, and then bishop of Geneva. The Order of the Visitation was founded under his direction. Painting in the Church of San Francesco di Paola, Milan by Cerano (1577–1633).

Clement's life, for not only did he make Robert Bellarmine (canonized in 1930) a cardinal, he also enjoyed the close friendship of Philip Neri (canonized in 1622). Not so happy, however, was his use of the Inquisition to condemn and execute the philosopher and controversialist, Giordano Bruno; and equally unfortunate was his nepotism which advanced two of his nephews and a 14-year-old grand-nephew to the cardinalate.

Nevertheless, at the time of his death, Clement could look with satisfaction at a Church which was renewed and strong at least partly because of the personal piety and spirited efforts of the popes of the 16th century, who had steered St Peter's barque through the high seas of reform and sailed into calmer waters.

One of the problems which had beset the papacy from its earliest years was that of avoiding control by the hand of the State. First the Eastern emperor, then the Holy Roman emperor and then the king of France had embodied that particular danger. During the 16th century these were being replaced by Spain, with France eager to exert not so much control over the papacy itself as management of her own ecclesiastical affairs. Spain was, for the time being, distracted by her empire in the Americas and wars in the Netherlands, and the popes themselves were preoccupied with religious revolution, especially in northern Europe, and their participation in and patronage of the Renaissance, which was reaching maturity during the 16th century, and so the significance of these threats to papal independence were not yet fully appreciated. The peculiar division of responsibility unique to the popes was also emphasized in those who held the office during this period: head of the universal Church on the one hand, and bishop of Rome on the other. Their eyes scanned the horizon one minute and focussed narrowly in front of them the next; and as pope after pope was chosen from Italy, that narrow focussing became more apparent, and the Protestant world's perception that Catholics were ruled merely by a blinkered 'bishop of Rome' began to find a faint echo in reality, despite the popes' constant attempts to encompass the wider sphere.

Leo XI
1605

Paul V
1605–1621

Gregory XV
1621–1623

Tomb of Leo XI by Algardi in St Peter's. When Leo died, according to Platina, his family was particularly grieved as its members had had no time to receive the honours the pope had destined for them.

LEO XI	
Nationality Italian, from Florence	ambassador in Rome, cardinal bishop, papal legate
Date of birth 2 June 1535	*Elected pope* 1 April 1605
Original name Alessandro Ottaviano de' Medici	*Age at election* 69
Family background Aristocratic	*Died* 27 April 1605
Early career Florentine	*Length of pontificate* 27 days

PAUL V	
Nationality Italian, from Rome	*Elected pope* 16 May 1605
Date of birth 17 September 1552	*Age at election* 52
Original name Camillo Borghese	*Died* 28 January 1621, of a stroke
Family background Son of a professor of law	*Length of pontificate* 15 years, 8 months, 12 days
Early career Cardinal priest	

LEO XI AND PAUL V

Paul was extremely tall with large, elegant arms and legs. His complexion was white and yellow, his eyes light blue.... His face was at once serious and calm, and in it were mingled dignity, charm, cheerfulness and severity.

Anon *Pauli V Vita*

The cardinals chose a Medici to succeed Pope Clement. **Leo XI** (1605) was a deeply religious man who, as a bishop, had worked hard to implement Tridentine reform and to restore Church discipline to a France ravaged by civil war. But he was 70 and delicate when they elected him and died within the month. So it was **Paul V** (1605–1621) who effectively succeeded Pope Clement and immediately fell into serious dispute with a number of Italian city-states over the Church's authority. Venice attempted to try two clerics in a secular rather than an ecclesiastical court. Pope Paul placed the city under an interdict (1606); Venice maintained he could not validly do so and expelled anyone who observed the pope's ruling. A pamphlet war ensued and catastrophe was averted only by the intervention of France. The episode badly dented papal prestige.

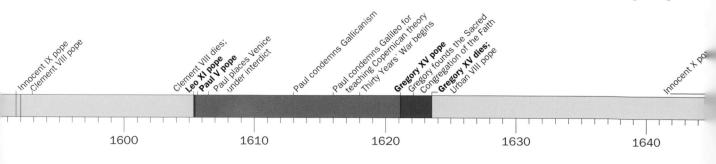

Innocent IX pope
Clement VIII pope
Clement VIII dies; **Leo XI pope**; **Paul V pope**
Paul places Venice under interdict
Paul condemns Gallicanism
Paul condemns Galileo for teaching Copernican theory
Thirty Years' War begins
Gregory XV pope
Gregory founds the Sacred Congregation of the Faith
Gregory XV dies; Urban VIII pope
Innocent X pope

1600　　1610　　1620　　1630　　1640

Bronze bust of Paul V by Bernini (Statens Museum for Art, Copenhagen). It is done in the traditional mode, with uncut eyeballs reminiscent of antique statues.

GREGORY XV	
Nationality Italian, from Bologna	*Length of pontificate* 2 years, 4 months, 27 days
Date of birth 9 January 1554	*Notable features* Gregory was the first pope to have been educated by the Jesuits. He laid down the rules for papal conclaves, and these have remained in operation mostly unaltered ever since
Original name Alessandro Ludovisi	
Family background Aristocratic	
Early career Cardinal priest	
Elected pope 9 February 1621	
Age at election 67	
Died 8 July 1623	

Paul did not learn caution, however, for in 1613 he proceeded to condemn France's claim to control the Church in French territory (a claim known as Gallicanism), and was answered in 1614 by a declaration that the French king held his crown from God and that the decrees of the Council of Trent would not be promulgated in France – a declaration modified somewhat by the French clergy who undertook to publish them via councils in the provinces. All this was a little depressing, but on the positive side one may note that Paul benefited Rome by restoring the aqueduct of Emperor Trajan, which was then renamed 'Acqua Paola', and by completing the nave, façade and portico of St Peter's. He also canonized Charles Borromeo and beatified (i.e. titled 'Blessed', a major step towards canonization) Ignatius of Loyola, Francis Xavier, Philip Neri and Teresa of Avila.

GREGORY XV

There was almost always in his complexion a dull brown colour tending very much to remind one of honey.

Accarisius *Vita Gregorii XV*, Book 3, chapter 21

Paul died of a stroke in January 1621 and was succeeded by **Gregory XV** (1621–1623), the first pope to have been educated by the Jesuits. The Thirty Years' War (1618–1648) in Germany had begun and Gregory was eager to support the Catholic powers involved and to achieve a restoration of the Faith in Germany. The war involved the Catholic emperor, Ferdinand II, and a Protestant contender for his title, Frederick V of Bohemia, with King Gustavus Adolphus of Sweden adding weight to the Protestant side. Aided by his representative, Cardinal Carlo Carafa, Gregory not only achieved reinstatement of Catholicism in Bohemia but also, in 1623, a transference of Frederick V's title to the Catholic Maximilian I of Bavaria. As France pursued anti-Calvinist policies at home, and even the British king tested the feasibility of a marriage between his heir and a Spanish princess, the pope's aim of uniting the Catholic princes of Europe and advancing the Faith in Protestant lands seemed to be faring well.

At home, Gregory finished one of Clement VIII's tasks by canonizing Teresa of Avila, Ignatius of Loyola, Francis Xavier and Philip Neri in 1622, and undertook the needful labour of revising the procedure of papal elections. This he did in such detail and so successfully – insisting upon election behind closed doors, for example, and by means of a written secret ballot – that with scarcely an alteration his is still the procedure followed today. It was Gregory, too, who founded the Sacred Congregation of the Faith in 1622 to guide and coordinate the Church's missionary work throughout the world. His pontificate, therefore, must be accounted a significant consolidation of the work of his predecessors.

Pope Gregory fell ill of a fever in June 1623 and died on 8 July, aged 70.

His acquisition of the Library of Heidelberg from Maximilian I was an event of the first importance for the Vatican Archives, while the artistic purchases made by his nephew, Ludovico Ludovisi, whom he made a cardinal, increased the number of ancient treasures in Rome. But the pontificate proved too short to allow Gregory much exercise as a patron, and it was left to his nephew to accumulate the finest collection of antiques Rome had ever seen, and to fill his new palace, the Villa Ludovisi, with remarkable works of art.

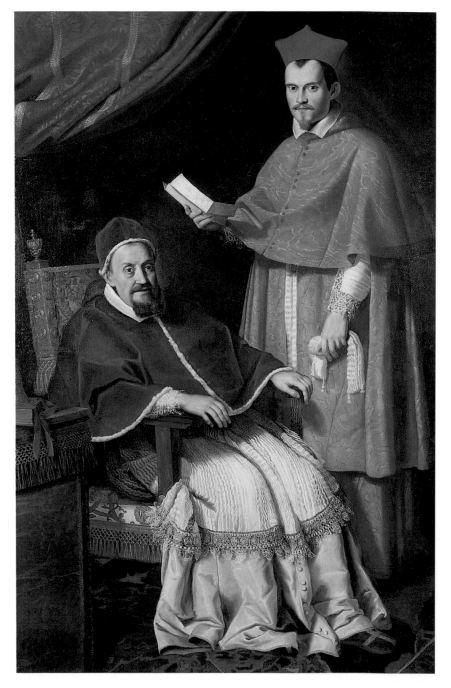

Portrait by Domenichino of Gregory XV and his nephew Ludovico Ludovisi, both of whom amassed valuable collections – Gregory of books for the Vatican Archives, and Ludovisi of ancient treasures (Musée des Beaux-Arts, Béziers). Gregory expanded the Vatican Archives, which had developed out of the preservation of title deeds and records of privileges held in St Peter's and the Lateran Palace, by adding Emperor Maximilian's library from Heidelberg to the archives. Ludovisi filled his palace, the Villa Ludovisi, with priceless antiques and works of art.

Urban VIII
1623–1644

Bernini's tomb of Urban VIII in St Peter's. The pope is giving an imperious sign of benediction. Barberini bees, emblems of Urban's family, can be seen on the pope's left shoulder and also appear on the sarcophagus and the base of the statue.

URBAN VIII	
Nationality Italian, from Florence	*Died* 29 July 1644
Date of birth April 1568	*Length of pontificate* 20 years, 11 months, 23 days
Original name Maffeo Barberini	*Notable feature* In order to ward off hostile celestial influences, Urban conducted a magical ceremony in the papal apartments with the help of Tommaso Campanella
Family background Wealthy merchants	
Early career Cardinal priest, papal legate	
Elected pope 6 August 1623	
Age at election 55	

The proportions of his body and limbs were nobly adjusted; his stature rather tall, his complexion olive, his figure rather muscular than fat. His head was large, giving evidence of a wonderful intellect and a most tenacious memory. His forehead was ample and serene, the colour of his eyes a light blue, the nose well proportioned, the cheeks round, but in his latter years greatly attenuated; ... his voice [was] sonorous and very agreeable.... From the time of his elevation to the prelacy he wore his beard of a moderate length and square form.

Andrea Nicoletti *Della Vita di Papa Urbano VIII*, Vol. 8

Urban VIII (1623–1644) was elected after a difficult conclave during which 10 cardinals went down with fever and one of the principal candidates, Cardinal Borghese, became so ill that he was forced to retire. Even the voting procedure went wrong, with 20 papers for 24 cardinals. At last, however, and in an atmosphere of teeth-gritting compromise, Urban received the required majority and began his pontificate. Perhaps understandably, after the ruses of the conclave, Urban chose to distance himself from the college of cardinals and rely upon his own judgment (which was not as acute as he thought), and on members of his own fam-

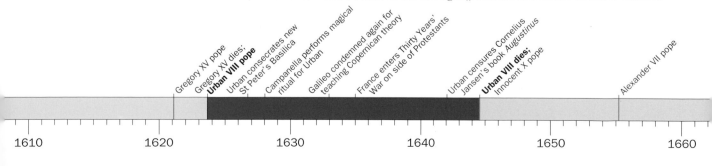

Gregory XV pope

Gregory XV dies; **Urban VIII pope**

Urban consecrates new St Peter's Basilica

Campanella performs magical ritual for Urban

Galileo condemned again for teaching Copernican theory

France enters Thirty Years' War on side of Protestants

Urban censures Cornelius Jansen's book *Augustinus*

Urban VIII dies; Innocent X pope

Alexander VII pope

1610   1620   1630   1640   1650   1660

CARDINAL RICHELIEU

Armand Jean du Plessis de Richelieu (1585–1642) came from a minor family of the French *noblesse* which had a history of royal service. When his elder brother, who had been destined for the bishopric of Luçon, entered a Carthusian monastery, Armand became bishop in his place (1607) and worked hard in his diocese to better conditions there for everyone. In 1616, he became secretary of State under the patronage of the queen mother, Marie de Medici, and in 1622 was rewarded with a cardinal's hat. Rapidly making himself indispensable to both King Louis XIII and the queen mother, Richelieu survived Marie's fall from power in 1630 and went on to form a remarkable political partnership with the king. Under their dual guidance, France rose to be the first power in Europe, extended her borders and subordinated her aristocracy to the centralized authority of the crown.

In religious affairs, Richelieu sought to curb the pretensions of the French Huguenots, laying siege to their stronghold of La Rochelle in 1627–1628 in order to do so. He also persuaded the king to dedicate France to the Virgin Mary in 1637, and published books supporting traditional Catholic teaching on asceticism and a defence of the Faith against certain French controversialists.

In foreign policy, however, Richelieu supported the Protestant German princes and King Gustavus Adolphus of Sweden against the Holy Roman emperor in an attempt to undermine the empire and thus make France the dominant power in Europe.

ily whom he advanced with prodigal abandon. Both self-reliance and nepotism brought trouble in their wake. At the end of his pontificate, for example, his trust of his greedy nephews propelled him into a local Italian conflict (1641–44) which drained papal finances and ruined the states' economies. As for the wider scene, unlike Pope Gregory, Urban chose to draw closer to France, largely because of his suspicion of Habsburg (imperial) ambitions in Italy. But, outfaced by France's minister of genius, Cardinal Richelieu, who intended to make France the greatest power in Europe, Urban failed to provide himself with a sufficient counterbalance to French ambitions, and thus watched helplessly in 1635 while Emperor Ferdinand II was forced to make peace with the German Protestants to free himself to deal with France, who had just entered the war on the Protestant side. Urban could only remark, 'If there is a God, Cardinal Richelieu will have much to answer for. If there is not, he has done very well.'

Ever suspicious of other people, Urban turned to magic for protection. Having had astrologers cast the horoscopes of cardinals resident in Rome to find out when they would die, and knowing that details of his own horoscope were common currency in every street, Urban ordered Tommaso Campanella to perform a magical ceremony to protect him from the effects of an imminent lunar eclipse. Campanella was a Dominican who had been arrested and imprisoned in 1589 for heresy

Terracota statue of Galileo by Andrea Boni of Milan (Science Museum, London). Famous for advocating that the sun revolved round the earth instead of vice versa, Galileo (1564–1642) was censured for teaching the Copernican theory by Paul V. Under Urban VIII, Galileo was again condemned as a heretic and forced to abjure his errors despite the fact that he was a personal friend of the pope.

(Right) 18th-century engraving of the magnificent Palazzo Barberini by Bernini. The Barberini family was the most generous patron of the arts in 17th-century Rome, and Bernini's career suffered for a while after the death of Urban VIII.

(Opposite) An astrological chart, showing the signs of the zodiac. The magical ceremony which Urban ordered Tommaso Campanella to perform to ward off harm from a lunar eclipse incorporated the signs of the zodiac into an elaborate, far-from-Christian ceremony.

and had been released only a short time before the pope sent for him at the beginning of 1628. In a ritual which Campanella seems to have devised for the occasion, a room in the Lateran Palace was sealed; its walls were hung with white silk, and sweet-smelling herbs and other substances were burned. Two large lamps represented the sun and moon, while other signs of the zodiac were present and astrological music, relating to Jupiter and Venus, was played by people immune to evil astral influences. The intention was to create an alternative model of the heavens with favourable conjunctions of the stars and planets, whereby the malign effects of the lunar eclipse would be negated.

Whatever the reasoning behind it, the ritual seems to have worked. But was it because of some sympathy for the magical cast of mind, which operated with a universe still conceived according to ancient astronomical theory, that Urban accepted the condemnation of Galileo in 1633 for questioning that very concept? Perhaps Urban was simply suspicious of notions which smacked of heresy, for in 1642 he censured a book by Cornelius Jansen which expounded certain controversial questions of theology raised long before by St Augustine, and which were to lie at the heart of a subsequent heretical movement called Jansenism.

The reign, which had begun with a conclave at loggerheads, ended with a city in riot. Urban's financial extravagance and his petty Italian wars had combined to make him deeply unpopular in Rome, and when he died there was rowdy celebration. Yet he had left a permanent mark on the city as the flowering of Roman baroque reached its climax. For during his pontificate, Bernini created the monumental *baldacchino* over the high altar in St Peter's – the bronze for which unfortunately came from the girders of the porch of the Pantheon; many churches were restored and embellished and his family home, the Palazzo Barberini, was reconstructed according to the most magnificent and sumptuous design.

Innocent X
1644–1655

Alexander VII
1655–1667

Clement IX
1667–1669

Clement X
1670–1676

Innocent XI
1676–1689

Alexander VIII
1689–1691

Innocent XII
1691–1700

Clement XI
1700–1721

Innocent XIII
1721–1724

Benedict XIII
1724–1730

Clement XII
1730–1740

Benedict XIV
1740–1758

Clement XIII
1758–1769

PAPAL NAMES	
INNOCENT X	Elected pope
Nationality	15 September
Italian, from Rome	1644
Date of birth	*Age at election*
7 May 1574	70
Original name	*Died*
Giambattista	1 January 1655
Pamfili	*Length of pontificate*
Early career	10 years, 3
Papal nuncio,	months, 17 days
cardinal priest	

The new pope, **Innocent X** (1644–1655), at once overturned his predecessor Urban's pro-French and pro-familial tendencies. The Barberini family was dispossessed of its property and wealth, and relations with the French cardinal Mazarin became somewhat strained as the pope made clear his preference for Spain and the Habsburgs. Out of deference to Spain, for example, Innocent refused to recognize Portugal's independence, or to acknowledge John IV of Braganza as its lawful king (1648). In 1647 when Naples revolted against Spanish control, Innocent rejected the notion of ruling the southern kingdom himself, because the suggestion to do so came from France. Not that his change of policy did him much good. When the Thirty Years' War ended in 1648, Innocent issued a bull which declared that articles in the peace treaty detrimental to the Catholic faith were null and void, but found himself ignored by each side of the conflict. More successful was his condemnation in 1653 of propositions from Cornelius Jansen's book, *Augustinus*, a censure which actually chimed with the disapproval of the French government and was thus a severe setback for the spread of Jansenism.

Innocent's principal adviser throughout his pontificate was his sister-in-law, Olimpia Maidalchini-Pamfili, a woman much reviled for her greed and leaping ambition. 'Olimpia's influence', wrote a contempo-

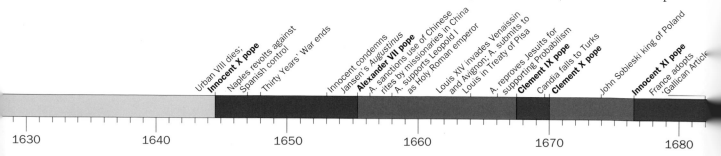

Bust of Innocent X by Algardi in the Palazzo Doria Pamfili, Rome. Innocent was generous to his people during the floods and famine of 1646–1647 which ravaged the Papal States.

Algardi's bust of Innocent X's domineering sister-in-law, Olimpia Pamfili (Palazzo Doria Pamfili, Rome). Her son, Camillo, built the Palazzo Pamfili in the Corso, and a large villa near the Porta San Pancrazio.

rary, 'grows every day. She visits the pope every other day and the whole world turns to her.' Olimpia sold benefices and civil and military offices to the highest bidder; her son was made a cardinal, and she nearly succeeded in overthrowing Cardinal Chigi, who had become Innocent's secretary of state in 1651. Stories about her relationship with the pope abounded, of course, but one must remember he was 80 when he died, and Olimpia's attitude towards him was then made abundantly clear when neither she nor her son would pay for his funeral. Indeed, they allowed his body to fester in a corner of St Peter's sacristy before it was buried (at someone else's expense), in the simplest style imaginable.

Cardinal Chigi succeeded Innocent as **Alexander VII** (1655–1667) after a conclave lasting for three months. But continuing Innocent's anti-French policy – for example, by supporting the election of Leopold I of Austria as Holy Roman emperor despite Cardinal Mazarin's vociferous opposition – proved to be a mistake, because Cardinal Mazarin then took every opportunity to support those Italian families who had a grudge against the papacy; and after Mazarin died, King Louis XIV extended French hostility by invading the papal estates in Avignon and Venaissin. Alexander could rally no friends and in 1664 submitted to Louis. This submission was followed the next year by a renewed papal declaration (in accordance with Louis's wishes) that Innocent X had been right to condemn certain Jansenist propositions, and that all clergy must accept the pope's decisions on these points. In 1666, he was able to act unsupervised and bared his teeth at the Jesuits, formally reproving them for supporting certain philosophical postulates called Probabilism, which he regarded as morally dubious and ethically undesirable.

But such matters gave Alexander little pleasure. He much preferred to enjoy events such as the conversion of the ex-queen of Sweden, the slightly eccentric Christina, who came to live in Rome after her abdication and enhanced the joys of the city by appearing in men's attire. The pope was charmed by her and, quite against convention, allowed her to lodge in the Vatican on the night of her formal entry. Alexander also delighted in patronizing the arts and employed Bernini both as sculptor and architect. Bernini built the great Scala Regia, which leads to the Sistine Chapel, and the immense colonnade of the piazza of St Peter's, his greatest architectural achievement and a masterpiece.

Edict of Nantes revoked

France and papacy on verge of schism

Alexander VIII pope

Innocent XII pope

Innocent publishes decree banning nepotism

Innocent renews condemnation of Jansenism

I. supports Philip of Anjou's claim to Spanish throne

Clement XI pope

War of Spanish Succession begins

C. forced to recognize Charles of Austria as king of Spain

Anti-Jansenist bull, *Unigenitus Dei Filius*, published

Turks declare war on Venice

C. forbids use of Chinese rites by missionaries

Jansenist leaders excommunicated

Innocent XIII pope

I. invests Charles VI with Sicily and Naples

Benedict XIII pope

Benedict makes Niccolò Coscia a cardinal

Clement XII pope

C. condemns Freemasonry

1690   1700   1710   1720   1730

(*Above*) Ex-Queen Christina of Sweden converting to Catholicism in 1655 before Alexander VII (National Museum, Stockholm). She shocked Rome by wearing male attire, and by the free way she tended to ignore convention.

(*Above*) Foundation medal of the Piazza of St Peter 1657 (British Museum) and (*above right*) part of the colonnade on the north side of the piazza. The piazza in front of St Peter's was begun in 1656 under the patronage of Alexander VII. Bernini designed it to accommodate the huge crowds which flocked every year to receive the pope's blessing *Urbi et Orbi* on Easter Sunday. The freestanding colonnades were his novel solution to the problem of enclosing the crowds without creating claustrophobia.

In August 1666, however, the pope suffered from pain in his kidneys. He was tortured by his ailments until, on 22 May 1667, he died.

His successor's reign was relatively short. **Clement IX** (1667–1669), unlike Alexander, managed to obtain and keep a certain degree of French goodwill, while still preserving an amity with Spain. During Alexander's pontificate, a fracas involving papal troops and the French ambassador had resulted in King Louis's demanding an apology in the form of a public monument recording the soldiers' guilt. This was now removed, although in fact it was only a minor victory, since a problem over Jansenist bishops and nuns in Paris was settled on the king's terms, in spite of attempts to disguise that unpalatable fact. Thus France continued to enjoy control over her own ecclesiastical appointments. French dominance in European politics, too, drew attention to the secular weakness of the papacy. When the Venetian defenders of Candia, the last

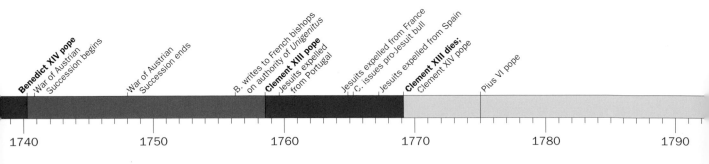

Benedict XIV pope
War of Austrian Succession begins

War of Austrian Succession ends

B. writes to French bishops on authority of *Unigenitus*
Clement XIII pope
Jesuits expelled from Portugal

Jesuits expelled from France
C. issues pro-Jesuit bull
Jesuits expelled from Spain

Clement XIII dies;
Clement XIV pope

Pius VI pope

1740   1750   1760   1770   1780   1790

[Hostile gossip about Pope Innocent XI.]

Innocent XI was accused of not giving audience, of harshness, cruelty, inflexible enmity to princes, of love of controversy, of irresolution and obstinacy, of being a destroyer of dioceses and ecclesiastical property because he remained many years without appointing to them.

Giovanni Lando: *Relatione di Roma,*
1691

Christian stronghold on Crete, which had been under attack by the Ottoman Turks since 1645, were in need of rescue, Clement signally failed to secure help from Louis, and when Candia fell on 5 September 1669, Clement was left to shoulder the financial burden attendant on that defeat. So perhaps it is not surprising that Clement was felled by a stroke in October 1669 and died five weeks later. He is unusual among popes in being the librettist of several operas. Indeed, he created the genre of sacred opera as well as writing libretti for some of the earliest comic operas. He possessed real gifts as a poet, and it was these in particular which had recommended him early in life to the powerful Barberini family and thus opened for him a route to advancement.

Five months after Clement's death, the cardinals elected a man in his 80th year, who took the name **Clement X** (1670–1676). Already infirm, Clement handed day-to-day control of the Church to Cardinal Paluzzi whose nephew had married Clement's niece. In Europe, John Sobieski decisively beat off a Turkish threat to Poland in 1673 and was elected as Polish king in 1674. This was good news for the pope. Louis XIV, on the other hand, full of plans to invade Holland, provided no assistance to Clement's efforts to stave off this Turkish menace, but allowed the pope to think that his plans for the conquest of Holland were motivated by a desire to restore Catholicism there. When the pope realized he had been duped, he turned towards Spain instead; whereupon Louis set about appropriating the revenues of French abbeys and vacant French bishoprics for his own war effort. Bullied by France – although other Catholic powers, too, were not above taking advantage of his weakness – Clement had a worrisome pontificate. He died of dropsy followed by a malignant fever, relieved to be freed from the burdens of his difficult office.

Abrasive relations with France continued during the pontificate of **Innocent XI** (1676–1689). In 1673 and 1675, Louis had exerted his claims over the French Church without evoking a protest from Pope Clement. Innocent, however, made plain his rejection of these pretensions and was met, in 1682, by the publication of the 'Gallican Articles', a list of propositions accepted by most of the French clergy, denying the pope any authority in secular affairs and declaring him subordinate to the power of a general council. Innocent immediately denounced these articles, and thus the gulf between pope and France deepened. Not even Louis's revocation of the Edict of Nantes in 1685, whereby the privileges hitherto accorded to the Protestant Huguenots were cancelled, thus opening their communities to persecution, persuaded Innocent that Louis was anything other than dangerous to papal interests. By 1688, a series of further disruptions between them had brought France to the verge of schism. Indeed, for a long time the French bore a grudge against Innocent and stopped the process of his canonization in 1744. Only in 1956 was he declared 'Blessed', and sainthood is still denied him.

Other foreign affairs, however, proved somewhat more satisfactory. The Ottoman Turks continued to threaten Europe, but in 1683 John III Sobieski of Poland pushed them back from Vienna and, with encourage-

The Catholic king James VII of Scotland and II of England fleeing to France in 1688 where he was forced to live as a pensioner of Louis XIV. The loss of this Catholic monarch was a blow to Pope Innocent XI. His court in exile was regarded as being religious, gloomy and faction-ridden.

17th-century bust of Alexander VIII, a popular pope when elected. He was kindly, courteous, gentle and cheerful, in marked contrast to his predecessor (Victoria and Albert Museum, London).

ment and subsidies from the pope, an imperial league drove them out of Hungary and liberated Belgrade. 1688 held disappointment, however, when the Catholic James VII of Scotland and II of England was driven from the throne by a political cabal and his Protestant daughter and her Protestant Dutch husband were invited to usurp his place. In June 1689, the pope succumbed to an attack of fever aggravated by gout. After he died, an autopsy revealed that he had been suffering from two large kidney stones as well. Frugal, devout and reformist, Innocent had been, in many ways, an excellent pope.

Nevertheless, the struggle with France had marred Innocent's pontificate and was to prove a continuing problem for **Alexander VIII** (1689–1691). Both Alexander and Louis XIV began by making conciliatory gestures to one another – Avignon and Venaissin which Louis had occupied were handed back; a Gallican bishop received a cardinal's hat – but coolness broke out afresh over Louis's further extension of Gallican claims, and even relations with Emperor Leopold I were not of the best. In theological matters, however, the pope was well able to exert his authority. Earlier in his career, Alexander had been head of the Roman Inquisition and this undoubtedly helped to mould his experience and led him to take a hard line on certain relaxed notions of moral philosophy still current among the Jesuits, to condemn (yet again) further Jansenist propositions, and to punish the followers of a Spanish priest, Miguel de Molinos, who had been censured by Innocent XI for Quietism – a declaration that religion can be found more truly in tranquillity of mind than in outward forms of worship.

The pope had been 79 when the cardinals elected him, but he was quite vigorous until January 1691 when it was discovered that one of his legs had turned gangrenous. He lingered until 1 February, having battled gamely but without success throughout his pontificate against the increasing secular weakness which was infecting the papacy.

Factionalism among the cardinals made the conclave which followed Alexander's death a long one, but at last, after five months, **Innocent XII** (1691–1700) was selected as a compromise candidate. The new pope chose his papal name out of admiration for Innocent XI, and at once proceeded to act after much the same fashion. He reintroduced frugality to the papal court, reformed many abuses or laxities in papal administration, and set up charitable institutions to look after the poor. Above all, in 1692 he dealt a deathblow to papal nepotism by publishing a decree which forbade popes from granting land, offices or revenue to any papal relative, a decree which met resistance from some of the cardinals. Innocent also made clear his disapproval of Jansenist teachings (1696), and in 1699 condemned – at the insistence of Louis XIV – certain mysti-

PAPAL NAMES

ALEXANDER VIII
Nationality
  Italian, from Venice
Date of birth
  22 April 1610
Original name
  Pietro Ottoboni
Family background
  Aristocratic
Early career
  Judge of the Rota,
  Inquisitor of Rome,
  cardinal bishop
Elected pope
  6 October 1689
Age at election
  79
Died
  1 February 1691
Length of pontificate
  1 year, 3 months,
  26 days

INNOCENT XII
Nationality
  Italian, from
  Spinazzola
Date of birth
  13 March 1615
Original name
  Antonio Pignatelli
Family background
  Aristocratic
Early career
  Archbishop of
  Naples, cardinal
  priest
Elected pope
  12 July 1691
Age at election
  76
Died
  27 September
  1700
Length of pontificate
  9 years, 2 months,
  16 days

CLEMENT XI
Nationality
  Italian, from Urbino
Date of birth
  23 July 1649
Original name
  Giovanni Francesco
  Albani
Family background
  Aristocratic
Status
  Clement was not
  ordained priest until
  September 1700
Early career
  Cardinal priest
Elected pope
  23 November 1700
Age at election
  51
Died
  19 March 1721
Length of pontificate
  20 years, 3
  months, 27 days

INNOCENT XIII
Nationality
  Italian, from Poli
Date of birth
  13 May 1655
Original name
  Michelangelo dei
  Conti
Family background
  Aristocratic
Early career
  Cardinal priest
Elected pope
  8 May 1721
Age at election
  65
Died
  7 March 1724
Length of pontificate
  2 years, 10 months

Portrait of Louis XIV of France by Rigaud (Louvre). Louis's long reign (1643–1715) overlapped the reigns of 9 popes. He revoked the Edict of Nantes, which had given limited rights to French Protestants, in 1685, but nevertheless came into conflict with many papal interests, to the point where the French crown and the papacy were almost completely divided during the reign of Innocent XI.

cal ideas taught by a French woman, Madame de Guyon, who was supported by Fénelon, the archbishop of Cambrai. What could one expect? Louis had seen six popes already during his long reign, and would have dealings with another after Innocent; so his will would be forcefully expressed and almost certain to predominate. Nevertheless, political circumstances had ranged much of Europe, especially the empire, against Louis, and so he decided to seek an amicable compromise with the pope. In return for allowing Innocent to make regular the positions of those French bishops who, since 1682, had suffered from the near breach between French crown and papacy, Innocent agreed to accept Louis's Gallican pretensions which left the crown more or less in control of the Church in France. It was not altogether a satisfactory situation, but at least it was a *modus vivendi*.

The pope's last major political act involved the throne of Spain. This had become vacant in 1699 and two candidates for it emerged: Archduke Charles of Austria and, by Spanish preference, King Louis's grandson, Philip of Anjou. The pope was consulted and recommended Philip, who thereupon became Philip V of Spain. Obviously, the sight of a Frenchman on the Spanish throne allied to (if not under the thumb of) Louis XIV sent Europe into paroxysms of resistance, and **Clement XI** (1700–1721), who inherited Innocent's choice, had to cope with a war which lasted for much of his reign.

Relations between the papacy and the empire had not been good since 1691, partly because of the overweening pretensions of the imperial ambassador in Rome. But when the War of the Spanish Succession flared between the empire and France and Spain, Clement did his best to remain neutral in order to preserve the possibility of his acting as a mediator. This, however, did not occur because the papacy was no longer regarded as a major political factor in Europe. Therefore, when imperial troops invaded the Papal States and conquered Naples,

An 18th-century engraving showing the Jansenists in heaven with God striking down the anti-Jansen bull *Unigenitus Dei Filius*. The Church found the élitism of Jansenist belief objectionable, and its invitation to raise the dictates of the individual conscience above the directives of the Church was equally unwelcome.

Engraving of the Italian Jesuits Michele Ruggieri and Matteo Ricci, who learned Chinese and gained the respect of the scholar-élite in China. Ricci established himself in Peking in 1601 and lived there for 18 years. The Jesuit missionaries favoured the adoption of Chinese beliefs and rituals to make the assimilation to the new religion easier. Clement XI banned these practices, however, causing the Chinese to turn against the Christian missionaries and the converted Chinese Christians. From A Kircher's *China Monumentis* (1667).

He [Innocent XIII] died on 7 March 1724 at the age of sixty-nine years. When urged, in his last moments, to fill the vacancies in the Sacred College, 'I am not of this world', he replied, and with these words he expired.

Abbé Darras *General History of the Catholic Church*, 443

Clement was forced in 1709 to abandon Philip V and recognize Charles as the legitimate king of Spain. Spain turned hostile, and when the war came to an end with the Treaty of Utrecht (1713), various papal fiefs, including Sardinia and Sicily, were handed over to new rulers without any regard to the pope. So enfeebled, indeed, was Clement's position that when the Turks declared war on Venice in 1714, he could not raise an effective alliance against them.

Louis XIV's long reign was coming to an end in 1715, with France much weaker in Europe than she had been while Louis was in his prime. Nevertheless, the king had been able to insist that the pope comprehensively condemn the Jansenist movement in a bull, *Unigenitus Dei Filius*, published in September 1713, followed by excommunication of some of the movement's leaders in 1718. Clement took another decision which had long-term consequences. For some time, Jesuit and Dominican missionaries in China had been arguing about whether it was proper, as a means of easing conversion, to adapt Chinese beliefs and ceremonies to Christian practice. Clement declared himself opposed to this in 1704 repeating the ruling in 1715, and as a result, the Chinese turned against the missionaries, persecuted Chinese Christians and closed down the missions themselves.

The conclave which elected Clement's successor was long and stormy as French and imperial supporters disputed with each other. At last **Innocent XIII** (1721–1724) was chosen, but his reign merely served to show how politically weak the papacy had become. He was obliged on the one hand to invest Emperor Charles VI with Sicily and Naples, despite the fact that these actually owed allegiance to himself as pope; and on the other to make a cardinal of Guillaume Dubois, principal minister of Louis XV's regent, a man altogether unsuitable for that advancement. He also issued what was rapidly becoming a regular papal condemnation of Jansenism, but then succumbed to the ill health which had troubled his entire pontificate, and died on 7 March 1724. The cardinals subsequently elected a Dominican, **Benedict XIII** (1724–1730), like his predecessor a member of one of Italy's grandest noble famil᠁s. Benedict, who needed to be persuaded to accept the papacy, continu᠁d to live the life of a friar after his election. Frugal beyond the examp᠁e even of the popes before him, he visited the sick and the dying, looked after the poor, and in general acted as if he were scarcely more than the bishop of Rome. In keeping with his principles, he also sought to curb some of the fashionable ostentation of many of the cardinals, announcing especially that he would not tolerate the wearing of wigs; and (an unheard of practice), he was accustomed to ride incognito out of the city without an escort so that he might take exercise uninterrupted.

When it came to more 'papal' affairs, however, Benedict's behaviour was less than happy. He reaffirmed condemnation of the Jansenists in 1725, which caused not a stir; but he provoked an international outcry by his manner of promoting the Feast Day of St Gregory VII, whereby he drew attention to Gregory's deposition of a Holy Roman emperor – a

Tomb of Benedict XIII in Santa Maria sopra Minerva, by Pietro Bracci. The pope is represented as an old man absorbed in private prayer.

piece of tactlessness which was exacerbated by his growing unpopularity. This he achieved unwittingly by his promotion of a scoundrel, Niccolò Coscia, to the cardinalate. Coscia and his cronies had little policy other than to enrich themselves by selling offices and accepting bribes, and to make sure that the pope received advice only from them. Hence it was that papal finances were weakened and that King Victor Amadeus II of Savoy and Emperor Charles VI were able to gain undue control over Church affairs in Sardinia and Sicily. It was a remarkably good example of the apparent rule that the more a pope devoted himself to being a pastor of his people, the more feeble his grip on secular affairs became, with attendant unhappy results for papal effectiveness outside purely Church concerns.

In 1732, Clement XII held a competition to design the Trevi fountain and Nicolo Salvi's design was accepted. Erection was completed in 1762, after Salvi's death. The water for the fountain comes from an aqueduct originally built by Agrippa in 19 BC.

St John Lateran is the cathedral of Rome and thus the principal church of the Roman Catholic world. It was the first Christian basilica to be built in Rome. The east façade was added by Clement XII in 1734.

Benedict died at the age of 81. What was by now the usual bad-tempered conclave dragged on for several months. At last the cardinals elected a man who was 79, frequently bedridden and, after 1732, completely blind. The choice of **Clement XII** (1730–1740) was perhaps a cynical manoeuvre to break the deadlock, but if that is so, the pope managed to outwit his electors by living for 10 more years.

The new pope's incapacities meant that he relied on other people to assist him, particularly his nephew, Cardinal Corsini. Together they arrested Cardinal Coscia, put him on trial, and had him committed to prison to serve a 10-year sentence. They then tried to untangle the mess of papal finances. But corruption was deeply entrenched in the administration and, despite their efforts, the level of debt continued to rise. Clement did use his family's considerable wealth to beautify Rome still further with such embellishments as the Trevi Fountain and the façade of St John Lateran.

The enfeeblement of papal prestige in secular affairs, however, continued apace. Whether it was virtual annexation of papal fiefs by Emperor Charles, war over who should succeed to the throne of Poland, or invasion of the Papal States by Spanish troops, Pope Clement's attempts to interfere, mediate, guide, control or indeed exercise any of the normal temporal powers of his office simply had no impact. Rather more effective were his condemnation of Freemasonry in 1738 – because he believed that Freemasonry's openness to all religious affiliations could lead to religious indifferentism, and that its oath of secrecy was a potential threat to Church and State; his interest in the work of foreign missions in fields as far apart as Ethiopia, Paraguay, Burma and Tibet; and his encouragement of the Lebanese Maronite Christians, an ancient Eastern Church, to adopt an ecclesiastical law and liturgy more in tune with those of Rome.

A combination of gout and hernia caused his doctors anxiety towards

The Lord died under Pilate. I shall probably die under Pontius.

Benedict XIV to his doctor, Pontio

the end of 1738, but the pope rallied until bladder trouble in January 1740 signalled his approaching death. His reign had been remarkable for his personal vigour in the face of his many physical disabilities. But it had also illustrated how fast the papacy was ceasing to be an effective secular power in a Europe of absolutist states. The choice of the next pope was therefore a difficult one, and it took the cardinals six months to make up their minds. When they did so, they elected **Benedict XIV** (1740–1758), who had not entered anyone's head as a candidate until the very last minute. At once Benedict set about coming to terms with the various points of abrasion which had caused trouble for his immediate predecessors. By conceding political realities, even if these were to the detriment of the papacy as a temporal power, he removed much of the recent difficulty with Spain and Portugal, although his touch with the Holy Roman empire proved somewhat less sure. Emperor Charles VI died in 1740 and a dispute over succession arose between Francis of Lorraine and Charles Albert of Bavaria. The former was married to Maria Theresa of Austria, daughter of Charles VI, who strongly pressed on the pope her husband's claim. Benedict dithered. First he supported Maria Theresa, then Charles Albert, thus alienating Austria and damaging the interests of the Church there. In Church affairs, Benedict was more successful. He improved papal finances, emphasized the duties of bishops, began a reform of the breviary, condemned the Jesuits' use of native rituals in China, reiterated Clement XII's fulmination against Freemasonry, censured the Jesuits in Portugal for neglecting their rule and involving themselves in trade, and issued a letter to the French bishops, reminding them of Clement XI's condemnation of Jansenism.

Benedict's personal interests lay in scholarship. He established four academies in Rome, devoted to various aspects of history and liturgy, all

Painting by Battoni showing Benedict XIV presenting the Encyclical *Ex Omnibus* to the Duc de Choiseul, the French ambassador (Minneapolis Institute of Art). This letter reiterated Clement XI's condemnation of Jansenism, but ruled that only those who publicly opposed the bull *Unigenitus* should be refused the sacraments.

Jesuits being expelled from Spain in 1767. The illustration purports to show them as 'the authors of pernicious leagues and plots'. Benedict XIV was said to look upon the Jesuits as follows: 'Benedict XIV, who had so many virtues and who said so many witty things, and whom we still miss long after his death, regarded the [Jesuits] as the janissaries of the Holy See, a body of soldiers who were restless and dangerous, but good servants.' Diderot *Encyclopédie*, s.v. 'Jésuite'.

of which attracted many of the most distinguished scholars of the day. In the University of Rome he created two new professorial chairs, one for higher mathematics, the other for chemistry; and in the University of Bologna he revived the practice of anatomical studies and founded a chair of surgery. To the Institute of Sciences in Bologna (his native city) he also gave his private library, which – together with that of Cardinal Monti, another benefactor – amounted to 80,000 volumes and 2,500 manuscripts. Such munificence, not only to Rome and Bologna but to other Italian cities, makes Benedict XIV one of the great Church patrons in the style, if not the preferred subject matter, of the Renaissance.

Benedict had been very ill in 1756, close to death in fact, but had recovered beyond expectation. In 1757, however, he fell prey to kidney disease and in spring 1758 to fever and inflammation of the lungs. He died quietly at midday on 3 May, regretted by many Protestants as well as Catholics. The conclave which followed produced a candidate who was vetoed by France. The successful choice, **Clement XIII** (1758–1769) was therefore a compromise. Strongly pro-Jesuit, in contrast with Benedict XIV who had been highly suspicious of the society, he was confronted within two months of his election by an anti-Jesuit scandal. Joseph I of Portugal was sure that Jesuits had been behind an attempt to assassinate him, and drove them out of the country in 1759. The pope protested, and Portugal broke off relations with the Holy See. France followed Portugal's lead, and in 1764 Jesuits were banished from there as well. Then Spain caught the fever. King Charles II became convinced that the Jesuits were planning to depose him, and on 2 April 1767 had 6,000 of them arrested and shipped to Italy. Naples and Parma imitated his example, and when the refugees tried to settle in Corsica they were thrown out of there, too. Finally these European powers, with the tacit support of Austria which refused to interfere, demanded that the pope dissolve the society. Clement appeared to capitulate and summoned a consistory for that purpose, but the day before it met he fell dead of a heart attack.

The heady days of secular power and corruption which had characterized the reigns of the early Renaissance popes were now far away and must have seemed almost incredible to anyone looking back two and a half centuries. By the dawn of the industrial age and the French Revolution, the papacy had changed considerably. Political weakness and personal integrity were now its characteristics, more or less the opposite of those of popes such as Alexander VI and Julius II. Gradually, it seems, a modern papacy was being born.

Clement XIV
1769–1774

Leo XIII
1878–1903

Benedict XV
1914–1922

Pius XII
1939–1958

Pius VI
1775–1799

Pius X
1903–1914

Pius XI
1922–1939

John XXIII
1958–1963

Pius VII
1800–1823

Paul VI
1963–1978

Leo XII
1823–1829

John Paul I
1978

Pius VIII
1829–1830

John Paul II
1978–

Gregory XVI
1831–1846

Pius IX
1846–1878

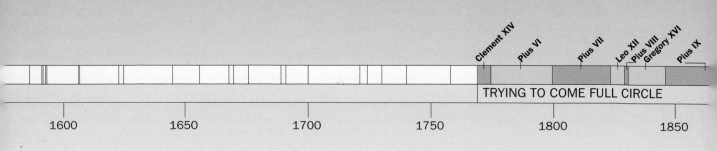

TRYING TO COME FULL CIRCLE

Clement XIV   Pius VI   Pius VII   Leo XII   Pius VIII   Gregory XVI   Pius IX

1600   1650   1700   1750   1800   1850

Pius VII   Leo XIII   John XXIII   John Paul II

TRYING TO COME FULL CIRCLE
AD 1769–1997

With the late 18th century, the papacy entered its latest stage of change. At first little appeared to be different when Napoleon Bonaparte rose to supplant Louis XIV as the manipulator of the pope and the dominant political power in Europe. But two things happened which caused great changes: the industrial and the French revolutions. Between them they confronted the world with explosive material inventions which would alter people's lives out of all recognition, and with the notion that a materialist philosophy was both 'correct' and preferable to any that had gone before.

This immense passion for new things and the materialist mentality which lay behind it presented the papacy with its greatest challenge since the Reformation, and during the 19th century the popes tried to shed the last remnants of their own secular powers and return to the roots of their office by seeking to become real pastors to their flock.

The 20th century offered further challenges: two world wars, Communism, a spread of materialism made ever more easy by cinema and television, and the need for the papacy to confront and adapt to change without surrendering the Faith have tested the nerve and skill of each pope in turn. An imperial, or even a princely papacy, could not have answered people's needs in such times in the same way as that of a father and a shepherd. Hence modern popes have turned back to their beginnings to find inspiration in the commands which started their mission: 'feed my lambs', 'feed my sheep'.

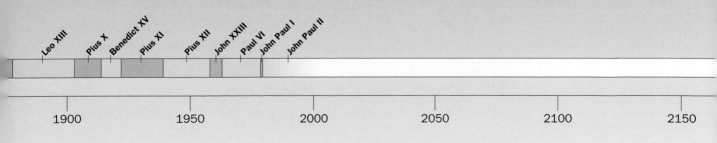

Leo XIII   Pius X   Benedict XV   Pius XI   Pius XII   John XXIII   Paul VI   John Paul I   John Paul II

1900   1950   2000   2050   2100   2150

Clement XIV
1769–1774

Pius VI
1775–1799

Pius VII
1800–1823

Leo XII
1823–1829

Pius VIII
1829–1830

Gregory XVI
1831–1846

Pius IX
1846–1878

Clement XIV died from fear of dying. Poison was his idée fixe, *and the sudden decomposition of his body was merely the result of the dreadful fright which killed him.*

Baron C.H. von Gleichen *Souvenirs*, 33

CLEMENT XIV	
Nationality	*Early career*
Italian, from Sant' Arcangelo near Rimini	Cardinal priest
	Elected pope
	19 May 1769
Date of birth	*Age at election*
31 October 1705	63
Original name	*Died*
Lorenzo Ganganelli	22 September 1774
Family background	*Length of pontificate*
Son of a village doctor	5 years, 4 months, 3 days
Status	
Franciscan friar	

CLEMENT XIV

I was talking yesterday to a monk of the Holy Apostles, who has always lived in the same place as the pope and knows him as well as he knows himself.... I was told that the pope's intelligence was quite extraordinary and encompassed several branches of learning such as theology, canon law, metaphysics, and history; and that he wrote with more erudition than elegance, although he was a born orator. If you speak to him, his conversation is rich, interesting, and full of images which capture your attention. When he was living in the cloister as a simple monk, he used to compare himself to a silkworm which starts to creep the moment it gets wings, and the day he was made a cardinal he joked that his work was finished since the worm had just turned into a butterfly.

Diderot *Lettres* (letter to the Abbé Galiani, June 1769)

When Clement XIII died, a crisis threatened the Church. The Catholic powers of Europe were ranged against the papacy demanding the suppression of the Society of Jesus, and **Clement XIV** (1769–1774) at last

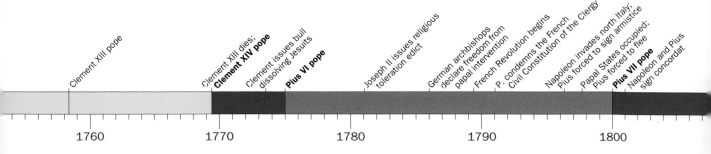

Clement XIII pope

Clement XIII dies; **Clement XIV pope**

Clement issues bull dissolving Jesuits

Pius VI pope

Joseph II issues religious toleration edict

German archbishops declare freedom from papal intervention

French Revolution begins

P. condemns the French Civil Constitution of the Clergy

Napoleon invades north Italy; Pius forced to sign armistice

Papal States occupied; Pius forced to flee

Pius VII pope

Napoleon and Pius sign concordat

1760   1770   1780   1790   1800

Marble bust of Clement XIV by Christopher Hewetson (Victoria and Albert Museum, London). In 1743, Clement published a theological treatise dedicated to St Ignatius of Loyola, with a foreword in praise of the Society of Jesus. His suppression of the society 30 years later, therefore, did not come easily to him.

gave way. He delayed for three years, full of nervous apprehensions that he might be poisoned, but in the end he dictated the fatal bull, *Dominus ac Redemptor noster*, and on 16 August 1773 the society was dissolved and its general imprisoned. The bull gave two reasons for the pope's decision. The ostensible reason – 'since [the society] can no longer bring forth the abundant fruits or be of the usefulness for which it was founded' – is followed by the real one – 'it is hardly, if at all, possible to restore a true and lasting peace to the Church as long as [the society] remains in existence' – and thus a major psychological break with the past was realized. The Jesuits had been formed as the shock troops of the papacy. A Church Militant had rounded upon the Reformation and, in the afterglow of an imperial apogee, had confidently sought to renew its teaching mission. Now that phase seemed to be over. The papacy was weak in the face of secular powers and had deprived itself of a potent weapon against the rising assaults of new philosophies – known as 'the Enlightenment' – which would combine with industrialization to produce a world radically different from that of the past. Jesuit missions were badly affected and European education received a shattering blow, for the Jesuits had been at the forefront of educational innovation. Only Russia and Prussia refused to implement the terms of the bull and in consequence afforded refuge to a significant Jesuit remnant from which restoration would be possible later on.

PIUS VI

The prestige of the papacy had perhaps never been so low, and yet the secular, often atheist tide of change which was sweeping over Europe demanded a papacy which could stand firm. **Pius VI** (1775–1799), unfortunately, was not equal to the fight. Indeed during his pontificate, the longest so far, the situation plummeted even further. Quite apart from Pius's personal mistakes – a reversion to nepotism and a fecklessness with money – three historical challenges rose to meet him and he was unable to deal with them effectively.

The first was the emperor Joseph II. He had come under the influence of ideas disseminated by the auxiliary bishop of Trier, among which were three attractive to any nationalist government: (i) the Church is not a monarchy; (ii) the popes claim many powers not actually given to them by Christ or exercised by the early Church; (iii) all bishops are equal. Adoption of these notions – known as Febronianism – would quickly lead to a diminution of respect for the papacy, a call for State

PIUS VI	
Nationality Italian, from Cesena	*Elected pope* 15 February 1775
Date of birth 25 December 1717	*Age at election* 67
Original name Giovanni Angelo Braschi	*Died* 29 August 1799, while a prisoner in the citadel of Valence
Family background Aristocratic	*Length of pontificate* 24 years, 6 months, 12 days
Early career Cardinal priest	

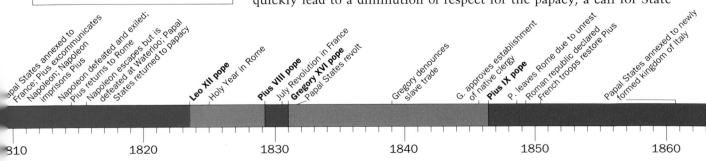

18th-century painting of Pius VI by Pompeo Battoni (Vatican Museums). After the election of Pius, two French cardinals wrote back to Paris that the new pope was an honest nobleman, well educated, of good morals, and without favourites. But they added: 'Only God knows the heart. Human beings are able to judge only by appearances. The way the new pope governs will show whether, before his election, we saw his face or only his mask.'

control of each national Church and a toleration of differences between Christian denominations. By an edict of 1781 Joseph set in motion just such a trend in the empire. By 1786, matters had reached such a pass that the pope was told by the German archbishops that he should not seek to interfere in their ecclesiastical jurisdiction. In the same year Joseph's brother, the grand duke of Tuscany, tried to introduce Febronianism into his domains, but here at last Pius had a small success in forcing the principal mover of these changes, Bishop de' Ricci, to resign.

Three years later, Pius faced his second major challenge, the French Revolution. At first he held his hand while the French clergy were reorganized and made salaried employees of the State. But when in 1791 they were required to swear an oath of loyalty to the State, he condemned the new arrangements, together with its Declaration of the Rights of Man. Relations between France and the papacy deteriorated considerably, and this led to Pius's third and biggest challenge, Napoleon Bonaparte.

In March 1796, Bonaparte had been entrusted by the French government with the task of invading northern Italy – part of a plan to take charge of the Papal States – and in May he entered Milan. From there he proclaimed his intention to restore a Roman republic. The economic and military situation in the Papal States was such that they could not mount a serious resistance, and the pope was forced to accept a humiliating armistice which cost a great deal of money, hundreds of works of art and manuscripts, and even more of the exiguous reserves of papal prestige. Yet it was not enough. In 1797, a French general was killed during rioting in Rome, thus providing a *casus belli* for the invasion and occupation of the Papal States, the proclamation of a Roman republic, and the deposition of the pope as head of State. Pius was obliged to flee and sought refuge in Florence, and for the next 18 months was moved, a virtual prisoner, from place to place in Italy and in France. The end came at daybreak on 29 August 1799, and a Paris newspaper rejoiced in the triumph of secularism. 'The death of Pius VI', it said, 'has, as it were, placed a seal on the glory of philosophy in modern times'.

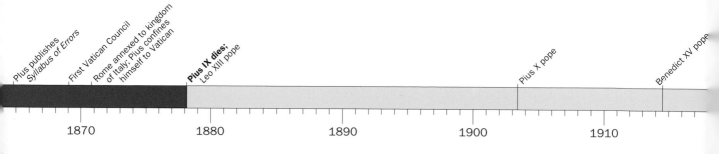

Pius publishes *Syllabus of Errors*

First Vatican Council

Rome annexed to kingdom of Italy; Pius confines himself to Vatican

Pius IX dies; Leo XIII pope

Pius X pope

Benedict XV pope

1870   1880   1890   1900   1910

NAPOLEON AND THE PAPACY

Napoleon's relations with the papacy blew hot and cold according to the dictates of the political moment. But he was always a Catholic, and his personal faith should be kept separate from his official dealings with the pope.

His campaign in Italy in 1796, as a general with the French revolutionary army, persuaded him of the Italians' devotion to the Church and therefore, despite his orders from the Directory to enter Rome and smash the papacy, he signed an armistice with the Holy See, which guaranteed papal neutrality on the one hand, and on the other assured Pius VI that he would be safe in Rome. In 1799, as First Consul, Bonaparte steered into French law a decree of religious liberty, and in 1800 he let it be known that he wished to discuss complete reconciliation between France and the Holy See. In return for recognizing limited papal authority in France and a restoration of some of the Papal States, Pius VII would recognize the legitimacy of Napoleon's government. An uneasy concordat was signed in 1801. The pope was alarmed, however, when he came to France in 1804 to preside at Bonaparte's coronation as emperor and found that subordination of the French Church to the French State was too bitter a pill to swallow. Relations between the pope and the emperor deteriorated during the period of Napoleonic expansion in Europe, and when Bonaparte sent a French general in 1808 to occupy Rome, and again annexed the Papal States in 1809, the pope had had enough. A bull of excommunication was issued. Bonaparte had the pope arrested and held in

Savona until 1812 when he was transferred to Fontainebleau where he remained until Bonaparte's first fall from power in 1814.

Bonaparte was sent into exile for a second time in 1815 and died in 1821. Pius VII, however, held no grudges and sent him a chaplain when he was dying – a recognition of that earlier re-establishment of the Church in France.

(Above) 'Remember to take off your hat' represents a certain British glee at the apparent humbling of the pope.

(Below) Painting by J-L David depicting Bonaparte crowning Josephine, with Pius VII reduced to the role of a mere spectator (Louvre). Bonaparte also crowned himself, contrary to an agreement with the pope.

PIUS VII	
Nationality	*Early career*
Italian, from Cesena	Bishop of Imola, cardinal priest
Date of birth	*Elected pope*
14 April 1742	14 March 1800
Original name	*Age at election*
Luigi Barnabà Chiaramonte	57
Family background	*Died*
Aristocratic	20 July 1823
Status	*Length of pontificate*
Benedictine monk	23 years, 4 months, 6 days

Portrait by Thomas Lawrence of Cardinal Consalvi (Windsor Castle). Consalvi was Pius VII's very able secretary of state, who helped the pope with the internal and international troubles that plagued his papacy.

PIUS VII

He was a sort of importunate bee, apt to sting from excess of sensibility, but equally ready to administer his own honey to remedy the wound he had made.

Gavazzi *My Recollections of the Last Four Popes,* 1858

Pius VII (1800–1823) was a compromise candidate, elected to break a stalemate fed by nationalist politics. With the help of his secretary of state, Cardinal Consalvi, some of the damage to papal and Catholic interests which had happened during the pontificate of Pius VI was mended after a fashion. Concordats were signed with France and the Roman republic, and in 1804 the pope even attended Bonaparte's coronation. This gesture, however, was not reciprocated by any easing of Bonaparte's determination to control the Church in France and to have Pius's cooperation during his wars in Europe; and further disagreements led to Pius's imprisonment at Savona, near Genoa (see feature p. 213). Such was his deterioration from his confinement that he gave way temporarily to humiliating demands for far-reaching concessions, including the removal of the papacy to France. But two months later he found sufficient strength to repudiate his signature, and with Bonaparte's eventual overthrow, was welcomed back to Rome. The flurry of the emperor's escape from captivity, restoration, and then defeat at Waterloo in 1815, proved to be short-lived.

Widespread admiration for the way the pope had withstood his captivity brought about remarkable changes. The Papal States were returned by agreement at the Congress of Vienna, the Inquisition and *Index* were revived, the Society of Jesus restored, and concordats with Russia and Prussia were signed. Pius issued condemnations of Protestant Bible Societies and Freemasonry, and in 1817 established a new Sacred Congregation of Propaganda, or, Propagation of the Faith. It is also to his credit that he offered refuge in Rome to members of Bonaparte's family

PIUS VII RETURNS TO ROME

He wore a white robe. His hair, which had remained black in spite of misfortune and years, formed a contrast with his hermit's pallor. On arriving at the Tomb of the Apostles, he prostrated himself. He stayed there without moving, as though dead, plunged in the depths of the counsels of Providence. The emotion was profound. Protestants who witnessed the scene wept scalding tears.

Chateaubriand *Mémoires d'outre-tombe,* Book 11

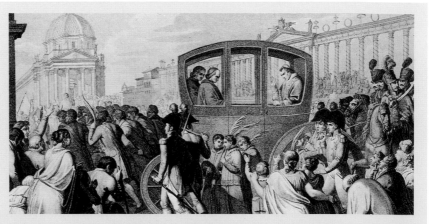

Thirty young men of the best families dragged Pius's coach to St Peter's on his return to Rome.

LEO XII	
Nationality	Bavaria, papal
Italian, from near	nuncio in Paris
Spoleto	*Elected pope*
Date of birth	28 September
22 August 1760	1823
Original name	*Age at election*
Annibale Sermattei	63
della Genga	*Died*
Family background	10 February 1829
Aristocratic	*Length of pontificate*
Early career	5 years, 4 months,
Papal nuncio in	13 days
Cologne and	

Statue of Leo XII by Giuseppe de Fabris in St Peter's Basilica, Rome, 1836. In his very first encyclical, Leo expressed his determination to raise the general standards of the clergy and to combat all dangerous teachings. His bull, *Quod divina sapientia* (1824), drew up regulations for Catholic education.

PIUS VIII	
Nationality	grand penitentiary,
Italian, from Cingoli	cardinal bishop
Date of birth	*Elected pope*
20 November 1761	31 March 1829
Original name	*Age at election*
Francesco Saverio	67
Castiglione	*Died*
Family background	30 November 1830
Aristocratic	*Length of pontificate*
Early career	1 year, 8 months
Bishop of Frascati,	

after 1815, and that he sought to intervene on the ex-emperor's behalf when he thought his captivity on the island of St Helena was too harsh.

A combination of papal courage and changing political fortunes resurrected papal prestige from the nadir of the previous two pontificates. Nevertheless, a subtle change can be discerned in emphasis. From now on the papacy, while still a political force in its own right, would seek more and more to draw attention to its spiritual and pastoral role.

LEO XII

Leo is tall and has a calm expression which is sad at the same time. He dresses simply in a white cassock. There is no splendour in his house. He lives in a poorly appointed room which has hardly any furniture. He eats next to nothing. Along with his cat he sustains life on a little polenta. He knows he is very ill.

Chateaubriand *Mémoires d'outre-tombe*, Book 12

The election of **Leo XII** (1823–1829) owed much to cardinals who wanted an emphasis on the pastoral role of the pope. Jesuit influence became strong; the society's educational system was restored; and Pius VII's strictures against Freemasonry, toleration and the notion that religious differences do not matter, were forcibly reiterated. Along with this, however, came a political conservatism which had less than happy effects. Minute surveillance of daily life in the Papal States, restoration of a feudal aristocracy and the restriction of Jews to ghettos meant that the economy stagnated, fear and suspicion were rampant, and the pope was regarded as a backward tyrant. Nevertheless, when it came to foreign policy, Leo was much more accommodating than his reputation suggested. Under the influence of Cardinal Consalvi – whose more liberal philosophy he had rejected outright in religious affairs – he maintained amicable relationships with Protestant as well as with Catholic powers, and vigorously supported any attempt in Britain to emancipate Catholics from the laws which discriminated against them. It was a curious performance, all in all, in which his efforts to awaken religion among the mass of Europe's peoples and to stem the advance of materialist philosophies were weakened by a domestic political outlook which was profoundly unsuited to the contemporary challenge.

PIUS VIII

The Romans liked him because he falsified the proverb Honores mutant mores *(honours change a person's behaviour), and did not forget as Pope that as cardinal he had loved the bottle of Orvieto, which he drank every day at an inn beyond Porta Pia.... Pius VIII died approved by all ... because if he had done no good he had, at least, done no harm to anyone.*

Gavazzi *My Recollections of the Last Four Popes*, 1858

Painting by François Gerard showing Louis Philippe accepting the French crown after the July revolution in 1830 (Versailles). Charles X abdicated on 2 August 1830 after a violent thunderstorm which had shaken Paris during the night. He abdicated in favour of the Duc de Bordeaux (Henri), but the Duc d'Orléans, Louis Philippe, was acclaimed king instead. Pius VIII acknowledged the new king, bestowing the traditional title 'Most Christian' on him.

Monument of Pius VIII by Pietro Tenerani, St Peter's Basilica, Rome. Pius VIII was in constant pain throughout his pontificate, and this made him somewhat irritable both in tone and appearance.

Pius VIII (1829–1830) firmly believed that it was religious indifference and Protestant missionary work, allied to secret societies such as the Freemasons and the Italian Carbonari, which were responsible for the breakdown of society. He therefore spoke out against them and, in an effort to shield children from the effects of mixed marriages, decreed that the Church would henceforth bless such marriages with reluctance and then only if their children were brought up as Catholics.

One event gave him pleasure, the passing of a Catholic Emancipation Act by the British Parliament in 1829. But perhaps the major event of his pontificate was the July revolution in France in 1830, which ended the reign of Charles X and brought Louis Philippe to the throne. Pius, bowing to realities, recognized Louis Philippe's title and paid him a traditional honour accorded to French kings, the title 'Most Christian', a gesture repaid by the new king's acceptance of a concordat between France and the papacy. But Pius's health, never good since his election, suddenly took a turn for the worse and he died on 30 November 1830.

GREGORY XVI

His features ... were large and rounded, and wanted those finer touches which suggest ideas of higher genius or delicate taste. But this judgment ceased the moment you came into closer contact and conversation with him.... His countenance then, and still more when discoursing on graver topics, lighted up, and was mantled with a glowing expression; his eyes became bright and animated and his intelli-

Gregory XVI, from an engraving by Henriquet-Dupont, after a drawing by Paul Delaroche. Forty-five cardinals took part in the conclave which elected Gregory XVI. The conclave lasted for 50 days and after the election Metternich, the Austrian chancellor, said he was pleased that the new pope had been born an Austrian subject.

GREGORY XVI	
Nationality Italian, from Belluno	Camaldolese Order, prefect of the
Date of birth 18 September 1765	Propaganda, cardinal priest
Original name Bartolomeo Alberto Cappellari	*Elected pope* 2 February 1831
Family background Aristocratic	*Age at election* 65
Status Camaldolese monk	*Died* 1 June 1846
Early career Vicar-general of the	*Length of pontificate* 15 years, 3 months, 27 days

gence and learning gave themselves utterance through his flowing and graceful language.

Cardinal Wiseman *Recollections of the Last Four Popes*

Gregory XVI (1831–1846), the last monk to sit on the papal throne, opposed all modern trends whether religious, philosophical or political. In consequence he found himself in difficulties both at home and abroad. The Papal States, for example, had been seething for several years and now burst into open revolt. With Austrian help, Gregory put down the insurgents but was not minded to initiate political reform. Fresh disturbances broke out and this time troops occupied the Papal States and remained there until 1838. Discontent sizzled for the rest of the pontificate, causing an endless drain on the papal treasury. Spain, Portugal and Switzerland became the objects of papal displeasure as they passed legislation which Gregory saw as anticlerical; and in 1832 and 1834 he saw fit vigorously to remind Prussia of Pius VIII's decree on mixed marriages.

Nor was he less stringent when it came to dealing with what he viewed as pernicious new ideas. In 1830, H.F.R. de Lammenais, a French priest of liberal notions, started a newspaper, *L'Avenir* (The Future), which advocated complete separation of Church and State, religious liberty, freedom of the Press, freedom of association, universal suffrage and decentralization of government. Lammenais received what amounted to little more than a slap on the wrist from the pope in August 1832, and then turned to more radical politics. By the beginning of 1834 he had ceased to function as a priest, and soon after abandoned the Church altogether. He found himself condemned and his books placed on the *Index*.

But Gregory was not entirely a figure of negative tendencies. During the 18th century, for example, the missionary work of the Church had declined to a disastrous extent. Gregory now reorganized the missions and brought them directly under papal control. He worked out guiding principles for them, and in 1845 approved the establishment of indigenous clergy in mission lands. He condemned slavery in 1839, while he exerted papal authority in the Americas, recognizing independence movements and establishing resident bishops in Latin America, and creating new dioceses in the north – 4 in Canada, 10 in the United States.

When Gregory died, a transitional period in the papacy came to an end. Since the low point of Clement XIV's unfortunate reign the popes had struggled to find a way of coming to terms with the materialist flood of the modern world. They thought they might succeed by turning back the political clock to an age before 'rationalism' took hold and by denying validity to any kind of innovation. This sometimes led to eccentricity. Gregory, for example, banned the railway in the Papal States, calling it the 'Hellway' (*chemin d'enfer*). But slowly the notion of compromise without capitulation was taking seed, and from now on the basic concern of the papacy to preserve the Faith and combat the deleterious aspects of modernism would be given freedom of expression without the hampering baggage of outmoded and restrictive political liabilities.

PIUS IX	
Nationality Italian, from Semigallia	Spoleto, cardinal priest
Date of birth 13 May 1792	*Elected pope* 16 June 1846
Original name Giovanni Maria Mastai-Ferretti	*Age at election* 54
Family background Aristocratic	*Died* 7 February 1878
Early career Archbishop of	*Length of pontificate* 31 years, 7 months, 22 days

Garibaldi showing Pius IX the cap of liberty. Pius, like Queen Victoria, was not amused.

PIUS IX

*If the council lasts much longer, I shall doubtless be infallible, but I shall also be bankrupt (*fallito*).*

Pius IX on the large number of people attending the First Vatican Council at his expense

Pius IX (1846–1878) endured rather than enjoyed the longest reign so far in papal history and presided over an extraordinary number of changes. He began his pontificate by declaring a political amnesty and set in train a number of reforms in the Papal States. But 1848 saw his initial popularity disappear when he held aloof from the Italian war against Austria which was still occupying the north of the country. With the political upheavals that followed the creation of the Roman republic in 1849 and then the kingdom of Italy in 1860, which incorporated Rome as its capital in 1870 (see box), the temporal princedom of the papacy shrank to the Vatican and its immediate environs, and thus it has remained ever since. The popes had returned to their roots (perforce, it is true), and the way was now clear for the office to exercise a purely spiritual authority unencumbered by the claims of secular government. Not that Pius surrendered quietly to this prospect. Angered by the apparent anti-clericalism of the Italian unification engineered by Camillo Cavour and Giuseppe Garibaldi, Pius declared he was their prisoner and from 1871 confined himself as such to the Vatican.

THE ROMAN REPUBLIC AND THE KINGDOM OF ITALY

In November 1848, alarmed at the political unrest, Pope Pius IX fled from Rome to Gaeta, south of Naples. On 9 February 1849, a republic was proclaimed in Rome. The new government abolished the

secular power of the pope, confiscated Church property and took over education. In July, a French army called in by the papal chancellor occupied Rome and enabled the pope to return. Thus restored, Pius took the opportunity to modernize the city and, with French help, kept things calm. Outside Rome, Count Camillo Cavour, chief minister of Piedmont, carefully engineered the rising tide of nationalism throughout Italy so that in 1860 the Papal States were annexed to the newly created kingdom of Italy leaving only Rome itself to the pope. In 1870, the French were obliged to retire from Rome to take part in the Franco-Prussian War. Soon after, soldiers led by Giuseppe Garibaldi, a republican patriot, occupied the city and the pope had to conclude an agreement with them. This left the Vatican independent of the new secular government, but its

independence was short-lived. After a plebiscite on 1 October 1870, Rome was annexed by the new kingdom of Italy and became its capital.

Many Romans acclaimed their new king, but just as many shouted for the pope.

THE DECREE OF PAPAL INFALLIBILITY

We teach and define as a divinely revealed dogma, that when the Roman pontiff speaks ex cathedra – that is, when he, using his office as pastor and teacher of all Christians, in virtue of his Apostolic office, defines a doctrine on faith and morals to be held by the whole Church – he, by the Divine assistance promised to him in the blessed Peter, possesses that infallibility with which the Divine Redeemer was pleased to invest his Church in the definition of doctrine on faith and morals, and that therefore such definitions of the Roman pontiff are irreformable in their own nature and not because of the consent of the Church.

Decree of Papal Infallibility

The 1860s and 70s were momentous years not just for Italy but for the whole Catholic Church. In December 1864, Pius published his most famous document, the *Syllabus of Errors*, which included a condemnation of those who said that 'the Roman pontiff can and should reconcile and harmonize himself with progress, with liberalism, and with recent civilization'. This, taken in context, clearly refers to the spoliation of the rights of the Church; but journalists and politicians misconstrued it as a deliberate preference for backwardness. No doubt it was this view of the *Syllabus* which caused the remarkable outburst from the *New York Herald* after Pius's death, 'The papacy has lived out its time. It has had the full thousand years of the life of a nation, a government or a system: and it must die'. Pius himself was astonished by reaction to the document. In 1869, he summoned a General Council of the Church (the First Vatican Council), whose decrees in 1870 further condemned contemporary materialism and atheism and included a declaration of papal infallibility: when the pope magisterially defines Church doctrine regarding a particular point of faith or morals, he will not be in error. Needless to say, this also caused a storm, but it can actually be seen as the logical conclusion to a question which had been exercising the Church for a very long time: is the pope or a general council the final arbiter of the Church's teaching? Indeed, it can also be seen as the triumph of ultramontanism, the overt centralization of Church authority in the papacy. Many countries in Europe raged and objected, but at least everyone now knew where he stood. The Church, stripped of its temporal powers, was offering itself as the alternative to the 'other' life of Europe, and with the regeneration of spiritual and pastoral values which was happening alongside the growth of materialism, the papacy was well-fitted (whether people liked its methods and pronouncements or not) to promote the new emphasis in its role – that of universal pastor.

(Right) The opening of the First Vatican Council summoned by Pius IX. The decrees issued from the council condemned modern-day materialism and atheism and included a declaration of papal infallibility. Pius had very strict views about Catholicism and the papacy and on 8 December 1854 he had proclaimed the dogma of the Immaculate Conception of the Virgin Mary, which says that she was born without taint of original sin. This point of faith was eagerly promoted by the Jesuits.

Leo XIII
1878–1903

Pius X
1903–1914

Photograph of Leo XIII taken in 1880. In two encyclicals (1888 and 1890), Leo urged the abolition of African slavery, and in 1899 he dedicated the whole of humanity to the Sacred Heart of Jesus.

LEO XIII	
Nationality Italian, from Carpentino	official who administers the Church during a papal vacancy), cardinal priest
Date of birth 2 March 1810	*Elected pope* 20 February 1878
Original name Gioacchino Vincenzo Pecci	*Age at election* 67
Family background Aristocratic	*Died* 20 July 1903
Early career Papal nuncio to Belgium, *camerlengo* (the	*Length of pontificate* 25 years, 4 months, 29 days

LEO XIII

Years of suffering, by lowering illness, had robbed the Pope, already in his sixty-fourth year, of many graces which adorned his earlier life.... His eye, however, and his voice, compensated for all. There was a softness and yet a penetration in the first, which gained at sight affection and excited awe ... and his voice was courteously bland and winning; he spoke without excitement, gently, deliberately, and yet flowingly.

Cardinal Wiseman *Recollections of the Last Four Popes*

The 19th century saw an enormous expansion of Catholicism, and both Pius IX and his successor, **Leo XIII** (1878–1903), established large numbers of dioceses and vicariates all over the world. Europe itself continued to be problematical. Leo reached accommodation with Germany, Belgium and Russia in an effort to allay the effects of anti-clerical or anti-Catholic laws, but the increasingly tense shifts in European political alliances undermined this progress, and his foreign policy must therefore be seen as the least successful part of his pontificate. More successful was his attempt to align the Church with trends in the modern world without compromising her traditional teaching. In letter after let-

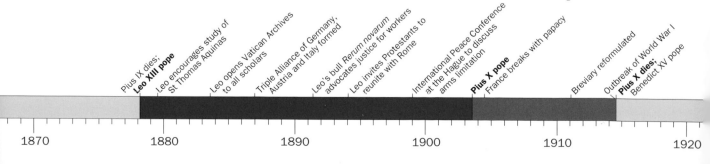

Pius IX dies; **Leo XIII pope**

Leo encourages study of St Thomas Aquinas

Leo opens Vatican Archives to all scholars

Triple Alliance of Germany, Austria and Italy formed

Leo's bull *Rerum novarum* advocates justice for workers

Leo invites Protestants to reunite with Rome

International Peace Conference at the Hague to discuss arms limitation

Pius X pope

France breaks with papacy

Breviary reformulated

Outbreak of World War I **Pius X dies;** Benedict XV pope

1870   1880   1890   1900   1910   1920

A contemporary triumphal poster showing the workers united, celebrating Pope Leo's *Rerum novarum* which advocated workers' rights and accepted trade unions.

ter he condemned, accepted and guided. Socialism, Communism and Freemasonry were condemned; democracy, workers' rights and trades' unions were accepted (these last in his most famous publication, *Rerum novarum*, 1891, which earned him the sobriquet, 'the workers' pope'); while the study of St Thomas Aquinas – to spread the doctrine that between true science and true religion there was no conflict – astronomy, natural sciences, and objective historical and Biblical research were all encouraged. Leo's attitude can be seen very clearly in his invitation to Orthodox Christians and Protestants. He spoke of them as 'our separated brethren' and invited them to reunite with Rome – a fraternal and pastoral gesture. But he also expected them to submit to Rome: accommodation would go so far, but not an inch further. A remarkable man, devoted to the Sacred Heart of Jesus and the Blessed Virgin Mary, Leo died at the age of 93, having retained his intellectual faculties to the end.

THE ELECTION OF LEO XIII

'Do you accept the election canonically made of you as Supreme Pontiff of the Catholic Church?' asks the sub-dean amid a stillness so painful that one might almost hear one's heart beat. Cardinal Pecci rises; his whole frame shakes with uncontrollable emotion. With a quivering voice, but steadily and distinctly, he affirms his own unworthiness. But seeing them all of one mind and determined in this matter, he bows to the divine will.

The sub-dean thereupon kneels before him; the master of ceremonies claps his hands, and at this signal all the cardinals rise and remain standing in homage to the new sovereign. Instantly all the canopies above the seats are lowered save that above the seat of the pope-elect. The sub-dean then asks: 'By what name do you wish to be called?' 'By the name of Leo XIII', is the prompt answer.

B. O'Reilly *Life of Leo XIII*, 311

PIUS X

As the long procession wended its way to the high altar, it paused three times, while the Monsignor Menghini, a papal master of ceremonies, holding aloft a silver brazier containing tow, set light to the flax, and making a genuflection towards the pope, cried aloud thrice, each time with a higher pitch of the voice, these solemn words: 'Pater Sancte! Sic transit gloria mundi'. [Holy Father, thus passes away the glory of the world.] The tow, however, could not be quenched, and it got brighter and brighter as the procession advanced, so that at last the master of ceremonies was obliged to throw the whole of the burning stuff on the ground, just under one of the bronze columns of the papal altar.

H. de la Garde Grissell *Sede Vacante*

PIUS X	
Nationality	*Early career*
Italian, from	Patriarch of Venice,
Riese	cardinal priest
Date of birth	*Elected pope*
2 June 1835	4 August 1903
Original name	*Age at election*
Giuseppe	68
Melchiorre Sarto	*Died*
Family background	20 August 1914
Son of a village	*Length of pontificate*
postman	11 years, 16 days

(*Right*) The canonization of Pius X by Pius XII on 29 May, 1954. The modern process of canonizing someone is quite protracted, involving a thorough scrutiny of every aspect of the candidate's life and sound evidence of miracles wrought by the candidate in life or after death. A Church official, popularly known as 'the Devil's Advocate', does his best to test the veracity of all the evidence and information relating to the candidate.

Pius X being carried in a ceremony in the Vatican. The huge fans (Latin, *vannus* = 'winnowing basket') originally had a practical purpose. They have now ceased to play even a ceremonial role in papal processions.

Leo XIII's pontificate was a difficult one to follow, and perhaps it is no accident that the next pope became the last pope to be canonized. Religious rather than political, **Pius X** (1903–1914) nevertheless made it clear that he would not yield one jot of what he regarded as the Church's rights, and in 1904 this led to a break with France where the government repudiated the concordat of 1801 which had conceded, in some measure, the pope's authority over French clergy. A similar rupture in Portugal was only just avoided, although Pius protested in the strongest terms in 1911 at the separation of Church and State, which took place there, too. In Italy, however, he was a little more accommodating. It was important that the Vatican reach some kind of amicable arrangement with the State, and so Pius permitted, at their bishops' discretion, Italian Catholics to take part in general elections in order to counterbalance what might otherwise be a preponderance of socialist votes.

Despite his condemnation of a group of liberal Catholics known as Modernists and a movement in France which sought to reconcile left-wing ideas with Catholic teaching, Pius had no hesitation about introducing change into the Church's daily life and administration. The Curia was reorganized, canon law revised and seminaries reformed – this last with the intention of improving the quality of Catholic clergy. He also encouraged the revision of Church music, advocating the Gregorian chant as a model, reformulated the breviary, urged frequent communion by the laity – including young children – made known his hope that Catholics might form action groups to promote social reform and justice, and was eager that lay people play an appropriate part in the apostolic life of the Church. When the First World War broke out Pius X was devastated, and died only a few days after hostilities had begun.

Benedict XV
1914–1922

Pius XI
1922–1939

Benedict XV suffered from delicate health as a child. One shoulder was noticeably higher than the other, and he walked with a limp. His temperament was kindly – he had charmed the Bolognese with his pastoral care for their welfare – and he was remarkably approachable.

General de Gaulle, who was 30 when Joan of Arc was canonized by Benedict XV, adopted the cross of her home province of Lorraine as the symbol of resistance to the Vichy government.

BENEDICT XV

It is Luther who has lost this war.

Benedict XV at the end of the
First World War

Benedict XV (1914–1922) was pope during most of the First World War and for the initial period of the uneasy peace which followed. During the conflict he tried to remain neutral while condemning atrocities and making arrangements to reunite prisoners-of-war with their families. In 1917, he proposed a plan for peace, but this was rejected by the warring governments, and when the Allies met in 1919 to arrange a peace settlement, the pope was ignored. From 1920 Benedict devoted himself to efforts at international reconciliation. Even France, cold towards the Holy See since at least 1910, resumed diplomatic relations, warmed perhaps by the pope's canonization of Joan of Arc in 1920. In Italy, too, Benedict did his best to encourage a friendlier relationship between the papacy and the government, and even in the midst of war Britain relaxed to the extent of sending a chargé d'affaires to the Vatican in 1915, the first for nearly 300 years.

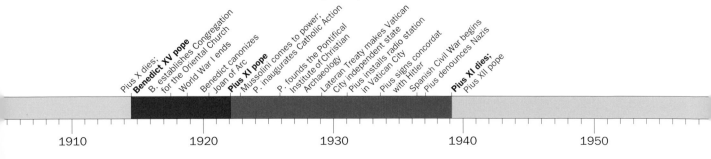

Pius X dies; **Benedict XV pope**
B. establishes Congregation for the Oriental Church
World War I ends
Benedict canonizes Joan of Arc
Pius XI pope
Mussolini comes to power; P. inaugurates Catholic Action
P. founds the Pontifical Institute of Christian Archaeology
Lateran Treaty makes Vatican City independent state
Pius installs radio station in Vatican City
Pius signs concordat with Hitler
Spanish Civil War begins
Pius denounces Nazis
Pius XI dies; Pius XII pope

1910   1920   1930   1940   1950

BENEDICT XV	
Nationality Italian, from Genno	Bologna, cardinal priest
Date of birth 21 November 1854	*Elected pope* 3 September 1914
Original name Giacomo Della Chiesa	*Age at election* 59
Family background Aristocratic	*Died* 22 January 1922, of pneumonia
Early career Secretary of state, archbishop of	*Length of pontificate* 7 years, 4 months, 20 days

Like Pius X, Benedict actively thrust forward Catholic missions, urging missionary bishops to ordain native clergy. The collapse of Russia in 1917 made Benedict think that the time was ripe for a reunification of the Western and Eastern Churches, and to this end he established the Congregation for the Oriental Church and the Pontifical Oriental Institute in Rome. Despite Benedict's many achievements, the horrors of the war prevented him from enjoying the respect and consideration which was really his due. To the Central Powers he was '*der französische Papst*'; to the Allies, '*le pape boche*'. The East, strangely enough, was more appreciative, however, since the Turks raised a statue to him in Istanbul in 1920.

PIUS XI	
Nationality Italian, from Desio	Milan, cardinal priest
Date of birth 31 May 1857	*Elected pope* 6 February 1922
Original name Ambrogio Damiano Achille Ratti	*Age at election* 64
Family background Son of a silk-factory manager	*Died* 10 February 1939
Early career Archbishop of	*Length of pontificate* 17 years, 2 days

PIUS XI

What struck me most about Pius XI was the authority which seemed to me to emanate from him; an authority which is neither stiff nor tense, and which imposes itself without effort because it is aware it has no need to do so.... Physically he does not yet look 74. He is, or seems to be, robust. His features, his expression, reflect energy, but an energy which is calm, 'in repose', so to speak. To rule must be natural to his temperament.

F. Charles-Roux *Huit Ans au Vatican*

Benedict XV died suddenly of pneumonia, and in his place the cardinals elected a scholar and a diplomat, the distinguished linguist and palaeographer Cardinal Achille Ratti. Taking the name **Pius XI** (1922–1939), the new pope set about the task of constructing a 'Pax Christiana' in a world still on edge and exhibiting the symptoms of a continuing hunger for war. He reorganized part of the Vatican Library, founded the Pontifical Institute of Christian Archaeology, built the Pinacoteca to house the Vatican's picture collection and removed the Vatican Observatory to the papal palace of Castel Gandolfo. In 1931, he installed radio in the Vatican City, and in 1936 founded the Pontifical Academy of Sciences. All these were indicative of his wish to ease tensions between the modern world and the papacy, and in this he managed to edge the Holy See further towards accommodation with modernist views than his immediate predecessors were either able or willing to go.

Pius XI was also intensely interested in promoting missionary work abroad, but he had to face a world falling apart and scrambling to fight itself. China, Japan, India and southeast Asia saw an immense advance in the numbers of native priests and bishops during his reign, and he pursued Benedict XV's attempt to encourage the Eastern Orthodox Churches to unite themselves with Rome. His terms, however, were submission, not compromise. Hence he was hostile to the growth of the Protestant ecumenical movement, remarking tartly in 1928 that Christ's Church could not consist of a number of independent

Pius XI seemed to have inexhaustible energy and attended vigorously to the smallest details of his official business.

On returning to the Palazzo Chigi after signing the Lateran agreements (*above*), Mussolini remarked that he did not much care for Pius XI. 'The fact is', he said, 'we both have a peasant mentality.'

A poster used during the Spanish Civil War, showing Italians, Germans and Moroccans supporting Franco against Communism: all in the same boat, with the priest representing the Church.

organizations believing completely different things. But it was his desire for lasting peace which dominated his pontificate, and lay behind his establishment of Catholic Action, a partnership of laity and clergy promoting the Church's mission; his frequent letters dealing with the practice of Christian ideals in all aspects of private and working life; his canonizations; his creation of the Feast Day of Christ the King; his efforts to offer guidance to the world as mass unemployment and the race to arm undermined society.

As soon as he had become pope, Pius had set about trying to resolve the question of the relationship between the Vatican and the kingdom of Italy. This resulted, after long negotiations with Mussolini, in the Lateran Treaty of 11 February 1929 whereby the Holy See recognized the kingdom of Italy and was in turn recognized by the kingdom as an independent, neutral state. Initially, Pius saw Communism as more damaging than the emergent National Socialism of Germany, and therefore he signed a concordat with Hitler in 1933. Nevertheless, it quickly became obvious that National Socialism was both oppressive and dangerous and so, after many protests addressed to the Nazi government, Pius denounced it in 1937 as anti-Christian and ordered his letter to be read from every Catholic pulpit. At the same time, he had to deal with the build-up to and the outbreak of civil war in Spain, while the increasing revelation of Fascism in Italy as a régime willing to adopt the racist doctrines of National Socialism caused his relations with Mussolini to deteriorate. In addition to these problems, the government of Mexico began a harsh and bloody persecution of the Catholic Church there, which Pius described as 'Diocletian' in reference to the outbreak of savagery against Christians under the 3rd-century Roman emperor.

Pius XII
1939–1958

John XXIII
1958–1963

Paul VI
1963–1978

John Paul I
1978

John Paul II
1978–

D'Arcy Osborne, British Minister to the Vatican during the Second World War, remarked on Pius XII's 'devastating combination of saintliness and charm'.

PIUS XII	
Nationality Italian, from Rome	law, secretary of state, cardinal
Date of birth 2 March 1876	priest *Elected pope*
Original name Eugenio Maria Giuseppe Giovanni Pacelli	2 March 1939 *Age at election* 63 *Died*
Family background Son of a lawyer	9 October 1958 *Length of pontificate*
Early career Professor of canon	19 years, 7 months, 7 days

PIUS XII

He spoke Latin, Italian, French, German, English, Spanish, Portuguese, Dutch, Slovak and Hungarian. At the end of his life he had even given himself the task of studying Arabic. He had a very great facility for learning the most diverse languages. He learned sufficient Portuguese in a few weeks, for example, to be able to speak to the Brazilian parliament.

R. Galeazzi-Lisi *Dans l'ombre et dans la lumière de Pie XII*, 1960

Pius XI died just before the outbreak of the Second World War, so like Benedict XV, **Pius XII** (1939–1958) had to guide the Church through an immense conflict which would leave much of the world shattered, and thereby create the need for subsequent reconciliation and reconstruction. In the few months before his election and the start of hostilities, Pius did his best to avert war by calling for an international conference, and broadcasting an appeal to the world to desist. Even after war had started, he did his best to keep Italy out of it, and throughout the war years took care to emphasize that he was 'impartial' rather than 'neutral', an important distinction. While war raged, he ran an immense pro-

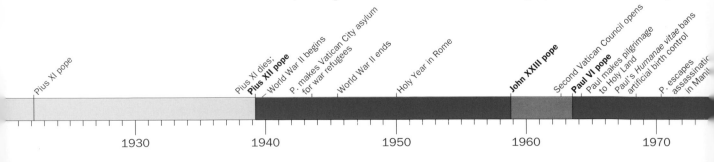

Pius XI pope

Pius XI dies;
Pius XII pope
World War II begins
P. makes Vatican City asylum
for war refugees
World War II ends
Holy Year in Rome
John XXIII pope
Second Vatican Council opens
Paul VI pope
Paul makes pilgrimage
to Holy Land
Paul's *Humanae vitae* bans
artificial birth control
P. escapes
assassinatio
in Manil

1930   1940   1950   1960   1970

MOTHER PASQUALINA

As well as being an excellent nurse, she [Pasqualina] was the devoted chatelaine of his [Pius XII's] household, devoted and energetic. On occasion, she was also capable in an emergency of being the pope's secretary and typist. There is no doubt that it is thanks to her that the pope has always been surrounded by a material existence which is tranquil and comfortable. She is the first woman to have directed a pope's household so well and for such a long time.

R. Galeazzi-Lisi *Dans l'ombre et dans la lumière de Pie XII*, 1960

Pius XII's household was run by a formidable Bavarian nun, Mother Pasqualina, who, thanks to the newspapers, achieved a certain notoriety during the pope's later years. She was, they suggested, too influential: 'the German corporal' was the unkind, and inaccurate, nickname visited upon her.

JOHN XXIII	
Nationality Italian, from Sotto il Monte, near Bergamo	France, patriarch of Venice, cardinal priest
Date of birth 25 November 1881	*Elected pope* 28 October 1958
Original name Angelo Giuseppe Roncalli	*Age at election* 76
Family background Peasant farmers	*Died* 3 June 1963
Early career Papal nuncio to	*Length of pontificate* 4 years, 7 months, 6 days

gramme for the relief of its victims – Jews, refugees, prisoners-of-war – although controversy sprang up afterwards over the degree of explicitness with which he had denounced the atrocities and genocide. When peace came at last, he accepted the Italians' choice of a republic rather than a monarchy, and indicated to the Roman nobility that the age of privilege was over. This was all of a part with his teaching (pursued throughout the war as well as after it) that social reform must seek above all to preserve the dignity, freedom and value of the individual. It is therefore not surprising that he saw Communism as a particularly dangerous force in the world, and sought to counter its theories by constant emphasis upon the importance of the family, and the subordination of the State's interests to those of the individual. Like Pius IX and Leo XIII in particular, he was devoted to the Blessed Virgin Mary and in 1950 – declared a Holy Year, which brought millions of pilgrims to Rome – he defined the Church's teaching on her bodily assumption into Heaven, and closed the Holy Year in Fátima, Portugal, one of the great Marian shrines of the Catholic world.

The range of the pope's teaching was enormous, including the Church's divine mission, the origin of humankind, artificial insemination, the validity of ordinations, Communism, radio, television and films, evolution, literary criticism and the concept of collective guilt. He was the first pope to become familiar to the world through radio and television. These made a considerable difference to his general reputation, aided perhaps by his appearance which suggested princely asceticism.

JOHN XXIII

When Pius XII died there was an outpouring of grief, followed by avid journalistic curiosity to know who would succeed him. Pius had created a large number of cardinals (well over 50), and as a result the college was now predominantly non-Italian. Nevertheless, an Italian was elected, **John XXIII** (1958–1963). He was nearly 77 when he became pope, having lived through both world wars and gained a great deal of diplomatic experience in Bulgaria, Greece, Turkey and France. Perhaps not unexpectedly his principal interest was Christian unity. To this end he established a Secretariat for Christian Unity in 1960, received the English archbishop of Canterbury in December of that year, sent fraternal greeting to the patriarch of Constantinople in 1961, and allowed Catholic observers to attend the World Council of Churches. He also proclaimed

John Paul I pope
John Paul II pope
John Paul shot
J. P. visits Britain
Berlin Wall dismantled
Catholic Lech Walesa president of Poland
Break up of the Soviet Union

1980   1990   2000   2010   2020

Pope John XXIII visiting a prison. When the new pope chose to be called 'John', he joked about it. 'It is the name which has been most used in the long series of Roman pontiffs. Nearly all of them had a brief pontificate.'

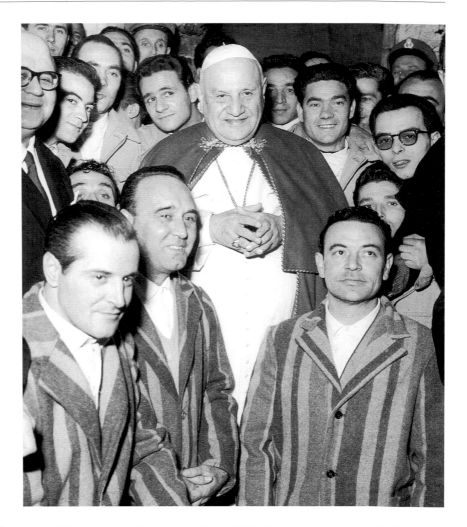

On nuclear weapons, Pope John wrote that in an atomic age, it was no longer sensible to think that war could be used to repair a violation of justice.

himself a pastor, and reiterated Leo XIII's description of non-Catholics as 'separated brethren'. Indeed, Leo XIII seems to have provided a deeply felt influence, since John pursued the social themes which Leo had set, and called for rich to help poor in a spirit of love and peace. The Western world was in the midst of the freezing animosity of the Cold War, but Pope John urged peaceful coexistence, despite his overt disapproval of Marxist theories; and the part he played in the Cuban missile crisis of 1962 won him respect from both Kruschev and Kennedy, as well as a prize for peace in 1963.

John XXIII's pontificate will be linked primarily with the Second Vatican Council (1962–1965), which he summoned in a sudden access of enthusiasm for modernizing the Church as a preliminary step to reunification with her 'separated brethren'. He started with a synod in Rome in 1960, and then set up preparatory working bodies before opening the first session of the council in October 1962. At the same time he established a pontifical commission to oversee a revision of canon law, a task which continued until 1983 when the new text was approved and published by Pope John Paul II.

PAUL VI	
Nationality Italian, from Concesio	archbishop of Milan, cardinal priest
Date of birth 26 September 1897	*Elected pope* 21 June 1963
Original name Giovanni Battista Montini	*Age at election* 65
Family background Son of a lawyer	*Died* 6 August 1978
Early career Secretary of state,	*Length of pontificate* 15 years, 1 month, 16 days

PAUL VI

On 8 December 1962, Pope John closed the first session of his council. It had discussed the liturgy, revelation and the Church, and was not due to reconvene for nine months. By the time it did, however, John was dead and it was left to **Paul VI** (1963–1978) to continue where he had left off. Paul had had a good deal of experience as archbishop of Milan in working with all manner of social problems, and he had travelled extensively during the 1950s and early 1960s, so he was well fitted to guide the council through its various sessions. These considered the Church, bishops, ecumenism, the liturgy and social communication in 1963; religious freedom, non-Christian religions, revelation, the apostolate of the laity, the modern world and Eastern Catholic Churches in 1964; and continued many of these in 1965, to which were added discussions on missionary activity, the priestly ministry, the religious life and Christian education. Paul started courageously to implement the new decrees, aware that he was setting afoot a revolution which must not be allowed to run away into division and rancour. One of the most immediately noticeable changes was that the liturgy would be conducted mainly in the vernacular instead of in Latin. Some people argued the benefits of comprehension for the laity; others regretted the loss of universality which the single language had afforded the Church's worship. The most vociferous of the latter was a French archbishop, Marcel Lefebvre, who rejected completely these and the other changes made by the council, and took many people with him.

John F. Kennedy was the first Catholic president of the United States of America. He met Paul VI in 1963. Paul went to the United Nations in New York in October 1965 to plead for peace, and celebrated a pontifical mass in the Yankee stadium.

Pope Paul VI with a special audience of Catholic Nigerians. Among the people canonized by Paul were the 22 martyrs of Uganda, put to death between 1885 and 1887.

JOHN PAUL I	
Nationality Italian, from Canale d'Agordo, near Belluno	*Elected pope* 26 August 1978 *Age at election* 65
Date of birth 17 October 1912	*Died* 28 September 1978, of a heart attack
Original name Albino Luciani	*Length of pontificate* 1 month, 3 days
Family background Humble	*Notable feature* Pope John Paul published a number of letters, *Illustrissimi*, addressed to authors and characters in fiction
Early career Vice-president of the Italian Conference of Bishops, patriarch of Venice, cardinal priest	

Meanwhile the pope produced a flood of documents dealing with various aspects of the topics covered by the council, and began to travel far beyond Rome in his pursuit of ecumenical understanding. Of these documents, none provided as much controversy as *Humanae vitae* in 1968, which condemned artificial methods of birth control. It ran contrary to the hopes that some form of relaxation of the Church's ban on contraception might be found, and was rejected out of hand by Anglican bishops. This, and his insistence upon priestly celibacy, rendered the last decade of Paul's pontificate careworn and increasingly stormy.

Nevertheless, the pope shouldered the burdens with a great deal of courage. The 1970s brought with them a surge of international terrorism, and when, in 1978, his friend the Italian politician Aldo Moro was kidnapped and murdered, the strain of the times could be seen in the pope's unsteadiness during the funeral mass; for Paul himself had been the object of an assassination attempt in Manila in 1970. But the very fact that he was in Manila points to the extensiveness of his journeys. He was the first pope to travel in aeroplanes and helicopters; the first modern pope to go to the Holy Land; the first to set foot in India; and the first to address the United Nations Assembly. It is an impressive record of innovation for a pope who was sometimes seen as over-conservative.

By mid-1978 the pope was worn out. He had been seriously ill on two occasions during the previous 18 months, and on 14 July went to Castel Gandolfo, aware that he might never return to Rome. On 6 August, mass was being said for him in the chapel next to his bedroom. He became agitated during the rite but managed to receive communion before lapsing into semi-consciousness. He died a few hours later. The agitation had been a massive heart attack.

JOHN PAUL I

Pope Paul VI had laid down strict rules for the election of his successor. Cardinals aged 80 and over, for example, were deprived of their vote in the conclave, and every attempt was made to ensure that proceedings would remain secret. What is more, the total number of cardinals had been raised dramatically to 138, most of whom were not Italian. Its natural conclusion, however – a non-Italian pope – did not happen yet. On the first day of the conclave, the cardinals elected **John Paul I** (1978), who broke with precedent in several ways. One was his choice of a double name; another was his refusal to be crowned. He chose instead to receive a pallium, the woollen vestment conferred upon archbishops in the Catholic Church, as a sign of humility and of the pastoral nature of his new office. He announced that he would continue to implement the decrees of the Second Vatican Council while maintaining the integrity of the Church's traditional discipline in the lives of the faithful, both clerical and lay. But just over three weeks after his inauguration, he was found dead in bed. A heart attack (rather than the poison of heated rumours) appeared to have been the cause.

The last picture to be taken of Pope John Paul I before he died. He is seated on the *sedia gestatoria*, the portable papal throne which was carried on the shoulders of 12 footmen. It enabled the pope to be seen easily above the heads of the crowd. The *sedia* has now been replaced by the curious white van gratingly known as 'the pope-mobile'.

JOHN PAUL II	
Nationality	army lieutenant
Polish, from	*Early career*
Wadowice	Archbishop of
Date of birth	Kraków, cardinal
18 May 1920	priest
Original name	*Elected pope*
Karol Wojtyla	16 October 1978
Family background	*Age at election*
Son of a retired	58

JOHN PAUL II

The cardinals then elected the first non-Italian pope for 456 years. **John Paul II** (1978–), the first Polish pope, made an immediate impression when he addressed the gathered masses in St Peter's Square a bare half-hour after his election. His references to his predecessor, to the Blessed Virgin, to 'your – our – Italian language', were greeted with an immense ovation, and from that point one of the most vigorous of all papacies was under way. John Paul is a formidable scholar, holding two doctorates (one in mystical theology, the other in philosophy), and speaking several languages fluently, especially Latin, these days a rare accomplishment. His background as a labourer in war-time Poland, a university lecturer, a bishop and then a cardinal prominent among the deliberations of the Second Vatican Council was excellent preparation for the role he was to play as pastor to the world.

Once elected Pope, he continued in the vein of his predecessors. Few countries have not received a papal visit, and indeed he has travelled almost frantically in an effort to fulfil what he called at the start of his

The bullet which nearly killed the pope miraculously (the word is that of his surgeons) missed the central aorta. Two tourists were badly wounded by the same bullet. A second bullet, however, passed harmlessly by. Despite the violence common to the 20th century, the attempted assassination of John Paul II in 1981 was felt to be particularly shocking.

reign 'our universal pastoral ministry'. Even the evident decline in his physical strength during recent years has had little effect on that punishing schedule. Like John XXIII and Paul VI, he has done his best to implement change in the Church while preserving its traditional core of teaching, a delicate task which almost invites dissension. But preserve it he does, summoning theologians with heterodox views to explain themselves in person, or forbidding them to teach if their answers are not to his satisfaction. Change balanced by conservatism is perhaps the distinctive note of his papacy. Like Leo XIII, Pope John Paul II has always taken care to emphasize the dignity of labour and the rights of working people, while condemning those philosophies, such as Marxism, which in practice if not in intention have subordinated individuals to the secular State. Thus perhaps his greatest contribution is to have played a major role in the downfall of Communism and the consequent changes of régime in many European countries – Poland in particular.

But the political terrorism rampant in the early years of his reign touched him closely when on 13 May 1981 he was felled by a pistol shot in the midst of St Peter's Square while he was greeting a vast concourse of pilgrims and tourists during his weekly general audience. John Paul made a remarkable recovery, but what would have happened had the pope been incapacitated or forced to undertake a long recuperation is a question that has never been answered. Canon law makes no provision for such a circumstance. In 1983, the pope visited the would-be assassin in his prison cell where the two men talked quietly in Italian for 20 minutes. What they said is not known, but the pope attributes his escape to a miracle by the Blessed Virgin of Fátima to whose shrine in Portugal he went in 1982 and again in 1991. The bullet which struck him now lodges among the diamonds of the Virgin's golden crown.

Whether or not John Paul succeeds in his declared aim to guide the papacy into the next millennium, the office he holds will have come more or less full circle. From its initiation 2,000 years ago with the commands, 'feed my lambs', 'feed my sheep', the papacy has travelled from pastoral mission to imperial power and back through Italian princedom to pastoral mission again. It is a fitting way to begin the next 1,000 years.

In my end is my beginning

SELECT BIBLIOGRAPHY

Alchermes J.D. 1995, 'Petrine politics: Pope Symmachus and the rotund of St. Andrew at old St. Peter's', *Catholic Historical Review* 81. pp. 1–40.

Baluze E. (ed. G. Mollat, 1914–1922), *Vitae Paparum Avenionensium*, 4 vols. Paris.

Barraclough G. 1968, *The Mediaeval Papacy*, Thames & Hudson, London and New York.

Bertomeu E.B. 1973, *Un Gran Aragonés*, Porter Libros, Barcelona.

Blumenthal U-R. 1982, *The Investiture Controversy*, University of America Press.

Bradford E. 1967, *The Great Betrayal*, Hodder & Stoughton, London.

Brown P. 1967, *Augustine of Hippo*, Faber and Faber, London.

Brundage J.A. 1995, *Mediaeval Canon Law*, Longman, London.

Burchard J. 1963, *At the Court of the Borgia*, ed. and trans. G. Parker, Faber, London.

Caillet L. 1975, *La Papauté d'Avignon et l'Eglise de France*, Presses Universitaires de France, Paris.

Cambridge Mediaeval History. 1967–69, 8 vols. Cambridge University Press, Cambridge.

Cecchelli M. (ed.) 1981, *Benedetto XIV*, 2 vols., Centro Studi, Ferrara.

Chadwick H. 1957, 'St. Peter and St. Paul in Rome', *Journal of Theological Studies*, n.s. 8.31–52.

Chadwick H. c. 1991, *Heresy and Orthodoxy in the Early Church*, Variorum.

Christie-Muney D. 1976, *A History of Heresy*, Oxford University Press, Oxford.

Davies R. 1989–95,*The Book of the Pontiffs (Liber Pontificalis)*, English trans. 3 vols., Liverpool University Press.

De Feo I. 1987, *Sisto V*, Mursia, Milan.

Eastman J.R. 1990, 'Giles of Rome and Celestine V', *Catholic Historical Review* 76, pp. 195–211.

Eberhardt N.C. 1961, *A Summary of Catholic History*, 2 vols., B. Herder Book Co, St. Louis.

Ellis G.M. (trans.) 1973, *Boso's Life of Alexander III*, Blackwell, Oxford.

Enciclopedia Cattolica 1948–54, 12 vols., Città del Vaticano.

Encyclopaedia of the Early Church. 1992, 2 vols., James Clarke & Co., Cambridge.

Eusebius *Ecclesiastical History*, Loeb ed. 2 vols., Harvard University Press, Cambridge, Mass.

Falconi C. 1967, *The Popes in the Twentieth Century*, English trans., Weidenfeld & Nicolson.

Falconi C. 1987, *Leone X*, Rusconi, Milan.

Fink K.A. 1981, *Papsttum und Kirche im abendländischen Mittelalter*, C.H. Beck, Munich.

Fontenelle R. 1938, *His Holiness Pope Pius XI*, English trans., Methuen, London.

Frazee C.A. 1983, *Catholics and Sultans*, Cambridge University Press, Cambridge.

Frend W.H.C. 1965, *Martyrdom and Persecution in the Early Church*, Blackwell, Oxford.

Frend W.H.C. 1984, *The Rise of Christianity*, Darton, Longman & Todd, London.

Gail M. 1969, *The Three Popes*, Simon & Schuster, New York.

Galeazzi-Lisi R. 1960, *Dans l'ombre et dans la lumière de Pie XII*, Flammarion, Paris.

Gill J. 1961, *Eugenius IV*, Burns & Oates, London.

Gill J. 1964, *Personalities of the Council of Florence*, Blackwell, Oxford.

Gill J. 1979, *Byzantium and the Papacy, 1198–1400*, Rutgers University Press, New Jersey.

Glasford A. 1965, *The Antipope: Benedict XIII*, Barrie & Rockliff, London.

Gleber H. 1936, *Papst Eugen III*, Gustav Fischer, Jena.

Grant M. 1993, *The Emperor Constantine*, Weidenfeld & Nicolson, London.

Greeley A.M. 1979, *The Making of the Popes*, Futura Publications, London.

Guarducci M. 1960, *The Tomb of St. Peter*, English trans., Harrap and Co., London.

Guillemain G. 1962, *La Cour Pontificale d'Avignon, 1309–1376*, Paris.

Gurgo O. 1982, *Celestino V*, Editoriale Nuova.

Halecki O. 1954, *Pius XII*, Weidenfeld & Nicolson, London.

Hales E.E.Y. 1954, 'The personality of Pio Nono', *History Today*, 4.113–120.

Hales E.E.Y. 1954, *Pio Nono*, Eyre & Spottiswoode, London.

Hales E.E.Y. 1960, *Revolution and the Papacy, 1769–1846*, Eyre & Spottiswoode, London.

Hales E.E.Y. 1962, *Napoleon and the Pope*, Eyre and Spottiswoode, London.

Hales E.E.Y. 1965, *Pope John and his Revolution*, Eyre & Spottiswoode, London.

Hatch A. 1967, *Pope Paul VI*, W.W. Allen, London.

Hebblethwaite P. 1984, *John XXIII*, Geoffrey Chapman, London.

Herde P. 1981, *Cölestin V*, A. Hiersemann, Stuttgart.

Hetherington P. 1994, *Mediaeval Rome*, Rubicon Press, London.

Hofman P. 1984, *Anatomy of the Vatican*, Robert Hale, London.

Holmes G. 1981, *The Papacy in the Modern World, 1914–1978*, Burns & Oates, London.

Holmes G. 1988, *The Oxford Illustrated History of Mediaeval Europe*, Oxford University Press, Oxford.

Holmes J.D. 1978, *The Triumph of the Holy See*, Burnes & Oates, London.

Housley N. 1986, *The Avignon Papacy and the Crusades*, Clarendon, Oxford.

Huskinson J. 1982, *Concordia Apostolorum*, BAR International Series, Oxford.

Johnson M. 1981, *The Borgias*, Macdonald, London.

Jones A.H.M. 1978, *Constantine and the Conversion of Europe*, University of Toronto.

Krautheimer R. 1980, *Rome, Profile of a City, 312–1308*, Princeton University Press.

Ladner G.B. 1983, *Images and Ideas in the Middle Ages*, 2 vols., Rome.

Landi A. 1985, *Il Papa Deposto: Pisa 1409*, Claudiano, Turin.

Lefton J. 1958, *Pie VII*, Librairie Plon,

Paris.

Le Goff J. 1985, English trans. 1993, *Intellectuals in the Middle Ages*, Blackwell, Oxford.

Llewellyn P. 1971, *Rome in the Dark Ages*, Faber, London.

Loomis L.R. (trans.) 1961, *The Council of Constance*, Columbia University Press, New York.

MacDonald A.J. 1932, *Hildebrand, a life of Gregory VII*, Methuen, London.

MacGregor G. 1958, *The Vatican Revolution*, Macmillan, London.

McKitterick R. 1994, *Carolingian Culture: Emulation and Innovation*, Cambridge University Press, Cambridge.

MacLagan M. 1968, *The City of Constantinople*, Thames & Hudson, London.

Maier C.T. 1994, *Preaching the Crusades*, Cambridge University Press, Cambridge.

Mango C. & Dagron G. (eds.) 1995, *Constantinople and its Hinterland*, Cambridge University Press, Cambridge.

Mann H.K. 1925–32, *The Lives of the Popes in the Early Middle Ages*, 18 vols., Kegan Paul, London.

Melloni A. 1990, *Innocenzo IV*, Marietti, Geneva.

Menestò E. (ed.) 1991, *Niccolò IV: un pontificato tra oriente ed occidente*, Spoleto.

Mollat G. 1963, *The Popes at Avignon*, English trans., Nelson, London.

Morris C. 1989, *The Papal Monarchy: the Western Church from 1050 to 1250*, Clarendon Press, Oxford.

Morrison K.F. 1969, *Tradition and Authority in the Western Church, 300–1140*, Princeton University Press.

Müller G. 1969, *Die römische Kurie und die Reformation, 1523–1534*, Gutersloher Verlagshaus Gerd Mohn, Heidelberg.

Naville C-E. 1984, *Enea Silvio Piccolomini*, Analisi.

New Catholic Encyclopaedia, 1967, 15 vols. and 2 supplements (1974, 1979), McGraw Hill.

Nielsen F. 1906, *The History of the Papacy in the XIXth Century*, vol. 2, John Murray, London.

Noble T.F.X. *c.* 1984, *The Republic of St. Peter*, University of Philadelphia.

O'Connor D.W. 1969, *Peter in Rome*, Columbia University Press, New York.

O'Dwyer M.M. 1985, *The Papacy in the Age of Napoleon and the Restoration*, University Press of America.

Pacaut M. 1956, *Alexandre III*, Paris.

Pardoe R. & D. 1988, *The Female Pope*, Crucible, Wellingborough.

Partner P. 1958, *The Papal State under Martin V*, British School at Rome, London.

Partner P. 1972, *The Lands of St. Peter*, Eyre Methuen, London.

Pastor L. 1891–1953, *The History of the Popes from the Close of the Middle Ages*, English trans. 40 vols., John Hodges, London.

Pennington K. 1984, *Pope and Bishops*, University of Pennsylvania.

Pesch R. 1980, *Simon-Petrus*, Anton Hiersemann, Stuttgart.

Pietri C. 1976, *Roma Christiana*, 2 vols., Ecole Française de Rome.

Powell J.M. (ed.) second ed. 1994, *Innocent III*, Catholic University of America Press, Washington DC.

Procopius (trans. 1981), *The Secret History*, Penguin Books, London.

Renouard Y. 1970, *The Avignon Papacy, 1305–1403*, English trans., Faber, London.

Rhodes A. 1973, *The Vatican in the Age of the Dictators, 1922–1945*, Hodder & Stoughton, London.

Richards J. 1980, *Consul of God*, Routledge & Kegan Paul, London.

Riley-Smith J (ed.) 1995, *The Oxford Illustrated History of the Crusades*, Oxford University Press, Oxford.

Rist J.M. 1994, *Augustine*, Cambridge University Press, Cambridge.

Robinson I.S. 1990, *The Papacy, 1073–1198*, Cambridge University Press, Cambridge.

Romanato G. 1992, *Pio X*, Rusconi, Milan.

Rope H.E.G. 1941, *Benedict XV*, John Gifford Ltd., London.

Sayers J. 1994, *Innocent III*, Longman, London.

Schimmelpfennig B. 1992, *The Papacy*, Columbia University Press, New York.

Schramm P.E. 1968–71, *Kaiser, Könige und Päpste*, 4 vols. in 5, Anton Hiersemann, Stuttgart.

Schüller-Piroli S. 1979, *Die Borgia Päpste Kalixt III und Alexander VI*, Vienna.

Setton K.M. 1976–84, *The Papacy and the Levant*, 4 vols., American Philosophical Society, Philadelphia.

Servatius C. 1979, *Paschalis II*, A. Hiersemann, Stuttgart.

Shaw C. 1993, *Julius II, the Warrior Pope*, Blackwell, Oxford.

Souchon M. 1970, *Die Papstwahlen in der Zeit des grossen Schismas*, Scientia Verlag Aalen, Darmstadt.

Southern R.W. 1970, *Western Society and the Church in the Middle Ages*, Penguin, London.

Stevenson J. 1978, *The Catacombs*, Thames & Hudson, London and New York.

Stroll M. 1987, *The Jewish Pope*, E.J. Brill, Leiden.

Szulc T. 1995, *Pope John Paul II*, Scribner, New York.

Tarugi L.R.S. (ed.) 1991, *Pio II e la cultura del suo tempo*, Guerini e associati, Milan.

Tessier G. 1967, *Charlemagne*, Albin Michel, Paris.

Thibault P.R. 1986, *Pope Gregory XI*, University Press of America.

Thomson J.A.F. 1980, *Popes and Princes, 1417–1517*, George Allen & Unwin, London.

Toynbee J. & Perkins J.W. 1956, *The Shrine of St. Peter and the Vatican Excavations*, Longman, London.

Ullman W. 1970, *The Growth of Papal Government in the Middle Ages*, 3rd ed., Methuen, London.

Wallace L.P. 1966, *Leo XIII and the Rise of Socialism*, Duke University Press.

Wallach L. 1959, *Alcuin and Charlemagne*, Cornell University Press.

Walsh J.E. 1983, *The Bones of St. Peter*, Victor Gollancz, London.

Wickham C. 1981, *Early Mediaeval Italy*, Macmillan, London.

Widmer B. *Enea Silvio Piccolomini, Papst Pius II*, Benno Schwabe & Co., Basel.

Wood D. 1989, *Clement VI*, Cambridge University Press, Cambridge.

ILLUSTRATION AND TEXT CREDITS

a = above, c = centre, b = bottom, l = left, r = right

The following abbreviations are used to identify sources and locate illustrations: AKG – Photo AKG London; BV – Foto Biblioteca Vaticana; BL – by permission of the British Library, London; BM – Copyright British Museum, London; BN – Cliché Bibliothèque Nationale de France, Paris.

1 I Musei Vaticani. 2 Scala. 5a–b Soprintendenza di Monumenti dei Lazio; Archivi Alinari; BM; The Royal Collection © Her Majesty Queen Elizabeth II. 6 Bibliothèque de l'Arsenale, Paris. 7 AKG. 8–9 ML Design. 11l–r AKG; A.F.E., Rome; BN; Stadtsbibliothek Trier. 12 Rhode Island School of Design, Providence. 13 Reproduced by courtesy of the Trustees, The National Gallery, London. 14 Staatliche Museen zu Berlin-Kulturbesitz Gemäldegalerie, Foto: Jörg P. Anders, © bpk, Berlin. 15 AKG. 16ar&bl Tracy Wellman. 18 Archivi Alinari. 19a A.F.E., Rome; b Universitätsbibliothek, Leiden. 20bl © bpk, Berlin; br Deutsches Archaeologische Institut, Rome. 23 BN. 24ar&l I Musei Vaticani; bl Reproduced by courtesy of the Trustees, The National Gallery, London. 26a I Musei Vaticani; b Archivi Alinari. 27ar AKG/Erich Lessing; al Hirmer Fotoarchiv; b AKG. 28a&b BN. 29 BN. 31 BN. 33 BN. 34 AKG. 36 AKG. 37 Gabinetto Fotografico Nazionale, Rome. 39a Hirmer Fotoarchiv; b Deutsches Archaeologische Institut, Rome. 41 Archivi Alinari. 42 Archivi Alinari. 43b Peter Clayton. 44 Hirmer Fotoarchiv. 45 Hirmer Fotoarchiv. 46 BL. 47a Museo Arqueologico Nacional, Madrid; b ML Design. 48 HirmerFotoarchiv. 50 Peter Clayton. 51 Stadtbibliothek Trier. 53l–r Scala; Scala; Scala; Domschatz, Aachen. 54 Hirmer Fotoarchiv. 55 Peter Clayton. 56a ML Design; b Topkapi Palace Museum, Istanbul; bc BL; br Österreichische Nationalbibliothek, Vienna. 59 Archivi Alinari. 60 BL. 61 BV. 63a ML Design; b AKG. 64 BV. 66a ML Design; bl Domschatz, Aachen; br Stadtbibliothek Trier. 67al&r AKG; b Tracy Wellman. 70 AKG. 71 Bibliothèque Royale Albert Ier, Brussels. 74 The Metropolitan Museum of Art, New York, Gift of George Blumenthal, 1941. 75 Foto Marburg. 76a Staatsbibliothek, Munich; b Domschatz, Aachen. 77 BL. 78 AKG/Erich Lessing. 80 Burgbibliothek, Bern. 81 BN. 83l–r © Photo R.M.N.; AKG; BN; Scala. 84 AKG. 85 Hirmer Fotoarchiv. 86 Scala. 87 Philip Winton after Conant. 88l BL; r BV. 89 Universitätsbibliothek, Jena. 90 BN. 91a Games Systems Inc.; b Sonia Halliday Photographs. 93a&b BV. 94 Scala. 95 ML Design. 96al Archives Nationales, Paris; bl Musée des Monuments Français, Paris; r Musée Condé, Chantilly. 97 AKG. 98l The Bodleian Library, University of Oxford. 99 BL. 100a Hessische Landesbibliothek, Fulda; b BN. 101 AKG. 102 Burgbibliothek, Bern. 103 Burgbibliothek, Bern. 104 Musée du Louvre, Paris. 105a The Conway Library, Courtauld Institute of Art, courtesy the Master and Fellows of Corpus Christi College, Cambridge; b MAS. 106a BN; b ML Design. 107al Adam Green; ar BL; b BN. 109 V&A Picture Library. 110a AKG/Stefan Diller; c BL; b BL. 111a AKG/Joseph Martin; bl AKG; br © Photo R.M.N. 112 AKG. 113 AKG. 114 The Conway Library, Courtauld Institute of Art, courtesy the Master and Fellows of Corpus Christi College, Cambridge. 116l AKG; r Tour Ferrande, Pernes. 117a Rosgartenmuseum,Constance; b Archivi Alinari. 119 BL. 120b BN. 121a MAS; b Canali. 123 © Photo R.M.N. 124 BL. 125 Archivi Alinari. 126 BL. 127 BL. 128 BL. 129 BL. 130 Fabbricca di San Pietro, Vatican. 131 Österreichische Nationalbibliothek, Vienna. 132 Scala. 133b Musée Calvet, Avignon. 134 BV. 135 I Musei Vaticani. 136 Tracy Wellman. 136–137 Giraudon. 137a&bl Giraudon; br Flammarion-Giraudon. 140 BL. 141a BL; b Scala. 142 Archivio di Stato, Siena. 143b BM. 144 Scala. 145 Germanisches Nationalmuseum, Nuremberg. 146 Scala. 147 AKG. 148 Reproduced by courtesy of the Trustees, The National Gallery, London. 150a Galleria degli Uffizi, Florence; b AKG. 151 AKG. 153a Archivi Alinari; b BM. 155l–r Scala; Scala; Photograph Claude Gourmanel, Musée des Beaux Arts, Béziers; AKG. 156 I Musei Vaticani. 157 Biblioteca Estense, Modena. 158a Scala; c Galleria Borghese, Rome; bl Galleria Carrara, Bergamo; br Scala. 159l–r Städelsches Kunstinstitut, Frankfurt-am-Main; Scala; Scala. 160 Tyroler Landesmuseum, Innsbruck. 161 Museo di San Marco, Florence. 162 AKG/Erich Lessing. 163 Stadt-u.Universitätsbibliothek, Bern. 164 BV. 165 Fabbricca di San Pietro, Vatican. 166a Galleria degli Uffizi, Florence; b BM. 167 AKG. 168 A.F. Kersting. 169 Archivi Alinari. 170a Scala; b BM. 171 Scala. 173 AKG. 174a&b AKG. 175a BV; b AKG. 176b Topkapi Palace Museum, Istanbul. 179 Museo di Capodimonte, Naples. 182 © Perth & Kinross Council, Perth Museum & Art Gallery, Scotland. 183l Stonyhurst College; r Museo Storico Navale di Venezia. 184 Archivio di Stato, Siena. 185a AKG; b © bpk, Berlin. 186 BM. 188a&b Scala. 189 Scala. 190 Fabbricca di San Pietro, Vatican. 191 AKG/Erich Lessing. 192 Photograph Claude Gourmanel, Musée des BeauxArts, Béziers. 193 Archivi Alinari. 194a&b BN. 195a The Science Museum, London. 197a&b Palazzo Doria Pamphili, Rome. 198al Nationalmuseum, Stockholm; ar A.F. Kersting; b BM. 200a BM; b V&A Picture Library. 201 AKG/Erich Lessing. 202 BN. 204a AKG; b A.F. Kersting. 205 A.F. Kersting. 206 Minneapolis Institute of Arts. 207 BM. 209l–r AKG Photo; Scala; AKG/Erich Lessing; AKG/AP. 211 V&A Picture Library. 212 Scala. 213a BM; b AKG/Erich Lessing. 214a The Royal Collection © Her Majesty Queen Elizabeth II. 215 Fabbricca di San Pietro, Vatican. 216a Scala; b Fabbricca di San Pietro, Vatican. 218a&br Punch Ltd; bl ML Design. 219 Scala. 220 AKG. 221 Moro, Roma. 222a&b Hulton Getty. 223a Hulton Getty; b V&A Picture Library. 224 AKG. 225a Archivio Mondadori; b Moro, Roma. 226 AKG. 228a Fotografie Pontificia Giordani, Rome; b Evening Standard/Solo. 229 Fotografie Pontificia Giordani, Rome. 230 Hulton Getty. 231 Hulton Getty. 232a Hulton Getty; b AKG/Dieter E. Hoppe.

Sources of quotations

The quotations used in this book are taken from the following sources. All translations are by the author unless otherwise stated.

Accarisius *Vita Gregorii XV* (used on p. 191).
Ammianus Marcellinus *History* (used on pp. 29, 30).
Anna Comnena *Alexiad* (used on p. 89).
Annales Lauresbamenses (used on p. 62).
Anon *Gesta Innocenti III Papae* (used on pp. 103–104).
Anon *Vita et Obitus Beati Petri Confessoris* (used on p. 123).
Anon *Vita Gregorii XV* (used on p. 191).
Apocryphal *Acts of Peter* (used on p. 12).
Bishop of Arezzo *Letters* (used on p. 165).
Benedict XIV *Letters* (used on p. 206).
Bernold of St Blaise *Chronicon* (used on p. 84).
Burchard & Conrad *Uspergensium Chronicon* (used on p. 97).
Burchard *Liber Notarum* (used on p. 163).
Canterbury monks *Letter* (used on p. 101).
St Catharine of Siena *Letters* (used on pp. 134, 135).
Cellini *Autobiography* (used on p. 177).
Charles-Roux *Huit Ans au Vatican* [Flammarion, Paris 1947] (used on p. 224).
Chateaubriand *Mémoires d'outre-tombe* [Paris 1849] (used on pp. 214, 215).
Continuation of *Gesta Episcoporum Virdunensium* (used on p. 108).
Continuatio Sanblasiana Chronici Ottoni Frisingensi (used on p. 115).
Continuatio Vindobonensis (used on p. 120).
St Peter Damian *De Abdicatione Episcopatus* (used on p. 78).
Dante *Inferno* (used on p. 140); *Purgatorio* (used on p. 118).
Abbé Darras *General History of the Catholic Church* (used on p. 203).
De la Garde Grissell H. *Sede Vacante* [Oxford & London, 1903] (used on p. 221).
Diderot *Encyclopédie* (used on p. 206); *Lettres* (used on p. 210).
Dionysius Exiguus *Decretals of the Roman Pontiffs* (used on p. 38).
Egidio di Viterbo *History* (used on p. 170).
Einhard *Vita Karoli Magni* (used on p. 63); *Annales Fuldenses* (used on p. 68).
Erasmus(?) *Julius Exclusus* (used on p. 166).
Eusebius *History of the Church* (used on pp. 20, 21).
Galeazzi-Lisi R. *Dans l'ombre et dans la lumière de Pie XII* [Paris, 1960] (used on pp. 226, 227).
Gavazzi A. *My Recollections of the Last Four Popes* [London, 1858] (used on pp. 214, 215).
Gerhoh *De Investigatione Antichristi* (used on p. 99).
Giovio *Vita Leonis X* (used on p. 172).
Gleichen C. H. von *Souvenirs* [Paris, 1868] (used on p. 210).
Gospel of St Luke Authorized Version (used on p. 14).
Gospel of St John Authorized Version (used on p. 12).
Gregorovius F. *Lucrezia Borgia* [Stuttgart, 1874] (used on p. 156).
Gregory I *Registrum Epistularum* (used on pp. 48, 50).
Gregory VII *Letters* (used on p. 88).
Guicciardini F. *Storia d'Italia*, English version of Leopold von Ranke, 3 vols. [London, 1908] (used on p. 161).
Heinrich the Seneschal of Dissenhoven *Vita Joannis XXII* (used on p. 128).
Innocent III *Regesta* (used on p. 104).
John the Deacon *Vita Sancti Gregorii Magni* (used on pp. 48, 51).
John XXI *De Oculo Liber* (used on p. 119).
Julius II *Papal Dispensation, 1503* (used on p. 168).
Lando G. *Relatione di Roma*, English version of Leopold von Ranke *The History of the Popes*, 3 vols. [London, 1908] (used on p. 199).
Leo I *Letters* (used on p. 37); *Sermons* (used on p. 36).
Leo IX *Letters* (used on p. 81).
Liber Pontificalis (used on pp. 17, 29, 57, 64–65).
Liberatus of Carthage *Breviarium* (used on p. 43).
Luther *Sermon*, from Kidd B.J. *Documents Illustrative of the Continental Reformation* [Oxford, 1911] (used on p. 128).
Nicoletti A. *Della Vita di Papa Urbino VIII*, English version of Leopold von Ranke *The History of the Popes*, 3 vols. [London, 1908] (used on p. 193).
O'Reilly B. *Life of Leo XIII* [London, 1887] (used on p. 221).
Paul the Deacon *History of the Lombards* (used on p. 46).
Pelagius II *Letters* (used on p. 45).
Peter the Deacon *Chronicon Casinense* (used on pp. 90–91, 92).
Philippe le Bel *Letter* (used on p. 127).
Pius IX *Decree of Papal Infallibility* (used on p. 219).
Platina *Lives of the Popes*, trans. P. Rycaut [London, 1685] (used on p. 163).
Prosper of Aquitaine *Chronicles to the year 445* (used on p. 36).
Procopius *Secret History* (used on p. 44).
Richard of Poitiers *Chronica* (used on p. 96).
Salimbene de Adam *Chronica* (used on p. 115).
Sanuto *I Diarii* (used on p. 164).
Siricius *Letters* (used on p. 32).
Von Troppau M. *Chronicle of the Popes and Emperors* (used on p. 91).
Walpole H. *Letters*, ed. Mrs Paget Toynbee, 16 vols. [Oxford, 1903–1905] (used on p. 206).
William of Malmesbury *Gesta Regum Anglorum* (used on p. 76).
Cardinal Wiseman *Recollections of the Last Four Popes* [London, 1858] (used on pp. 216–217, 220).

INDEX

Page numbers in *italic* refer to illustrations on the relevant pages

(p) pope